CUTTING EDGE TECHNOLOGIES AND MICROCOMPUTER APPLICATIONS FOR DEVELOPING COUNTRIES

ABOUT THE BOOK

This report covers microcomputer applications in cutting edge technologies for developing countries. For those developing countries with experience in microcomputer use, it provides information on important new areas. These include advanced computer concepts, artificial intelligence, computer-aided design and manufacture, applied expert systems, and geographic information systems. For developing countries initiating use of microcomputers, this report can help set priorities by providing awareness of the unique ways that problems in resource assessment, resource utilization, and communication can be approached using newly developed hardware and software.

For all developing countries, microcomputers can assist government and industrial planning with extensive guidance on options and outcomes. Microcomputers have a special role in development because they can provide access to new technologies and facilitate the implementation of these technologies. Because of these dual functions in technology and planning, microcomputers can speed the incorporation of science and technology into both government and industrial planning and maximize its benefits.

Preparation of this report was coordinated by the Board on Science and Technology for International Development in response to a request from the U. S. Agency for International Development.

Published in cooperation with
the Board on Science and Technology
for International Development,
Office of International Affairs,
National Research Council
and
the National Board for Scientific
and Technological Research
and
the Luso-American Development
Foundation of Portugal

CUTTING EDGE TECHNOLOGIES AND MICROCOMPUTER APPLICATIONS FOR DEVELOPING COUNTRIES

Report of an
Ad Hoc Panel
on the Use of
Microcomputers for
Developing Countries

LONDON AND NEW YORK

First publishing 1988 by Westview Press, Inc.

Published 2018 by Routledge
52 Vanderbilt Avenue, New York, NY 10017
2 Park Square, Milton Park, Abingdon, Oxon OX14 4RN

Routledge is an imprint of the Taylor & Francis Group, an informa business

Copyright © 1988 by the National Academy of Sciences

All rights reserved. No part of this book may be reprinted or reproduced or utilised in any form or by any electronic, mechanical, or other means, now known or hereafter invented, including photocopying and recording, or in any information storage or retrieval system, without permission in writing from the publishers.

Notice:
Product or corporate names may be trademarks or registered trademarks, and are used only for identification and explanation without intent to infringe.

Library of Congress Cataloging-in-Publication Data:
Cutting edge technologies and microcomputer applications for Developing Countries / written by the members of BOSTID (Board on Science and Technology for International Development).
    p. cm.—(Westview special studies in science, technology, and public policy)
  ISBN 0-8133-7645-9
  1. High technology—Developing countries. 2. Microcomputers—Developing countries. I. National Research Council (U.S.). Board on Science and Technology for International Development.
II. Series.
T49.5.C87 1988
004′.09172′4—dc19   88-5714
                                                                                    CIP

British Library Cataloguing in Publication Data:
A CIP catalogue record of this book is available from the British Library
ISBN (U.K.): 1-85339-090-0

ISBN 13: 978-0-367-01266-3 (hbk)
ISBN 13: 978-0-367-16253-5 (pbk)

NOTICE: The project that is the subject of this report was approved by the Governing Board of the National Research Council, whose members are drawn from the councils of the National Academy of Sciences, the National Academy of Engineering, and the Institute of Medicine. The members of the committee responsible for the report were chosen for their special competences and with regard for appropriate balance.

This report has been reviewed by a group other than the authors according to procedures approved by a Report Review Committee consisting of members of the National Academy of Sciences, the National Academy of Engineering, and the Institute of Medicine.

The National Academy of Sciences is a private, nonprofit, self-perpetuating society of distinguished scholars engaged in scientific and engineering research, dedicated to the furtherance of science and technology and to their use for the general welfare. Upon the authority of the charter granted to it by the Congress in 1863, the Academy has a mandate that requires it to advise the federal government on scientific and technical matters. Dr. Frank Press is president of the National Academy of Sciences.

The National Academy of Engineering was established in 1964, under the charter of the National Academy of Sciences, as a parallel organization of outstanding engineers. It is autonomous in its administration and in the selection of its members, sharing with the National Academy of Sciences the responsibility for advising the federal government. The National Academy of Engineering also sponsors engineering programs aimed at meeting national needs, encourages education and research, and recognizes the superior achievement of engineers. Dr. Robert M. White is president of the National Academy of Engineering.

The Institute of Medicine was established in 1970 by the National Academy of Sciences to secure the services of eminent members of appropriate professions in the examination of policy matters pertaining to the health of the public. The Institute acts under the responsibility given to the National Academy of Sciences by its congressional charter to be an adviser to the federal government and, upon its own initiative, to identify issues of medical care, research, and education. Dr. Samuel O. Thier is president of the Institute of Medicine.

The National Research Council was organized by the National Academy of Sciences in 1916 to associate the broad community of science and technology with the Academy's purposes of furthering knowledge and advising the federal government. Functioning in accordance with general policies determined by the Academy, the Council has become the principal operating agency of both the National Academy of Sciences and the National Academy of Engineering in providing services to the government, the public, and the scientific and engineering communities. The Council is administered jointly by both Academies and the Institute of Medicine. Dr. Frank Press and Dr. Robert M. White are chairman and vice chairman, respectively, of the National Research Council.

The Board on Science and Technology for International Development (BOSTID) of the Office of International Affairs addresses a range of issues arising from the ways in which science and technology in developing countries can stimulate and complement the complex processes of social and economic development. It oversees a broad program of activities with scientific organizations in developing countries, and examines ways to apply science and technology to problems of economic and social development through various programs, research grants, and mechanisms. BOSTID's Advisory Committee on Technology Innovation publishes topical reviews of technical processes and biological resources of potential importance to developing countries.

These proceedings have been prepared by the Board on Science and Technology for International Development, Office of International Affairs, National Research Council, under Grant No. DAN-5538-G-SS-1023-00 from the U.S. Agency for International Development.

PANEL ON MICROCOMPUTERS FOR DEVELOPING COUNTRIES

WILLIAM J. LAWLESS, JR., (Chairman) Cognitronics Corporation, Stamford, Connecticut

JAMES S. McCULLOUGH, (Vice Chairman) Research Triangle Institute, Research Triangle Park, North Carolina

RUTH M. DAVIS, The Pymatuning Group, Inc., Arlington, Virginia

BARBARA DISKIN, International Statistical Program Center, Bureau of the Census, U.S. Department of Commerce, Washington, D.C.

NATHANIEL FIELDS, Institute for International Development, Vienna, Virgina

HARRY HUSKEY, Board of Studies in Computer and Information Sciences, University of California, Santa Cruz, California

DONALD T. LAURIA, Department of Environmental Sciences and Engineering, School of Public Health, University of North Carolina, Chapel Hill, North Carolina

HAROLD LIEBOWITZ, School of Engineering and Applied Sciences, The George Washington University, Washington, D.C.

KURT D. MOSES, Academy for Educational Development, International Division, Washington, D.C.

MOHAN MUNASINGHE, The World Bank, Washington, D.C.

PHILIP F. PALMEDO, Energy Development International, Setauket, New York

KILUBA PEMBAMOTO, McDonald Douglas Payment Service Co., Chevy Chase, Maryland

ROBERT TEXTOR, Department of Anthropology, Stanford University, Stanford, Palo Alto, California

MICHAEL WEBER, Department of Agricultural Economics, Michigan State University, East Lansing, Michigan

KARL WIIG, Arthur D. Little Inc., Cambridge, Massachusetts

NATIONAL RESEARCH COUNCIL STAFF

Michael Dow, Associate Director, BOSTID
Jack Fritz, Senior Program Officer
Augustus Nasmith, Senior Program Officer
Griffin Shay, Senior Program Officer
F. R. Ruskin, BOSTID Editor
Michael Heasley, Consulting Editor
Hertha Hanu, Administrative Secretary
Elizabeth Mouzon, Administrative Secretary
Monique Vandamme, Program Assistant

JNICT STAFF

Manuela Loureiro, Program Director

Contents

Introduction, *William J. Lawless, Jr* 3

Overview, *João Cravinho and A. D. Figueiredo* 9

Conclusions and Recommendations 19

SECTION 1
THE TECHNOLOGIES

1. Advanced Computer Concepts, *Harry D. Huskey* 25
2. The Impact of Memory Technology Advances on Microcomputers, *Richard Dubbe and Durkee Richards* . 41
3. Artificial Intelligence: An Overview, *Eugénio Oliveira* 61
4. Prolog for Artificial Intelligence Projects: The Portuguese Experience, *Luís Damas and Miguel Filgueiras* 67
5. Computer-Aided Design: A Primer, *Glenn A. Hart* ... 73
6. Applied Expert Systems, *Raoul N. Smith* 99
7. Computer Vision, *Anil K. Jain* 109
8. A Multiple Microprocessor Architecture for Real-Time Visual Inspection, *A. J. Padilha and J. C. D. Marques dos Santos* 119

SECTION 2
RESOURCE ASSESSMENT

9. An Integrated Microcomputer Processing System for Census and Survey Data, *Barbara N. Diskin* 129

10. The Microcomputer in the Brazilian Health Information System, *Marcio Humberto Montagna Cammarota* 145
11. Population Program Applications of Expert Systems, *John Daly* 163
12. A Growing-with-the-User Expert System for Clinical Use, *José Negrete* 171
13. Disease Control in the Community: Toward Microcomputer-Supported Decision Models for Health Centers, *Teodoro Briz* 183
14. SIGUS: A Microcomputer-Based Management System for Primary Health Care Centers, *Alexandre Vieira Abrantes* 189
15. Computer Technology and Biomedical Instrumentation, *Murray Eden* 199
16. A Distributed Processing Architecture for Real-Time Biological Data Analysis, *Pedro Guedes de Oliveira, José Carlos Príncipe, and António Nunes de Cruz* ... 221
17. Natural Resource Analysis, Assessment, and Management, *T. M. Albert* 227
18. Geographic Information Systems, *Vincent B. Robinson* 249
19. Super Microcomputer Networks for a National Geographic Information System, *António Sousa da Câmara, António da Silva e Castro, and Rui Gonçalves Henriques* 259
20. Microcomputers in Agricultural Development, *F. J. Tilak Viegas* 265

SECTION 3
RESOURCE UTILIZATION

21. Expert Systems for Design and Manufacture, *David C. Brown* 275
22. Microcomputers for Industrial Automation in Small- and Medium-Sized Industries in Brazil, *Flavio Grynszpan* 293
23. A Microprocessor-Based Sequence Controller, *Engelbert T. Kapuya, R. K. Appiah, and S. M. Kundishora* 309

24. The Field Limitations of Diagnostics
    in Processor-Controlled Industrial Systems,
    A. D. V. Nihal Kularatne 321
25. Computer-Aided Power System Design,
    Sridhar Mitta 331
26. Applications of Microcomputers in Water Resources
    Engineering, *Don Charles Henry Senarath* 339
27. Intelligent Programs for Public Investments in
    Community Water Supply and Sanitation Systems,
    Donald T. Lauria 349
28. Applications of Artificial Intelligence in Civil
    Engineering, *Brian Brademeyer and Fred
    Moavenzadeh*... 367
29. An Expert System for Time-Series Statistical
    Analysis, *Pablo Noriega B. V., Carlos del Cueto M.,
    Luis M. Rodríguez P., and Ileana Gutiérrez R.* 383

SECTION 4
COMMUNICATION

30. Intelligent Interface, *Andrew C. Kapusto* 399
31. English to Thai Machine Translation,
    Wanchai Rivepiboon 407
32. The Need for Standards in Computer Graphics,
    João Duarte Cunha 415
33. Network-Based Information Systems: A Role for
    Intelligent Workstations, *Joseph F. P. Luhukay* 421
34. Application-Driven Networks, *Kiluba Pembamoto* 435
35. The Use of Microcomputers to Improve Telephone
    Service, *Augusto Júlio Casaca* 451
36. Loop Signaling for PCM Equipment,
    Vasco Lagarto and Lusitana Delgado 459
37. Design and Manufacture of Modern
    Telecommunication Equipment in Portugal,
    Candido M. Lopes Manso 465
38. The Use of Expert Systems in Educational
    Software, *Ernesto Costa* 471

Contributors 481

Introduction

Introduction

This report is based on the third of four conferences on the applications of microcomputers in development sponsored by the U.S. Agency for International Development and the U.S. National Academy of Sciences in collaboration with a host country. The joint sponsor for this third meeting is the National Board for Scientific and Technological Research - Junta Nacional de Investigação Cientifica e Tecnologica (JNICT). The role of the JNICT is to plan, coordinate, and promote scientific and technological research in Portugal. Additional financial support has been provided by the Luso-American Development Foundation. This foundation contributes to Portugal's economic and social development by promoting cooperation between Portugal and the United States in scientific, cultural, educational, and commercial fields.

In the previous two conferences,* experts in the application of microcomputers to agriculture, health, population, energy, and education described current and prospective uses in the respective sectors of developing countries. The predictions of these experts were, in general, extrapolations from present practice in which the availability of computers with greater power and lower cost was presumed. The experts were more conversant with applications than with technologies.

---

* See *Microcomputers and Their Applications for Developing Countries* and *Microcomputer Applications in Education and Training for Developing Countries.*

The focus of the third meeting described in this report is on emerging technologies. Through presentations and discussions, areas are identified in which departures from existing practice can provide generically new solutions to development problems. Problems inherent in these new technologies are also described. These issues are most capably defined by those who have helped shape the advanced technologies.

There is a real need for this kind of advice. Not surprisingly, relatively few decision-makers in development assistance agencies and developing countries have the expertise to assess the risks and benefits of cutting-edge technologies in microcomputers. An unbiased critical assessment of potential impacts and priorities in this field is important to these decision-makers.

Recommendations on special research and development priorities for developing countries are also needed. Research and development in industrialized countries is driven by demands unrelated to the technological requirements of developing countries. Developing countries must be aware of the nature and direction of industrialized research and development, however, to use and build on it.

Although the prices of microcomputers have decreased dramatically, these costs are still not inconsequential for developing countries. It is therefore important that microcomputer investments be made with a clear understanding of their immediate and future uses, of which capabilities will be enhanced, and of which new tasks will be performed.

It is vital in this situation that decision-makers in developing countries consider these advanced technologies in their planning. Many developing countries can benefit from adopting or adapting elements of currently available, knowledge-based graphic, design, or expert systems. In fact, many such applications have more to contribute in developing countries. Because many of these advanced applications are at the beginning of their growth curves, particularly in the utilization of microcomputers, an opportunity exists for scientists and engineers in developing countries to take the lead in some of these areas.

The advanced hardware concepts that will soon be realized will allow increasingly complex systems to be used with microcomputers. The combined advances in hardware and software represent a tremendous opportunity for developing countries to move forward more quickly, to embrace a field in its entirety and transform it to match their needs.

The purpose of this report is to facilitate this process.

William J. Lawless, Jr.

Overview

Overview

The purpose of this report is to explore the opportunities offered by advanced microcomputer technologies to developing countries. This exploration begins with an examination of the character of these technologies and proceeds with information on how these technologies relate to resource assessment, resource utilization, and communication in developing countries. In each of these sections, there are surveys of recent developments, reports on specific applications, and investigations of microcomputer use in new areas. The conclusions and recommendations of the participants in this meeting are presented in the following section.

THE TECHNOLOGIES

In the broadest sense, the new technologies are concerned with information and its acquisition, manipulation, and transfer. These new technologies are truly revolutionary because they provide computer systems with historically unique capabilities.

For example:

- They are superior to all previous information handling systems, usually in orders of magnitude and across several dimensions.
- They are intrinsically capable of integrating systems and concepts to unify conventionally disparate activities.
- They enlarge the domain of feasible achievements in many spheres of human activity.

These and other characteristics of computer systems will affect present and future generations. Computers are entering a new phase in their existence. The capacity for rapid calculation, endless iteration, and other well-structured applications is being succeeded by the integrative processing of many different types of applications in more flexible environments. Integrative processing enables a computer system to serve as an expert in a wide variety of areas by interacting with the user to provide the guidance normally given by a highly trained and experienced consultant.

In their initial applications, microcomputers were essentially used as stand-alone machines. A rapid transition is now being made from stand-alone uses to microcomputer networks. In a parallel movement, the communications power of microcomputers is being developed in a number of areas.

This networking process, and its increasing communications content, is changing the way people live and work. It also has the power to penetrate traditional frontiers between activities, businesses, and geographic regions. The use of computer networks on a sectoral, national, or global scale has become a significant policy issue. The continued growth of networking and communication raises concerns that such expansion may be disadvantageous for developing countries outside the loop of shared information.

New technologies create new activities. Computer-based production systems have special relevance for developing countries. In some cases, these systems are being used to modernize mature industries in developed countries and reduce the amount of labor-intensive processing now farmed out to developing countries. There are indications that developing countries may no longer have a comparative advantage in the semiconductor, clothing, and metal-processing industries because of the advances made in computer-aided engineering. Developing-country strategies for a stable manufacturing economy can become obsolete in an economy of innovation. These countries must examine and introduce some of these new technologies in their operations to remain competitive.

The first paper on technologies, "Advanced Computer Concepts" by Harry Huskey, traces the history of computers from the concepts of Babbage to today's supercomputers; the cost-performance pattern for computers is clearly defined and implicitly projected. This provides the context for the next paper, "The Impact of Memory Technology Advances on Microcomputers" by

Richard Dubbe and Durkee Richards. This paper examines developments in low-cost mass storage—the technology that initially made microcomputers practical and is now making them powerful.

In "Artificial Intelligence: An Overview," Eugénio Oliveira examines the development and application of this concept, defines accomplishments, and suggests future trends. The following paper, "Prolog for Artificial Intelligence Projects: The Portuguese Experience," by Luís Damas and Miguel Filgueiras, describes the features of the Prolog programming language that contributed to its wide use in Portuguese artificial intelligence projects.

In "Computer-Aided Design: A Primer," Glenn Hart introduces the capabilities of this technique together with information on the basic hardware and software required for its implementation and the cost savings that may result.

In "Applied Expert Systems," Raoul Smith describes the architecture, software tools, development issues, and market for expert systems. Particular emphasis is placed on "make or buy" decisions and some of the issues involved are considered.

The various uses of computers in image processing are covered in "Computer Vision" by Anil K. Jain. Diverse applications in document processing, industrial automation, remote sensing, medicine, nondestructive testing, scientific analysis, agriculture, and personal identification are indicated and basic information on how the systems are created is provided. The special value of visual sensors in industrial automation is described by A. J. Padilha and J. C. D. Marques dos Santos in the next paper, "A Multiple Microprocessor Architecture for Real-Time Visual Inspection."

RESOURCE ASSESSMENT

Human and natural resources are the prime assets of every country. Accurate qualitative and quantitative information on these resources is required for effective national planning. In addition, because neither one of these assets is static, a country's status, direction, and potential can be determined only if data on human and natural resources are periodically gathered and analyzed. This type of information flow can help focus on critical aspects in development and provide the guidance essential for national planning. It is especially important that decision-makers in developing countries have an understanding of the computer technologies that can assist in dealing with the complexities of planning.

Demographics that include health, education, employment, and income are needed to study populations. Renewable and nonrenewable resources must also be considered. Renewable resources, as represented by forestry and agriculture, must be analyzed to determine their stability and capacity for sustained use. Watercourses, as potential sources for hydropower and irrigation, must also be monitored. The extent and value of nonrenewable minerals and fossil fuels must be determined.

A more valid plan for national development can evolve when timely and accurate data on human and natural resources are combined. Microcomputers can play a major role in the attainment of this goal. Eight papers on human resources are provided in this section, ranging from the collection and analysis of population data to consideration of health care on a national, community, and individual basis. Four papers on natural resources help define the new tools available for gathering and analyzing geographic information.

The first paper on human resources is "An Integrated Microcomputer Processing System for Census and Survey Data" by Barbara N. Diskin. This report describes the development of microcomputer software for a processing system, including data entry, editing, tabulation, statistical analysis, demographic analysis, and operational control modules.

The role of the microcomputer in the administration of the Brazilian Health Information System is described in a paper by Marcio Humberto Montagna Cammarota. Microcomputers facilitate information flow to help improve the efficiency and reduce the cost of the services provided. In addition, centralization-decentralization issues can be examined to determine the optimal management and funding levels.

In "Population Program Applications of Expert Systems," John Daly examines the practical aspects of whether computers can emulate the performance of health care professionals in population programs and other medical applications. In "A Growing-with-the-User Expert System for Clinical Use," José Negrete describes how developing countries can build innovative expert systems through a participative effort of computer scientists and users. These systems are developed around a core algorithm and tested by simulating the environment.

Two papers, "Disease Control in the Community: Toward Microcomputer-Supported Decision Models for Health Centers" by Teodoro Briz and "SIGUS: A Microcomputer-Based Management System for Primary Health Care Centers" by Alexandre Abrantes, focus on community health care. Briz defines the objectives of health care centers and the special value of microcomputers in their operation; Abrantes relates experience in the development and introduction of a system for the administration of a community health center.

The wide range of current and potential uses of microcomputers and other electronic equipment in diagnosis and patient monitoring is discussed by Murray Eden in "Computer Technology and Biomedical Instrumentation." Additional studies on the analysis of biological signals are reported in "A Distributed Processing Architecture for Real-Time Biological Data Analysis" by Pedro Guedes de Oliveira, José Carlos Príncipe, and António Nunes de Cruz.

In "Natural Resource Analysis, Assessment, and Management," Ted Albert examines the use of microcomputers in the inventory and utilization of natural resources. Several expert systems to be used in natural resource development are described and geographic information systems are introduced.

In "Geographic Information Systems," Vincent Robinson elaborates on the characteristics of geographic information systems and provides two examples of their use in developing countries. The implementation and impact of Portugal's geographic information system is described in "Super Microcomputer Networks for a National Geographic Information System," by António Sousa da Câmara, António da Silva e Castro, and Rui Gonçalves Henriques.

In "Microcomputers in Agricultural Development," F. J. Tilak Viegas describes the applications and limitations of microcomputers in farm management, in the planning of agricultural development, and in project monitoring and evaluation in Portuguese agriculture.

RESOURCE UTILIZATION

The productive and economic utilization of a country's resources can also be guided by advanced microcomputer technologies. Expert systems can help in almost all phases of production in various industrial processes, from product design to quality and inventory control.

In "Expert Systems for Design and Manufacture," David C. Brown reviews the applications of expert systems in these areas and defines some of the preconditions for and benefits of their use. Specific examples of these systems are provided and the special value of their use in developing countries is described.

In "Microcomputers for Industrial Automation in Small- and Medium-Sized Industries in Brazil," Flavio Grynszpan places the new microcomputer-based technologies in the context of countries where unemployment may be high, the level of industrial development low, and the technological infrastructure poor. The paper gives three examples of automation in different industries and describes some of the social consequences.

A flexible system for industrial process control has been developed at the University of Zimbabwe that uses locally available components. The design and use of this programmable logic controller is described in "A Microprocessor-Based Sequence Controller" by Engelbert T. Kapuya, R. K. Appiah, and S. M. Kundishora.

One of the special uses of expert systems is in the diagnosis of problems in industrial processes or complex networks, especially when failures may occur infrequently or in the absence of a human expert. In "The Field Limitations of Diagnostics in Processor-Controlled Industrial Systems," A. D. V. Nihal Kularatne provides examples of field responses to rare problems.

Industrial progress in developing countries depends on assured and increasing power supplies. Generating stations, transmission lines, and distribution systems are required for electric power. The complexities and interactions in such systems and the use of microcomputer-based software in their design is covered in "Computer-Aided Power System Design" by Sridhar Mitta.

Like electricity, water is a valuable commodity that must be distributed where and when it is needed to facilitate development. The use of microcomputers in the design, construction, operation, and management of water resource systems is covered in "Applications of Microcomputers in Water Resources Engineering" by Don Charles Henry Senarath.

Broad decisions on the timing, size, and construction of water supply and sanitation systems in developing countries can be guided by programs that draw on the experience of other countries. Information on this application of microcomputers is provided in

"Intelligent Programs for Public Investments in Community Water Supply and Sanitation Systems" by Donald T. Lauria.

In "Applications of Artificial Intelligence in Civil Engineering," Brian Brademeyer and Fred Moavenzadeh examine not only computer-aided design and drafting in this field, but applications of automated condition assessment and robotics. Computers can interpret complex sensor data on building sites to assist design before construction and to guide maintenance after construction. Construction can be automated to some degree through the use of robotics. The special relevance of these applications in developing countries is discussed.

Statistical expertise is often a scarce and costly resource in developing countries. In "An Expert System for Time-Series Statistical Analysis," Pablo Noriega B. V., Carlos del Cueto M., Luis M. Rodríguez P., and Ileana Gutiérrez R. describe a system that will act as an on-line expert advisor to diagnose the specific analytical needs of the user and recommend appropriate tests or analysis for the data.

COMMUNICATIONS

Communications and information transfer are areas in which computer use is highly developed. The capacity of computers to store and organize information is of little value if data cannot be effectively and efficiently transmitted to the user.

Although continuous progress is being made in improving communication within computer systems, improvements in communication between users and computers are proceeding more slowly. The paper "Intelligent Interface," by Andrew C. Kapusto discusses the practical applications of natural language in computerized information exchange systems, including voice recognition and voice response.

Computer-aided translation is a special form of communication. In the paper "English to Thai Machine Translation," Wanchai Rivepiboon describes the mechanisms used by an existing translation system and discusses the directions for future research.

Another example of language in communication is provided in "The Need for Standards in Computer Graphics" by João Duarte

Cunha. The consequences of the few standards that exist in computer graphics for developing countries and recent work in standards development are discussed.

Computer networks enable resources to be shared and processing to be distributed. A strategy to distribute tasks and computing power on a network geared toward balanced application loads is discussed in "Network-Based Information Systems: A Role for Intelligent Workstations" by Joseph F. P. Luhukay. A design approach that results in a network in which the application functions and the network support functions are fully integrated is described in "Application-Driven Networks" by Kiluba Pembamoto.

The papers "The Use of Microcomputers to Improve Telephone Service" by Augusto Júlio Casaca, "Loop Signaling for PCM Equipment" by Vasco Lagarto and Lusitana Delgado, and "Design and Manufacture of Modern Telecommunication Equipment in Portugal" by Candido M. Lopes Manso all address important aspects of the Portuguese telecommunications network. Casaca covers the introduction of digital hardware in the network for supervision and maintenance purposes, Lagarto and Delgado describe improvements in signalling techniques that can ease the transition to a digital network, and Lopes Manso suggests research and development strategies in this field.

Some considerations involved in the substitution of computers for teachers in education are the subject of the final paper on communications–"The Use of Expert Systems in Educational Software" by Ernesto Costa.

João Cravinho
A. D. Figueiredo

Conclusions and Recommendations

Conclusions and Recommendations

CONCLUSIONS

The Green Revolution had its impact through the introduction of new crop varieties and agricultural techniques. A Gray Revolution is now beginning. Human reasoning—the use of the brain's gray matter—is being simulated by computers in a field broadly defined as Artificial Intelligence (AI), which introduces new techniques to address development problems. Past progress in computer use and power, although rapid, has been evolutionary. Current and future applications of AI are revolutionary.

Conventional computer uses expand human capacities in number manipulation and text processing. New AI systems mimic human capacities in problem solving, sight, hearing, speech, and various motor functions. Although most administrators realize that computers can be used in labor-intensive record-keeping and accounting, few recognize their potential role in knowledge-intensive planning and management. The traditional use of computers in data analysis has now been augmented by newer applications in data evaluation and by the more impressive use of expert systems in making decisions based on these data.

Expert systems allow the use of special-purpose consultants when and where they are needed. Problems that arise infrequently or that require unavailable knowledge or experience, for example, can be solved through the use of expert systems. In addition, less demanding but repetitive and tedious tasks can be handled even in conditions that make human involvement undesirable. The range of applications for expert systems is broad and is increasing with many sectoral opportunities in manufacturing, medicine, agriculture, and education. It is perhaps more important that uses for expert systems and other cutting-edge technologies abound in national planning.

Strategic planning for developing countries requires economic data, qualitative and quantitative information on human and natural resources, and guidance on options in resource utilization. As described in the papers presented at this meeting, cutting edge technologies can be applied in strategic planning in each of these areas. Applications of these new technologies in asssessing human resources exist in census operations, health care, and family planning. Geographic information systems can form the basis for planning the development of a country's natural resources. Computer-assisted design, computer-assisted manufacture, computer vision and sensing, and robotics can be used in resource utilization. In addition, the use of computers in communications can enhance the information flow and management of all of these operations.

The use of these cutting-edge computer technologies in developing countries is not predicated on earlier uses of less advanced computer technologies. Familiarity with basic computer theory and use is advantageous in understanding these new technologies, but it is no more necessary than to have driven a car before flying an airplane. The automobile/airplane analogy is apt in another way: these advanced computer technologies allow activities and accomplishments that were not previously possible.

It is surprising that many of these newer technologies are easier to use than traditional computer applications. Natural language commands can be used, allowance can be made for missing data, and some systems can explain their actions and even their problems with built-in diagnostics.

Direct and immediate applications for these new technologies exist in developing countries. Obstacles to these applications are not inherent in the technologies, but in their selection, in identifying and defining the problems that need to be addressed, and in matching or modifying available cutting-edge technologies for their solution. Access to the technologies may also be difficult in some countries.

Thus, technologies exist that can provide significant benefits for developing countries. Development assistance agencies and their clients need to understand the vital importance of these technologies for developing countries and to provide the assistance required to introduce and support their use. All developing countries should have at least a minimal capacity to utilize these technologies. They cannot afford less.

RECOMMENDATIONS

Although there are many potential applications for computer-based cutting-edge technologies in developing countries, these technologies should be selected and their use guided by policy-makers within those countries. This requires that these administrators be aware of the possibilities and options in this field. Development assistance groups should recognize that transposing (or imposing) technical solutions is often counterproductive. Locally initiated solutions should be encouraged and supported. Assistance agencies should therefore:

- Organize workshops and seminars to demonstrate these new technologies and their applications. Participants in these meetings should be decision-makers—the senior administrators that have the authority to introduce new programs.
- Support participation in conventions and trade shows that focus on new computer technologies. Participation in these meetings is important for those who must implement new programs so that information can be gained on a broad spectrum of hardware, software, and suppliers.
- Assist scientists and engineers in developing countries with relevant formal graduate and undergraduate training. This training is important for those who will support these new systems, and will help develop the capacity to devise new or modified applications.
- Facilitate access to periodicals, texts, hardware, software, supplies, spare parts, and equipment repair. This access is important at all levels to maintain and expand operations and applications, and to stay up-to-date in new areas.
- Establish regional networks for cooperation among developing country groups in applying these technologies.

- Create linkages between centers of excellence in these fields in developed countries and appropriate institutions in developing countries.

These linkages and networks could serve many valuable purposes. Regional centers could be established in existing developing country institutions. After an initial emphasis on problems and service, their long-term efforts would be focused on resource and knowledge sharing, in providing on- and off-line guidance for network participants, and in developing local expertise.

Libraries for lending equipment as well as books, manuals, and software could be developed. Guidance on maintenance and repair could be provided. This type of facility could also become a contact point for vendors, provide training, and serve as a center for homegrown experts. It could also provide feedback to manufacturers on special equipment needs or protection for hostile physical environments. Software could be created or modified to serve regional needs. These centers could also track successes and failures in various applications and share experiences with other regional centers.

New computer technologies present opportunities for developing countries to speed up many traditionally cumbersome or inexact bureaucratic processes. For developing countries to gain from advances in these technologies, an effective means to share information on their use and provide assistance for their implementation must be provided. These recommendations offer a way in which this can be accomplished.

The Technologies

1

Advanced Computer Concepts

HARRY D. HUSKEY

The first proposed automatic computer was the difference engine of Charles Babbage (1822). Of more interest is his proposed analytical engine, which in today's terminology would be called a tape-sequenced von Neumann computer.

Such automatic computers can be classified on several bases. One such basis is in terms of storage of information; another is relative to the kind of logic circuits used. Perhaps of more importance is the means of controlling the sequence of operations.

Little happened with respect to automatic digital computation until about 1940 in Germany and 1944 in the United States. Konrad Zuse's Z3 computer was fully functional in 1941; however, it was destroyed in an air raid and was never used for routine computing. In the United States, the Harvard Mark I, a punched-paper, tape-sequenced computer that used mechanical registers, was dedicated. The first electronic general-purpose computer–the 18,000-tube ENIAC at the University of Pennsylvania–was dedicated in 1946.

During the design of the ENIAC computer, the group at the University of Pennsylvania conceived of a stored program computer (instructions and data stored in the same media) called EDVAC that used acoustic delay lines for memory. John von Neumann visited this group and wrote his well-known "EDVAC

Report." In 1946, Wilkes attended the summer course at the University of Pennsylvania and returned to Cambridge to build the EDSAC. Eckert and Mauchly left the ENIAC-EDVAC project and started a company to build UNIVACs. Hughes Aircraft tied together some IBM punched-card machines to perform general computation. IBM marketed this computer as the Card Programmed Calculator (CPC); the first deliveries were made in 1949. These developments are summarized in the following table:

	Conceived	*Operational*	*Produced*
Automatic computer	1833 Babbage	1941 Zuse (Germany) 1944 Harvard Mark I	1949 IBM CPC
Electronic computer		1946 ENIAC	
Stored program computer	1944 EDVAC	1949 EDSAC Cambridge	1951 UNIVAC

The stored program computer, in which instructions were placed in memory in the same way as numbers, was important because it was the only flexible way to control the sequence of operations at rates comparable to the availability of operands. Of much more importance was the fact that this system enabled one to "compute" on programs, which led to compiler development and the whole field of computer languages.

The growth of computer memory from 1945 to 1955 is shown in the following table. (One word equals approximately 4 bytes; 1 byte equals 8 bits.)

Computer	*Year*	*Memory Capacity (Words)*
ENIAC	1946	20 (electronic)
SWAC	1950	256 (William's tube)
SEAC	1950	512 (delay line)
UNIVAC	1951	1,000 (delay line)
IBM 701	1952	4,096 (William's tube)
IBM 704	1955	8,192 (magnetic core)

Core memories reached a capacity of about 4 Mbytes (million bytes) with cycle times of one microsecond (IBM 360-85, 1969). All mainframe computers since about 1970 have used semiconductor memories. Microcomputers were introduced in 1975 with 16 to 64 Kbytes (1,000 bytes) of memory. Many personal computers today are offered with a minimum of 640 Kbytes of memory.

DATA STORAGE

Punched Cards

Although Babbage conceived of using punched cards to control the sequencing of operations in 1835, their use in data processing had to wait until the 1980 census. Most large computing systems used punched cards for shelf storage and for input and output until the 1980s.

Magnetic Tape

The use of magnetic tape for auxiliary and shelf storage dates from the 1950s. The IBM 9-track tape was the industry standard for many years. Magnetic tapes are still used for archival storage and companies recently have been offering high-performance cassette systems. The use of magnetic tape for archival storage may be displaced by optical disks.

Magnetic Disks

In 1956, IBM offered the first on-line disk; it stored 5 million characters on 50 "platters." Disks have since improved in performance and declined in cost. Large disks currently hold from 15 to 5,000 Mbytes and small hard disks hold from 10 to 300 Mbytes. Since 1970, floppy disks have become available with capacities of 0.14 to 1.2 Mbytes. Floppy disks have also declined in cost; disks are currently available for $1.

Optical Disks

Optical disks have a higher capacity and are lower in cost than magnetic disks. Unlike magnetic tape, optical disks can be accessed randomly. They are removable from the drive like floppy disks. They are also very rugged and can be mailed. The reading head does not come close to the surface, so there is no wear and less sensitivity to dust particles. Optical disks are currently slower than magnetic disks and the lack of standards is slowing their development.

About 6,000 optical disk drives were produced worldwide in 1985. Almost all of these were write-once disks. A 14-inch, write-once optimal disk can store the contents of 50 reels of standard 6,250 bits per inch (bpi) 9-track computer tape. Several companies expected to have a manufacturing capacity of 500,000 to 1,000,000 disks by the end of 1986. One Japanese company claims it is now making 10,000 5-1/4 inch disks per month with yields of 70 to 80 percent. About 20 firms worldwide are developing "jukeboxes" to automatically change optical disks. Others are making optical tape cartridges that hold 2.5 to 20 Gbytes (gigabytes or billion bytes) of information. A Japanese company offers a drive that stores 1.2 Gbytes on a 12-inch removable cartridge.

One company offers a write-once, read-only (WORM) 400-Mbyte controller and drive for about the same price as a 40-Mbyte hard disk. The replaceable disk cartridge costs about $150—a price that will come down as volume develops. Although drives are being developed for 3-1/2, 5-1/4, and 8-inch drives, one consultant says that 90 percent of all optical drives will be 5-1/4 inches by 1990.

Ninety-five percent of business information is stored on paper; this is the target of the optical disk industry. Optical disks for personal computers (PCs) therefore represent a small share of the market.

Companies are also offering compact disk, read-only memory (CD-ROM) disk drives. One model stores 600 Mbytes on a disk drive that is 3-1/4 × 4-1/4 × 8 inches. This is equivalent to more than 1,500 floppy disks. Such disks are ideal for reference information; an encyclopedia is available on CD-ROM. The disks cost $199 and a drive, disk, and access software package is $1,395. A New York company is planning a CD-ROM-based telephone directory. The April 1986 issue of *IEEE Spectrum* lists 68 data bases available on CD-ROM and lists 11 companies that supply drives. Prices range from $500 to $2,500. Master disks cost from $3,000 to $5,000 and copies are $10 each in quantities of 1,000 (summer 1986 prices). The 3M Corporation offers a read-write 5-1/4 inch removable optical disk that stores 300 to 500 Mbytes.

COMPUTER LOGIC

Before 1950, electronic computers used dual-control grid tubes (a two-input NAND gate) or multiple cathode followers (positive OR, negative AND) for logic functions. Computers finished in the 1950s began to use semiconductor diodes (germanium) for logic gates. Silicon diodes with better performance and greater reliability soon appeared. The first transistors appeared in computers in 1954 (TRADIC, Bell Laboratories) and in production computers in 1955. Integration followed in 1969 and more and more logical units were placed on a single chip. Depending on the number of units, the circuits were classified more or less as follows:

Integration	Logical Elements	Year
Small-scale	2-64	1959
Medium-scale	64-2,000	1966
Large-scale	2,000-64,000	1973
Very large-scale	64,000-2,000,000	1984
Ultra large-scale	2,000,000-64,000,000	?

In the next decade, switching devices that are currently 2 micrometers in size will become so small that switching energies will be comparable to that of stray alpha particles. This means that all circuits will have to use error-correcting techniques that depend not only on memory but on logical functions. Whether the upper limits shown in the previous table will soon be reached depends on such pragmatic questions as:

- Can 100 million transistors, each dissipating 10 microwatts (1 kilowatt), be packaged on a single chip?
- At 5 volts, can currents of 200 amperes lead to reduced reliability without associated electromigration effects?

For example, the Cray 2 dissipates 150 kilowatts in about one cubic meter.

Some authors have noted that IC designers were producing a few hundred circuits per day in 1984. This sounds like the number of lines of debugged code that system programmers produce. Assuming the number is 500 circuits, a 64,000 transistor chip would require 500 man-years of effort. This places a great premium on design automation and silicon compilers.

ARCHITECTURE

The architecture of the first computers was as simple as possible; emphasis was placed on the sentiment "Let's get something that works!" The difference between processing and input-output speeds led to overlapping operations. Binary number systems promised more computing power per dollar; consequently, two lines of computers were developed: scientific computers and data processing computers (e.g., the IBM 704 and 705 computers).

The high cost of computer systems led to the development of operating systems that "kept the hardware busy." Problems were therefore run in batch mode. The difference in speed of input and output versus processing speeds led to overlapping input, output, and computation with queues existing between each stage. Early systems called "spooling" systems used magnetic tape to buffer the process. Magnetic disks replaced magnetic tape for this purpose in the 1960s. Even though disks were more efficient than tape systems, the time to get a small job (e.g., one minute of computation) through the system might have been several hours. This poor turn-about led to interest in time-sharing, which is discussed later. The development of the ALGOL language led to the use of stacks.

The relative decline in the cost of logic brought the two computer lines together. Thus, the Burroughs 5,000 and the IBM 360 series had features for both scientific and business computation. There are exceptions; the CDC computers were optimized for scientific computation.

The mid-1960s saw the development of time-sharing. The Massachusetts Institute of Technology developed MULTICS, the University of California developed the SDS940, IBM produced the model 67, and Digital Equipment Corporation (DEC) produced its PDP11 series (1970). The idea was that several users would sit at terminals and a scheduling program would successively give each a few milliseconds of computing time.

The following are three examples of recent architectures:

	IBM 370/168	*DEC VAX-11/780*	*INTEL iAPX-432*
Year	1973	1978	1982
Instruction size	2 to 6 bytes	2 to 57 bytes	6 to 321 bits
Control memory	420 Kbytes	480 Kbytes	64 Kbytes
Number of instructions	208	303	222
Cache size	64 Kbytes	64 Kbytes	0

All three architectures use microprogramming. The Intel 432 never made it!

Reduced instruction set computers (RISC) have been recently proposed on the basis that, being simpler, they can run faster and give more through-put than conventional architectures. The characteristics of three RISC computers are as follows:

	IBM 801	SCI	MIPS
Year	1980	1982	1983
Number of instructions	120	39	55

These RISC computers do not use microprogramming; control is "hard-wired," each instruction is 32 bits, and execution is register-to-register (the references to memory are LOAD and STORE instructions). The design of these computers and their associated compilers has been integrated to improve performance.

In January of 1986, IBM announced the PC RT. Its claimed performance is comparable with the INtel 80386 and with the DEC VAX 11/780 minicomputer. Another approach is to offer a board-level RISC computer that can be plugged into Multibus II (Intel), which can deliver 3 to 8 million instructions per second at prices between $3,000 and $8,000. The CPU has 102 fixed format instructions, 32 general-purpose instructions, 32 bit registers, a five-stage pipeline, and a cache control for 8 Kbytes of data or instructions.

USER LANGUAGES

Because the developers of the first stored program computers in 1950 were primarily concerned with whether they would work, most of their efforts went into memory design and the design of arithmetic circuits. Instruction sets were limited to general-purpose computation. Little attention was paid to how the user would solve a problem.

Although some work had been performed on computer languages, the first significant event was the release of FORTRAN by IBM in 1957. This was soon followed by a committee-designed ALGOL and a U.S. Government-sponsored COBOL. FORTRAN and COBOL survive today without significant changes. It is probably true that more lines of code exist in these languages than in all other computer languages.

The arrival of time-sharing systems in the 1960s led to the development of BASIC. This language was simpler than FORTRAN or COBOL, but it had a superb user support environment. Incomplete fragments of code could be tried and variables could be inspected. BASIC was interpretive, so changes could be made and tested quickly. Its drawback was that execution was extremely slow.

In response to ALGOL, IBM developed PL/1. The development of ALGOL 68 followed. Like its predecessor, ALGOL 68 was not attractive to mainstream computer users. An alternate, PASCAL, was more widely accepted, particularly among small computer users and in the academic community.

The difficulties of correctly writing large programs that could be maintained and easily explained to others led to great interest in so-called structured programs. The ALGOL-PASCAL developments supported this idea.

These difficulties with large programs led the U.S. Department of Defense to support the development of a new language called Ada. Irrespective of its technical merits, about which there are great arguments, its forced use by a major customer guarantees its existence.

The boom in personal computers has generated a market for special-purpose programs. For example, more than 700,000 copies of WordStar (an editor-formatter) and VISICALC (a spreadsheet program) have been sold. Another word processor, MULTIMATE, now outsells WordStar. The dBase II and dBase III systems are the most popular data base systems. It has been reported that PC users run one program 80 percent of the time and that 85 percent of the PCs are used for word processing.

OPERATING SYSTEMS

An operating system is a program that controls the allotment of resources to the users. Although earlier systems existed, IBM's OS360 and Bell Telephone Laboratories' UNIX serve as examples. The IBM OS360 was developed for large batch-processing systems and UNIX was developed for time-sharing systems.

The first microcomputer operating system was CP/M (1976),

but MS-DOS has become the most popular system. Versions of UNIX (developed by AT&T for minicomputers) recently have become available, and there are prospects that a version of VM (IBM's big machine operating system) will become available for microcomputers. Currently, 100,000 computers run UNIX and about 7,000,000 run MS-DOS. Some observers think that UNIX will not become popular and that MS-DOS (particularly with improved versions) will continue to lead the field. It is expected that MS-DOS 5 will permit physical memories of up to 3 Mbytes to be addressed and an MS-DOS 6 is expected for the 80386.

USER INTERFACE

Input

Almost all PCs use a conventional keyboard. In control applications other sensors may be directly connected. Development is under way for voice input systems. Currently, 100-word vocabularies work and 1,000-word vocabularies will soon be available. Computer-game systems have been developed in which joy-stick inputs allow one to position a cursor any place on the display. "Mouse" systems allow a user to move a hand-held device over a table surface, which moves the display cursor accordingly. "Painting" systems are available that allow a user to paint pictures and letter words, which are useful features for making slides for lecture presentations.

Output

The first low-cost printers for PCs were dot matrix printers. If one wanted letter-quality printing, then one bought a daisy wheel printer. Now with more printing pins and more strokes per character, the dot matrix printers print near letter-quality work. They print draft-quality work at a higher speed with fewer strokes. Dot matrix printers have been advertised for $98.

Ink jet printers print near letter quality at 110 characters per second and are very quiet. They print draft-quality work at a speed of up to 220 characters per second.

Laser printers are being offered that print 300 × 300 dots to the inch and print 12 pages per minute; the price is $3,499.

Dot matrix printers are being offered for color printing. They use multicolor ribbons that when mixed produce seven colors and black. They print at speeds of 100 letter-quality and up to 400 draft-quality characters per second.

Thermal printers produce brilliant colors, but are noticeably slow. The paper is also still expensive at 30 to 40 cents per page.

Video displays have been improving in step with other developments. Current PC video displays provide resolutions of about 640 × 400 pixels (picture points). Pictures developed on such displays show the individual points, but the characters do not have curves as smooth as one would like. Displays of 1,000 × 1,000 are available, but they are expensive and are primarily used in so-called work stations. However, the resulting pictures are much more realistic. Memory used to be a limitation in display quality—a 640 × 400 color display using 8 bits per pixel requires 256 Kbytes of memory.

PERSONAL COMPUTERS

The first personal computers—the MITS Altair and the Apple I—were introduced in 1975. The development of personal computers is summarized in the following table.

Personal Computer Introductions

1975	Jan MITS Altair	1982	Aug Commodore 64
	Apr Altair BASIC		
		1983	Jan Apple Lisa
1976	Mar CP/M		Jan Lotus 1-2-3
			Mar IBM PC XT
1977	May Apple II		Nov IBM PCjr
	Aug Radio Shack TRS-80		
	Sep Commodore PET	1984	Jan Apple Macintosh
			Jun Lotus Symphony
1979	Apr WordStar		Jun dBase III
	Jun VisiCalc		Jul Atari ST
1980	Jan ZORK		Sep Commodore Amiga
	May Apple III		
		1986	Jan IBM RT PC
1981	Jan CP/M-86		
	Feb dBASE II		
	Apr Osborne I		
	Aug IBM PC		
	Aug MS-DOS		

Most personal computers use the Intel 8088 or 8086 central processors or their descendents (the 80286 or 80386). The Apple used the Motorola 6502. The Apple Macintosh, the Commodore Amiga, and the Atari ST use the M68000. Speed has increased; the 6502 ran at 1.2 Mhz, the 8088 at 4.77 Mhz, and the 80286 and M68000 at about 8 Mhz. The xePIX company in New Hampshire offers a computer that uses the M68020 running at 12.5 Mhz, with a 20-Mbyte hard disk, serial and parallel ports, the UNIX operating system, and up to 5 Mbytes of RAM for $4,995. The company claims that the computer runs at 3 million instructions per second. Intel has announced hypercube combinations of 80286s, which can theoretically do 424 million operations per second. In practice, users do well to have programs that get more than 10 percent of the maximum speed in such computer systems.

The first IBM PC had 16 Kbytes of random-access memory (RAM). The original Intel 8080 addressed 64 Kbytes of memory, whereas the Intel 68020 and the 80386 computers address 4 Gbytes of memory. The Intel 80386 can address up to 64 trillion bytes of virtual memory and can run 2 to 3 million instructions per second. During its development, the memory of the Intel 80386 has improved in speed by 20 times and the address space has increased by 100,000. The Intel 8088 and 8086 computers address memory in blocks of 64 Kbytes; the use of segment registers extends this range to 1 Mbyte. However, operating system constraints lessen the availability of memory to the user; for example, MS-DOS gives the user a maximum of 640 Kbytes. Memory costs less than one-fifth of what it did 2 years ago. Consequently, basic computers are being delivered that have 640 Kbytes of memory.

Floppy disks have similarly improved. The first Apple disks stored 143 Kbytes. Now 5-1/4-inch disks store up to 1.2 Mbytes. At the same time, hard disks have improved in performance and declined dramatically in price. Hard disks are now available in 10 to 30 Mbytes for $400 to $1,000. One Japanese company has announced a 4-Mbyte, 3-1/2-inch drive that uses so-called perpendicular recording.

Software products have become increasingly oriented toward novice or intermittent users to make manuals unnecessary. Software products therefore offer menus and "help" pages.

Several computer companies are offering portable computers that weigh 10 to 15 pounds. One model has a 25 × 80 LDC display with an electroluminescent background, 640 Kbytes of RAM, two

3-1/2-inch floppy disk drives, serial and parallel ports, a 5-hour rechargeable battery, a weight of 12 pounds, and a price of $2,399. Zenith, Toshiba, and Hitachi offer similar models.

Desk-top PCs are declining in price. The clone market that manufactures PCs that are compatible with the de facto standard IBM PC offered (summer 1986) computers for $1,250 with 640 Kbytes of memory, 1.2-Mbyte floppy disk drives, and a UNIX-style operating system. Hard disks are available with capacities from 20 to 40 Mbytes and a 39-millisecond access time at prices from $549 to $699. One company has advertised a 120 Mbyte hard disk for $388. It seems that every month someone advertises systems or components for less.

THE CURRENT MICRO-MINI-MAINFRAME SITUATION

New mainframes are becoming more powerful through the use of parallelism and cache memories to make operands more quickly available. For example, the Cray-2 mainframe can execute 64-bit floating point instructions at a rate of more than 1 billion per second. The following are examples of high-performance computers:

	Processor	*Memory*	*Processors*	*Operations (M)*
Cray-2	1-4	2,000 Mbcom		1,000F
Multimax	2-20	4-32 Mbcom	NS32032	20
Sequent	2-12	-28 Mbcom	NS32032	20
Flex/32	-20	1-4 Mb/cpu	NS32032+FP	
iPSC	32-128	0.5 Mb/cpu	80286+7	
System 14	16-256	1 Mb/cpu	80286+7	
Ncube/ten	1,024	0.25 Mb/cpu	new chip	500F

[1,000F means 1 billion floating point operations per second]

The last three computers listed in the table have so-called hypercube structures. A processor at each node is connected only to its nearest neighbors. Processors at the corners of a cube would each be connected to three neighbors. In a hypercube configuration with 1,024 processors, each would be connected to 10 neighbors. Each node of the Ncube/ten computer consists of a processor chip and memory chips only. The processor is a 2.5-micron, 160,000-transistor, 10-Mhz chip that includes a 32-bit general processor, a 64-bit floating point processor, a memory interface with error correction, and 22 direct memory access channels. Because hardware costs are essentially per chip costs, powerful computers of this design can be relatively cheap.

Just as mainframe computers have been increasing in power, so have minicomputers. The increasing power of very large-scale integrated (VLSI) processors and the declining costs of memory have blurred the distinction between micro-, supermicro-, mini-, and mainframe computers. Problems that formerly required a minicomputer can now be run on the micro- or supermicrocomputer. For example, a microcomputer with 1 Mbyte of memory can run a simulation of a circuit with 10,000 gates in about a day. Faster 32-bit computers will reduce this time, and with larger address spaces can run even larger simulations. Who needs a minicomputer, much less a large mainframe?

The Microcomputer

The microcomputer has become pervasive. Apple Computer was recently shipping 10,000 Macintosh computers each month. For the cost of a cheap automobile one can buy three systems, each with 512 Kbytes of fast memory, a back-up floppy disk drive, a 20-Mbyte hard disk, a color cathode ray tube (CRT) with graphic capability, and a printer capable of printing 50 to 100 characters a second. The microcomputer has changed the character of time-sharing systems and has made local area networks a hot subject.

Most computers use the Intel 8088, which cycles at 4.77 Mhz. Second-generation models of the Intel 8088 or 80286 can run at 8 Mhz, which is faster than the IBM PC-AT. Companies are offering "accelerator" boards that can be plugged into the PC. These boards provide greater speed; some of them have up to 2 Mbytes of memory and cost less than $1,500. However, because most PCs and disks are limited by input-output speeds, fast central processing units are not important to most users.

The trend in the integrated circuit industry is to place more functions on a single chip; prices will therefore decline even further. As automation increases, even complicated mechanical devices will decline in price.

Networks

CS Net is a computer science network with 89 nodes, or sites (1984), 90 percent of which are academic. It carried 800 to 1,500 messages a day, the lengths of which ranged from 1,500 to 4,000 bytes.

In business environments, a network allows a user to have access to more expensive peripherals such as a laser printer or to a data base that must be kept current. Data bases that need infrequent updating will migrate to CD-ROMs.

Data Bases

Many commercial data base companies are offering access to their information by way of personal computers. For example, Mead Data Central offers LEXIS, a 25 Gbyte file of legal information. Each week 65,000 documents are added to the file. Another file, NEXIS, contains the complete text of more than 100 newspapers and magazines. A search for particular information may take a couple of minutes, cost $20, and produce 100 to 200 hits.

Dozens of companies, including Automatic Data Processing, Interactive Data Corporation (IDC), I.P. Sharp, and Wharton Economic Forecasting Associates, make commercial data bases available to PC users. The financial data bases of IDC cover 10,000 companies, 14,000 banks, 250 utilities, 60,000 North American securities, 26,000 non-North American securities, and 1,700,000 municipal bonds. Access charges typically involve a minimum charge and hourly charges that may depend on the time of day and the data base accessed. Some data base companies charge new customers against their credit cards.

Automation

The development of VLSI circuits has made it practical to automate production lines. An example can be found in the computer area. Printers are complicated devices with many parts that require close tolerances. The Oki Electronic Industry Company of Japan has described an automated production facility for dot matrix printers that became operational in November of 1983. Of the 269 parts of the ET-88300 printer, more than 80 percent are assembled by robots. Ten thousand printers are assembled each month using only 27 assembly persons. Oki reports that assembly costs, exclusive of materials, are one-tenth that of previous costs and, even more interesting, the failure rate at the customer site is also one-tenth that of previous rates. IBM announced that a printer manufacturing facility completed in 1986 was "one of the world's most highly automated" facilities.

Apple Computer says that 85 percent of the components of the Macintosh computer are placed by insertion machines and that half of the 31 remaining parts are placed by robots. Labor therefore represents about 1 percent of the cost of assembling a Macintosh computer.

SUMMARY

Microcomputers, minicomputers, and mainframe computers are all increasing in power and declining in cost. Personal computers are available for less than $1,000 and are able to perform satisfactory computation or file management. Printers are available for under $300 and quality printers for $500. Computer power is increasing dramatically; desk top computers now compete with minicomputers.

Disk drives are increasing in size and decreasing in price; 20 to 30 Mbytes of memory are available for about $500. Optical disks are now entering the market. Read-only (CD-ROM) disks that hold 600 Mbytes of memory are available. Write-once and read-write disks of a similar capacity are promised. Read-write optical disks have also been announced. As the market develops, the prices will decline substantially.

The increased on-line storage capacity opens up a new realm of applications and the increase in computing power will satisfy most users without access to minicomputers or large-scale computing systems.

REFERENCES

Bell, C. G. "The Mini and Micro Industries," *Computer*, IEEE CS, Vol. 17, no. 10, October 1984, pp. 14-30.

Burger, R. M., et al. "The Impact of ICs on Computer Technology," *Computer*, IEEE CS, Vol. 17, no. 10, October 1984, pp. 88-95.

Fuerst, I. "Gimme the Turbos," *Datamation*, Vol. 32, No. 6, March 15, 1986, pp. 30-32.

Patterson, D. A. "Reduced Instruction Set Computers," *CACM*, Vol. 28, no. 1, January 1985, pp. 8-21.

Pohm, A. V. "High Speed Memory Systems," *Computer*, IEEE CS, Vol. 17, no. 10, October 1984, pp. 162-171.

Rothchild, E. S. "An Eye on Optical Disks," *Datamation*, Vol. 32, no. 5, March 1, 1986, pp. 73-74.

Tanimoto, H. "Factory Automation: An Assembly Line for the Manufacture of Printers," *Computer*, IEEE CS, Vol. 17, no. 12, December 1984, pp. 50-68.

Voelcker, J. "Microprocessors," *IEEE Spectrum*, Vol. 23, no. 1, January 1986, pp. 46-48.

Voelcker, J. "Microprocessors," *IEEE Spectrum*, Vol. 23, no. 1, January 1986, pp. 46-48.

Zorpette, G. "Personal Computers," *IEEE Spectrum*, Vol. 23, no. 1, January 1986, pp. 40-42.

2

The Impact of Memory Technology Advances on Microcomputers

RICHARD DUBBE AND DURKEE RICHARDS

The dramatic reductions in the cost and physical size of mass storage have been a major force in making microcomputers possible. Low-cost mass storage has given microcomputers the capability to handle a wide range of applications heretofore possible only on large machines. An attempt is made in this paper to trace the progress of memory technology and to identify the trends that will determine the point at which microcomputer mass storage capacities might be at the end of this decade, as shown in Figure 1.

The built-in, solid-state random access memory (RAM) is the operational part of the microcomputer. It is limited by size, cost, and volatility. It loses its memory when the electrical power is interrupted. Mass storage systems, such as diskette drives, rigid disk drives, tape cartridge drives and optical disks, are the "permanent-until-altered" memory of the computer. With the exception of most rigid disks, all mass storage systems have removable media.

Typical microcomputer solid-state memory capacity has grown by a factor of eight in 5 years, from 64 kilobytes to 512 kilobytes. The capacity of diskette drives typically used for software distribution has grown in the same period by about a factor of four, from 125-kilobyte to 500-kilobyte unformatted capacity, although larger capacity drives (up to 1.6 megabytes) have been available and are frequently used with microcomputers. If both types of memory maintain their current growth rates through 1990, the capacity of solid-state memories used with microcomputers will then essentially match that of the highest capacity diskette drives available for use with microcomputers. However, because diskettes are removable, their capacity can be multiplied by the number of diskettes employed and limited by the time and logistics of handling numerous diskettes.

Many microcomputer systems are now incorporating rigid disks to increase speed and capacity. A typical rigid disk drive currently offers 20 megabytes, and systems with over 60 megabytes should be common by the year 1990.

A strong demand continues to exist for more memory capacity, both for the solid-state RAM and the peripheral devices. This demand exists in part because better, and more user-friendly, software has increased the range of applications for microcomputers. Much of the increase in capacity of peripheral devices has been accomplished through increases in the areal recording density. Areal density trends are shown for rigid disk and diskette drives in Figure 2.

The technology advances that have allowed these increases in areal density have also helped reduce the size and cost of the system. Examples of drive cost reductions are shown in Figure 3. These reductions in the size and cost of peripheral memory devices have contributed greatly to the growth of the microcomputer industry.

HISTORY

The operating memory of early computers, circa 1950, used vacuum tubes, and magnetic drums were used for storage. Both were nonremovable. Magnetic tape, in which a flexible plastic substrate is used, has been an important removable mass storage medium for computers since its introduction by 3M and IBM in the early 1950s. Magnetic tape, together with punched cards and paper tape, performed input/output, program load, backup, and archival functions. Although punched cards and paper tape have been replaced by diskettes, 10 1/2-inch reels of 1/2-inch wide computer tape remain the main backup and archival storage means for medium to large computer systems. Reels of computer tape also have provided the primary means of exchanging data between systems.

In 1963, solid-state electronics replaced vacuum tubes, and IBM introduced magnetic disks to replace many of the operating memory functions performed by magnetic computer tape. However, tape remained the medium of interchange, backup, and archiving.

By 1967, IBM had developed removable disk packs that largely supplanted magnetic tape functions except interchange and archiving. The removable nature of the disk packs allowed the memory size to be expanded and enabled some interchange, even though the packs were large, expensive, and could easily be damaged.

In 1971, IBM introduced their "Winchester" technology. These permanently mounted disk drives provided far greater storage density per unit volume at a lower cost and with greater reliability. However, the removability feature was sacrificed. In the same period, the floppy disk was developed by IBM. The floppy disk was originally intended to load programs, but soon after its utility for input/output was recognized, it rapidly replaced punched tape in these applications. Both the Winchester and diskette technologies were destined to play a major role in the microcomputer industry.

The current microcomputer, often called a personal computer or desk-top computer, took form in the mid 1970s when the newly introduced microprocessor silicon chip was combined with an IBM invention, the 8-inch flexible or "floppy" disk that was made available to users in 1973. In 1976, Allan Shugart introduced a 5 1/4-inch floppy disk that rapidly became the microcomputer standard. A 3 1/2-inch diskette, originated by Sony and featuring a rigid plastic shell, is now beginning to challenge the dominance of the 5 1/4-inch disk. The combination of an inexpensive computer-on-a-chip with a small diskette drive enabled a desk-top computer system to be developed with performance comparable to earlier mainframe computer systems. The diskette drive performed the functions of the rigid disk and tape drives used with the mainframe computers: on-line mass storage, archival storage, software distribution, and exchange of data. These desk-top computers in turn spawned the creation of a software industry in which many software publishers competed to create more powerful and user-friendly programs with applications that ranged from word processing to accounting and finance with increasingly sophisticated graphics capabilities. The size of software packages has grown rapidly to take advantage of the increased memory capacity of the microcomputers. For example, early spreadsheet programs for the Apple II microcomputer (e.g., Visicalc by Visi-Corp) used about 30 kilobytes of memory, whereas current programs for the Apple Macintosh range from 69 kilobytes for word processing (Microsoft Word) to 300 kilobytes for an integrated program including graphics (Microsoft Excel). Future UNIX-based software is expected to need 20 to 40 megabytes of storage, and computer-aided design and other graphics-type applications will need 100 megabytes or more.

A saying in the computer industry is, "The world has an insatiable appetite for memory." Around 1981, several microcomputer manufacturers began installing rigid disks internal to their computers. Other "value-added-manufacturers" began offering plug-in accessories, including rigid disks and a device new to microcomputers: a tape cartridge backup system. Besides greatly expanding the memory size, the rigid disk provided much faster access to the required information. This in turn increased the demand for more powerful applications, software, and graphics. The nonremovable rigid disk, which employed IBM "Winchester" technology, created an urgent need—backup—to assure users that, regardless of operator errors or physical damage to the rigid disk, their data would still be protected and retrievable.

The 3M Company's Data Cartridge, the first reliable tape cartridge system available to this industry segment, has gained wide acceptance in providing the larger capacity needed for backup and achiving microcomputers that use fixed rigid disks. In some systems, the issue of backup has been addressed through the use of removable, rigid disk cartridge drives, or Iomega Bernoulli Box drives, that employ removable cartridges that contain flexible media.

Today, microcomputers use various combinations of, and sometimes all of, three mass memory systems: (1) diskettes (floppy disks), (2) rigid disks (Winchesters), and (3) magnetic tape (Data Cartridge). The key technical trends of each of these technologies are discussed in the following section of this paper.

TECHNICAL TRENDS

Diskettes

One of the key factors in the success of diskette drives has been their very low entry-level cost. This demanding cost goal has influenced the technology advances that were used to achieve the improved performance in these drives. For example, most diskette drives use full-length recording with little or no equalization in the read/write channel to minimize complexity and cost. They also include no error correction (although error detection is routinely employed), and the relatively low linear bit densities and spindle speeds give rather modest data transfer rates. The majority of drives do not include track-following servos, which are automatic systems for accurately locating the read/write head on the intended track. It is clear that future generations of diskette drives with significantly higher performance will still adhere to this rigorous cost goal even though they will incorporate much more sophisticated technology.

This does not mean that the storage of data on diskettes is inexpensive relative to other available technologies. The cost per megabyte of on-line data storage on diskettes is typically one to two orders of magnitude higher than that of large disk systems. The mean file service time is also at least one order of magnitude longer. However, this is not a problem for most diskette users, because the typical file sizes stored on diskettes are less than 1 megabyte, and diskette drives are not used to serve several networked microcomputers as rigid disks often are.

There have been rapid increases in the areal density of diskette drives. However, the capacity of diskette drives has not increased as rapidly because of a second trend—a continued migration to physically smaller drives. The latter trend has been important to the marketing of diskette drives. Because they are typically used in desk-top microcomputer systems, the diskette drives must compete for space with the other components of the system, and the total "footprint" of the computer system is steadily shrinking. The combined effect of an increase in areal density and a reduction in size can be seen in the capacity migration shown in Figure 4.

Most development efforts are currently concentrated on increasing the capacity of the 3 1/2-inch diskette. Major microcomputer systems manufacturers such as IBM are introducing

TABLE 1. Diskette Track and Linear Bit Densities

Year	Drive Type	Track Density TPI	Max. Bit Density kBPI	Coating Caliper μM	Storage Capacity MByte	Areal Density Megabits per sq inch
1973	8" SS, SD	48	3.3	2.5	0.4	0.16
1976	8" DS, SD	48	3.3	2.5	0.8	0.16
1977	8" DS, DD	48	6.5	2.5	1.6	0.31
1976	5 1/4" SS, SD	48	2.8	2.5	0.1	0.13
1977	5 1/4" SS, DD	48	5.6	2.5	0.3	0.27
1979	5 1/4" DS, DD	48	5.6	2.5	0.5	0.27
1980	5 1/4" DS, DD	96	5.6	2.5	1.0	0.53
1981	5 1/4" - H.D.	96	9.3	1.3	1.6	0.89
1983	5 1/4" - H.D.	192	9.3	1.3	3.3	1.78
1982	3 1/2" SS	135	8.7	1.9	0.5	1.18
1984	3 1/2" DS	135	8.7	1.9	1.0	1.18
1986	3 1/2" DS	135	17.4	0.9	2.0	2.35
1981	8" Iomega (RLL)	325	24.4	1.3 - 1.9	10.0	7.93
1983	5" Iomega (MFM)	434	18.3	1.3 - 1.9	5.0	7.94
1985	8" Iomega (RLL)	600	24.4	1.3 - 1.9	20.0	14.63

(SS: Single Sided; DS: Double Sided; SD: Single Density; DD: Double Density)

products that incorporate 3 1/2-inch diskette drives, thus ensuring widespread acceptance of the 3 1/2-inch format. Sales of new 8-inch drives have fallen, and 5 1/4-inch drive sales are expected to flatten soon in favor of the 3 1/2-inch diskette. The 3 1/2-inch, 2.0-megabyte diskette, which is also available in 1.6-megabyte versions, is nearing introduction and should find widespread use. This increase in capacity will be achieved by increasing the linear bit density (number of flux changes per inch along the magnetic track). The history of linear bit density and track densities in diskette drives is summarized in Table 1. Data for the Iomega Bernoulli Boxes are also included for comparison in Table 1 because they use flexible media that are similar to those used in 5 1/4-inch density and 3 1/2-inch diskette drives. However, the Iomega drives perform much better and cost more than diskette drives, and therefore compete in the rigid disk market.

By 1990, the 3 1/2-inch diskette is expected to have at least a 4.0-megabyte capacity. This increase in areal density can be accomplished through increases in either linear bit density or track density. The nature of the key technical problems that must be solved is quite different for these two approaches. An increase in the linear bit density will require advances in three general areas:

1. The redesign of the head/media interface to maintain the usable output, signal to noise ratio, and error rate.
2. The adoption of a new interface standard with a higher data transfer rate. (Otherwise the spindle speed would have to be reduced, which would increase the rotational latency and reduce the read-head signal.)
3. The control of the head alignment to tighter tolerances to prevent azimuth errors, unless the track density is also increased. (An azimuth error occurs when the gap in the recording head is not parallel to the recorded transition on the medium.)

The use of full-depth recording will require that the medium coating thickness be reduced in proportion to the increase in linear bit density. At some point, the required coating thickness will become impracticably small, and the drive designers will have to adopt the use of partial penetration recording. Although this method complicates the magnetic head design and possibly the electronics, it allows one to use magnetic coatings far thicker and more practical than those dictated by present saturation recording, in which the flux transition is recorded through the entire coating thickness. The coating thickness for 2.0-megabyte diskette media is about 1 μm. It appears doubtful that the linear bit density could be doubled and still retain the use of full-depth recording because the required coating thickness would then be about 0.5 μm.

The gap length of the read/write head must also be reduced as the linear bit density is increased. Early diskette drives used gap lengths of about 1.5 μm. The 2.0- megabyte drives will use 6.0-μm gap lengths. This is still larger than the head gaps used in video systems today, so it should not carry any significant cost penalty. Newer magnetic recording materials such as barium ferrite or small metal particles will probably be incorporated in the design of drives intended for use above 30 kFCI (12 kFC/cm). Thin metal films, although magnetically attractive for these high linear bit densities, currently lack the durability and flexure characteristics needed for diskette applications.

The azimuth problem mentioned earlier is important for any removable medium system. It must be possible to write a diskette on any drive in a given population and read it back on any other drive in the same population. The degree of control required on head alignment is related to the ratio of the track width to bit length. Most drives in use today control the head alignment to ± 12 minutes of angle. This can be done with automated assembly techniques. A doubling of linear bit density at the same track density would reduce this tolerance to about ± 7.5 minutes, which would probably require a head alignment step during the manufacturing process.

Increasing the track density will involve a different set of problems, including media dimensional changes as a result of changes in temperature and humidity, media centering errors, and head positioning errors.

These factors combine to effectively limit the track density that can realistically be used on a drive without closed-loop track following servo. The drive can be designed to match the mean thermal expansion coefficient of the medium. However, the thermal expansion of the polyethylene terepthalate (PET) substrate is not isotropic. Therefore, a track written at one temperature will become elliptical at any other temperature. The drive cannot compensate for this without the addition of some sort of track following. The materials used in the construction of the drive do not generally respond to changes in humidity. Therefore, the hydroscopic expansion of the medium (also anisotropic) will also contribute to off-track errors.

Media mis-centering has been reduced in the 3 1/2-inch drives through the use of a metal hub on the diskette that allows tighter tolerances to be maintained at the hub/spindle interface. Typical mis-centering errors for these drives are about 5 μm. This is about one-half the error for earlier generations of diskette drives that used a punched hole in the center of the diskette. It is expected that these sources of off-track error will limit 3 1/2-inch diskette drives to less than 200 tracks per inch (TPI), or 79 tracks per centimeter, unless track-following servos are used.

It is not yet clear which approach will be adopted by the industry to increase the capacity of the next generation of diskette drives. Toshiba has announced a 4.0-megabyte drive that uses barium ferrite media. They have chosen to increase the linear bit density (using partial-penetration recording) and keep the track density fixed at 135 TPI. Other drive manufacturers have discussed the possibility of using the 2.0-megabyte media at the same linear bit density and adding a track-following servo to give 270 TPI.

It has also been suggested that in this case the capacity should be increased beyond 4.0 megabytes to reduce the impact of the track-following cost.

Rigid Disks: "Winchesters"

In 1986, 20 percent of the new microcomputers will be either shipped with an internal rigid disk drive or sold with an auxiliary memory that contains a rigid disk drive. Half of the microcomputers sold by the year 1990 are expected to use fixed rigid disk drives. The rapid increase in the use of rigid disks is a result of their improving cost-effectiveness and the continued increase in the internal memory capacity and computing speed of the microprocessor.

The terms "rigid" and "hard" are synonymous for these drives, which use an aluminum substrate coated with either magnetic oxide particles or a magnetic thin film applied by plating or sputter deposition. These small hard disk drives are often called "Winchesters," which was a name used by IBM during the development of this technology. The distinguishing features of this technology were as follows:

- A great reduction (more than an order of magnitude) of the mass of the flying head and of the spring constant of the arm that forces the head toward the disk surface;
- The use of surface lubricants on the disk, which, when combined with the low mass and lightly loaded head, allowed the head to land on the disk surface when the drive was powered down; and
- The use of an extremely clean sealed container with constant submicrometer air filtration.

The Winchester technology was a logical choice for building small, high-performance drives for several reasons. Previous generations of head technology required the heads to be lifted and moved off to the side of the disks whenever the drive was powered down. The head carriage and actuator assembly for Winchester drives have a shorter stroke than the older drives, which helps reduce the size of the drive. The larger size of the previous heads also meant that they could not fly as close to the outer edge of the disk as the Winchester heads. The Winchester heads therefore could allow more tracks on the same size disk. The relative importance of this difference increases as the size of the disk medium decreases. The small, lightly loaded Winchester heads could also be safely flown closer to the disk surface than the older heads, which allowed the use of significantly higher linear bit densities. The resulting improvements in storage density and reductions in the size and costs of rigid disk drives have caused them to almost completely replace the disk packs that were used for many years as the main mass storage memory of computers.

The recording density of rigid disk drives has been achieved by increasing both the number of TPI and the number of encoded bits per inch (BPI). These changes are shown in Figure 6 as a function of time for the large disk drive systems introduced by IBM. The technology advances developed for these large drives tend to be quickly incorporated into the smaller rigid disk drives that are marketed for use with microcomputers.

Increasing the recording density lowers the system cost by reducing the number of magnetic heads and disk surfaces required for a given capacity. The higher recording density can also be used to reduce the size of the drive because a disk smaller in diameter can still have the same capacity. The use of physically smaller drives helps reduce system cost through the use of smaller motors that use less power, smaller castings and bearings, and so forth. More information packed at a greater density can also contribute to higher transfer rates and, together with magnetic head positioner advances, faster access times.

The reduction in the physical volume occupied by disk drives is shown in Figure 7. The charts in Figure 8 depict the rapid transition of the 3 1/2-inch "form factor."

The recent widespread acceptance of rigid disks for microcomputers represents a recognition of their improved performance in terms of greater capacity, with lower mean access time, and a higher data transfer rate. This improvement in performance has been accompanied by a steady reduction in the size and cost of rigid disks and improvements in reliability. Unfortunately, fixed rigid disk memory size is not "expandable" in the sense that diskette or tape cartridge drive capacities can be increased by the number of media units that one is willing to use. One also cannot practically remove the information and store it, as is done for backup and archiving, without some type of drive. It is also impractical to directly interchange information stored on a fixed disk drive unless the drives are connected to a communications link. A removable memory is needed to perform these functions. Removable rigid disk cartridges and Bernoulli disk cartridges are two new technologies that were designed to deliver the performance of a fixed rigid disk drive and also be removable.

Magnetic Tape

Tape drive systems remain the cheapest form of mass storage (on a cost per bit basis) in widespread use today. They have other attributes that help make them a good choice for the backup of rigid disk drives. The function of a rigid disk backup should ideally be performed by a medium that can be removed from the microcomputer and stored in a secure location. It should have a very low off-line cost per bit. The media should occupy minimum storage space, and should be rugged, reliable, and able to withstand frequent handling. Many tape cartridge systems have been developed for rigid disk backup in recent years. The relative drive system cost per megabyte of data for various removable media systems in use today is shown in Figure 9.

The Philips tape cassette was used for input/output and program loading by some of the smaller computer systems that began to appear in the late 1960s and early 1970s. Early in the 1970s, 3M developed the 1/4-inch tape Data Cartridge with the objective of making an extremely reliable tape package. It was intended for computer input/output applications. However, the 8-inch diskette introduced by IBM in the same time period became a popular choice for the same applications. The rapid adaptation of rigid disk drives to microcomputers created a new need for data backup means for the Winchester rigid disks in microcomputers. Future applications are expected to be the input/output of files too large to be conveniently stored on diskettes and archival storage.

Advances in tape technology are continuing. Higher areal densities are being developed into products that can therefore offer various combinations of higher capacity and lower system size. Higher data transfer rates will also become common. Capacities of 500 to 1,000 megabytes should be available by the end of this decade.

FUTURE MASS STORAGE TECHNOLOGY

The mass storage industry is very large. The size of the total industry in 1985 is shown in Figure 11. This chart represents all mass storage memory devices for all types of computers.

Many computer experts have suggested that increasing the performance of magnetic mass storage systems is becoming more difficult, and that the industry is ready for a new replacement technology, such as optical recording. The great impact some industry observers believe optical media will have by the year 1990 is shown in Figure 12.

Optical disk recording has yet to be standardized and has many forms, such as:

Function	Disk Size	Recording Method
1. Read only CD ROM	4.72 inches	Mastering
2. Write once	10, 11, and 12 inches	Bubble, pit, phase change
	5 1/4 inches	Pit
3. Erasable	3 1/2 and 5 1/4 inches	Magneto-optic (exp. phase change, dye)

The 3M Company, the world's largest magnetic media manufacturer, is also investing heavily in optical disk recording, which is an area that it pioneered. Current commercially successful optical disk systems for computers are "write once." They are used for very large files that usually contain image information. These systems are quite specialized and are very expensive in comparison to microcomputer systems. Because of the rapid consumer acceptance of the optical compact disk (CD) for music replication and distribution, many are optimistic that the CD optical disk and associated low-cost players will provide a large, 100- to 500-megabyte, inexpensive memory for microcomputers. Software manufacturers are also interested in the compact disk to provide protection from widespread illicit copying of their proprietary software.

Current limitations to the optical disk's acceptability for microcomputers are: (1) the lack of erasable media systems with a low entry-level cost that can function as an on-line mass memory, and (2) the lack of suitable software and low-cost player systems to provide a useful function for read-only applications.

Many companies are working in both areas, and microcomputer product introductions can be expected within the next few years. The acceptability and success of these products will depend on the usefulness of the software provided, which can be limited by the hardware performance.

Technical problems for erasable optical disk systems are the development of low-cost, reliable erasable media; processes that yield consistent laser diodes; and optical assemblies capable of fast access times.

Problems for the read-only systems are slow access time and software organization for use with large, slow-access memories.

Considerable progress undoubtedly will be made in solving these optical disk limitations within the next few years. It is envisioned that a read-only memory adaptation of the low-cost CD player could make large libraries of information available to the microcomputer user. Examples of such libraries are:

- Medical and pharmaceutical data such as drug interactions;
- Graphics of all kinds, including maps, geophysical surveys, and medical x-rays;
- Legal libraries; and
- Parts lists for servicing equipment and inventories of all kinds.

The promise of optical recording remains great. However, magnetic recording continues to make rapid advances that challenge the potential of optical recording. To this day, magnetic recording remains the universally accepted mass storage technology.

REFERENCES

Engh, J. T. "The IBM Diskette and Diskette Drive," *IBM J. Res. Develop.*, Vol. 25, no. 5, September 1981.

1985 DISK/TREND (tm) REPORT, DISK/TREND, Inc., 5150 El Camino Real, Suite B-20, Los Altos, California 94022.

Freeman Reports: Computer Tape Outlook Half-Inch Products, Freeman Associates, Inc., 311 East Carillo Street, Santa Barbara, California 93101.

Friedman, S. "Mass Storage Migration, All Paths Lead to PC's," *Micro-Product Review*, June 16, 1986.

Gardner, R. N., Rinehart, T. A., Johnson, L. H., Freese, R. P., Lund, R. A. "Characteristic of A New High C/N Magneto-Optic Media," SPIE Optical Mass Data Storage Conference, June 1983.

Harker, J. M., Brede, D. W., Pattison, R. E., Santana, G. R., and Taft, L. G. "A Quarter Century of Disk File Innovation," *IBM J. Res. Develop.*, Vol. 25, No. 5, September 1981.

Harris, J. P., Phillips, W. B., Wells, J. F., and Winger, W. D. "Innovations in the Design of Magnetic Tape Subsystems," *IBM J. Res. Develop.*, Vol. 25, no. 5, September 1981.

Imamura, N. "Research Applies Magnetic Thin Films and the Magneto-Optical Effect in Storage Devices," *JEE*, March 1983.

Magnetic Media International Newsletter, Vol. III, No. 4, Magnetic Media Information Services, Suite 1100, 980 North Michigan Avenue, Chicago, Illinois 60611.

Mass Storage Current Analysis Service, InfoCorp, 20833 Stevens Creek Boulevard, Cupertino, California 95014-2107.

Mulvany, R. B., and Thompson, L. H. "Innovations in Disk File Manufacturing," *IBM J. Res. Develop.*, Vol. 25, no. 5, September 1981.

Optical Memory's Impact on Magnetic Storage and Computer System Architecture, Electronic Trend Publications, 10080 N. Wolfe Road, Suite 372, Cupertino, California 95014.

Stevens, L. D. "The Evolution of Magnetic Storage," *IBM J. Res. Develop.*, Vol. 25, no. 5, September 1981.

The DATEK DIGITAL STORAGE Monthly, Vol. 2, no. 2, February 1985.

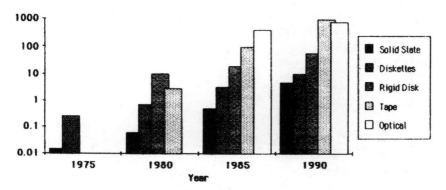

FIGURE 1   Microcomputer memory systems—Capacity in megabytes.

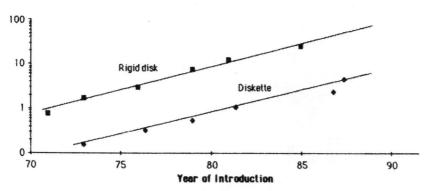

FIGURE 2   Disk area density—Megabytes/square inch.

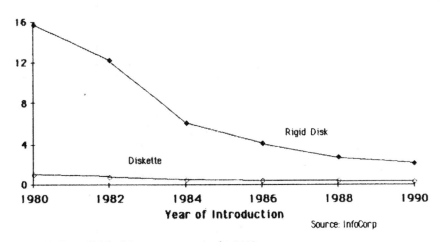

FIGURE 3 Disk drive user cost in $1,000's.

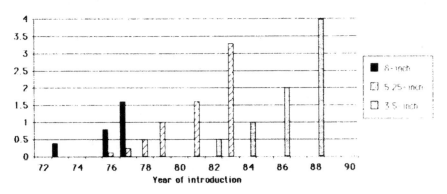

FIGURE 4 Diskette capacity migration in megabytes.

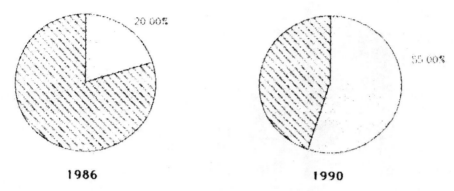

FIGURE 5 Percentage of microcomputers equipped with rigid disks.

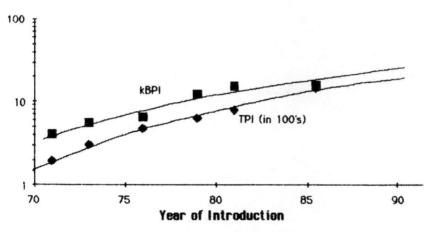

FIGURE 6 Rigid disk track and bit density.

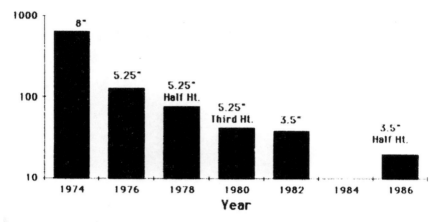

FIGURE 7 Physical drive volume in cubic inches.

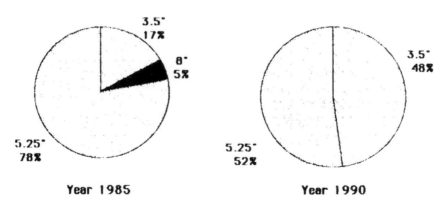

FIGURE 8 Percentages of diskette and rigid disk drives under 30 megabytes.

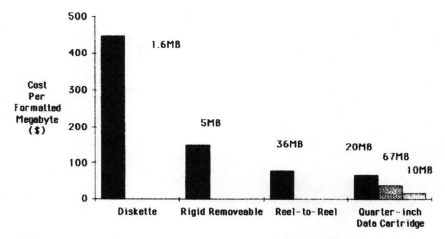

FIGURE 9   Hardware costs of various backup media systems.

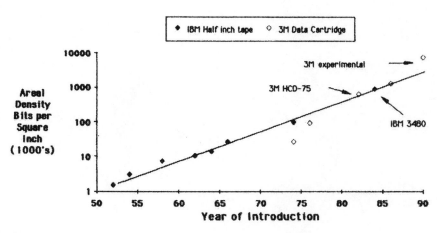

FIGURE 10   Advances in tape data storage systems.

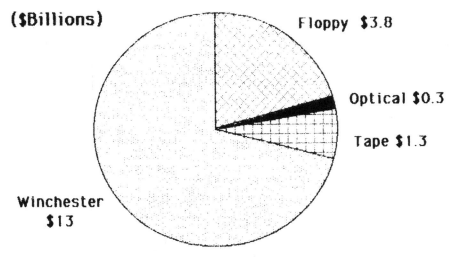

FIGURE 11 Distribution of 1985 mass storage market (in $Billions).

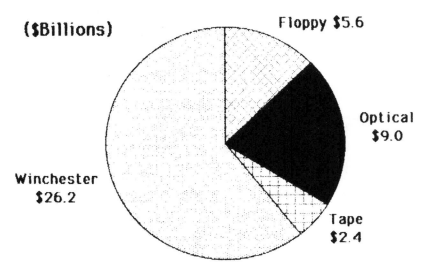

FIGURE 12 Projected distribution of 1990 mass storage market (in $Billions).

3

Artificial Intelligence: An Overview
Eugénio Oliveira

The concept of artificial intelligence (AI) has yet to be definitively accepted. The mimicry of human intelligence and modeling of mental processes, although important to understanding intelligent behavior, are not the core of this computer science discipline. The development and application of techniques that enable computers to simulate human skills appears to be the simplest definition, and at least one of the main guidelines, of AI studies.

LESSONS

Besides the promotion of creativity, earlier concerns of AI in the late 1950s were shown to be unrealistic. Attempts at machine translation were abandoned after a large investment because of incipient contextual knowledge and lack of representation mechanisms. Simplistic programs, like Weizenbaum's ELIZA, that naively simulated the interaction between doctor and patient proved to be nothing but a curiosity. The use of key recognition words in a sentence proved to be an erroneous technique to deal with the natural language understanding problem.

The success of game playing has led scientists in other fields to consider its AI algorithms an accurate representation of real-world problems.

Finally, a program like Newell and Simon's General Problem Solving (GPS), although replete with brilliant ideas (e.g., Means Ends Analysis), has yet to be applied because it was found to be too general and unable to solve concrete problems in real situations.

AI became much more complex than expected; a heuristic search and the use of more contextual knowledge appeared to be of major importance. Broad domains and general-purpose strategies were much too difficult to handle and were abandoned by most researchers.

In the mid 1970s, the paradigm "knowledge is more important than algorithms" generated the first relatively successful AI system; it embodied expert knowledge in restricted domains like blood infections or mineral sites.

Friendly interfaces like natural language and clever interactions as suitable methods of explanation (closely related with knowledge engineering applications) have been developed to improve expert systems performance.

The main directions of AI research and development currently include:

- Specific hard and soft environment development for AI;
- Deep knowledge in intelligent, knowledge-based systems;
- The integration and cooperation of intelligent, knowledge-based systems; and
- Learning algorithms.

AI LANGUAGES

Three different models support AI languages as privileged vehicles for knowledge, heuristics, and inference:

- Functional languages like Lisp;
- Object-oriented programs like Small Talk; and
- Logic programming like Prolog.

The computation of functions or relations is different from the exchange of messages between objects. Being based in Lambda calculus is not the same as being in first-order predicate logic. Nevertheless, some features are shared by these languages, mainly Lisp and Prolog. Among these features are the simplicity of data structures (lists, terms, etc.), natural recursive programming, and the ability to deal with data and programs in the same way.

AI language interpreters and compilers, expert system shells, and various other applications are already available for microcomputers, although more sophisticated systems need higher levels of hardware and software support.

Knowledge Representation

Knowledge representation (KR) is a key technique in AI. The "equation" KR = Knowledge + Access makes the point that structures should embody as much knowledge as possible, and that the efficient access and manipulation of this knowledge must also be considered.

Frames, associative networks, production rules, or predicate calculus are some of the more common knowledge structures. They tend to be combined in advanced knowledge-based systems.

Search

Another important set of techniques and methodologies in AI deals with search problems. Search is the process of navigation among states that represent possible problem situations. Well-known algorithms are Depth-First, Breadth-First, Hill-Climbing, Best-First, Branch-and-Bound, A*, Minimax, and Alpha-Beta Pruning. Although all these algorithms try to avoid combinational explosion, most of their performance depends on good heuristics to inform evaluation functions.

OTHER AREAS OF RESEARCH

Man-machine interface is another subfield in which AI has made significant progress. Several knowledge-based systems have at least a subset of a natural language interface in that AI work stations permit the use of enhanced graphics and speech recognition, although this remains a subject of intensive research.

Learning algorithms have been presented as the quintessence of real (artificial) intelligence. Several attempts to implement learning systems have not yet proved to be significant in terms of real-life and real-size problems. Nevertheless, recent progress in learning algorithms makes it one of the most promising areas of research. Learning approaches include algorithms to acquire new knowledge by analogy, by examples, by experience, and by being told, among others.

Finally, some trends in the near future of AI include the following:

- The use of parallel computing and formalisms;
- VLSI knowledge bases and inference mechanisms;
- The cooperation of knowledge-based systems through networks;
- Learning and powerful knowledge bases; and
- Complete autonomous decision-making in sensor-based robots.

MAJOR PORTUGUESE ISSUES

It should be emphasized that what follows is a single perspective on the key issues, concerns, and hopes of a substantial part of the Portuguese research and development (R&D) community.

It should first be stressed that as a community Portugal remains able to detect and master its own social and economic problems. However, it is also recognized that Portugal would be in a better position if it could cooperate on an equal basis with more advanced countries.

Research and development in Portugal have too many imbalances. Universities compete with industry; Lisbon competes with the rest of the country. Portugal has many capable and renowned researchers and research groups. Single accomplishments have been made in fields such as physics, electronics, artifical intelligence, and biotechnology. But these individual accomplishments do not help much to solve Portugal's structural problems.

The real problem is to cross the threshold of a critical quantitative mass in which the previous singularities should be based and inseminate society with competence and literacy in advanced technologies. If this is not done, brain drain will occur. It is extremely important to avoid this phenomenon by investing heavily in the research and development of Portugal's own projects aimed at solving its own problems. This approach also could be profitable to other similar countries.

Portugal needs assistance in gaining acceptance and funding from international agencies for its own projects, and in giving incentives to advanced countries' R&D teams to cooperate with it and become interested in its proposals.

Portugal has already developed sophisticated prototypes in several domains; AI systems are only one example. But all too often the incompetence of managers, politicians, and industrialists impedes progress. What frequently happens is that there is no follow-up after these pioneer efforts. Most companies are aware that it is not worthwhile to invest in sophisticated technologies and products if there is no infrastructure in place to ensure the effective acceptance of and follow-up on all the processes.

Portugal needs to work on its own expertise and develop suitable interfaces between the R&D community and industry to help ensure that conditions attractive to experts and researchers exist. Fortunately, some interesting examples of such interfaces exist in Portugal.

A panel such as this cannot be more than a forum of good intentions and generalities, and its discussions and conclusions may have no lasting value. Nevertheless, it is important to note that Portugal must trust its capabilities. At the same time, it needs cooperation. This cooperation should not be selective, but should take place at different levels of knowledge and at different scientific, industrial, and educational levels. This cooperation should mainly take place within Portugal's institutions or with a greater involvement than merely lending manpower.

Portugal is able to master advanced tools once it has become acquainted with them, but this learning process should take place from the beginning, not when these tools have become closed commercial products.

Portugal must convince its science managers, public institutions, and industries that they must either invest in the intelligent automation of factories or be left behind by it. Creativity would cease to exist if this investment is not made. This is not simply a reference to the use of such tools but to the understanding of the concepts involved.

Finally, Portugal is still in a good position to contribute to world progress and to promote approximation among different cultures and societies. However, as technology advances more rapidly, Portugal may find itself responsible for a great failure if it is unable to convince those in power (money, science, technology, etc.) to help it prepare for the future.

Research and development make education attractive, make the upgrading of industry less risky, and promote immeasurable creativity.

4

Prolog for Artificial Intelligence Projects: The Portuguese Experience

LUÍS DAMAS AND MIGUEL FILGUEIRAS

A comparatively large number of workers are employed in artificial intelligence (AI) in Portugal. It is clear that the Prolog language played a very important role in this development. A discussion is provided of the features of Prolog that contributed to this development, particularly those that were relevant in Portugal.

There are some indications (Warren, 1982) that Prolog (Clocksin and Mellish, 1981) will have a significant impact on programming technology. The future of Prolog is not discussed in this paper, but rather the impact that Prolog has already made in AI research in Portugal. In fact, Prolog has become the programming language used by most groups working in AI in Portugal, and it has played a vital role in developing AI research.

The main reason behind the widespread use of Prolog is that some Portuguese researchers were involved in the development of two of the more popular Prolog implementations, namely DEC-10 Prolog (Pereira, Pereira, and Warren, 1978) and C-Prolog (Pereira, 1983). Logic programming has also been one of the main topics of AI research in Portugal. Although this involvement can account for the relatively widespread familiarity with Prolog, other programming languages are even more widely known, and this is not a complete explanation.

The distinctive features of Prolog as a programming system that helped Portuguese AI researchers to overcome some of the difficulties that still exist will be examined in the next section of this paper.

ARTIFICIAL INTELLIGENCE RESEARCH IN PORTUGAL

Artificial Intelligence research in Portugal has been mainly of an academic nature and has been conducted mostly by university teachers who had to combine research with their lecturing and administrative duties. This is still true today.

The scarcity of funds was responsible for the lack of staff and suitable equipment. Research teams, if the word "team" can be applied in such extreme situations, were formed by two or three enthusiasts who had to develop the concepts, implement them, and start the process again when concepts proved to be unworthy. Implementation in this context means that the programs had to be written, typed (or punched), and debugged, which was a lengthy and boring sequence of steps in the programming environments available at the time. The few computers available were either very small or did not have some of the basic features one would expect them to have. For instance, the University of Porto had a respectable machine that never had a multiplexer to allow for a time-sharing facility. The price of the multiplexer was obviously ridiculous when compared to the price of the equipment in use.

This gloomy picture is, or has been, the same for many developing countries. In spite of this, the amount and quality of work produced by AI researchers in the past years in Portugal has increased in a way that cannot be simply explained by the improvement in circumstances.

Difficulties in recruiting researchers still remain. Although research teams have more enthusiastic participants, they cannot afford the luxury of contracting personnel to perform minor tasks. With few exceptions, the equipment available today (mostly in the range of micro- or super-microcomputers) is still not expensive, even though it is much more powerful.

PROLOG

Prolog was originally introduced by A. Colmerauer in 1972 at the University of Marseille, and was based on R. Kowalski's concept of "logic programming" (Kowalski, 1979).

One of the distinctive features of Prolog as a programming language is that it is modeled after a powerful but simple mathematical model, namely the semi-decidable set of Horn clauses of first-order predicate calculus. Prolog presents a clearly understood semantics based only on the concepts of unification and depth-first search with backtracking. However, in contrast to other programming languages, "pure" Prolog can be used for large programs with a small loss of efficiency, which allows implementations to be kept very close to the original model.

Another feature of Prolog is that it introduced the concept of the logical variable, which behaves as a kind of assign-once variable and allows for such programming techniques as the deferred filling of parts of data structures and the sharing of information among distinct data structures. Prolog also includes a built-in backtracking mechanism that is useful for implementing search procedures.

A Prolog program consists of a set of predicate definitions, each of which is a set of clauses; roughly speaking, each clause is usually a small and possibly void sequence of calls to predicates.

From the point of view of a programming discipline, the two main features of Prolog are as follows:

- The nonexistence of global variables, which enforces modular programming through the exclusive use of parameters for passing information around.
- The concept of logic variables combined with the nonexistence of global variables and the recursive nature of definitions, which makes program verification easier. In fact, apart from termination considerations, to verify a program one must only convince oneself that each clause for a predicate is "true" and that all the relevant cases are scattered in the proper order.

It should be noted that Prolog is not some kind of problem-solver; it is a powerful programming language for which there are implementations that not only provide efficiency, but sophisticated programming environments.

These characteristics explain why programming in Prolog is easy to learn. The concepts involved can be understood without any reference to models of computer architecture, and the novice is not confronted with the difficult problem of implementing the pattern-matching and search procedures that are necessary in almost every AI program.

The modularity offered by Prolog precludes the need to write all the parts of a program for it to run (obviously with limitations). One can partially define a predicate simply to test an idea, knowing that it will not work in all cases. This allows for a kind of incremental programming, in which the programmer starts from a small set of clauses, tests them, and adds new clauses until the program is complete and known to work.

Most Prolog systems provide a fast turn-around cycle. Prolog programs are consulted at a high speed, and little time is therefore needed to leave the program, correct it, and run it again.

Debugging facilities normally include provisions for step-by-step inspection of the program execution, as well as spying of selected predicates. Moreover, most debuggers allow for the preservation of all the computation history so that it can be examined to find the origin of an error. Algorithms are also available for fault-finding in Prolog programs (Pereira, 1984). All this allows for extremely fast program development.

As was stated earlier, most implementations follow the original Prolog theoretic model. It should be stressed that this property offers the user a clear semantics that is vital for predicting and understanding the program's behavior. We hope that future extensions to Prolog, namely those that allow for parallel computation, will preserve this property.

PROLOG AND ARTIFICIAL INTELLIGENCE RESEARCH

Given the small size of research teams and the scarcity of trained AI programmers, the ease of learning to program in Prolog is very important. For the same reasons, the relative compactness and readability of Prolog programs is also crucial. For instance, it is easier for a single researcher to write and debug a 30-page as opposed to a 200-page natural language front-end in a reasonable time.

As was mentioned earlier, Prolog offers a modular and incremental programming style. This means that programs can grow consistently from a small set of clauses, with the obvious benefit of less debugging work. Another consequence is that the programmer can quickly see the results of the program being built. This process also has the stunning psychological side effect of causing work addiction. Modularity, combined with good debugging facilities, enables even large programs to be tested predicate by predicate (from the lower level to the top level).

Fast turn-around cycles and good debugging facilities enabled the experimental method to be fully applied to programming; ideas can be checked in the "real" world of computation and either accepted, discarded, or adapted to that world. Because the programming effort is reduced, no compromise is made with earlier versions, and improvements to programs can be willfully made.

CONCLUSION

The intensive use of certain Prolog systems has strongly contributed to the progress of AI research in Portugal. Some of the distinctive features of Prolog systems that make them especially suited for use as programming tools for AI research have been reviewed. Many benefits can be derived through AI research in developing countries by adopting a suitable Prolog system.

REFERENCES

Clocksin, W., Mellish, C. *Programming in Prolog.* Springer Verlag, 1981.
Kowalski, R. *Logic for Problem Solving.* North Holland, 1979.
Pereira, F. (ed.). "C-Prolog User's Manual," SRI International, 1983.
Pereira, L. M. "Rational Debugging," Universidade Nova de Lisboa, 1984.
Pereira, L. M., Pereira, F., and Warren, D.H.D. "User's Guide to DECSystem-10 Prolog," Department of Artificial Intelligence, University of Edinburgh, 1978.
Warren, D.H.D. "A View of Fifth Generation and Its Impact," Technical Note 265, SRI International, 1982.

5

Computer-Aided Design: A Primer

GLENN A. HART

The purpose of this paper is to introduce computer-aided design (CAD) to those who are not yet familiar with either its capabilities or the computer hardware and software necessary for its implementation. Although the benefits to be derived from CAD are considerable in terms of both improved image quality and cost savings, there is an unusually high number of factors to consider. Microcomputer CAD systems now offer most of the functions of large minicomputer and mainframe installations at a small fraction of the cost. They are now available to a much wider spectrum of users in smaller firms and developing countries. It is hoped that this primer will provide information to help those desiring the benefits of CAD to proceed with full awareness of the many issues involved.

THE ALPHABET SOUP: CAD, CADD, CAE, AND CAM

Sometimes it seems that the key to understanding new developments in computers is another TLA—a new Three-Letter Abbreviation! Although acronyms can serve as a shorthand for effective communication, they also often obscure meaning to the noninitiate.

CAD is usually defined as computer-aided design, but the

same abbreviation is also used to refer to computer-aided drafting. Both definitions are valid. The acronym CADD is sometimes used to indicate both attributes, as in computer-aided design and drafting. Several other abbreviations are used in conjunction with CAD, including CAE for computer-aided engineering and CAM for computer-aided manufacturing. For the most part, CAE and CAM refer to tools that are outside the CAD environment but that are often integrated with it to perform a set of functions. Examples of such external tools include FEA (finite element analysis, which is used to judge the demands placed upon and safety of proposed structures), NC (numerical control, in which CAD is used to design a part and generate instructions to control the computerized machinery that actually creates the finished product), and so forth.

GENERAL DEFINITION

An analogy between CAD and word processing is often drawn, and it is an appropriate one in many respects. At its most basic level, processing can be considered the storage of keystrokes; the reentering of the same keystrokes as changes are made is avoided, text is moved from one place to another, and formatting is added or modified. Obviously, there are many enhancements that further ease the manipulation of characters, reduce manual effort, and assist in the preparation of elegant and accurate textual material, but the core of word processing is a simple concept.

The concept of CAD is similar in that it involves the storage of graphical primitives. Just as in word processing, entities (lines, arcs, circles, ellipses, etc.) are entered into the system, with various tools to ease and speed the process, and can then be edited in a variety of ways. Just as the daisy wheel or laser printer produces high-quality output, the CAD system's plotter generates flawless hard copy graphics.

An understanding of this intrinsic nature of CAD systems immediately eliminates one common misconception. No one would assert that a word processor actually writes anything; it is obviously only a tool used by an author to translate ideas into words more quickly, more cost-effectively, and with superior results. Computer-aided design also serves as an assistant, with very much the same objectives. In fact, CAD systems allow some kinds of images to be prepared quickly by assembling or collating predefined drawings in the same way that word processor users doing repetitive work often prepare boiler-plate text that they can quickly combine into longer documents. However, CAD should not be considered automation in any sense in which the term is usually employed.

ADVANTAGES

The benefits to be derived from CAD systems encompass all stages of the design, drafting, and production process. There is no monolithic, across-the-board improvement; the efficiencies instead vary from phase to phase and also vary depending on the discipline.

The earliest stages of a project usually result from some new idea or requirement that must be translated into a tangible form for further evaluation and development. Many CAD users believe that CAD is least useful at this stage. The mechanics of operating the computer may interfere with the creative process in capturing at least some form of the concept on paper. In general, only if the designer is familiar and facile with the CAD system can the computer perform transparently. In some disciplines, CAD techniques can assist in product visualization, but for the most part, the benefits of CAD come later in the cycle.

The next phase is usually a first pass at a production drawing. Several CAD techniques influence this process dramatically.

Initial entry is much faster and easier with the drawing aids commonly provided. A grid of points sets an accurate framework, snap features force the operator to draw from accurately spaced locations, and entities are drawn precisely. Depending on the option chosen, the operator simply cannot be inaccurate; this precision is attained without operator strain or delay.

The documentation of the image with explanatory text, often a very time-consuming operation, is much faster, and lettering quality is precise and identical. Cross-hatching and solid area fills, another slow and dreary process, is similarly enhanced. The automatic calculation and drawing of dimensioning information greatly eases the accuracy and speed of yet another tedious chore.

If the drawings have any repetitive aspects or utilize subassemblies, major time savings can be derived through the use of predefined parts, symbols, or blocks. A chip that is used a dozen times in a printed circuit board, a symbol that is repeatedly in a schematic, a window that appears often throughout a building, and standardized desks, chairs, and furnishings can all be inserted in a second or two instead of monotonously redrawing them.

Nevertheless, initial drawing entry essentially remains a cognitive activity in which operator creativity and thought is required. The most significant improvements wrought by CAD occur during the next stage of processing: preparing and editing working drawings. This phase is more drawing-intensive, so the shortcuts provided by CAD pay the most dramatic dividends. To recall the text-processing analogy, CAD is similar to word processing in that productivity improves more in the editing process than during initial text entry. Making changes to existing drawings, which usually requires mass erasures and redrawing, is perhaps the biggest bottleneck in the entire design process. Such CAD tools as erasure, moving, rotating, scaling, stretching, and duplicating make image editing fast and gratifying. Productivity gains of four to five times are not uncommon in the editing and correction process when compared to manual updates.

Other CAD techniques improve productivity later in the cycle. Many serious CADs include systems that can extract data from the drawing to indicate how many times certain assemblies or parts are used. Ancillary programs can be written to prepare complete bills of materials and other reports useful in job cost quotations and client billing. Most CADs can perform calculations that are helpful in determining area utilization or, in the case of mechanical drawings, checking clearances and other factors with calculations of moment of inertia, radii of gyration, and so forth.

CAD also offers a general consistency of style from one designer or draftsman to another. Lettering, dimensioning techniques and styles, symbols, and entire subassemblies that are inserted from prepared libraries will be identical, assuming that the same CAD software is used, in spite of differing individual abilities.

WHO CAN USE CAD?

CAD is appropriate for a wide range of design and drafting disciplines:

- Architecture;
- Civil engineering;
- Interior design and office layout;
- Landscape design;

- Mechanical design;
- Printed circuit board design;
- Schematics; and
- Surveying.

WHAT IS NEEDED TO RUN A CAD SYSTEM?

The Computer Itself: Hard Disks Versus Floppy Disks

Two main alternatives are available for the storage of CAD software and the drawing images and symbol libraries that are purchased or created. Both have advantages and disadvantages.

Floppy disks are small circles of polyester coated with magnetic oxide. They are conceptually akin to audio cassettes in that they can be recorded and played back or, in computer terms, written to or read from. The data stored is permanent unless it is erased. The disk rotates at a speed of about 300 revolutions per minute (rpm). The tape head that writes and reads the data signal is mounted on an arm that moves over the surface of the disk. The head actually touches the magnetic surface.

Floppy disk systems are available in single-sided and double-sided configurations. In a double-sided system, two heads contact both the upper and lower surface of the disk through appropriate openings in the disk envelope. Double-sided drives obviously hold twice as much as single-sided drives. Floppy disks intended for double-sided use are slightly more expensive because both surfaces must be certified as perfect.

Floppy systems also vary based on the density or concentration of the data. Single- and double-density systems are common, and quad density is also available. Higher densities store more data per disk, but media quality and proper maintenance of the disk drive beome more critical.

Floppy disk systems are commonly available in three sizes. Although disks 8 inches in diameter are still used in minicomputers and mainframe computers, they are not often seen in modern microcomputers. The current standard is a 5 1/4-inch disk. An IBM PC drive stores 360 kilobytes on standard double-sided disks of this size, whereas the high-density drive in the IBM AT stores 1.2 megabytes on special high-density floppies.

Floppies that are 3 1/2 inches in diameter are becoming increasingly popular. The magnetic disk is housed in a hard plastic shell with a sliding shutter that seals the disk from the environment. Very high recording densities allow capacities up to 800 kilobytes or more. First introduced on the Apple Macintosh, 3 1/2-inch floppies are now used on many IBM-compatible portable computers as well.

Although floppy disks offer a very low cost, data portability, and other advantages, they are relatively slow in transferring data. Floppy disks are also a contact system, because the tape head (or heads) makes physical contact with the magnetic surface. As such, they will wear out over time and could potentially lose data.

Hard or fixed disks solve many of these problems. A hard disk consists of an aluminum or glass disk that is coated with magnetic material. Various alternative coating methods and head technologies exist, but the operating principles are similar in all. Because the platter is rigid, it can be spun at much higher speeds, usually around 3,600 rpm.

The tape head does not actually touch the surface but is maintained at a very small but fixed distance above the disk surface. The same phenomenon causes the ground effect noted by airplane pilots that tends to hold a plane up in the immediate vicinity of the ground. This "flying head" is close enough to write and read the data, but the deleterious effects of friction are eliminated. The gap is so small that any particle of smoke or other foreign substance would clog the works. Hard disks are therefore hermetically sealed in a clean room during manufacture.

The sealed operating environment also allows very high track densities and data storage capabilities. Five- and 10-megabyte capacities are currently the smallest available, 20 to 30 megabyte capacities are common, and up to 250-megabyte capacities are now available for microcomputers, even in 5 1/4-inch hard disks. The high rotation speed also means that data transfer rates are high.

At one time, hard disks were somewhat fragile, but great strides have been made in reliability. Even portable computers are now available with hard disks. The main disadvantage to hard disks is their cost, although prices are dropping rapidly. Hard disks also are fixed in position; data interchange and backup must still involve the use of removable media like floppy disks or tape cartridges.

Another alternative that is especially attractive in the CAD environment (given the large drawing files that are created and retained) is the Bernoulli Box from IOMEGA Corporation. In many senses, this device offers the best of both worlds. Basically a floppy disk technology, Bernoulli cartridges are removable and transportable like floppy disks, but they store 10 or 20 megabytes of data each and operate at hard disk speeds. Their only drawback is that their cost is relatively high compared to floppy or hard disk systems.

Microprocessor and Clock Speed Considerations

Various microprocessors are available within the IBM environment. Intel's 8088, used in the base IBM PC and compatibles, is basically an 8-bit chip with 16-bit internal processing, whereas Intel's 8086 is a full 16-bit processor. Intel's newer processors, the 80186 and 80286, which are used in the IBM AT and compatibles, are 16-bit chips with internal 32-bit processing. Japan's NEC has introduced counterparts to many of the Intel processors that operate slightly faster and offer some other advantages. However, the NEC chips are not yet widely used and legal action clouds their continued availability.

A new generation of Intel microprocessors recently emerged that was expected to be widely available in late 1986 and early 1987. The new 80386 central processing unit (CPU) is a full 32-bit microprocessor with many advantages. Although the 80386 can run current software written for the 80286 and 8088/8086, new software will be required to fully utilize its capabilities.

The various processors can be run at differing clock rates. High clock speed requires not only special processor chips, but faster memory and other circuitry. IBM PCs operate at 4.77 MHz, whereas standard IBM ATs now run at 8 MHz. Many competitive systems now offer faster speeds, of up to 12 MHz or more for some 80286 AT-type systems.

A full 32-bit CPU also exists for the Motorola family used in the Macintosh. Designated the 68020, it is just beginning to be used in third-party add-ons for the Macintosh, but Apple has not yet introduced any system based on it.

Computer-aided design software is processor-intensive, which means that more capable processors running at higher speeds translate almost directly into improved throughput and efficiency. Accordingly, the extra investment required to acquire high-speed 80286 systems is quickly returned.

Math Coprocessors

The tremendous number of floating-point calculations required by CAD software places heavy demands on the computing capabilities of the computer system. Although such calculations can be performed by the system's software, special hardware can execute these calculations much faster. Math coprocessors are processor chips that relieve the main CPU of math calculations and can execute them very quickly while the CPU is performing other tasks.

The Intel coprocessors have been designated the 8087 for PC-type, 8088- and 8086-based computers and the 80287 for AT-type 80286 systems. As with CPUs, these chips are available in a range of clock speeds; the extra cost of the faster versions is well worth the investment. An empty socket is present on almost all IBM-compatible computers to allow for the installation of a math coprocessor, although special hardware is usually required for the higher speed chips. An equivalent math coprocessor, the 68881, exists for the Motorola family. No available Macintosh CAD software makes use of it yet.

Math coprocessors are so useful in CAD applications that many IBM-compatible CAD programs are now requiring them to operate. Be sure to check this requirement when purchasing computer hardware.

Maximized RAM

Computer-aided design software uses a certain amount of the computer memory for the actual program instruction. The remaining memory stores the data base of drawing instructions that, in aggregate, form the image. Some CAD programs must store the entire image in memory. Although this results in the fastest operation, the complexity of the image that can be accommodated is ultimately limited. Other CAD programs store what they can in memory but save any overflow on floppy or hard disks. Such programs can manage a drawing of essentially unlimited complexity (limited only by available disk space), but the process for "paging" data to and from the disk takes a finite amount of time and can slow the operation.

In either case, more RAM is always better. In addition, as CAD programs add features, the amount of RAM required for the program itself continues to expand. Fortunately, the price of additional RAM memory has declined rapidly and will continue to do so. Therefore, all CAD systems should be configured with the maximum amount of RAM that can be installed. The maximum amount of RAM available for current versions of PC/MS-DOS is 640 kilobytes. The Apple Macintosh Plus contains 1 megabyte of RAM as standard, but can readily be expanded to 4 megabytes with third-party add-ons. New versions of DOS expected next year will allow much more RAM, but it will probably be some time before CAD software can use this added memory.

In the meantime, several manufacturers have developed a method of accessing RAM beyond the 640-kilobyte barrier. The Lotus-Intel Microsoft (LIM) expanded memory standard allows installation and use of up to 8 megabytes of additional RAM. Most current CAD software cannot use this extra memory, although the newest version of AutoCAD can manipulate this memory, and other CADs are also expected to add this feature. The speed increases gained by adding LIM memory are real, but do not seem significant enough to merit the extra expense at this time.

Input/Output Ports

Two types of input/output ports are generally available for microcomputers: serial and parallel. Serial ports transmit data one bit at a time, whereas parallel ports transmit a complete byte of 8 bits at one time. Parallel ports are therefore faster than serial ports. Serial ports operate at varying speeds and with several different configurations, and the cable wiring between the computer and peripheral device is not completely standardized. Parallel cabling is almost always consistent. Parallel ports therefore have many advantages in both initial configuration and operation. However, most peripheral devices necessary for CAD systems use the serial interface method. Although a few plotters offer both serial and parallel ports, it is generally necessary to have two serial ports, one for the digitizing device and one for the output device.

Video Display Options

The video display devices selected for a CAD microcomputer are a prime determinant of the overall cost of the system, because acceptable alternatives range from perhaps $600 to well over $5,000 (list price in U.S. dollars).

Two factors explain this wide divergence in cost. First, the video system may be either monochrome or color. Monochrome video offers higher resolution per dollar, and the monitors used are both much less costly and more critically sharp. Color systems visually differentiate between layers of a drawing or between individual entities. (Layers are analogous to acetate overlays in conventional drawings.)

The type of drawings to be made dictates the need for color. If layering is needed, an individual color can be assigned to a layer to make the drawing easier to work with (although there are methods of turning on and off the display of different layers to attempt to differentiate them on monochrome displays). Similarly, if color is to be used in the final output (i.e., on a contour map), a color screen is convenient and even essential.

Another cost factor is screen resolution. The larger the number of pixels (picture elements) displayed on the screen, the smaller the detail that can be easily distinguished. Although all CAD software allows details to be enlarged by zooming into an area or a drawing, higher resolutions are more convenient, faster (and therefore more cost-efficient), and easier on the operator's eyes. The only negative aspects of higher resolution are the extra initial cost and the drawing speed; it takes a finite amount of time to draw each pixel, so more capable CPUs and higher clock rates are increasingly more important with higher resolution screens. It should be remembered that screen resolution has nothing to do with the resolution and detail of the final plotted or printed output. The output device and to some degree the software determine this precision, not the screen resolution.

The basic IBM monochrome adapter system is a text-only device that has no graphics capability of any kind. A third-party system developed by Hercules to address this shortcoming has become something of a de facto standard and is widely supported. Hercules graphics cards from both the original designer and other companies now sell in the $300 range and require only standard IBM TTL-type monochrome monitors. IBM's own such monitor and third-party monitors like the Princeton Graphics MAX-12, Amdek 310A, and others are suitable choices. Such monitors are commonly available only in the standard 23-inch screen size.

Hercules-type systems offer 720 (horizontal) by 348 (vertical) resolution, which is acceptable for most CAD uses.

Two monochrome adapter card/monitor systems have recently become available that offer significantly higher resolution. The WYSE 700 system displays 1,280 by 800 resolution on a 15-inch monitor for approximately $1,800. The Moniterm Viking One system is capable of 1,280 by 968 resolution on a large 19-inch monochrome monitor for about $2,200. Both systems can be used with standard DOS software, but special software drivers are required for their high resolution modes. Drivers are currently available for AutoCAD and a few other microcomputer CAD software packages.

In terms of color display systems, IBM offers three levels of resolution and color capability in their CP-compatible line. The original IBM Color Graphics Adapter (CGA) displays either 320 by 200 in four colors or 640 by 200 in two colors (essentially black on white). Although almost all CAD software supports the CGA, even the higher 640 by 200 resolution is simply too coarse for comfortable CAD or conventional software use. The CGA is therefore not recommended; a low-cost microcomputer CAD system is better with a Hercules monochrome display.

IBM's newer Enhanced Graphics Adapter (EGA) is emerging as a standard for color text and graphics applications. Its 640 by 350 resolution is acceptable for CAD, and the EGA displays text of acceptable quality for use with non-CAD software. The EGA can display 16 colors simultaneously from a palette of 64 colors if the card is equipped with the full 256 kilobytes of display memory. It should be noted that this memory is dedicated to use by the display system and has nothing to do with the RAM used for program and drawing storage. IBM's own EGA sells for approximately $1,000 with a full complement of memory, but many third-party equivalents are now available in the $300 to $600 range. EGA systems require special color monitors that are somewhat more costly than CGA-type monitors, but complete video systems still cost only $1,100 to $1,800.

The next level of color resolution is 640 by 480, which is noticeably better for CAD. IBM's Professional Graphics Adapter (PGA) offers this resolution, as do many systems from companies like Verticom, Vermont Graphics, and others. Until recently, such systems cost up to $3,000, but a few companies are now offering 640 by 480 systems for as little as $1,600, most notably new adapters from Tseng Laboratories, NEC, Vega, and others, all of which are used with an NEC Multi-Sync color monitor. Most 640 by 480 systems are downward compatible only with the CGA standard and do not run EGA-compatible software, but the Tseng, NEC, and Vega emulate the EGA as well.

Still higher resolution color systems are available at resolutions of up to 1,024 by 1,024 or even higher. At this level, special graphics processors are used to speed drawing to the screen, and costly and heavy monitors are required. The phosphors on such monitors are often not as bright as those used in conventional color monitors, which some users find bothersome in brightly lit working environments. These systems are often capable of displaying more colors simultaneously, which is not usually terribly important in most CAD applications. The cost of such systems is currently $5,000 or more, but, as with all computer hardware, the cost is likely to decline over time. In general, the very high color resolution systems are extremely pleasant to use and reduce the need for time-consuming zooms, but the heavy additional cost is not merited for most CAD needs.

The Operating System

The unquestioned standard in microcomputer CAD systems is Microsoft/IBM DOS. The great number of systems that use this operating system has allowed software companies to invest heavily in the development of CAD programs for the DOS/IBM PC-compatible environment. Although current versions of DOS are single-user, with no multi-tasking or multi-user capability, 1987 versions of DS should have added these functions. In any case, multi-user features can be added by way of local area networking.

The Apple Macintosh is the only alternative microcomputer operating system/hardware system with any significant development in the CAD area. It appears that this graphics-oriented system would be a natural fit with CAD, but the available CAD software is rather limited to date. Apple has announced a major effort to encourage CAD development of the Macintosh, and this system bears watching.

Input Devices

In addition to entering text and commands by way of the

keyboard like any computer software, CAD programs require the operator to enter graphic coordinates. Most CAD systems allow numeric coordinates to be input directly from the keyboard when appropriate, but the majority of positional inputs is entered by pointing at a position on the screen.

Many programs allow the cursor movement keys on the computer's keypad to position the on-screen graphics cursor, but this is generally an unsatisfactory method. It is slow, awkward, and counterintuitive when compared to devices that allow the operator to simply point to the desired position.

The least costly pointing device is the joystick. Similar and sometimes identical to the joysticks used for computer games, most joysticks connect to special game ports that must be added to the computer instead of normal serial interfaces. Joysticks are not particularly intuitive, and it is not always easy to position the cursor accurately; they are not recommended.

Light pens are perhaps the most intuitive pointing device. A light pen is a stylus attached by a wire to a special port provided on some, but not all, video adapter cards. The graphics cursor is positioned by actually touching the stylus to the display screen at the point desired. Besides the fact that they do not work with some displays and, in some cases, limited resolution, many users find light pens physically fatiguing. Not all CAD programs support light pens either. Although light pens can be quite pleasant for entering limited selections from menus and the like (especially by untrained users), as in hospital systems, they are not generally used in CAD systems.

The fastest growing pointing device is the mouse. Two popular mouse designs are mechanical and optical. Mechanical mice are like a reverse of the trackball used in video games. A rotating ball moves internal rollers by way of friction as the mouse is moved over any desk surface, and the movement of the rollers is translated into the movement of the screen cursor. Optical mice have no rollers. Instead, the mouse is moved over a small inscribed pad while infrared light is reflected off the pad. The movement is calculated and translated into the movement of the screen cursor.

Proponents of the optical mouse enjoy its lack of friction and its reliability, whereas advocates of mechanical mice disdain the need for the special pad. In fact, either method works well and is reliable.

Mice are available in one-, two-, or three-button designs. Although valid arguments can be made for each style in terms of ease of use as opposed to flexibility, the Microsoft Mouse, by far the industry's largest seller, is a two-button design, and most PC software assumes this design. The Macintosh mouse is a single-button device, and software for that system is adjusted accordingly.

Most mice use a normal serial interface port, although some connect to a special interface card that must be plugged into the computer. The Microsoft Mouse is available in either form. The interface card saves the need for another serial port, but occupies an expansion slot. Again, either method works fine. In addition to the Microsoft Mouse, mice from companies like Logimouse, Torrington, Maynard, and others are quite acceptable.

The prime virtues of a mouse are its low-cost ($100 to $200) compatibility with a wide range of both CAD and general-purpose software. On the negative side, mice are by definition relative devices. In other words, they track the direction and usually the speed of movement, but they have no intrinsic frame of reference.

Digitizing tablets, on the other hand, are absolute devices. A digitizing tablet is a flat surface over which either a stylus or puck is moved. The stylus resembles a pen, whereas the puck looks similar to a mouse with one to sixteen buttons on the top. (Some CAD software recognizes the buttons and allows the operator to directly issue commands by pressing a given button.) In either case, moving the pointer to a given position always sends the same coordinates to the computer. There are several methods by which digitizing tablets recognize the movement of the pointer, but these engineering alternatives are not of great significance to the average CAD user.

This absolute reference provides one of the digitizing tablet's greatest strengths: the ability to use template overlays. An overlay is a plastic or paper form that is taped to the tablet. The surface is divided into small boxes, each of which can be programmed to send a CAD command to the computer. A user can simply point at a box to perform a complex series of actions that would otherwise require the use of some other means, such as keyboard entry. Not all CAD software offers the option of a template, but its use can improve productivity by 30 to 40 percent or more.

Tablets are available in a wide range of sizes, from 6 by 6 inches (not recommended) up to drafting table size (36 by 48 inches or more). The larger sizes are intended primarily for tracing preexisting drawings. Tracing can be done with smaller tablets by tracing a section for a drawing and repositioning the paper image repeatedly, but this process is tedious and prone to error. In fact, tracing old drawings is always a cumbersome and monotonous process, because many corrections and editing steps are usually required. It is often easier to simply redraw old images or use a commercial service that uses scanning devices to translate existing drawings directly to the format required by a given CAD program.

In any case, by far the most common tablet size is about 12 by 12 inches. Most template designs assume this tablet size. The larger tablets can actually be less convenient to use, because the distances the operator must span are proportionally larger, and the larger devices cost much more (up to $5,000 for the largest sizes).

Tablets are available in 200 and 1,000 steps per inch resolutions; the higher resolution is desirable. Prices for 12 by 12 tablets are dropping rapidly; high-resolution units of an excellent quality are now approaching the $500 mark. The extra cost, as opposed to the use of mice, is well worth the investment.

Plotters

The pen plotter is the primary output device for CAD systems. A plotter is, in a real sense, a robotic analog of a human hand that moves a pen over paper or other media surfaces to actually draw the final image.

Three main designs accomplish this objective. Flatbed plotters are perhaps the closest equivalent to the human drawing process. The medium is fastened onto a flat drawing surface. A system of pulleys and motors moves an arm along a horizontal rail to provide X-axis movement. The pen head is mounted on this arm; it in turn moves along the arm vertically to provide movement along to provide Y-axis movement. The pen can thus access any portion of the medium. Another motor or solenoid raises and lowers the pen head.

Various methods are used to ensure that the medium does not move during this process. The medium can simply be taped to the bed with special masking tape circles made especially for this purpose. Some plotters have strips of sticky material to which the medium adheres; these strips eventually must be replaced after they lose their adhesive properties. If the plot bed is ferrous, flexible magnetic strips can be used to hold the edges of the medium. The best but most costly method is known as electrostatic holddown. A charge of static electricity is applied to cause the medium to cling lightly to the bed.

Alternative plotter designs move the medium along one axis and move the pen head along the other axis, thus providing equal access to the entire medium surface. The oldest such designs fastened the medium on the opposite edges of a rotating cylindrical drum. This design is not commonly seen now, having been replaced by plotters that grasp the edges of the medium by way of some combination of rubber capstans and wheels that are either coated with gritty material or etched with patterns of grooves. These wheels grasp the medium firmly and move it forward and backward while the pen head moves from side to side.

One might expect that keeping the medium stationary would be more precise than flapping the medium around, but tests reveal that this is not the case. Excellent results can be achieved with either method; in fact, various mechanical considerations often lead to more accurate results with moving paper designs. In addition, flatbed plotters capable of drawing the largest plots would be prohibitively large and unwieldy. Moving paper plotters therefore dominate the large plotter segment of the market.

The maximum plot size that can be drawn is the major determinant of plotter cost. Both International Standard Organization (ISO) and American National Standards Institute (ANSI) designations of plot size exist, but ANSI measurements will be used here. The smallest plotters accommodate only A-size media (8 1/2 by 11 inches), but A- and B-size plotters (11 by 17 inches) are also common. A few C-size plotters exist, but D-size (24 by 36 inches) and E-size (36 by 48 inches) plotters are most often used in professional environments. Obviously, plotters that can draw these larger sizes are physically bigger and require both more powerful and more precise motors and drive systems to maintain full accuracy while moving large sheets of media.

Most plotters handle a single sheet of media at one time. Sheet-feeding plotters exist that can automatically insert sheets of small media for continuous operation, and many larger plotters are available in versions that accommodate continuous rolls of media. These options add significantly to the device's cost and are merited only if a very high volume is forecast and the driving software can manage batch operations.

The term "medium" as opposed to "paper" has been used in this discussion because several popular drawing substances exist. Common bond paper or paper coated with a clay surface for extra gloss can be used; they are often acceptable for presentation materials and draft plots. Special papers are available and widely used for certain types of drawings (vellum is the most common). However, paper is subject to dimensional instability according to changes in temperature and humidity, and therefore may not be suitable for critical drawings. Mylar film is often used in cases in which drawing accuracy must be maintained over time. Another type of film is used to prepare transparencies to project business charts.

Many types of pens are available that vary in the type of material used for the pen tip and the type of ink employed. Each pen type is most suitable for a given type of medium and also operates best at a certain range of plotting speeds. Fiber-tipped pens are perhaps the most common type. The nylon fibers and vivid inks yield excellent results at moderate to high speeds on paper. These pens are also available with different inks for overhead transparency plotting. Ceramic and ball-point pens can also be used with various inks, often at high plot speeds.

The ultimate in plot quality and flexibility is obtained with liquid ink pens, although at slow plot speeds. Various tips are available to match specific media, and inks are available in a wide range of colors and drying speeds. These pens require that ink be transferred from a storage bottle to a reservoir in the pen by way of suction. The inks tend to dry quickly and scrupulous cleaning and maintenance is required. Disposable liquid ink pens have been recently developed that provide many of the benefits of liquid ink without the mess. Prices are somewhat higher than other types, but the quality often makes the incremental cost worthwhile for important plots.

Plotters can be further distinguished by the number of pens that can be stored and accessed automatically. Multiple pens are obviously required for color plots, but they can also be necessary or desirable for mixing pens of differing tip width (i.e., thicker tips are used for headings and outlines). Single-pen plotters can be used in such cases by instructing the software to pause and prompt the operator whenever the pen must be changed, but this requires the operator to stand by during the often lengthy plotting process.

Several multi-pen access designs are available. Some store the pens in a row along one edge of the plotting area; others use a rotating carousel. In some cases, the pens actually travel with the moving pen head. There are minor advantages and disadvantages to each design, but any mechanism is acceptable. More important is whether the pen tips are capped while in storage. If not, the pens tend to dry out or clog, which can ruin the results. It is not overstating the case to say that automatic pen capping is mandatory for an acceptable multi-pen plotter.

Plotters also vary widely in their speed and, to a lesser extent, their accuracy. These factors overlap in that it is easier to design a plotter that can deliver greater accuracy at slower speeds. The achievement of both high accuracy and fast drawing speed, especially in larger media units, requires heavier-duty and more costly motors and control systems. High-speed ratings translate directly to shorter plot times, assuming the computer system and CAD software can drive the plotter at maximum speed. Many users find that the higher initial investment in a faster plotter pays off if the work volume is high or plots are complex and lengthy. It is difficult to assess the interaction of speed and plot quality simply from manufacturer's specifications; the author's extended review of nearly 40 plotters (*PC Magazine*, December 1985 and October 1986) can provide detailed guidance. In general, plotters from leading manufacturers like Hewlett-Packard, Houston Instruments, and Calcomp are sound choices.

Printers

Although plotters are the universal output device of choice for quality CAD drawings, printers can provide lower-quality, hardcopy output that is useful for checking work progress, archival documentation, and other purposes. In many cases the printed output can be produced more quickly than plots. Because most printers are also less costly than plotters, it is often efficient in multiple work station environments to give each worker a printer and have all workers share a large and costly plotter for the final output. The dot matrix printer design is most commonly used for this purpose.

Most dot matrix printers now have some graphics capability,

and often adhere to standards set by Epson and IBM in their PC-compatible small printer line. The most common secondary graphics standards are set by Okidata and Toshiba. Suitable dot matrix printers, in either 8-inch or 15-inch wide carriage formats, range in price from about $500 to $1,800. In general, graphics output places heavy demands on a dot matrix printer's print mechanisms, and it is wise to purchase reasonably heavy-duty units as opposed to off-brand units. Dot matrix printers are capable of resolutions up to around 200 by 200 dots per square inch, which yields acceptable draft-quality output. Although color output can be produced with multicolor ribbons and multiple passes of the printhead, the quality is generally mediocre, the cost is higher than black-and-white printers, and the speed also suffers.

Laser printers are generally 300 by 300 dot devices in which each dot is both smaller and more accurately positioned than that of dot matrix printers; the output quality is therefore far better. Laser printers are much quieter and generally faster than dot matrix devices. The main drawbacks of laser printers for CAD use are media size and cost. Current laser printers are strictly black-and-white, although color laser printers were due to be introduced in 1987 at much higher prices. Current laser printers handle only 8 1/2- by 11-inch paper. More importantly, laser printers are page printers, which means that the entire image of the page output must be stored internally in the printer. This requires over 1 megabyte of memory at full 300-dots-per-inch resolution, which increases costs dramatically. Many text-oriented laser printers have much less memory and can print only small areas of graphics at full resolution.

Several laser printers have recently been introduced that are aimed specifically at the CAD market. The Laser Master printer, for example, is supplied with a hardware interface board and software drivers for several leading microcomputer CAD packages and can produce a finished page of graphics in only a couple of minutes. Another approach, typified by AST's TurboLaser printer, is to include the HPGL graphics language used in Hewlett-Packard's plotters. This allows the CAD software to drive the printer as if it were a plotter; it also produces finished output in 1 or 2 minutes. Both these printers sell for over $4,500, which is clearly too costly for producing CAD output unless they are shared by several users.

Several other printer technologies are capable of graphics output and can be used in CAD systems. Ink-jet printers are available in a wide range of resolutions and in both black-and-white and color. Special coated paper is generally desirable because the ink tends to blot and spread on conventional bond papers. Thermal transfer printers can also produce high-quality color output. However, neither type of printer has established a firm foothold in the CAD arena, given their cost and throughput limitations when compared to more conventional technologies.

DISADVANTAGES

Cost

As was outlined earlier, CAD is an intensive application that places extraordinary demands on the computer system. There is a clear trend toward the demand for more and more computing resources as CAD programs continue to add functionality; computing power requirements are therefore likely to increase rather than decrease over time.

Most CAD programs show a significant increase in performance as computing power is increased. More RAM generally reduces the need for relatively slow disk accesses, and hard disks are obviously faster than floppies. Some CAD programs have recently begun to use Lotus-Intel Microsoft expanded memory and the new generations of DOS in 1987 will almost certainly avail themselves of both expanded and AT-type extended memory.

Perhaps the most significant issue is that in which incremental investment in more powerful computer hardware results in sufficient efficiency improvement (primarily through faster drawing, fewer time-consuming zooms with higher resolution displays, etc.) to pay for the added cost. A generalization useful in evaluating this situation is known as the "Rule of 6,000." A standard work year consists of about 2,000 hours. Computer systems are often considered to have a 3-year life span (at least from an accounting point of view); the functional life span of the computer can therefore be considered to be 6,000 working hours. Dividing the cost of a high-end computer with more costly display facilities, hard disk, and so forth by the cost of a more bare-bones, low-end system often yields a cost differential of only $1 or $2 an hour. If the added efficiency and throughput of the more costly system (even ignoring such intangible factors as operator satisfaction and fatigue) factored with the labor cost of the operator saves at least this amount, the superior system makes economic sense.

The more costly systems generally have been found to be efficient. The return on investment for more costly hardware is paid back relatively quickly. For these reasons, PC/XT-class machines are not recommended for serious CAD environments unless cost constraints are unusually severe. The AT-class machines, although higher in initial cost, are strongly suggested. Digitizer tablets are also more desirable than lower cost mice, and faster plotters ease what is often one of the most significant bottlenecks in CAD operations.

Specific CAD software is not recommended here; the author's reviews in the March 1985 and other issues of *PC Magazine* investigate many microcomputer CADs in detail. However, higher-cost CAD software is again generally recommended. In recent months, the microcomputer CAD software market has divided into two price categories. Low-end programs are available in a range from under $100 to perhaps $500 (suggested U.S. list prices), whereas the high-end programs are priced between $2,000 and $3,000. Although several computer programs exist in the lower price bracket (e.g., EasyCAD, Drafix, and In*A* Vision), for the most part such programs are not usually in the best long-term interests of most serious CAD users.

High-end programs like AutoCAD, VersaCAD, Cadvance, IBM's new CADWrite, and others offer more features, improved performance, and many other benefits. If the "6,000 Rule" is applied again, the incremental hourly cost of such programs is almost insignificant; the cost can be measured in cents.

Another major factor is the availability of third-party ancillary programs that add functionality to the base CAD program. The more costly programs are supported to a far greater degree by such outside software developers. For example, well over 200 add-on programs are available for AutoCAD, the market share leader in the United States. The CAD programs themselves are usually general in nature so as to appeal to the widest possible audience. The third-party programs are therefore often highly desirable and sometimes even necessary to customize the CAD environment for the specific needs of a given discipline. The acquisition of full-featured, high-end CAD software is once again suggested, in spite of the extra initial investment.

The Learning Curve and Training

It is axiomatic that "with flexibility comes complexity," and few classes of software are as flexible as a full-featured CAD program. Computer-aided design programs include a large number of powerful commands and features to accommodate the various disciplines that commonly employ CAD and to provide as wide a spectrum of entity entry, editing, and measurement commands to allow intrinsically unforeseen visual manipulations.

The productivity increases that CAD can provide come only after the user attains transparency. Transparency is assumed when the CAD program and its command syntax and operating procedures disappear, and the user feels intimately connected to the screen. The flow of visual ideas is enhanced, rather than encumbered, by the technology.

This level of skill does not come quickly or easily. Depending on the cost of labor, the investment in training a user in the use of the software can sometimes contribute to a significant portion of the total system cost. It is essential that both management and the user understand the steepness of this learning curve. Management must allow sufficient training time before applying undue pressure on the staff. Because there is a period during which most drawings could probably be created faster by traditional hand methods, management must consider the throughput demands placed on the staff and adjust work loads accordingly. Without such measures, users tend to build negative attitudes that can further impede learning.

Unfortunately, the training tools available for many CAD programs are limited. The most obvious source is the documentation that accompanies the software. Most manuals are reference-oriented. Like much microcomputer documentation, the manuals make sense and become helpful only after the user has learned the program somewhat. Several CAD vendors, in recognition of this situation, have begun to include printed tutorial lessons that introduce a new user to the software. No disk-based interactive tutorials (such as those provided with the Lotus 1-2-3 spreadsheet program and some other applications) exist to date.

A few of the more successful CAD programs have attracted third-party training support. Tutorial books are available for several programs. Some audio tape and book programs have also appeared. Innovative video tape training courses are available for a few programs. Given the visual nature of CAD, these are perhaps the most appropriate training vehicles at this time, although they are costly and more oriented toward lecture and demonstration than they are interactive. Of course, they also require appropriate video playback and monitoring equipment, preferably in the immediate vicinity of the microcomputer. Interactive video disk and CD-ROM training materials may appear within the next 2 or 3 years that will be superior to current video methodologies.

All these self-training methods have the obvious benefit of being operational in any location, however remote. Although they can be very helpful and are far better than nothing, the best results have been attained with hands-on, in-person training sessions. Two basic approaches exist: classroom sessions, often with a computer for every one or two students, and on-site instruction in the end user's operating environment. Classroom instruction can be effective, but there are several drawbacks to its use. The teacher usually must be general and not focus on any particular discipline. There are so many commands to be learned that it is often unreasonable to expect the average student to assimilate them all in a 1- or 2-day course.

Experience has shown that far better results are usually obtained from on-site training. Students feel more comfortable in their normal environment, the same equipment configuration used in production is used in training (and any idiosyncrasies can be taught), and the course can be slanted toward the actual needs of the user. It has also been found that the best results are obtained from not attempting to cram the entire range of commands and procedures into a 1- or 2-day course. It is instead better to schedule three 4- or 6-hour classes separated by a week. This reduces the amount that must be absorbed in one session and allows the students to experiment with and assimilate the material between each session. They are then ready to absorb more when the next class occurs.

It has been proven over time that this technique compresses the learning curve dramatically. Students actually generate production-quality drawings at the conclusion of a 3-week period as opposed to months of experimentation. In a domestic situation, costs do not widely diverge from many classroom alternatives, depending on the location and the number of users to be trained on-site. However, the extra travel time could be prohibitive in a remote site.

In any case, managers of CAD sites believe that making the users familiar with the system quickly makes economic sense and improves user's attitudes and productivity. Training costs are not often considered in determining the overall system cost. Management should investigate the training options available in a given location and incorporate the costs into the overall system budget.

COMPATIBILITY

Microcomputer CAD installations can be divided into two categories: those whose output must be interfaced with or transferred to other CAD systems and those that stand alone and whose drawings are totally created within the microcomputer system.

Linking microcomputers and minicomputers or mainframes is a complex subject, especially in cases in which bidirectional data transfer is required. Fortunately, so-called "micro-mainframe links" are more often used to transfer financial data; the situation is somewhat less murky in the CAD arena.

Several manufacturers of CAD packages that normally reside on large systems have released microcomputer versions that maintain some level of file interchangeability with their larger brethren. The targets for such micro packages are primarily users of large system installations who would like to add compatible work stations at a lower cost or without further burdening the large computer. In some cases, subcontractors are being asked to use compatible micro CAD programs so the subcontractor can incorporate the farmed-out work directly. The large CAD systems in this category include IBM's CADAM/MicroCADAM and the ANVIL series.

However, these programs have not yet established a major impact on the microcomputer market. By far the most common method of CAD interchange is file conversion by way of a software translation program. Several established standards specify an interchange format, the most popular of which is IGES. Several microcomputer CADs include IGES translation as a standard option or at an extra cost, and third-party vendors also offer such convertors.

The dominant microcomputer CAD program, Autodesk's AutoCAD, includes its own interchange format, known as DXF. The DXF format has emerged as somewhat of a de facto standard, and is now supported by many other micro-, mini-, and mainframe CAD systems and third-party software developers.

It is strongly suggested that the availability of DXF transfers be considered in evaluating potential CAD software acquisition. Even if no immediate need is seen for the exchange of image data with outside systems, many third-party programs require or use DXF; of course, needs may change in the future.

SUMMARY

Microcomputer CAD systems are available for affordable prices and return significant economic and intangible dividends in efficiency, consistency, and overall drawing quality. They are suitable for a wide range of design and drafting disciplines.

Potential users should consider a wide range of issues in determining which hardware and CAD software is most appropriate to their specific needs. The least expensive alternatives are generally not attractive when compared to the somewhat more costly options.

For the most part, the considerations discussed in this paper apply equally well to both developed and developing countries. The normal concerns of reliable electrical power, environmental conditions, equipment availability, and service are universal. Special attention should be paid to the availability of training and product support, either through the vendor or by way of third-party products. This tends to indicate the selection of successful market leaders instead of secondary products.

6

Applied Expert Systems

RAOUL N. SMITH

INTRODUCTION

Computers in artificial intelligence have a radically different viewpoint from traditional computer science, and even from much of business data processing, because they are considered not as numeric calculators but rather as symbol processors. It is this perspective that has liberated many researchers in computer science and has led to the current revolution which we call Artificial Intelligence (AI).

Probably the most commercially successful field within AI is that of expert systems. What is meant by success here is the broad acceptance and application by industry of a technology that has been transferred from the academic or industrial research laboratory to the marketplace. Thus, the field of expert systems has become the most applied area within artificial intelligence and incorporates the subfields of knowledge representation, reasoning, planning, natural language understanding, cognitive modeling, and, sometimes, robotics and vision.

As a basis for discussion, let us define an expert system as: a computer program that contains knowledge of a problem domain and has rules of reasoning that can simulate the skills of an expert in that domain. In order to accomplish this, expert systems perform a variety of tasks. They reason through symbol manipulation and heuristics. They use stored knowledge about the domain as well as new deductions made by the system and data supplied by sensory instruments. A few have some built-in common sense and many of them, especially commercial products, are able to explain their reasoning.

Expert systems have been used to function in a variety of tasks such as interpreting, predicting, diagnosing, designing, planning, monitoring, debugging, repairing, teaching, and controlling. Systems performing each of these tasks are already in existence.

The major difference between expert systems and conventional programs is that expert systems represent and use knowledge rather than data. They operate heuristically rather than algorithmically. Their method of processing is more referential, they proceed along empirical lines rather than repetitious calculations, and they have the ability to explain.

Some practical considerations in deciding whether to attack a problem by means of an expert system (especially in less developed countries) include evidence that experts in the domain do exist. In addition, if this expertise is rare and costly, that would be added motivation for development. Having an expert who is voluble and is easy to debrief is also important as is the fact that the task should be more cognitive than physical.

EXPERT SYSTEM ARCHITECTURE

When deciding on the purchase of an expert system or on its design, one has to know about the five basic components of any expert system. These are:

- Knowledge base of rules and facts
- Inference engine for reasoning
- Knowledge acquisition module
- Explanation subsystem
- Appropriate user interface.

Major technical issues involved in the construction of each of these modules deserve some discussion.

Major Knowledge Representation Techniques

Production rules are the most widely used form of knowledge representation in expert systems. These are IF-THEN rules, commonly used to perform reasoning toward a stated goal. Examples of expert system building tools using this methodology are EMYCIN and OPS5. Another representation scheme focuses on frames, which capture prototypical knowledge and which allow for the inheritance of properties and for attachment of procedures. Example of tools using this method are FRL and SRL. LISP, as a language, is another representation tool. It allows for procedure and function-oriented representations that utilize nested subroutines to organize and control program execution. PROLOG, another programming language used rather extensively in AI, emphasizes the logical statement of the problems. It uses predicate calculus-like notation to structure statements and guide execution.

Two other forms of representation are becoming popular. These are object-oriented and access-oriented. The first is epitomized in SMALL-TALK, a language that operates on symbolic objects that communicate with one another via messages. The latter is exemplified in LOOPS, a tool whose computations are triggered by changes in input data.

Major Reasoning Techniques

Two factors must be considered in building or evaluating the inference engine. One is the type of inferencing scheme and the other is the type of control structure. Two standard types of inferencing are "modus ponens" and resolution. Typical control structures include backward and forward changing, depth-first and breadth-first search, and monotonic versus non-monotonic reasoning.

The most common control structure is backward and forward chaining. Forward chaining starts from the current state(s) and moves toward the goal. Backward chaining moves from the current state back toward known conditions. Deciding on which form of chaining to use clearly depends on the shape of the search space, desired performance, and purpose. If the control structure is simple or the search space converges to a small set of goals, then forward chaining is appropriate. If a hypothesis is being tested or the search space diverges from a small set of facts, it is probably wise to use backward chaining. In either case, a combination of the two can be used.

Explanation Capability

A user often wants to know why a system came to a particular conclusion. A simple way of getting this information is to keep a history of the path traversed by the space search in arriving at a conclusion. This can be displayed by rule number, or a text generation module can be adapted to interpret the meaning of the rule and generate an English text.

Knowledge Acquisition

Very few, if any, expert systems have a learning module (although recent results in connectionist theory suggest these are profitable models in learning). Most of the knowledge acquisition is accomplished by manual input. More proactive approaches will have to be developed in order to make these components productive.

User Interface

One of the most important, but often neglected, aspects of all computer systems is their user interfaces. The interface is, however, what the user will be exposed to first and what will greatly determine the usefulness of the system. Recently, more effort has been placed on building good user interface with expert systems. For example, the expert system building tool KEE has facilities for building task-appropriate, iconic-based user interface.

SOFTWARE TOOLS FOR BUILDING EXPERT SYSTEMS

This subject can be divided into two separate, but related, categories—programming languages and development tools.

Expert System Programming Languages

Any programming language can be used for writing an expert system. That includes FORTRAN and COBOL, and both have been used exactly for this purpose. COBOL in particular is gaining acceptance in building expert systems in MIS shops. Pascal and C are used more, but the two languages of choice on AI—LISP in its many forms and PROLOG—are the most frequently used languages. However, SMALL-TALK is gaining acceptance.

Two points to consider when choosing an expert system development language are convenience and efficiency. From a functional point of view, one should look for a language that supports data types such as lists, trees, and logical operators. Control structures that allow for recursion and backtracking are also important. In addition, fast pattern matching capabilities should be available.

Expert System Development Tools

There are two categories of tools that can be used here: knowledge engineering languages and system-building aids. The system-building aids include Expert-Ease, Rule Master, and Timm; all are used in acquiring knowledge, and Plume is used in building natural language interfaces. The general-purpose knowledge languages that are available today include ART, DUCK, KEE, KES, M.1, OPS5, S.1, and SRL+. The majority are rule-based and operate on large DEC, Symbolics, or Xerox hardware. They are still very expensive, with prices of $50K not being unusual. A few systems are available on microcomputers but they are small and have a narrower set of functions available.

In evaluating a language or tool, managers may find the following checklist useful:

- Development states
  - The system is debugged
  - There are manuals for the system
  - It is currently supported
- Hardware on which the system will operate
  - The system can run on local machines
  - The user community is a good size
  - It is an expedient system
- Software environment
  - The system can support graphics
  - The system has good editing facilities
  - The system has good debugging facilities.

DEVELOPMENT ISSUES IN EXPERT SYSTEMS

The cost of software development continues to increase while that of hardware decreases. But it is reassuring to note that over the past fifteen years, because of shared experiences, the amount of time necessary to develop expert systems has decreased. This has helped to lower the cost. Rough estimates for expert system development costs in the U.S. suggest that a small system of up to 350 rules takes about one-quarter to one-half person-years to complete and costs $40-50K. A large system of up to 3,000 rules takes 1-2 person-years and costs $500K-1M, and a very large system of 10,000 rules takes about 3-5 person-years and cost $2-5M. Clearly, actual costs depend on the experience of the developers, the cost of experts that need to be debriefed, the need to purchase new hardware or software, etc.

On the average, one can predict that selecting a problem in order to produce a commercial expert system takes about one to three months. Developing the prototype takes about six months, if all goes well. The development of the complete system, including user interface and documentation, takes another twelve to eighteen months. Testing and evaluation are next, and finally the system is ready for commercial use.

Justification for Development

Because of what could be a costly project, especially for developing countries, a manager must have a good reason for proposing the development or purchase of an expert system. Any of the following reasons should be considered sufficient:

- Expertise in that field in the country is scarce and important
- The number of experts in the field is decreasing
- Many locations need the expertise and it is rare
- Implementation could mean a high return on investment
- The environment in which it is to be used is very hostile to humans.

Before embarking on the development of an expert system, the following conditions exist:

- Experts must exist in the field
- The task should be well understood

- Cognitive and physical skills are required (unless the expert system is linked to a robot)
- There is a general consensus among the experts about the solution
- The experts can be easily debriefed.

A development project where all of these conditions are not met is not likely to succeed.

Resources Required

There at least three types of resources that must be considered in the development of an expert system: software, hardware, and human. In developed countries, hardware and software resources are often distinguished into two groups—research and production. But in developing countries it seems wiser to emphasize production environments. In such an environment, one has to consider non-specialized users who, as much as possible, should not have to learn many new software systems especially with documentation in a non-native language. In addition, hardware should be rugged, dependable, and inexpensive.

As for human resources, expert system development groups need project managers, system engineers, knowledge engineers, and domain experts. In the United States, it is estimated that only 5 percent of computer scientists work on knowledge-based systems in a variety of capacities. Trained knowledge engineers constitute an even smaller percentage of knowledge-based systems engineers. The situation in developing countries must be even more difficult. Characteristics of a good knowledge engineer include not only being learned in knowledge-based systems but also include excellent communication and debriefing skills.

THE MARKET FOR EXPERT SYSTEMS

The conditions mentioned earlier concerning justification for a build-or-buy decision on an expert system are especially acute for developing countries. And, because the scarcity and resultant cost for expertise is so great in those countries, expert systems may be the only visible solution to acquiring and utilizing that expertise. Therefore the market for many types of expert systems should be very high. If these same developing countries produce their own systems, then they will have produced valuable export commodities.

SUMMARY

Less developed countries appear to be a fertile ground for the use of expert systems. The basic decision of whether to build or buy an expert system requires answers to a variety of questions. Clearly, the understanding of the technical aspects of expert systems must be understood by the decision makers in order for them to make a proper decision concerning what type of features to build into or look for in the construction or acquisition of an expert system. Once a problem to be solved is decided upon, many of the technical characteristics of a proposed expert system are readily available. But there are many local political, economic, and social considerations that must come into play. Purchasing or building an expert system just for the sake of having one, because it is a status symbol for an organization, is hardly a noteworthy reason.

The interplay of political, social, and technical considerations is complex and special to individual conditions. Decisions must be made as to which of these four considerations must be given priority so that other decisions will fall into place.

PUBLISHED RESOURCES ON EXPERT SYSTEMS

Alty, Jim and M. Coombs, *Expert Systems: Concepts and Examples*. Manchester, UK, NCC Publications, 1984.

Harmon, Paul and D. King. *Expert Systems*. New York: John Wiley and Sons, Inc., 1985.

Hayes-Roth, Frederick, D.A. Waterman, and D.B. Lenat. *Building Expert Systems*. Reading, MA: Addison-Wesley Publishing Co., Inc., 1983.

Hewett, Julian and R. Sasson. *Expert Systems 1986*, Vol. I: USA and Canada. London, England: Ovum, Ltd., 1986.

Jackson, Peter. *Introduction to Expert Systems*. Workingham, England. Addison-Welsey Publishing Co., 1986.

Reitman, Walter, ed. *Artificial Intelligence Applications for Business*. Norwood, N.J.: Ablex Publishing Co., 1984.

Waterman, Donald A. *A Guide to Expert Systems*. Reading, MA: Addison-Welsey Publishing Co., 1986.

Journals

AI Expert
AI Magazine
Applied Artificial Intelligence
Artificial Intelligence in Engineering
Communications of the ACM
Computer
Expert Systems User

Newsletters, Surveys, etc.

AI Alert, Management Roundtable, Inc.
AI Capsule, Writers Group
AI Markets Newsletter, Aim Publications, Inc.
AI: Through the Looking Glass, Henry Firdman & Associates, Lexington, MA
Applied Artificial Intelligence Reporter, University of Miami Intelligent Systems Research Institute
The Artificial Intelligence Report, Artificial Intelligence Publications
Expert Systems 1986: An Assessment of Technology and Applications, SEAI Technical Publications, Madison, GA
Expert Systems Strategies, Cutter Information Corporation.
The International Directory of Artificial Intelligence Companies, Artificial Intelligence Software, Rovigo, Italy
Knowledge Engineering, Richmond Publishing Corporation
SIGART Newsletter

7

Computer Vision
Anil K. Jain

Computer vision techniques augment the human visual analysis of images or photographs. The terms picture processing, machine vision, computer vision, scene analysis, and image understanding also refer to the processing and interpretation of images using digital computers (Ballard and Brown, 1982). Modern scientific equipment in many disciplines has automated the image data-gathering process; photography, television, electron scanning microscopes, x-rays, multispectral scanners, bubble chambers, and ultrasonic devices all produce images that can be subjected to computerized or digital image processing. The collection of computer techniques known as image processing allows much of the routine analysis of pictorial data to be automated, thus freeing individual scientists to perform the more challenging and productive aspects of their work. In some cases, computer programs can recognize features or objects in pictures, a process called pattern recognition, or enhance a poor image. The best known example of computer-image enhancement is the satellite photography of the moon and Mars; the computer-enhanced images are a significant improvement over the originally transmitted data.

Two main reasons to digitally process images are to improve image quality to facilitate human interpretation and to automatically determine the presence or absence of objects in an image.

In remote sensing, images are gathered by satellites and transmitted to earth (Hord, 1982). These images are analyzed by trained photointerpreters to derive information in such areas as land-use categories, mineral deposits, wet lands, crop disease, and forest inventory. These images need to be corrected for the earth's curvature and brought into geographic alignment. Distortions in these images, such as shading effects and scattered light from the atmosphere, need to be removed. Digital image processing allows images to be efficiently processed to eliminate various forms of degradation and noise. This makes the job of a human photointerpreter much easier. However, even a thoroughly trained photointerpreter cannot process a great number of images in a consistent and reliable manner. Therefore, the remotely sensed images are also automatically classified into various categories depending on the particular application.

APPLICATIONS OF COMPUTER VISION

Recent concerns over productivity and quality control in developed countries have led to an upsurge in computer vision activity. Virtually every segment of the industry in developed countries has either employed or investigated the use of image processing for automated assembly and inspection. Most of the robots that are currently used in industrial plants are preprogrammed and do not have any "intelligence." The new generation of robots has a computerized vision system that enables them to "see" and recognize things (Hollingum, 1982). This capability allows a system to inspect a part and determine if it is defective.

One example of such a system is CONSIGHT (Ward, 1979), which has been developed to locate and inspect the automatic alignment of integrated circuit chips during various manufacturing processes at the Delco Electronics Division of General Motors. This system is currently in use in production and achieves the required production accuracy within acceptable costs. Other industrial applications of the machine vision methodology are parts verification, process control, materials handling, sorting, the proper location and orientation of parts, and assembly automation.

The applications of computer vision are not restricted to manufacturing processes or inspection techniques. In fact, these applications are recent compared to remote sensing and medical applications. Satellite images have been used to determine crop yields and monitor environmental factors, land-use planning, oil and mineral exploration, and water pollution. Various applications of image processing can be categorized under the following major areas:

- *Document Processing*: The recognition of printed or written characters in such applications as reading machines for the blind, the sorting of objects using bar codes, and the automatic input of printed text in processing systems.
- *Industrial Automation*: The inspection and assembly of complex objects in such applications as printed-circuit board inspection, high-speed inspection of small machine parts, and inspection of fuel gauges and speedometers.
- *Remote Sensing*: The observation of Earth by sensors aboard satellites or aircraft for forecasting crop yield, planning land use, monitoring the environment, meteorology, mineral exploration, and topographic mapping.
- *Medicine and Biology*: The processing of various medical images and signals as in counting blood cells, detecting the presence of tumors in chest x-rays, characterizing tissue using ultrasonics, and analyzing chromosome images.
- *Nondestructive Testing*: The detection of flaws and defects in materials and components before failures occur as in eddy current inspection for cracks in heat exchanger tubes, ultrasonics for cracks in pressure vessels, and radiography for voids and inclusions in pipeline welds.
- *Personal Identification*: The detection of unauthorized entry in secure installations in the form of speech and face recognition and fingerprint identification.
- *Scientific Applications*: These include the interpretation of seismic waves to predict earthquakes, the identification of tracks in bubble chamber photographs, and the analysis of molecular composition from electron microscope images.
- *Agriculture Applications*: These include the guidance of equipment, the inspection of products, and the sorting and packing of products.

Many of these applications are discussed in detail by Fu (1982). Although the images associated with any of these applications can be examined and interpreted by a trained human operator, the automation of the interpretation process by use of pattern recognition and image processing algorithms implemented on a digital computer has almost always led to improved accuracy in less time and at a lower cost.

COMPUTER VISION TECHNIQUES

Computer vision converts images or pictures from a camera into usable data through the use of digital computers. A typical image processing application consists of three fundamental operations:

- The acquisition of images;
- The processing and quantitative assessment of features in an image; and
- The formulation of decisions based on this information.

The field of image processing therefore deals with the acquisition, storage, enhancement, restoration, and interpretation of images.

In a typical computer vision application, the image of the scene to be interpreted is acquired by sensors. The analog or continuous image (signal) is digitized so that the image can be entered into a digital computer; the intensities in the image are then quantized to a finite number of gray levels. The image is then enhanced to remove or reduce noise and degradation. At the third stage, image points or pixels with similar properties are grouped to form regions or segments. Regions are described by such properties as shape, area, texture, and color. Relationships (adjacency, left, right, surround) among the various scene components or regions are then used to recognize the objects and interpret the scene. At each stage of processing, certain assumptions are made that do not arise from the sensed data itself. For example, a priori assumptions about the imaging noise are made in the enhancement stage. Assumptions are also made about the smooth variation of object boundaries and the uniform intensity of object interiors in the segmentation stage. The various stages in a typical image processing system are described in the following sections (Hall, 1979; Pavlidis, 1982).

Image Acquisition

Three devices are commonly used to electronically record an image: the vidicon tube, the solid-state camera, and the multispectral scanner. Most image sensors are passive in that they record emitted energy. However, active sensing is necessary in many applications. Laser scanners used to measure depth and x-ray and ultrasonic sensors used in biomedical applications are examples of active sensors. Solid-state cameras are more appropriate for industrial applications, particularly robotics, because they are lightweight and rugged and use little power. Solid-state cameras are now available with a higher resolution and a lower cost. A good survey on image sensors is provided by Nagy (1983).

Image Digitization

Image digitization refers to the process of converting an image or picture into a set of numbers so that it can be entered into a digital computer. The following are two important aspects in the conversion of an image into digital form:

- Spatial resolution refers to the spatial detail captured during the sampling process in which an image is converted into an N × N array or grid of pixels. The physical size of the pixel depends on the camera optics and the distance of the camera from the object. The Landsat-2 satellite produces images with a pixel size of 80 meters by 80 meters. Pixel size is measured in micrometers in biomedical applications.
- Gray level resolution refers to the range of densities or reflections to which the image scanner responds and how finely it divides the range. Most digitizers and scanners will code each intensity value into 256 possible intensity encodings. For industrial tasks in which illumination can be controlled, 16 levels of intensity information are sufficient.

Image Enhancement

A digital image usually contains several kinds of noise and degradation that make it difficult to interpret the image. Some sources of distortion are sensor noise, motion blur, lens aberrations, noise introduced during the transmission of the image, nonuniform illumination, and specular reflection. Image enhancement and restoration refers to a collection of techniques that improve the quality of a noisy and degraded image, either for human inspection or subsequent automatic analysis.

Image Segmentation

Once an acquired image has been processed to improve its quality, it is often desirable to automatically isolate regions of interest in the image. For example, given a digital image obtained from a Landsat satellite, the desired output is a map of the region that shows specific types of terrain features (e.g., forest, urban areas, or water bodies). The output requires the location and identification of the desired terrain types. Image segmentation refers to the partitioning of an image into regions in such a way that pixels that belong to a region are more similar to each other than pixels that belong to other regions. What criterion should be used to group the pixels? In the context of remote sensing, the similarity between two pixels is measured in terms of the gray values in several spectral bands.

Region Description

Regions or segments in an image can be distinguished and classified based on their color, shape, and texture. A useful description of an object should be independent of its size (viewing distance), orientation, and position. The color, shape, and textural properties of a region are therefore used to derive features needed by a pattern recognition or classification system.

IMAGE INTERPRETATION

Image interpretation refers to a symbolic description of an image. Interpretation not only requires that the individual objects present in the image be identified, but that the spatial relationship between the objects be defined. The difference between image processing and image interpretation can be illustrated by the following example.

Given an aerial image of a scene, an image processing system would label or classify each pixel into one of several prespecified categories. An image interpretation system, on the other hand, is capable of generating a narrative from the image that could read something like: "The image contains two major highways with a river in the southeast corner. There are two bridges on this river." The system must understand the concept of highway, bridge, and river to generate this narrative. The difficulty lies in representing this knowledge so that it can be used efficiently in the analysis of an image. It is now generally agreed that to interpret a complex image the image processing system must utilize the same knowledge about the image domain that a human expert uses.

COMPUTER VISION HARDWARE AND SOFTWARE

Applications of computer vision methodology require a critical mass of hardware, software, and personnel. It is an interdisciplinary activity that requires close interaction among computer scientists, engineers, and experts in the application area. For example, image processing experts must work in close cooperation with meteorologists to develop a system to analyze and interpret satellite and aerial images for meteorological applications. The processing of images requires complex software that consists of algorithms for two-dimensional filtering, edge detection, region growing, shape analysis, texture, and classification. A typical image is composed of 512 × 512 pixels, each with 256 gray levels, that require approximately 2 million bits of storage. Even a simple operation like 3 × 3 averaging or smoothing can take several minutes on a super minicomputer. A dedicated and interactive computing facility is therefore required for computer vision work. Many of these algorithms are often implemented in hardware to speed the processing.

Hardware

Computer vision systems are commercially available in a variety of forms ranging from simple image manipulation capabilities to the high-volume processing power needed in remote sensing. The price of such systems ranges from $10,000 to $500,000. The more a system costs, the faster and more flexible it will be in handling the data.

An image processing system, irrespective of its size and cost, must have the capability to handle the following tasks:

- *Image digitization.* Analog pictorial information must be converted into digital form.
- *Image storage.* Large disks and tape drives are needed to store digital images.
- *Image display.* A display is needed to view input and processed images.

- *Processing.* A processor is needed to execute various enhancement and classification tasks.

An interactive computer environment is essential for image processing. This environment facilitates the interplay between man and machine to interpret, understand, and classify images (Gini and Gini, 1985). Early image processing systems that were used in industrial applications were binary systems because of limitations in speed, cost, and computer memory. Current computer technology allows gray scale processing at a reasonable cost. Color systems are now being developed that will further increase application potential, especially in agriculture.

The simplest image processing system requires an investment of about $4,000 for a personal computer, $500 for a camera, and $2,000 for a board to "grab" and filter the frames from the camera. Some vendors sell a complete desk-top image processing system for about $20,000. Novini (1985) makes several recommendations for potential buyers of a vision system. Introductory information, a list of vendors, and exhibition dates for vision and robotics systems can be obtained from the Machine Vision Association of SME, One SME Drive, P.O. Box 930, Dearborn, Michigan 48121.

Software

Different processing strategies are needed for images from different domains. For example, the nature and source of noise and distortion in the ultrasonic images in biomedical applications are different from those in the x-ray images of welds in nondestructive testing. This explains the large number of processing and classification techniques available in the literature. There is no optimal sequence or set of processing steps. The given images influence the choice of image processing techniques. It is therefore important that a user have access to a large variety of algorithms for image transformation, enhancement, edge and line detection, texture analysis, segmentation, shape, and registration. The best way to get started is to purchase a comprehensive software package that is available from several vendors. This will eliminate the large amount of resources needed to write and test the software in-house.

SUMMARY

Image processing is useful for improving the quality of an image to aid human interpretation and to make automatic decisions about the objects present in the image. One of the first applications of digital image processing was to remove the noise and degradation of the images of Mars and the moon transmitted to Earth by satellite. Image processing has been routinely used since then to process and interpret images in a number of fields, such as remote sensing, astronomy, medicine, chemistry, physics, agriculture, and industrial inspection. The current vitality in this area stems from its important role in robotics, in which image processing is needed to analyze three-dimensional indoor and outdoor scenes. It is already revolutionizing the manufacturing and inspection processes in most developed countries. It is important that developing countries understand the applications of this advanced technology to their own industries and production problems.

REFERENCES

Ballard, B. and Brown C., Computer Vision, Prentice Hall, 1982.
Fu, K.S. ed., Applications of Pattern Recognition, CRC Press, 1982.
Gini, G., and Gini, M., "A software laboratory for visual inspection and recognition," Pattern Recognition, Vol. 18, 1985, pp. 43-51.
Hall, E., Computer Image Processing and Recognition, Academic Press, 1979.
Hollingum, J., Machine Vision: The Eyes of Automation, Springer Verlag, 1982.
Hord, R., Digital Image Processing for Remotely Sensed Data, Academic Press, 1982.
Nagy, G., "Optimal scanning digitizers," Computer, May 1983, pp. 13-23.
Novini, A., "Before you buy a vision system...," Manufacturing Engineering, March 1985, pp. 42-48.
Pavlidis, T., Algorithms for Graphics and Image Processing, Computer Science Press, 1982.
Ward, et al., "CONSIGHT: A practical vision-based robot guidance system," Proceedings 9th International Symposium Industrial Robots, Society of Manufacturing Engineers and Robot Institute of America, Washington, D.C., March 1979, pp. 195-212.

8

A Multiple Microprocessor Architecture for Real-Time Visual Inspection

A.J. PADILHA and J.C.D. MARQUES DOS SANTOS

The performance and flexibility of industrial automation systems can be improved by the addition of several types of sensor devices, including visual sensors. Visual sensors can perform an important function by enabling many benefits to be realized, namely:

- Cost reduction, by eliminating or reducing the need for complex feeding, positioning, and alignment devices that are required by rigid automation systems;
- Quality improvement, by allowing a 100 percent inspection with capabilities for precise dimensional measurement, rejection of defective parts, and detection of qualitative surface properties; and
- Compatibility with computer-integrated manufacturing systems by exploring the facilities for communication and interaction with other automation devices and systems.

Computer vision systems can identify shapes, measure distances, determine position and orientation, quantify movement, and detect surface properties.

In terms of operational design, the implementation of the previously mentioned functions could be straightforward in current commercial systems; however, in practical applications, the cost and speed requirements may call for specially tailored systems. The large variety of technical objectives and requirements makes each application a new, distinct problem, that demands costly and time-consuming design and development. Many potential applications consequently must be abandoned for lack of economic justification.

The multiple microprocessor architecture hereafter described is an important piece of a development system that is designed to allow the introduction of automatic visual inspection systems in cases in which only moderate technical and economic resources exist.

The SPAI general-purpose laboratory system is an interactive development tool for the generation of image processing and analysis algorithms suited to each particular application. The algorithmic structure thus obtained can easily be transposed to a multiple microprocessor architecture, AMIVA, that is capable of real time operation. The cost and execution speed of the future prototype is then readily available. The actual implementation of the prototype requires only the installation and physical interconnection of standard nodules.

APPLICATION DEVELOPMENT

The SPAI laboratory system consists of a low-cost conventional LSI-11 microcomputer and a special-purpose hardware unit, the interface, that enables it to communicate with a standard TV camera and monitor (Figure 1). This interface contains a video controller, a frame buffer memory, analog/digital and digital/analog conversion circuits, and hardware for communication with the microcomputer by way of its standard input/output parallel port. Image acquisition is performed in real time to a square matrix of 128×128 8-bit pixels; the same format is used for image display.

The operation of the SPAI is determined by a set of programs that collectively obey the flow graph of Figure 2. The user controls the system by way of an interactive command language that lets the user execute the following classes of commands: utilities, image acquisition and display, image processing, and image analysis.

The utilities class is composed of several commands to store and retrieve images from flexible disks, generate and recall macrocommands and programs of commands, invoke auxiliary images, insert text, print data on the terminal, and so forth.

The image acquisition and display commands perform the sampling and quantization of the video signal from the camera, the display of the frame buffer image on the TV monitor, and the hard copy of images on the microplotter.

Image processing commands operate on a point, local (3 × 3 neighborhood), or global basis. Each elementary command performs a trivial transformation; more elaborate functions are obtained by the appropriate association of elementary commands.

Image features, such as areas, perimeters, projections, and counts, are extracted by analysis commands and used for object or scene classification purposes.

The current set of commands and the facilities for grouping them in sequences, macrocommands, and programs of commands have been found adequate for a great variety of applications. Algorithm development is greatly improved because of the possibility of following, step by step, the results of the adopted processing strategy.

REAL TIME IMPLEMENTATION

Laboratory tests conducted in SPAI may result in establishing the conditions of a given application's viability, in operational terms, and in defining a processing strategy suited for the achievement of specific goals.

Cost and speed requirements must be considered when a dedicated system is being built for routine operation in the application environment. More often than not, these requirements cannot be met by SPAI itself. The cost and time duration for the design and implementation of the dedicated system may then be excessively high and difficult to predict accurately.

The AMIVA modular system was designed with the primary goals of reducing the design effort of dedicated systems and eliminating the uncertainty of their cost and performance. The performance and associated cost of the AMIVA system to implement a given processing strategy, as obtained in SPAI, is readily available. Furthermore, the actual construction of a prototype system is straightforward, because it only requires that a number of standard modules be assembled.

This assembly results in an organization that directly reflects the application algorithm designed in SPAI. This algorithm can be expressed in a graph of operations like the one shown in Figure 3, in which the arrows represent the flow of image data between elementary commands of SPAI, GP, TH, and BQ. If one assigns the execution of each of these elementary operations to one distinct module, the AMIVA structure that is implementing the algorithm can be described by a similar graph, as shown in Figure 4, in which the arrows correspond to the physical connection of modules.

Each AMIVA is composed of one processor submodule and one memory submodule. Each submodule of a given type has three access ports to an equal number of submodules of the other type. In this way, a processor submodule can have direct communications with six other processors by way of three memory submodules, as shown in Figure 5.

AMIVA structures can implement all algorithms developed in SPAI and are efficient when the same algorithm is repeatedly applied to a succession of images, which is frequently the situation in many practical problems. The basic speed of an AMIVA system is two images a second (of about 100 × 100 pixels each); the speed can be doubled by, at most, doubling the cost.

THE OPERATION OF AMIVA STRUCTURES

AMIVA submodules are interconnected by means of cables to establish a configuration that is a material version of the algorithmic structure expressed in SPAI command language. The operation of the processing chain is supervised and controlled by an operating system, each module of which contains and executes one copy. The global flow graph of the operating system is shown in Figure 6.

During the initialization phase, the modules execute a self-identification process. Each processor assigns itself a distinct identity and collects information on the communication paths to the other processors. Data transfer from one module to another is then accomplished by message passing, directed by the target processor's identity.

The application programs (called external programs in Figure 6) that correspond to SPAI commands, can permanently reside in each module, or they can be transferred by means of specific messages from one module to all others.

The functioning of the chain is self-synchronized in normal operations. When one processor terminates its function over an image, it sends a message to the following processor(s) in the chain to signal the availability of new image data. The processor then enters a wait loop until it receives a message from the previous processor(s) in the chain to process a new image.

Writing application programs is a trivial task because the operating system provides auxiliary subroutines to help handle the message exchange procedures.

CONCLUSION

An integrated system for applications development in automatic inspection is described that provides facilities for laboratory research of the image processing and analysis algorithms suited to a particular problem. The system also provides means to transpose those algorithms to prototypes capable of real time operation. The system has been fully implemented and tested.

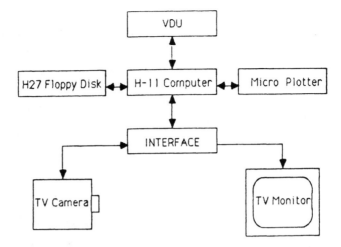

FIGURE 1   Microcomputer interface with TV camera and monitor.

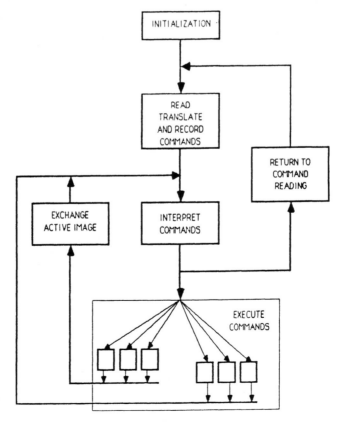

FIGURE 2   Operational flow chart.

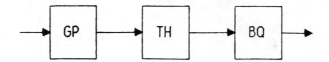

FIGURE 3 Image data flow.

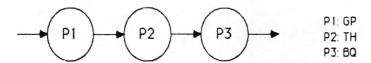

P1: GP
P2: TH
P3: BQ

FIGURE 4 Physical connection of the modules.

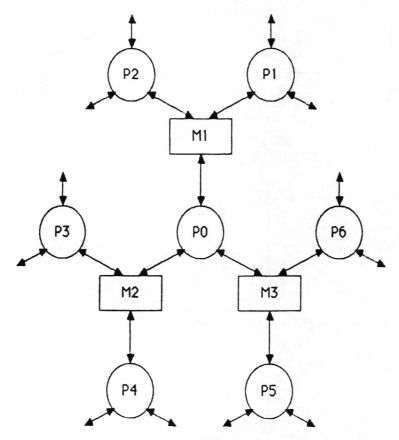

FIGURE 5 Each processor submodule can be connected with six other processors through three memory submodules.

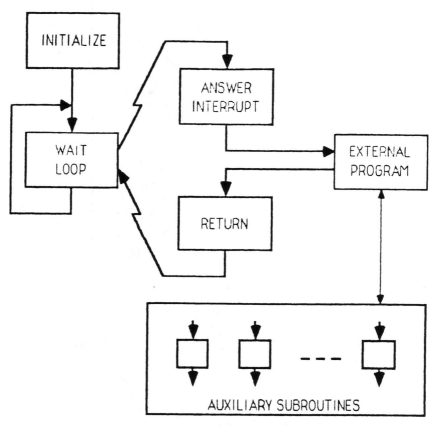

FIGURE 6 Global flow graph of the operating system.

Resource Assessment

9

An Integrated Microcomputer Processing System for Census and Survey Data

BARBARA N. DISKIN

COMPUTER PROCESSING IN THE STATISTICAL OFFICES OF DEVELOPING COUNTRIES

Although it is impossible to offer a universal description of computing in the national statistical offices (NSOs) of developing countries, some similarities deserve mention. The biggest task for an NSO is invariably the population census that normally takes place every 10 years. It is the volume of data, not necessarily the complexity of the job, that makes this such a formidable task. A census of population and housing typically results in one record of data for each individual enumerated and a record of each household identified during the census. Twenty questions are typically asked about each person, and twelve questions about each housing unit. The first major processing task is to capture the data in machine-readable form. The next step is to rectify missing and incomplete data. The final phase of processing involves the generation of the myriad of cross-tabulations of data, preferably in a form that is suitable for direct printing.

Many NSOs attempt to supplement the data collected in a national census by conducting an ongoing program of household sample surveys. Although only a small portion of the population is interviewed during a round of a typical survey, the questionnaires tend to be longer than census questionnaires. Moreover, the data often have a greater urgency because they may serve to generate such statistics as unemployment rates and consumer price indices. The processing steps include those identified earlier for processing a census as a core. In addition, the NSO will calculate variances to determine the degree of sampling error.

National censuses and sample surveys are by no means the only work of an NSO, but they are activities that typically demand the greatest use of data processing resources.

Mainframe Problems

Many NSOs depend exclusively on a mainframe computer that is either in-house or at a national computer center for their processing support. Although these large machines have proven to be real workhorses in processing censuses and surveys, this arrangement has several inherent problems that make it difficult to accomplish the processing in a timely manner.

Access to the computer is often limited because of conflicting priorities for computer resources and the limited number of jobs that can be run simultaneously. The internal politics and management of the computing center have a significant effect on the speed with which jobs are run.

The mainframe hardware found in developing countries is not often the latest model. Furthermore, the machine is often the only one of its kind in the country, and it is too costly to keep a complete set of spare parts. Electricity is unstable in many developing countries. The power requirements of mainframe computers make the cost of backup power systems high, sometimes prohibitively so. For these reasons, computer users experience considerable downtime while the parts are being ordered, the machine is being repaired, or electricity is unavailable. In such cases, processing comes to a complete stop. Mainframe computers demand environmental conditioners. Raised floors and powerful air conditioners are standard requirements for these large machines.

Perhaps the greatest problem associated with mainframe computing is attracting, training, and retaining computer professionals. Systems analysts, computer programmers, and computer operators often use the NSO as a training ground and then move on to better-paying positions in the private sector. Before professionals can be productive, they must have an understanding of the operating system, one or more high-level programming languages, and whatever packaged software exists, as well as the capability to read technical manuals that are usually written in English.

Many mainframe computers are rented because the cost of purchasing them is prohibitive. Furthermore, such a commitment would lock the NSO into fixed technology for many years. Rental costs can run up to $1,000,000 a year; in one way or another, the monetary outlay for mainframe computing is significant.

Most mainframe applications require a significant amount of customized programming. Packaged software for mainframe computers is not plentiful, certainly not in developing countries. Some of the packages on the market require a monthly or yearly rental fee that developing countries simply cannot afford. The existing packages are for the most part oriented toward programmers and are not considered user-friendly.

The existence of these mainframe computing problems has contributed to data processing being the weak link in meeting the schedules of surveys and censuses. Too many factors are out of the control of the end user.

The Use of Microcomputers

Developing countries are embracing microcomputer technology as a solution to many of the previously described problems. The low cost of microcomputers often makes it possible to buy multiple machines and to locate them in a decentralized manner that enhances their accessibility. Most microcomputers function well in a normal office environment. Good microcomputer software is written to minimize the inhibition the user experiences when interacting with the microcomputer. It therefore no longer takes a data processor to use the machine effectively. Finally, the modularity of microcomputers has fostered an entirely new approach to maintenance in which components are simply swapped in and out by the user to accomplish repairs.

This is not to say that the use of a microcomputer is trouble-free. The most common problem is the frustration of getting started. The solution to this problem may involve a completely new approach to processing that accounts for the strengths and weaknesses of a microcomputer system. This approach is to identify appropriate software packages and become comfortable with their use. In the isolation of a developing country NSO, however, the selection of appropriate software may be particularly difficult because no other person in the country may have any knowledge of the software.

As the NSO user becomes more proficient in the use of the microcomputer and its associated software repertoire, it becomes evident that the standard software offerings do not address many of the processing needs of censuses and surveys. When the software does exist, the pieces do not always fit together to form a coherent processing system.

Trends

Since microcomputers were introduced in the mid-1970s, their use has rapidly grown in every country of the world. The enthusiasm of microcomputer users has resulted in a repeated reduction in the size and cost of microcomputers and an exponential increase in power and available microcomputer software. Recent developments in memory and storage expansion, such as removable hard disks at the board level, enhance the feasibility of the largest-scale processing. The use of local area networks now makes it possible to consider sharing large data bases and costly peripherals.

National statistical offices are looking to microcomputers to augment their total computer environment. They are asking for communication and compatibility with larger computers to take advantage of the best resource for the task at hand. They are constantly searching for software to facilitate their processing tasks.

A CASE FOR INTEGRATED SOFTWARE PACKAGES

The advent of the microcomputer has spawned a new breed of user that does not think in terms of bits, bytes, operating systems, and positional operands. The user instead wants to communicate with the computer in an English-like style and let software take care of the drudgery of communication. The primary objective is to get a task done as effortlessly as possible without extensive computer knowledge.

The term software integration was coined to describe a set of desirable functions or modules that are brought together under one "umbrella." The user interface is typically in the form of a series of menus from which the desired modules are requested. The overhead of making the output from one module recognizable as input to another module is taken care of by the software package.

This approach is particularly appealing to NSO users who may not be experienced data processors. It means that scarce programming time can be freed for those tasks that require it; other tasks such as intelligent data entry can proceed and analysts can look at summary data in the meantime.

The development of integrated software is expensive and time-consuming. For the result to be effective, the developers must have a thorough understanding of the user's needs. A provision must also be made for intended users to actually test the system at significant stages of its development.

The Integrated Microcomputer Processing System of the International Statistical Programs Center (ISPC)

Several years ago, the ISPC identified the lack of appropriate software to perform the tasks typically associated with census and survey processing on microcomputers. National statistical offices were beginning to acquire microcomputers and to consider how they could be used most productively. Packages like dBase III for data base work and LOTUS 1-2-3 for the generation of spreadsheets were already available and quite popular. However, packages like ISPC's CONCOR for editing and CENTS 4 for tabulation were not available for microcomputers. Furthermore, the concept of software integration was just becoming a reality.

ISPC has embarked on a software project to fill this void. An integrated microcomputer processing system and usable intermediate products for surveys and censuses are being developed incrementally. The result will be an integrated system of modules that addresses the most important tasks in census and survey processing.

The Components of Census and Survey Data Processing

The processing of census and survey data involves several major tasks. Data entry involves capturing the data in machine-readable form. It can be achieved by keying the data or by using an optical mark and character reader to transfer the data to a magnetic medium. Data entry is closely followed by editing to correct errors introduced in filling out the questionnaires or in entering the data. It is desirable to do a considerable amount of editing at the time data are entered to take advantage of the presence of the questionnaires to resolve errors. When the quantities of data are great, the longest delays often occur in the entry and editing stages, especially in cases in which editing is done in repeated passes of the data through an edit program, followed by review of error listings and subsequent manual corrections.

Once the data have been edited, they are ready for tabulation and further analysis. Tabulation generally requires that the data be passed multiple times to produce descriptive statistics by crosstabulating two or more variables in each table. Analysis involves a broad range of calculations, including regression, life tables, projections, and estimates of sampling errors.

Operational control is especially significant when large volumes of data are involved. The NSO must track work units of data from the initial collection through each stage of processing, and a mechanism must exist to accurately reflect the status of processing.

Many of the tasks associated with census and survey processing can be generalized; they do not vary significantly from one processing effort to the next. The extensive use of the U.S. Census Bureau's CONCOR and CENTS 4 packages for editing and tabulation on mainframes attests to this fact. The ISPC's integrated microcomputer processing system will result in the equivalent of these packages and additional software modules to address the other processing tasks mentioned earlier.

Overall Design and Objectives

The key to the success of the system lies in taking a careful look at what NSO users need and in what form it will be most useful. The following points summarize the consensus of potential users:

- The system should be designed for a standard configuration of the most common microcomputer hardware that runs a proven operating system.
- At a minimum, the system should address data entry, editing, tabulation, statistical analysis, demographic analysis, and operational control.

- The system should be modular to the degree that the user should be able to use one module or any number of modules.
- The user should be able to interface with custom programs for specialized processing not provided for by the system.
- A common data dictionary should be shared by at least the editing and tabulation modules.
- The system should be menu-driven and offer the user additional support in the form of on-line "help" information.
- The system should provide effective error-trapping and recovery routines.
- It should automatically provide any reformatting necessary to move data from one module to another.
- Comprehensive documentation should include written manuals and tutorials for user orientation.
- The system should be designed in such a way that modules can be easily modified or swapped as software improvements are recognized. The system should be written in a high-level language that allows it to migrate to other operating systems, because operating systems are still evolving.

Choice of Target Hardware

Deciding which microcomputer to use as a target machine was one of the initial tasks of the ISPC. The popularity of the IBM Personal Computer (PC) made it a good candidate. The worldwide network of IBM support, the choice of the PC by numerous software developers, and the growth of the PC-compatible industry further recommended it as the target machine. The integrated system was designed for an IBM PC model XT or AT (or compatible) that had a minimum of 256 kilobytes of memory, a 10-megabyte hard disk, and a printer.

Data Entry

Since the beginning of computerized data processing, it has not been the writing of programs that typically delayed the overall processing of censuses and surveys, but the capturing of data in machine-readable form. This problem exists for small surveys, but becomes even more severe when a large number of questionnaires are to be entered, such as those associated with a national population census. Data entry can greatly affect the success of any processing effort from the standpoint of timeliness and quality. Careful attention therefore should be given to the data entry component to maximize the success of overall processing.

The goal of data entry in the interactive environment of the microcomputer is to enter the data and perform as many edit checks as possible without seriously degrading the speed of the operation. The overall requirement is for a package that provides ease of use, speed, and the necessary functions.

The ISPC evaluated existing data entry software packages for the IBM PC and compatibles in an effort to identify the best candidates for census and survey data entry. The evaluation criteria included the following capabilities:

- The processing of data in identifiable batches, with batch control checking allowed;
- The automatic duplication of fields such as identification fields;
- Range checking, with a provision for noncontiguous ranges;
- A programmable cursor control that allowed another part of the questionnaire to be skipped to, depending on a particular response;
- Consistency editing;
- Table look-up, including external files;
- Recoding;
- The handling of hierarchical files, such as those made up of housing and population records;
- Record retrieval and modification capability;
- Verification that would ideally allow selected fields to be verified;
- An audit trail for errors and corrections made;
- Performance reporting statistics; and
- Foreign language support or a potential for support.

The evaluation resulted in the identification of two packages with the proper balance of functionality and ease of use. The ENTRYPOINTS package from Datalex, Inc., provides the greatest flexibility in design and is easy to learn and set up. It has reasonable documentation and a user-friendly menu system. Its screen refreshment and logic processing are somewhat slower than desirable, especially on an IBM PC with 256 kilobytes of memory.

The set-up style and sophistication of ENTRYPOINT make it appealing to computer programmers. It costs $845 for the "designer" version, which allows screens and edits to be defined, and $545 for the "operator" version, which simply allows production keying.

The RODE/PC package facilitates high-speed keying. The documentation is adequate, but inferior to that of ENTRYPOINT. Its menu system during the design phase is exceptionally good. The user-friendly menus make this package especially good for non-data processing personnel who are responsible for the set-up of applications. A Spanish version was available in 1986. The initial copy of RODE/PC costs $595; additional copies cost $395.

Although both packages have capabilities necessary for census and survey data entry, they do not perform all of the functions equally well. An evaluation by the ISPC identifies the strengths and weaknesses of each package.

Editing

A need exists for editing beyond that provided at the time of data entry. These edits could include structure edits (i.e., to ensure the completeness of a questionnaire), interrecord and intrarecord consistency checking, and imputation of missing data. The success of the ISPC's generalized CONCOR editing system on mainframe computers and minicomputers recommended its choice as the editing module in the integrated microcomputer processing system.

The following are important features of CONCOR:

- An English-like structured command language;
- A range and consistency editing capability;
- An interrecord editing capability;
- An automatic correction capability;
- Comprehensive edit reports; and
- Complete system documentation.

CONCOR was successfully converted to run on an IBM PC (model XT or AT) and compatibles. The key to its successful operation on the microcomputer was the identification of the REALIA COBOL compiler, a microcomputer compiler with mainframe features and performance.

Tabulation

National statistical offices worldwide have successfully used the ISPC's CENTS 4 tabulation package on mainframe computers and minicomputers. The important features of CENTS 4 include:

- The ability to produce multiple publication-quality tables in one data pass;
- The flexibility of report formats;
- The ability to perform basic statistical calculations;
- The production of tables by geographic hierarchy; and
- Comprehensive system documentation.

The CENTS 4 package will form the basis of the tabulation module of the integrated microcomputer processing system. Such portions of the package as table layout will eventually be redesigned to take advantage of the interactive nature of the microcomputer.

The CENTS 4 package was successfully converted to run on the IBM PC (model XT or AT). Once again, the REALIA COBOL compiler facilitated the conversion of the software and contributed to its efficiency on the microcomputer. Benchmark processing has shown that CENTS 4 on the IBM PC-AT can tabulate data (13 tables) from over 2,000 80-character records in about 1 minute. This level of performance exceeds that of some mainframe computers and most minicomputers.

Statistical Analysis

National statistical offices perform many surveys for which calculations of sampling errors are never made, usually because the resources are not available to write customized variance programs. With this in mind, an important module of the system will facilitate the calculation of sampling error and other statistics associated with complex sample surveys. The availability of this information should make survey results more meaningful.

The ISPC was familiar with the capabilities of SUPER CARP, a mainframe computer package from Iowa State University (ISU), to meet the need for this type of statistics from surveys with complex sample designs. The ISPC worked with ISU staff to develop a project to convert SUPER CARP to run on the IBM PC-XT, and to simultaneously redesign the package to be more interactive. The following algorithms will be available in PC-CARP:

- A total estimator;
- A ratio estimator;
- Two-stage samples;
- Collapse of strata;
- Subpopulation means and totals;
- A test of goodness and fit;
- A test of independence for a two-way table;
- Regression;
- Ordinary design effects for simple estimators; and
- A coefficient of variation for simple estimators.

Demographic Analysis

The Computer Programs for Demographic Analysis (CPDA) will form the core of the demographic analysis module of the integrated microcomputer processing system. These programs were written for mainframe computers by the Bureau of the Census in the early 1970s. They were successfully converted to run on an IBM PC by Westinghouse Public Applied Systems under their USAID Demographic Data for Development Project.

The CPDA is actually a group of subroutines that supports the following functions:

- Curve Fitting, Smoothing, and Graduation
    - Equalize the number of age groups in two distributions.
    - Separate grouped data into five parts.
    - Make a linear or exponential interpolation.
    - Rank a set of values and give the median.
    - Smooth a population in 5-year age groups.
    - Smooth a population distribution of 5-year age groups.
    - Calculate age and sex ratios.
    - Adjust age-sex population distributions.
    - Compare two age-group distributions.
    - Construct a population pyramid.
    - Make a population rejuvenation.
    - Evaluate age group 0 to 4 in a population distribution.
- Fertility
    - Change the level of age-specific fertility rates.
    - Modified Brass fertility estimation technique.

- Calculate age-specific fertility rates.
- Mortality
  - Calculate a life table for both sexes combined.
  - Modified Brass mortality estimation technique.
  - Calculate an abridged life table from Mx or Qx values.
  - Compare two sets of survival rates.
  - Calculate a Coale-Demeny model life table by sex.
  - Calculate a set of survival rates.
  - Select a pattern of mortality from the Coale-Demeny tables.
  - Estimate a set of Qx life table values.
  - Calculate a set of survival rates for open-ended age groups.
  - Calculate survival rates.
  - Life table and crude rates from two population distributions.
- Projections
  - Make a population projection.
- Stable Population
  - Estimate quasi-stable crude vital rates.
  - Calculate an intrinsic growth rate.
  - Calculate a stable population.
  - Calculate stable or quasi-stable parameters.

In addition to these routines from the CPDA, the demographic analysis module can draw on programs from the United Nations' mortality measurement software (MORTPAK) to accomplish the following tasks:

- Generate life tables from empirical data;
- Evaluate empirical data relative to model life tables;
- Generate model life tables that correspond to a mortality level, such as life expectancy at birth;
- Indirectly estimate infant and child mortality given "children ever born, children surviving" data;
- Indirectly estimate adult female mortality given "maternal survivorship" data; and
- Indirectly estimate adult mortality given "spouse survivorship" data.

Operational Control

The CONTROL Census Management System will form a module to answer the needs of operational control. This system is intended to complement the editing and tabulation process. The CONTROL management reporting system is designed to monitor various activities of a census or large survey and to provide timely information on the progress of the census or survey. The information is provided in tabular and graphic form by major phases of the project. It shows where bottlenecks occur and reports on the timeliness of production schedules. The system keeps track of all census geographic areas and shows missing and duplicate areas. The CONTROL system was converted to run on an IBM PC in 1986.

APPLICATION OF THE INTEGRATED MICROCOMPUTER PROCESSING SYSTEM

In any software development effort it is necessary to clearly define the intended user group and the means by which the software will be introduced, taught, and maintained.

Potential Users

The ISPC's integrated microcomputer processing system is intended to be used by the national statistical offices of developing countries. The nature of the software will allow both data processors and statisticians to be potential users. The ISPC is aware that microcomputers are likely to play a significant role in the 1990 round of world population censuses. The software development cycle, with a completion date of 1988, is timed to give most developing countries the opportunity to avail themselves of some or all of the modules in support of these census efforts.

Alternate Utilization Scenarios

A number of factors will influence how a national statistical office makes use of the ISPC's integrated system. The current mix of hardware and software, staff experience, number of questionnaires, and budget are important factors in determining the applicability of the software. However, as microcomputers become more common in the NSOs, the functions made possible by the integrated system will become increasingly appealing.

Some NSOs will use microcomputers only for data entry, which provides for data capture with some concurrent editing. The ISPC has identified the existence of user-friendly software that minimizes the programming needed for intelligent data entry. More importantly, the microcomputers will be available for other tasks when data entry needs have diminished. In this scenario, the NSO may want to consider the use of magnetic tape or microcomputer-mainframe communication to move the data between the microcomputers and the mainframe computer.

The capability of the CONCOR and CENTS 4 packages to run on the IBM PC and compatibles now makes it possible for programs to be developed in an environment in which a programmer can be most productive: with a machine dedicated to his use. The fact that identical commands will be available in the mainframe and microcomputer versions of the software means that CONCOR and CENTS 4 programs that are developed and tested on a microcomputer can simply be passed to the mainframe for production processing. This approach makes sense when large quantities of data are involved and mainframe computer time is available.

Other NSOs might use the microcomputer to actually edit and tabulate the data from censuses and surveys, especially in countries with relatively small populations. National statistical offices with obsolete or nonexistent access to mainframe computer resources will increasingly attempt to use the microcomputer to effect production processing.

The decision to use one or more microcomputers for production processing implies that careful thought should be given to speed and storage. National statistical offices should consider the added performance of the IBM PC-AT and compatibles. Although it is possible to transfer data on diskettes, it is easy to lose control of the data, especially when large volumes of data are involved. High-volume storage media such as the Bernoulli box, which is removable and holds up to 30 megabytes of data, are ideal for maintaining and moving data between microcomputers. Local area networks offer an alternative for data access and transfer by allowing data to reside on central disks and offering easy communication between nodes on the network.

Analysis has often been neglected because of its low priority against other data processing tasks or because analysts were unable to interface with the computer. The availability of user-friendly software on microcomputers may cause an increase in the attention given to analysis. One can envision a scenario in which the majority of processing is done on other computers and summary data is down-loaded to microcomputers to be analyzed.

A microcomputer is ideal for performing operational control. All of the necessary data to monitor the phases of collecting, processing, and analyzing a census or survey can easily be kept on a hard disk. The ease of access makes it convenient to keep the information current and to produce status reports as they are needed.

The previous utilization scenarios are not mutually exclusive. It is possible that the integrated system could serve all of these needs, perhaps at different times. This simply reiterates the idea that the user can select one or more modules that meet the needs of the application at hand.

Potential Problems

Those NSOs that elect to take advantage of ISPC's integrated microcomputer processing system will need to confront the issues of training and support. Thought should be given to these issues before the fact to help ensure the successful application of the software.

The ISPC has envisioned several forms of training to give NSO staff the requisite knowledge to make effective use of the integrated system. Formal workshops of several weeks in duration can give data processors and statisticians a thorough introduction to the various modules. A program of on-the-job training that leads them through an actual application of the software is the ideal training mechanism. The eventual development of programmed instruction through tutorials that are developed for use on the IBM PC and compatibles would make it possible for one to use the system with little or no formal introduction or hand-holding.

The ISPC will support the use of the integrated microcomputer processing system in the same way that it has supported the use of CONCOR and CENTS 4 on various mainframe computers and minicomputers. This support will include making new releases available to users of the software as improvements are made, and responding to inquiries communicated in person or by mail, cable, or telephone.

CONCLUSIONS

The ISPC hopes that the integrated microcomputer processing system will fill a conspicuous microcomputer software void in the national statistical offices of developing countries. These offices will have powerful software modules at their disposal that are appropriate for the most important tasks associated with census and survey processing. The availability of this software will be a significant contribution to the timely and efficient processing of survey and census data.

REFERENCES

Del Pinal, Jorge. 1985. *Manual for the Microcomputer Version of Computer Programs for Demographic Analysis.* Columbia, Maryland: Westinghouse Public Applied Systems.

Diskin, Barbara. 1985. "Microcomputers in Developing Country Statistical Offices: Current Use and a Look to the Future." *Proceedings of the 45th Session of the International Statistical Institute* 51(3):22.1-22.1.14.

___. 1986. "Evaluation of Data Entry Software Packages for Microcomputers." Draft of report being prepared for the Agency for International Development.

Fuller, Wayne; Schnell, Dan; Sullivan, Gary; and Kennedy, William J. 1986. "P.C. CARP: Variance Estimation for Complex Surveys." Paper presented at the 18th Symposium on the Interface.

Kirmeyer, Sharon. 1985. Letter describing capabilities of United Nations' MORTPAK.

10

The Microcomputer in the Brazilian Health Information System

MARCIO HUMBERTO MONTAGNA CAMMAROTA

The use of microcomputers in the Health Information Network will be the foundation of the Brazilian Health Information System that is currently being developed by the Ministry of Health. The microcomputer is not considered an isolated instrument that allows autonomous groups to satisfy their needs in terms of informatics. It is considered an integral and essential part of an information network based on teleprocessing that is required to modernize the health system in Brazil.

The microcomputer therefore will not lose the basic features that have made it an indispensable instrument to administration and management. It will instead reach a new level of productivity through its connection with a mainframe and large data banks, and its importance to the health system in Brazil will increase. Its low cost and independent status allow it to be integrated with larger systems without losing its functions.

CHANGES IN THE HEALTH SECTOR IN BRAZIL

Brazil is a Federal Republic that occupies approximately 8.5 million square kilometers in Latin America with a population currently estimated at 130 million. It is politically divided into

26 federated units or states that are further subdivided into 4,107 municipalities.

Brazil has traditionally been a unitary country motivated by its economical and social development needs. Over the years, the federal government has used all of its power to assign itself the responsibility and the resources to solve nearly all of the country's problems, thereby reducing the authority of the state and municipal powers.

Such excessive centralization, coupled with the increasing distrust of the local authorities, generated a large and complex bureaucratic system that became inefficient and extremely expensive to operate. Issues relating to the welfare of all Brazilians, such as food, health, and education, were directly affected by this transformation. Steps are currently being taken to reverse the situation.

The health system in Brazil is one of the sectors currently undergoing a major transformation as a result of the trend toward decentralization. Because of its dimensions, population characteristics, potential, development status, and organizational level, Brazil cannot continue to coexist with systems that show a low level of efficiency.

Proposals are being consolidated toward that end to accelerate the health system reformulation. In their most developed form, such proposals arrive at what has been called the United Health System. This proposal, currently in its final stage, attempts to offer health services for the population on a satisfactory level of quality and quantity, without discrimination, by requiring a more equitable participation of the power levels.

The proposed reformulation of the health system must be far-reaching. The role of the state in the system and the restructuring of the devices that allow the development of the health sector must be redefined to improve the efficiency of the system. The basic guidelines for the proposed health system are as follows:

- Unification of the political command of the health system into a sole ministry that articulates with the other ministries through academic bodies;
- Intersectorial integration to unify the health activities performed by several sectors;
- Integration of efforts currently separated by preventive/remedial or individual/collective dichotomies;

- Decentralization of the responsibilities for the operation of health activities to the state and municipal levels;
- Decentralization of the planning for these health programs in coordination with the central level;
- Regionalization and hierarchization of the services in a unified and functionally articulated network;
- Popular participation in the formulation and execution of health policies;
- Access of the less-privileged classes to quality health services; and
- Restructuring of the sector's financing devices with a higher inversion of resources in terms of the percentile of gross national product participation.

This information will therefore be the result of political maturation and properly structured policies. Such policies will allow for the advancement of the health system, which must be achieved step by step to modify the cultural factors responsible for the current situation.

THE INFORMATION SYSTEM AS A TOOL FOR CHANGE

The tools and policies required for the operation of the health system must be reevaluated and rewritten so that they can become the catalyst for change. The following issues therefore must be evaluated as they relate to either the public sector or private enterprise:

- The structural capacity of the medical and sanitary welfare services;
- The efficiency of the services rendered;
- The cost of such services;
- The allocation of funds transferred to the states and municipalities;
- The nonregressive financing of the health system;
- Pharmaceutical aid;
- The management models used; and
- The compatibility of staff, working rules, and professional careers.

THE BRAZILIAN SYSTEM OF HEALTH INFORMATION

The concept of the Brazilian System of Health Information is based on the general theory of systems; it tries to establish, in a macro way, the general definition of the system and its subsystems. The following requirements were taken into account to arrive at such a definition:

- Scope;
- Intersectorial integration;
- Interinstitutional and institutional integration;
- Decentralization; and
- Regionalization and hierarchy.

Only two of these aspects are of interest to the scope of this paper.

Decentralization

Because the health sector is an area in which government action occurs at all levels, the Brazilian System of Health Information should be associated with the state and municipal requirements. It is hoped that the decentralization of these actions will be aimed at the federal states. Furthermore, the current concept of the Brazilian System of Health Information should not be the result of efforts centralized in the federal government, because data that would be of interest to the system would most likely originate at the state and municipal levels.

The Brazilian System of Health Information will become a strong instrument in the decentralization process. It is estimated that this system should be defined in concurrence with one of the state systems to make this idea feasible.

Regionalization and Hierarchization

In an effort to decentralize the health activities and responsibilities involved, the Brazilian System of Health Information must look to the interior of the states to reach the health regions (*Regionais de Saude*) and the municipalities themselves, including the small health posts.

The levels of attention in the Unified Health System are adequately correlated with the operational structures. The basic activities must be supplied at the local level, whereas secondary and tertiary activities should be more adequately managed by the regional and state levels. It is then implied that intermediate levels of management must have adequate decision-making information in accordance with their responsibilities.

This hierarchy also distinguishes the various types of health institutions according to their degree of complexity and attention rendered. Once again, the system must provide required information to the management of such units and forward to other levels the information required for the management of the entire system.

The basic precepts behind the system's concept allowed the establishment of one of its elementary premises: "The Brazilian System of Health Information means the aggregate of the state systems of health information, harmonized among themselves and adjusted at the federal level."

An initial study is to be performed from the point of view of the Brazilian System of Health Information's subdivisions that will generally express its integration characteristics. This concept is illustrated in Figure 1; the subsystems can be summarized as follows:

- Food and nutrition;
- Medical and sanitary care;
- Pharmaceutical care;
- Control and eradication of transmittable diseases;
- Sanitary vigilance; and
- Administrative information.

There are subsystems in the proposed study that comprise the Brazilian System of Health Information. Other subsystems will be considered that are included in the scope of this system in a complementary way. Although these subsystems are under the influence of the Ministry of Health, they are also performed by other ministries, some of which bear responsibility for them. This is true of the following information subsystems:

- Planning;
- Science and technology;
- Human resources;
- Sanitation;
- Environmental protection; and
- Workers' health.

CENTRALIZATION VERSUS DECENTRALIZATION OF INFORMATION

Once the principles that characterize the changes in the health system are established, aspects that have characterized the evolution of the informatics technology and their influence on the reformulation of the health system will be studied. One of the basic questions in the restructuring of the Brazilian System of Health Information is where and how the information is to be stored.

In the early 1970s, systems of this kind were based on large computers that centralized all information processing. It was an age of centralization in which all applications of an institution were processed with only one computer and mainly in batches. This method of data processing proved to be precarious, especially as a result of the inability of the technicians to obtain answers that met the users' requirements. The mainframes were difficult to reprogram and were therefore unable to keep up with the technological advances.

After the arrival of the microcomputer, the situation was reversed; the user became aware of the possibility of solving problems himself, thus becoming independent from the mainframe. This step has revolutionized data processing and has popularized the use of informatics.

Simplified languages and programs that did not require in-depth technical knowledge of informatics to use microcomputers followed. This was viewed as a "boom" for the microcomputer. It was an age of great decentralization that dominates most of data processing to this day.

The microcomputer spawned great independence from the mainframe, but one quality of this independence was an isolation characteristic that restricted its use to specific problems. Another factor in the evaluation of the use of microcomputers in this kind of system is capacity. Even with the use of memory expansions through the use of "Winchester" disks, many systems are reaching a point of saturation.

Computer manufacturers who paid attention to the evolution of the market tried to solve this problem by developing programs that provide the user with the same advantages as a microcomputer integrated to a mainframe. This concept favors the idea of work through a teleprocessing network, and it represents the future for all users of microcomputers that work increasingly complex systems.

This revolution has had many positive developments in terms of software. The emergence of fourth-generation languages and user-friendly software that try to reapproximate the user to the mainframe, illustrates the reaction of the suppliers of these systems to the many uses of the microcomputer.

All these factors were evaluated, and the microcomputer was considered an indispensable element to the future of the Brazilian System of Health Information.

THE MICROCOMPUTER-MAINFRAME CONNECTION

The arrival on the market of data-processing equipment for the personal computer (PC) opened a new horizon for the evolution of microinformatics, because it enabled a highly professional relationship to exist between this kind of equipment and the host installation.

This connection allows for the acquisition of a series of functions essential in all fields of microcomputer applications, including business, research, production, and commercial development. The use of microcomputers in the Health Information Network must serve the following functions:

- Allow local processing;
- Allow access to data banks;
- Share centralized systems;
- Communicate with other users; and
- Allow the microcomputer to be used as a terminal in multifunctional environments.

Aspects that relate to a cost-benefit analysis of microcomputers must be examined. The question of specificity of the application in use and the evaluation of the efficiency of this interconnection must also be examined.

Three levels of probable communication exist between the microcomputer and the mainframe, all of which are obtained from the emulation of the microcomputer:

- The microcomputer emulated as a terminal;
- The emulation of a terminal with a link; and

- Cooperative processing.

Emulation is the process by which special hardware boards, and in some instances, specialized software, are introduced into the microcomputer to link the functions of this equipment with the mainframe.

The Brazilian market has several boards that enable the previously mentioned types of interconnections and that can be used in either domestic or imported equipment. It is therefore possible to interconnect locally manufactured microcomputers with imported mainframes, such as the IBM. These plates are available for both local and remote connections.

The Microcomputer Emulated as a Terminal

The microcomputer emulated as a terminal is the most simplified type of interconnection of the microcomputer with the mainframe. In this case, the microcomputer acts as a terminal for the mainframe in the functions on which the connection is active. The application program sends information to the PC to keep it under screen control. It then starts to act as a single terminal that is unable to use the typical functions of the PC on the data received. The PC can be used as a stand-alone only when the connection is inactive.

The basic feature of this type of connection is that while it is active it ignores the software available in the microcomputer, thereby keeping it a slave of the mainframe's software. The following advantages can be derived from this type of connection:

- *Simplicity*. The microcomputer is utilized as a terminal. It starts to answer directly to the mainframe with an increase of resources and without difficulty.
- *Communication capacity*. The microcomputer is able to communicate rapidly with the mainframe applications.
- *Multiple facets*. The PC can be supported by several networks.

The following are the disadvantages of this type of connection:

- The host files are not available for use by the microcomputer after it is disconnected.
- It is not possible to use the microcomputer's resources simultaneously with those of the mainframe.

A scheme of this type of interconnection is shown in Figure 2.

Emulation of a Terminal with a Link

The emulation of the microcomputer as a terminal with a link has the characteristic of enabling the central files to be transferred and processed by it, even after disconnection. The data received from the central files is kept on the disk (diskettes or Winchester) for local processing, even in batch. After being processed, they can be transferred to the mainframe, also by batch. The microcomputer is able to store the data for its own processing and does not need to stay on-line all of the time. This kind of application is recommended for users who do not need to constantly send or receive data from the host.

The following are the advantages of this kind of connection:

- It does not need to remain on-line with the mainframe during the entire operation.
- It has the capacity to access centralized files.
- It has the capacity to communicate with other users.

The following are its disadvantages:

- The microcomputer loses its computer capacity while it is on-line.
- It needs to convert its data structure (ASCII to EBCDIC).
- In some cases, it is necessary to develop an adequate program to serve as an interface.

This kind of connection is shown in Figure 3.

Cooperative Processing

Cooperative processing is the most complete interconnection between the microcomputer and the mainframe. Everything occurs to the user as if the connection were transparent in that the microcomputer presents all resources available in the mainframe by simulating it as if it were an extension. It also allows the host to store files or applications currently in use on the PC in addition to its own files, thereby increasing the safety of the data.

The following are the advantages of this kind of connection:

- The capacity of microcomputer is limited.
- Access to the mainframe is transparent.

- It has the capacity to exchange information with other users.
- It is capable of accessing and handling centralized files.

The following are its disadvantages:

- The cost of this kind of interconnection is high.
- It is a complex and specialized interconnection.

This kind of connection is shown in Figure 4.

THE HEALTH INFORMATION NETWORK

The Ministry of Health must be physically connected to the states of the Federal Republic of Brazil for the Brazilian System of Health Information to be operational. At the current stage of development, the flow of information between the state and federal levels is done by means of forms that are difficult to enter into a computer. However, some states already have data processing equipment and teleprocessing networks that interconnect the State Secretariats of Health with the *Regionais de Saude* (health regions that have several municipalities).

The Health Information Network is being established to promote the connection of the Ministry of Health with the State Secretariats of Health. As the states develop their teleprocessing networks and become interconnected to the Ministry of Health, a national network will be formed. The objective of this network is to reach, in the near future, municipalities and larger health bodies, such as hospitals and health units.

The Health Information Network will be composed of the following three levels:

1. An interconnection between the Ministry of Health and the state Secretariats of Health;
2. An interconnection between the State Secretariats of Health and their *Regionais de Saude*; and
3. An interconnection between the *Regionais de Saude* and the municipalities and health units.

Taking into account the network hierarchy and the great number of existing bodies at the second and third levels, the redefinition of the use of microcomputers in the Health Information Network is important.

In addition to the basic features of the network, the intermediate levels need to have their own data processing capabilities. The Health Information Network is therefore composed of a mainframe with a network of terminals. The success of the Health Information Network requires that a comprehensive study be undertaken of the remote interconnection between the mainframe and the microcomputer. It is feasible to use other equipment such as minicomputers or superminicomputers at the intermediate levels. The possibilities for using multiprocessing systems between the host equipment and other network equipment will also be studied.

The physical interconnection of the various types of equipment will be made through "RENPAC," the Brazilian Network of Package Switching that allows a telephone interconnection to be made between this equipment through special data communication protocols.

THE USE OF MICROCOMPUTERS IN THE HEALTH INFORMATION NETWORK

After considering the several types of interconnections possible between the mainframe and the microcomputer in the Health Information Network, emulation as a terminal was selected as the level of interconnection. Emulation as a terminal will be employed in microcomputers at points where there is a high level of data entry and a low index of inquiry and where there is a need for local data processing. The microcomputer will be useful for the procurement of answers to inquiries and for the processing of local information independent of on-line connections.

Emulation with link will be used to obtain, through the microcomputer, information contained in the central data bases that will be useful for local processing. This type of utilization is typical of decentralized planning units and corresponds to the needs of the State Secretariats of Health and of the State *Regionais de Saude*.

Cooperative processing will be used at those Information Centers of the Health Information Network that have more complex responsibilities and that therefore require more computer resources. Specialized units dedicated to the resolution of specific and complex problems will have cooperative processing available to allow the microcomputer to have access to all of the mainframe's available resources.

Strategy for Implementation

It is foreseen that the Health Information Network will be primarily implemented with local connections in the Ministry of Health followed by the interconnection of several states. The use of fourth-generation languages that simplify the communication among the available data bases will also be considered. Several fourth-generation languages were studied and IBM's AS-Application System language was chosen for use in the mainframe.

This language gives the system the advantage of allowing the integrated processing of several functions, such as the management of data banks, project control, financial monitoring, statistics, graphics, and text editing.

The Application System language will be used in the Health Information Network through the emulation of microcomputers as terminals. It will primarily be used to update the centralized data bases and to handle inquiries when the emulation is with the link. This will allow the local processing of the information obtained by access to the file obtained in the mainframe.

From the point of view of physical implementation, the states included in the Northeast Project will initially be interconnected. The initial phase of the project is financed by the World Bank and seeks to support the development of health activities in four states of the northeast region of Brazil, namely Rio Grande do Norte, Piaui, Bahia, and part of Minas Gerais. The project's budget allocates funds for the acquisition of equipment for data processing, especially microcomputers. The projected interconnections necessary for the Health Information Network to meet the Northeast Project are shown in Figure 5. It is intended that the equipment obtained through this project be compatible with and connected to the specifications of the Health Information Network.

CONCLUSION

One of the main conclusions is the influence of the technology evolution in reaching viable political solutions. The proposed reformulation of the health system is being facilitated by the fact that the development of informatics favors the intended solutions. Therefore, the universalization of aid to the health sector, the decentralization of that sector, and the regionalization and hierarchy of the services, which are the object of the change, are facilitated when the dominant technology is able to support these objectives.

In the case under study, the use of microcomputers emulated to the Health Information Network greatly facilitates the solution of the topological problems posed by such objectives. The Health Information Network has the integration and decentralization features required for the informational aspects of the intended reform. It is hoped that this kind of solution will help other developing countries with similar problems.

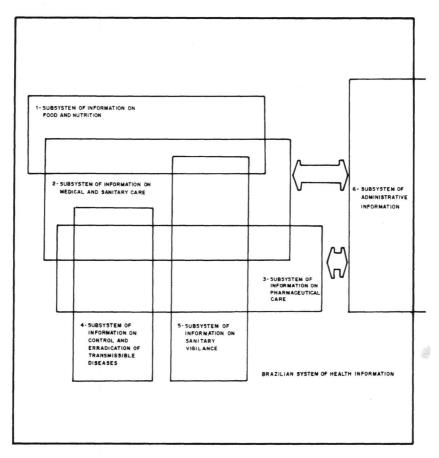

FIGURE 1 Brazilian health information system.

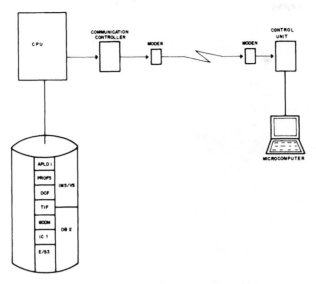

FIGURE 2 Emulation of a terminal by a computer.

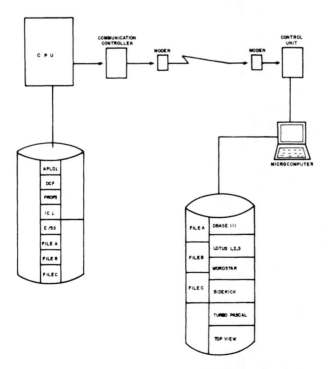

FIGURE 3 Emulation of a terminal with a link by a microcomputer.

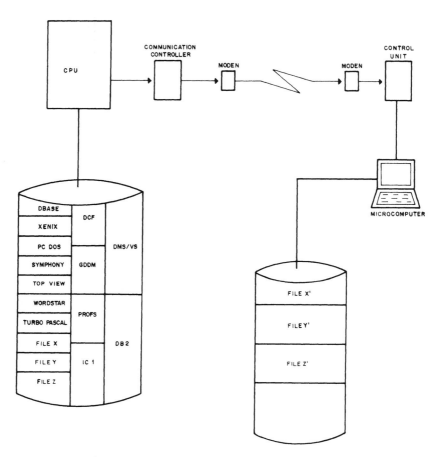

FIGURE 4 Cooperative processing.

FIGURE 5 Health information network in Northeast Brazil.

11

Population Program Applications of Expert Systems

JOHN DALY

One of the hottest areas of computer science is expert systems. An expert system is a computer system that can substitute in performance for a human expert. Many researchers have been trying, for example, to develop computers that can simulate the accuracy of physicians in aspects of medical diagnosis and prescription (Barr and Feigenbaum, 1982). In the context of population programs, this technology could be very useful in Latin America in the future.

One may ask if computers can learn to emulate the performance of physicians and professional health service administrators in selected tasks of population programs. In terms of actual Latin American programs that serve the majority of the people, can expert systems improve the performance of paraprofessionals?

Inherent in this concern is a belief that microcomputers powerful enough to implement such systems will soon be available at a cost low enough to allow them to be widely used in developing countries. The fact that the cost of hardware has dropped by one-half every 2 or 3 years for decades lends credence to this belief. Moreover, the intense effort to develop fifth generation technology suggests that technological progress will be especially fast in the areas of computer artificial intelligence (Feigenbaum and McCormack, 1983). Finally, it appears likely that medical expert systems may soon be available in packages small enough to be hand carried by health workers in the field.

Computers tend to be thought of as number crunchers or word processors, but they are also logical engines. With appropriate programming, computers can logically deduce conclusions from specified premises and rules of inference. In other words, given a set of if-then relationships, an appropriate computer system can deduce the conclusions that follow from a given set of postulates. An expert system is fundamentally a system that has been provided with a set of if-then relationships that emulate those used by human experts.

EXPERT SYSTEMS IN CLINICAL PRACTICE

The Office of the Science Advisor of the United States Agency for International Development (USAID) has funded Dr. Chandler Dawson of the University of California and his colleagues at IBM and Rutgers University to develop an expert system for ophthalmological diagnosis (Kastner et al., 1984). The idea is to develop a system that can be implemented on a hand-held computer. This system can be used by paramedicals at the primary health-care level to decide if a patient needs eye treatment and, if so, whether the patient can be treated locally or should be referred to a health center.

A physician would normally approach such a problem in two steps. He would use information on the signs and symptoms of the patient and on the pattern of disease in the locality to make a diagnosis. Then, based on the diagnosis, the signs and symptoms of the patient, and the applicable norm for medical practice, he would prescribe a regimen of care. In performing this task, the physician intuitively may be using inferential rules, such as "if a chemical has splashed in the eye of the patient, and if the patient's cornea is cloudy or hazy, then the patient may have a chemical burn to the cornea." The follow-up rules might be, "for a potential chemical burn to the cornea, the eye should be irrigated, an antibiotic ointment should be applied, and the patient should make a follow-up visit." A general-practice physician may have thousands of such inferential rules to cover the variety of conditions and patients he sees.

In the case of the primary health-care worker, the situation can be dramatically simplified. The system deals only with a specific class of medical problem. A detailed and definitive diagnosis need not be made to decide whether to treat the patient in the village or to refer him to a more skilled practitioner. The computer programs to be tested in Tunisia and Egypt by Dr. Dawson and his colleagues will therefore be relatively simple.

A total of 49 observations of patient-specific findings can correctly be entered into the computer by the user. In practice, according to the initial responses, the user is only asked to enter about a dozen observations. The computer uses 77 rules to deduce which of 26 treatments or actions are to be recommended. In fact, the programs to be field-tested are written in BASIC to allow them to be easily transported from microcomputer to microcomputer.

The programs currently require less than 32,000 characters of memory that are primarily devoted to text to explain questions and recommendations to paraprofessional healthworkers.

The logic was developed on a specialized computer system, "Expert" (Barr and Feigenbaum, 1982), that was developed by Sholom Weiss and Casimir Kulikowski and that runs on the relatively large VAX 785 and DEC-20 computer system of Rutgers. The Expert system facilitates the introduction of rules by the human medical expert and the tracing of the logical process followed by the computer to categorize a sample of real patients. In this case, Dr. Dawson and his colleagues entered data of hundreds of real patients with acute ophthalmological disease to ensure that the recommendations made by the computer system are correct and to simplify the inferential rules of the system.

It appears likely that if Dr. Dawson is able to develop a clinical algorithm for primary ophthalmological care, one could also develop a hand-held expert system for primary family planning services. Such a system might, for example, incorporate a body of inferential rules on the contra-indications of various contraceptive devices and help front-line workers advise couples more expertly on which type of contraception is appropriate to their needs and preferences.

EXPERT SYSTEMS AS KNOWLEDGE, ATTITUDE, AND PRACTICE SURVEY INSTRUMENTS

Another appealing application is to use the expert system as a survey device. In family planning knowledge, attitude, and practice surveys, for example, there is normally a limit to the quality of information one can obtain due to the practical limits of the complexity of a survey instrument. The substitution of a questionnaire with an expert system that embodies the rules of inference an anthropologist might use to predict whether or not a respondent would use family planning services could be considered.

Some expert systems have a very sophisticated logic. They can identify and seek the information they need to reach a conclusion. If the original premises in these systems are inadequate, in terms of the given rules of inference, to allow a deduction to be drawn, the systems use artificial intelligence. For example, some systems can review the available rules and identify a small number of rules which, if invoked, would complement the available information and allow the deduction to be completed. The expert system can then ask the interviewer if the premises for those rules are met! The artificial intelligence in this case is obvious and advantageous.

A computer system could, in the case of contraceptive practice, review the information it currently has on a respondent and select a question that would be most likely to allow a conclusion to be drawn as to whether or not that respondent would use a specific contraceptive technology. In theory, not only would such a survey instrument give far more accurate information on the demand for contraception, it might also give more accurate information on the key factors that limit the demand. After the first few questions, the expert system could develop a unique interview for each respondent, ask only those questions relevant to that respondent, and provide information on the respondent instead of data on the interview responses.

OTHER POTENTIAL APPLICATIONS TO POPULATION PROGRAMS

It has been estimated that 1,000 or more expert systems are currently in operation or under development. Although none are known to be specifically designed for population programs, it appears likely that they will have important applications in the future. Expert system technology should allow personnel with relatively little training to function in specific, limited domains with a fair degree of sophistication.

Expert systems should help Latin American population organizations deal better with rapidly changing technical needs in the 1990s. For example, the Digital Equipment Corporation, which manufactures small computers, had difficulties in that its sales force frequently made errors in specifying custom systems of the computers and peripherals that they manufactured. Sales engineers not only had to master many intricate rules as to which devices and connectors could be paired, but these rules changed quickly as new equipment was introduced and outmoded equipment was discontinued. The company therefore developed an expert system that helps the engineer correctly specify custom systems (Feigenbaum and McCormack, 1983). As new products are marketed, old products are dropped, and system configurations are modified, sales offices can be updated by simply sending an updated version of the design rules. In a like manner, properly designed and tested expert systems could eventually help technicians in population programs in a number of tasks, ranging from vehicle maintenance, to the repair of medical equipment, to the planning of initial inventories of new family planning clinics.

Administrative applications may be in many ways easier to promote than clinical applications because the element of ethical concern for the safety and convenience of the patient is absent. An expert system could help an administrator of family planning services in a health-care center to perform his or her duties more efficiently. One could therefore focus on the expertise involved in inventory control or in the marketing of family planning services.

Scores of applications for expert systems can be envisioned. Educational software that incorporates expert system technology could be developed to quickly diagnose false hypotheses and allow remedial information to be supplied. Expert systems for project planners could be developed to incorporate knowledge gained about factors that determine the success or failure of population projects. Finally, systems that facilitate the use of demographic projections could be developed for use by planners to help them infer from data and estimates the appropriate parameters for models and projections.

The reader should be cautious, however. Real limitations exist on the use of such systems. A major part of the art of the successful expert system engineer is the selection of appropriate problems. An expert system should be used in a well-delineated area of human endeavor, one that has established norms and standards that can be embodied in the system. In the case of Dr. Dawson's ophthalmological system, the World Health Organization and other medical organizations had carefully defined diagnostic and primary care treatment standards. Moreover, the number of rules and the complexity of the task should not be too great.

A key problem is how to test the systems. Expert systems are proposed for tasks that are so ambiguous that they cannot be embodied in quantitative algorithms. If a sufficiently complex and ambiguous area of application is important enough to justify the cost of developing an expert system, how does one convince oneself that the system is sufficiently expert? In the case of Dr. Dawson, the diagnosis and prescriptions made by the system have been checked against those of practicing physicians in hundreds of real cases from several different areas of the world, and the validation is continuing. Nevertheless, the nightmare of any clinical system designer is the inclusion of an error in the system that is not manifest in the trial population but results in damage to patients when introduced into practice.

The limitations of expert systems are sufficiently severe and the difficulty of developing them sufficiently grave that many more eager announcements of their potential are made than practical field applications of the technology. Furthermore, one may question when the economics of such systems will justify their applications in developing countries. Economic justification will surely lag behind technical feasibility. Nevertheless, the advantages of automating the reasoning process to allow paraprofessionals to work at a more expert level and the rapidly decreasing cost and increasing availability of computers in Latin America suggest that this is a fruitful area for research.

Latin American computer and health professionals should collaborate in the research necessary to develop and test such systems for population programs. If this is not done, Latin America will be faced with the choice of going without such systems or using systems designed and oriented toward different patients, health systems, and cultures.

REFERENCES

"Applications-Oriented AI Research: Medicine," in Barr, Avron and E. A. Feigenbaum, *The Handbook of Artificial Intelligence;* Vol. 2. William Kaufman, Inc., Los Altos, California, 1982.

Feigenbaum, E. A. and P. McCormack, *The Fifth Generation: Artificial Intelligence and Japan's Computer Challenge to the World,* Addison-Wesley Publishing Co., Reading, Mass., 1983.

Kastner, J. K., C. R. Dawson, S. M. Weiss, K. B. Kern, and C. A. Kulikowski; "An Expert Consultation System for Frontline Health Workers in Primary Eye Care," Journal of Medical Systems, Vol. 8, No. 5, 1984, pp. 389-97.

12

A Growing-with-the-User Expert System for Clinical Use

José Negrete

The following is a description of a viable strategy to promote the emergence of useful expert systems in developing countries. The strategy is based on the microsociological assumptions that people (1) want to use tools that they understand in their own terms, (2) prefer to use tools developed under their own authorship, (3) prefer to use tools they have become accustomed to, (4) do not want to use tools that threaten their expertise or status, (5) want immediate results with little investment, (6) want tools that solve problems even in extremely poor conditions or uncertainty, and (7) prefer to view the use of computers in their professional environment as tools instead of thinking companions.

It is postulated that a "growing-with-the-user" strategy of a participative nature will focus attention on the previously mentioned assumptions. The problem still remains, however, of how to implement this strategy without defeating these assumptions.

GETTING ACQUAINTED WITH A COMPUTER AS A PROBLEM-SOLVER

The strategy should begin with the use of a problem-solving graciously degenerable algorithm (GDA), such as a program that can give advice on solving a trouble-shooting problem even with scarce information (see Figure 1).

The expert on the right in Figure 1 will be able to test and reform by using actual problem algorithms in a production environment (i.e., industry, hospital, school, or bank). If the expert is successful, he or she can also become a user or convince others to use it because of his or her new-found expertise and status. New users should also be able to test and reform the algorithm.

Understanding the Expert Task

In the second step, a trouble-shooting simulating system (TSSS) should be built to make clear to future users the nature of the problems faced when building an expert system. The TSSS must provide data that, organized and transformed by the expert on the left in Figure 1, can provide the expected inputs of the GDA to test the TSSS. The TSSS should be able to be modified by the GDA's recommendation or by the expert's implementation.

A Trial Expert System Prototype

In this stage, one is tempted to recommend the use of an expert system as a quick substitution for the "inferior" mental mechanics of the expert and concentrate on the typical problems of knowledge engineering: the production rules.

However, this imposes a straitjacket on the nature and abilities of the expert systems versus the possibility of the construction of a more flexible prototype tailored to the productive environment with the participation of experts and users.

The Growing-with-the-User Expert System

The prototype, together with the type of knowledge the expert system will use, must revolve around the participation of the users. The evaluation of the expert system's progress can be tested by the TSSS and by using actual problems (see Figure 2). The TSSS can be used not only to test the expert system but also as an important part of the expert system that solves problems through searches.

The expert system project shown in Figure 3 is to be implemented in the participative, productive environment of a hospital in Mexico. The algorithm proposed as a starting point is a cardiovascular, biophysical, and qualitative model that will call on an expert system to "satisfy" its inputs (the prototype or the expert system is reread when finished). The GDA will search for an etiology system that will produce an algorithmic search. Whether the search for an etiology algorithm was successful or not, the GDA will produce a diagnosis through a diagnostic function that uses the qualitative information parameters and the etiological facts gathered. The more developed part of this specific project is the TSSS Vascular Patient Simulator, which makes use of a small inner expert system.

Cryptic-database (CRY-DB) generating systems are defined here as:

- A system that generates a data base with conditioned accessibility from a source data base.
- The data alone condition accessibility. The cryptic properties of these data are as follows:
  - Some data are "spontaneously" produced.
  - Some data are directly available by queries.
  - Some data are only available in encoded form.
  - Some data are not available.

As was shown elsewhere, the CRY-DB system is a particular kind of cryptic-data generating system.

Theoretically, a medical text should be able to generate a dynamic clinical case. An attempt is made in this discussion to use a clinical text as a source. Clinical texts provide two kinds of data for this purpose: empirical knowledge and basic science knowledge. Empirical knowledge is in the form of symptoms-disease correlations, symptoms-parameter correlations, and systems-variable correlations. Basic science knowledge is in the form of causal assertions and biophysical models.

Both kinds of information found in clinical textbooks were used. However, the system had to be provided with information that could not be found in clinical texts: the cryptic properties of the data.

THE TRANSLATION OF A CLINICAL TEXT INTO A SOURCE DATA BASE

The structure selected for the source data base in CRY-DB

was a tree-like structure known in artificial intelligence (AI) as a frame. The first level in the structure (slots) consists of the terms Diagnosis, Sex, Age, Motive-of-the-visit, Inspection, Antecedents, Signs, and Laboratory data. The second level consists of either the word's value or value # (# is a number) or generic words like thyroid-gland-palpation, pulse, "radio-immuno-assay."

The third level carries the menu of items, at least one of which can be associated with every second level item in the cryptic frame. These values can be simple text, expressions with systemic functions, or newly defined functions.

The following is an example of the source data base:

Frame H-H
Diagnosis:
    Value; (ENCODE Hyperthyroidism)
Sex:
    Value; (SEX (female 7, male 1))
Age
    Value; (AGE (30, 80))
Motive-of-visit:
Value 1 Excessive sweating; Hyperdefecation; Difficulty-when-climbing stairs; Heat-intolerance; Goiter.
Value 2
If sex=female AND 42 GREATER age THEN (CHOOSERND (amenorrhea, oligomenorrhea, normal-menstruation)
Value 3
    Tremor-of-fingers; Nervousness
Inspection:
Value 1
    Fine-Hair; Widened-palpebral fissures;
    Exophthalmic
Value 2
    Thyroid-enlargement
Antecedents:
    Value
        Hyperkinesis; Weight-loss;
        Mother-with-same-disease
Signs:
    Thyroid-gland-palpation
    Diffuse-hypertrophy; Symmetric-hypertrophy

Skin
   Peau-d'orange
Radial-Pulse
   '(PULSE increased)
Laboratory-data
   Nuclear-Medicine-Tests
      '(T3 increased)
TRH
   IF 9 GREATER T3 THEN '(TRH +)
Model:
   Value
   IF sex=female AND IF 40 GREATER age THEN begin LOAD cardio-vascular-model AND rules cardio-vasc.; LET right-cardiac-contractility = (RND (1.5, 2.5)) TIMES right-cardiac-contractility; LET arterial-system-compliance TIMES (RND (0.5, 0.8)); LET chronicity=(RND (9, 0.5 TIMES Age)); end.

Frame H-H has nine slots. The first eight slots correspond to the clinical text's empirical knowledge. The last slot is concerned with basic science knowledge representation: the last slot is actually the conditional LOADing of the equations of a cardiovascular model and a set of rules that is designed to give clinical sense to the variables of the model. The last slot is also the setting of the abnormal parameters for the model.

Frame H-H is a three-level structure (LISP). The third level of the structure handles system functions (in caps) and ex-professo-defined functions followed by their arguments (both within parentheses). Note that some functions are preceded by a single quote mark.

THE FIRST STEP IN THE GENERATION OF THE CRYPTIC DATA BASE

A frame source was transformed into a second-level cryptic frame CASE by the procedure (function) CRY-DB GENERATOR (Figure 4). This function randomly chooses at least one of the third-level items for every second-level item to generate the corresponding structure of the new frame. When the item is a non-quoted function, the function is evaluated and its value is placed into the new frame. Quoted functions are transferred verbatim to the frame CASE. One of the many possible initial cryptic frames CASE is as follows:

Frame CASE
  Diagnosis:
    Value 2367
  Sex:
    Value female
  Age:
    Value 41
  Motive-of-the-visit:
    Value difficulty-when-climbing-stairs; Value amenorrhea
  Inspection:
    Value Exophthalmic; Value Fine-hair
  Antecedents:
    Value weight-loss; Value mother-with-same-disease
  Signs:
    Thyroid-gland-palpation symmetric-hypertrophy;
      Skin peau-d'orange; Radial-pulse (PULSE increased)
      Laboratory-data: (T3 increased) Model: Value NIL

Second-level items in CASE are chosen directly from the third-level texts or from function values in H-H, and always in the "at-least-one" fashion. In the example the patient has amenorrhea because (1) the function SEX with argument (female 7 male 1) produced a "female" value and (2) the function AGE with arguments (30 to 80) produced 41 years old, and (3) the function SPECIFY at slot Motive-of-the-visit chose to evaluate the function: IF sex=female, THEN CHOOSERND with arguments (amenorrhea, etc.). The final value was amenorrhea.

Also note that the selection of the quoted function (T3 increased) caused its verbatim incorporation into the laboratory data.

Finally, note that the third-level name in the source frame is transferred to the second level of the cryptic frame, as a second item at every second-level value.

The cryptic nature of frame CASE is granted by:

- Procedure SPECIFY, because it automatically prints out the case slots sex, age, motive-of-the-visit, and inspection, but not the others.
- Diagnosis, model explications, and name of modified parameters are not available in CASE.

- Quoted functions will produce their values (encoded) but not their arguments when consulted throughout procedure INQUIRY.

THE SECOND STEP (DYNAMIC) IN THE GENERATION OF THE CRYPTIC DATA BASE

The MODEL EVAL procedure calculates the value of the variables of the equations. In the example, the steady-state values of the nine variables of a cardiovascular model proposed by Randall as a training tool. A procedure DEDUCE, together with the set of rules-cardio-vasc., constructs a new cryptic frame CASE #.

An example of a CASE-T1 frame is as follows:

Frame CASE-T1
Antecedents:
Value *nocturnal-paroxistic-coughing; value Orthopnea
Signs:
Chest-auscultation: discrete-basal-pulmonary-rates;

value Diastolic-arterial-pressure: 60; value Sistolic-arterial-pressure: 150; Ankle-pressing: Edema-pedal; XR: (Chest-XR heart-failure).

The expert system function CONCLUDE, called by DEDUCE, incorporates these conclusion "antecedents: *nocturnal-paroxistic-coughing" when rule 27 premise "VP2 GREATER 7.5 AND 8 GREATER VP2 was found TRUE. (VP2 is the variable systemic-venous-pressure calculated by the procedure MODEL.)

The cryptic nature of this CASE-T1 frame is granted because:

A CONCLUDE prints-out the message nocturnal-paroxistic-coughing because this conclusion is preceded by an asterisk. Neither "chest-auscultation:" nor "Diastolic-arterial-pressure:" nor "Systolic-arterial-pressure:" are printed out, although they were produced by similar rules.

B Some rules "produce" changes in parameters, thereby simulating a pathology in process (the dynamics). The parameter change is not an available datum. The following is the rule that was used by the system for this encoding: Rule 29: IF (systolic-arterial-pressure MINUS diastolic-arterial-pressure) GREATER 70 AND chronicity GREATER 20 THEN LET cardiac-contractility = cardiac-contractility TIMES 1.10.

C   Rules can also produce quoted functions. None exist in the example.

If requested, the system can recycle through MODEL EVAL to a new calculation. The result will be the production of a new frame CASE-T2.

In the example, CASE-T2 is identical to CASE-T1 except for the increased arterial differential pressure. However, the combined change of parameters produced by Rule 29 generates the new frame CASE-T4 in visit 4, which is a frame different from the previous ones:

Frame CASE-T4
Antecedents: Severe-exertional-dyspnea
Signs: (Chest-XR advanced-failure)

The new data in CASE-T4 was indirectly triggered by the production of a rule:
IF 500 GREATER right-cardiac-contractility AND arterial-pressure-systemic GREATER 100 THEN LET left-cardiac-contractility = 500.

The situation mimics the often-found right heart failure following left heart failure. The resulting frame is a result of the calculation of the MODEL EVAL. Note the disappearance of pulmonary congestion, the remaining severe dyspnea, and the presence of a new function of a roentgenographic finding.

THE LINGUISTIC SUBSYSTEM WITHIN THE EXPERT SYSTEM

Every time the MODEL-DEDUCE cycle ends, the system waits for the procedure INQUIRE to be used. The information available at the third level is obtained through this procedure by specifying the first level and the preceding text (generic) of the third level.

The system should have a natural-language interface to perform optimally, but this has not yet been provided. A multiple-choice menu was formulated instead. It contains the generic preceding text of the third level of the last CASE frame together with "garbage text" taken from source frames that are not pertinent to the current simulated patient.

In an inquiring session with the same example, the question on "lab T3" would produce a laboratory report, which is the value of the function T3 increased. This mechanism preserves the cryptic nature of the frame; the recovery of the original data therefore is a matter of interpretation. Other functions like CHEST-XR hypertensive-heart (Figure 5) or EKG hypertensive-heart (Figure 6) provide graphic information that must be interpreted by the user.

An associated compartmental pharmacodynamic model (DYNAMICS PARAM. MODF in Figure 4) can be triggered together with a menu of drugs to be used to modify the parameters of the model, thus simulating therapeutical or iatrogenic effects.

A minor tutorial discussion is available (TUTORIAL in Figure 4) because the system can check if the student can answer correctly on the antecedents of those rules used by the inner expert system at any moment of the consultation. The linguistic interface can print the data that were spontaneously produced by the system in addition to discovered-by-the-user "treatments given" at any moment of the consultation.

REFERENCES

Negrete-Martinez, J., Gutierrez-Lopez, A., and Ariza-Gomez, E., Patient Simulation Through Dynamic Cryptic Data Base Generating System (CRY-DB) Medinfo86, 903-905 (1986).

Ingbar, H.I. and Woeber, K.A., Diseases of the thyroid in Harrison's Principles of International Medicine. McGraw Hill, N.Y. (1980).

Charniak, E., Artificial Intelligence (1978) 225.

Randall, J.F., Microcomputers and physiological simulation, Addison-Wesley, Reading (1980).

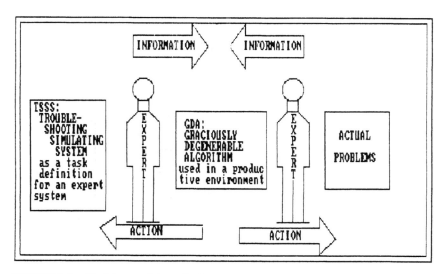

FIGURE 1 Problem-solving strategy.

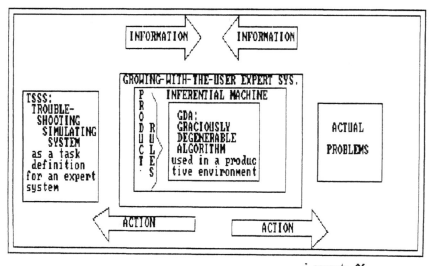

FIGURE 2 Evaluation of expert system.

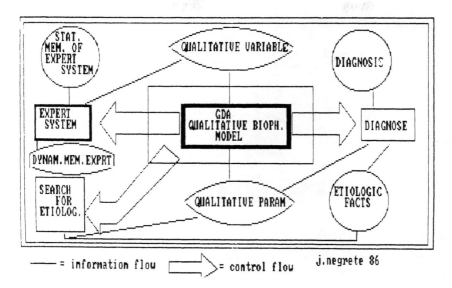

FIGURE 3 Expert system project.

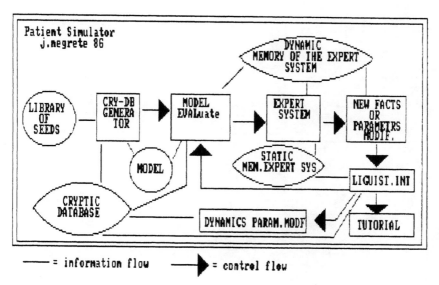

FIGURE 4 Patient simulator.

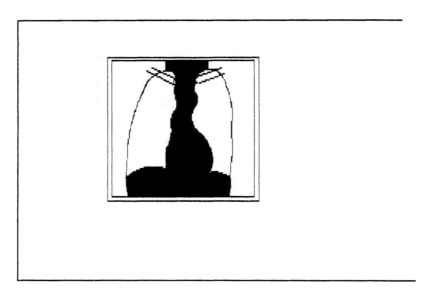

FIGURE 5 Graphic information on heart X-ray.

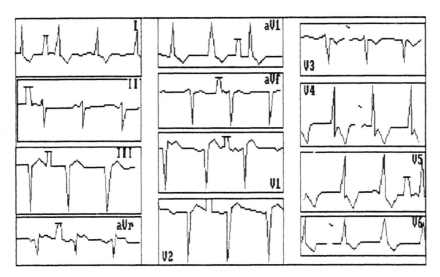

FIGURE 6 Graphic information on heart EKG.

13

Disease Control in the Community: Toward Microcomputer-Supported Decision Models for Health Centers

TEODORO BRIZ

THE OBJECTIVES OF COMMUNITY HEALTH CENTERS

Recent advances in the knowledge of the natural history of disease, clinical sciences, epidemiology, social and behavioral sciences, administration sciences, and information technologies have completely changed the future of health care services, which act as a front line for contact with communities.

In fact, it is generally accepted that following the traditional approach of fighting disease by responding systematically and only with clinical care to repeated individual demands leaves unattended those health care needs that were not expressed by individuals. Furthermore, resource consumption is mainly guided by a subjective perception of needs, which is an uncomprehensive and biased individual approach that results in a waste of resources. Meanwhile, the disease in the community remains an unknown entity that creates more and more patients. Little or no resources remain that can be invested either in the promotion of the health status of the community or in service innovation (Barker and Rose, 1979; Grundy and Reinke, 1973).

The traditional restricted view, therefore, tends to be replaced with a multifocal view of community health center objectives worldwide. Although they are primarily concerned with the control of individual health problems, health centers also must deal with the control of the disease itself and the promotion of community health. These objectives require careful management of the available resources to optimize them in terms of an objective community-based determination of needs. Because the health center information system must provide support for decision-making at all these levels, it necessarily reflects such differences of focus (Thompson and Handelman, 1978).

Although the evidence that health needs expand much more quickly and easily than resources is a universal truth, its implications are more dramatic in developing countries. This reinforces the belief that a global multifocal approach in these countries is urgent.

OPTIMAL RESOURCE ALLOCATION IN A GLOBAL APPROACH TO HEALTH

Health and disease evolve in the community with dynamics that do not respect the limitations of time and space. They interact with other dynamic phenomena, namely the evolution of risk factors and the development of health services. The best guides for predicting the relative success of alternative interventions on risk factors are therefore the degree of effect of each risk factor on the health of the community and the size of population groups that share the particular risk factors. Only those risk factors that may be vulnerable to the action of community health centers are of interest, whatever their nature may be (Backett et al., 1984; Grundy and Reinke, 1973).

Although this approach envisions a positive effect of the health center's activities on the community, the correct management of these resources ensures that the delivery of care is more economical and efficient. Finally, maximum consistency of the health center's work is achieved if the management of individual health problems is truly oriented toward problems and risk factors.

The risk approach to community health administration is based on two important epidemiological concepts: the relative risk and the attributable risk. A relative risk expresses the degree of association between a given risk factor and a certain outcome;

its value may vary from community to community for the same risk factor. An attributable risk expresses the relative amount of disease frequency in the community that can be attributed to a given risk factor. An attributable risk is a function of both the relative risk and the proportion of the population that is exposed to that risk factor. A more detailed exploration of these concepts was undertaken by A. and D. Lilienfeld (1980) and an excellent description of their practical interest in community health administration can be found in Backett et al. (1984).

THE RISK CONCEPT APPLICATION MADE ACCESSIBLE: THE ATTRACTIVE FEATURES OF MICROCOMPUTERS

The use of attributable risk to support decisions in community health administrations assumes that a cross-sectional set of population-based data is available on file, either concerning the total population or a representative sample of it. In this file, the variables relate the exposure status to pertinent risk factors and the pertinent health and disease statuses; a single risk factor may have several levels of intensity.

Different possibilities may arise, according to the combination among several levels in a single risk factor. For example, several risk factors with one level each or several risk factors with several levels each is one possibility, and one or several outcomes is another possibility (Backett et al., 1984; Epstein and Holland, 1983).

The calculation of a relative risk estimate for each risk factor or level and the calculation of the proportion of the total population sharing each risk factor or level allow an approximation to be made of the expected impact of each alternative intervention of services on each risk factor or level. That is given by the corresponding attributable risk that can be computed from the previous parameters. If a vulnerability score for each risk factor level is taken into account, the population group that maximizes the intervention on a risk factor or a combination of risk factors can be identified. This group may then be either submitted to an ad hoc intervention in the community, such as a health care center initiative, or be subject to a preferential reception when those individuals seek care on their own initiative. A similar reasoning applies to other units of observation, such as the family, school, or place of work.

As more risk factors and outcomes are considered, both the

calculations and the interpretation of their results tend to be more complicated and confusing. Such procedures become clumsy and threaten the possibility of using this approach on a routine and large scale. This is particularly true if further dimensions are taken into account, such as risk factor interaction estimates and the degree of priority of different outcomes.

Microcomputers are of great value at this point. They not only make it easy to handle and process all the required information, but they can also suggest the best choices according to decision models based on those parameters. In addition, they can simulate the expected community impact of the health administrator's suggestions and hints about interventions on risk factors or levels that can be constructed from other criteria.

The increasingly lower price and higher performance of microcomputers have made them attractive instruments in this field. An interesting paradox is developing in that cutting-edge technology is matching the enhanced needs of developing countries for the rational use of their primary health care resources (Davis, 1981; Sundararajan and Romensky, 1985; Tremblay and Bunt, 1979).

Microcomputers could contribute to the development of both computer-assisted decision models and human skills. When enough experience has been accumulated and human expertise is mature in this field, the possibility for developing real expert systems can be considered.

The use of microcomputer-supported models for reducing the risks of undesired future health outcomes in individuals, based on the concept of relative risk, is already being explored and improved. These models are usually applied to population elements who have the initiative to come to the health services. The primary usefulness of these models is in the maximization of individuals' health by advising them on their risk factor profiles. This approach also tends to contribute to the improvement of community health. It does not, however, lead to preferential care intended for those groups of the population who are experiencing an objectively determined higher risk of disease, which is undoubtedly pertinent and often urgent, especially if strong resource constraints exist (Black and Ashton, 1985; Evans, 1985; and Raines and Ellis, 1982).

CONCLUSIONS

Developing countries are on the verge of reaping enormous benefit from the improvement of microcomputer-supported decision models for the administration of community health centers.

These models are primarily based on the concept of attributable risk of disease as a proxy for the health needs of the community. The models offer good prospects for improving the level of community health because they assist the community health center administration in formulating a rational and economical use of the available health resources. There is great interest in microcomputers in places where severe resource constraints turn decision-making on alternative interventions on risk factors into a real puzzle.

In this way, increasingly powerful and less expensive microcomputers create new and promising opportunities for the development of both the community and the health centers in the context of innovation and objective decision-making.

REFERENCES

Backett, E., Davies, A., and Petros-Barvazian, A. "The Risk Approach in Health Care (With Special Reference to Maternal and Child Health, Including Family Planning)" Geneva, World Health Organization, 1984.

Barker, D. J. and Rose, G. "Epidemiology in Medical Practice" London, Longman Group Ltd., 1979.

Black, G. and Ashton, A. "Health Risk Appraisal in Primary Care" Primary Care, 12 (3), p. 557, 1985.

Davis, G. "Introduction to Computers" Tokyo, McGraw-Hill International Book Company, 1981.

Epstein, F. and Holland, W. "Prevention of Chronic Diseases in the Community - One-Disease versus Multiple-Disease Strategies" International Journal of Epidemiology, 12 (2), p. 135, 1983.

Evans, S. "Decision Support Systems for the Outpatient Office: Two Examples of Medical Expert Systems" Primary Care, 12 (3), p. 445, 1985.

Grundy, F. and Reinke, W. "Recherche en Organisation Sanitaire et Techniques de Management" Geneva, World Health Organization, 1973.

Lilienfeld, A. and Lilienfeld, D. "Foundations of Epidemiology" New York, Oxford University Press, 1980.

Raines, J. and Ellis, L. "A Conversational Microcomputer-Based Health Risk Appraisal" Computer Programs In Biomedicine, 14, p. 175, 1982.

Sundararajan, S. and Romensky, A. "Comprehensive Microcomputer-Based System for Primary Health Care Settings: A Possible Model" Communication to the Workshop on Appropriate Technology for Primary Health Care Development, Lisbon, 1985.

Thompson, G. and Handelman, I. "Health Data and Information Management" London, Butterworth Publishers, Inc., 1978.

Tremblay, J. P. and Bunt, R. "An Introduction to Computer Science: An Algorithmic Approach" Tokyo, McGraw-Hill Kogakusha Ltd., 1979.

14

SIGUS: A Microcomputer-Based Management System for Primary Health Care Centers

ALEXANDRE VIEIRA ABRANTES

Information processing and communications are essential activities at primary health care (PHC) centers. Physicians and nurses base their decisions on information they collect from the patient and records. They communicate with colleagues, laboratories, and hospitals. A community physician's major activity consists of assembling data and processing it into meaningful information that can assist rational decision-making in public health promotion. Finally, health administrators analyze data to assess community health needs, the performance of health services, and the outcome of health center activities.

A great amount of data is assembled, stored, retrieved, and processed. The process is cumbersome, time-consuming, and prone to frequent error. Computers perform these tasks quickly, accurately, and efficiently. Several pilot systems have automated these functions; COSTAR is usually chosen as a historical example (Barnett, 1976). Until recently, automated health care information systems had to be supported by large computers and were limited to hospitals, whereas primary health care services lagged behind. They were front-line services that were based on simple technology. They tended to be small, isolated, and immature organizations that could hardly support one of the large and sophisticated forerunner systems.

Microcomputers have made automation simpler, and health centers have grown larger and more sophisticated. Microcomputers therefore have a great potential to assist operations at PHC centers. The SIGUS research and development project was developed in Lisbon in 1985 to create five prototypes of automated information systems for Portuguese health centers. The SIGUS project provided industry with specifications of what was needed, and it is hoped that it will give Portuguese firms a competitive edge when health centers decide to automate some of their functions.

An outline is provided of how the SIGUS project started and its major outputs and hardware specifications. A framework is also suggested for a "post-SIGUS" project.

THE DEVELOPMENT OF SIGUS

The SIGUS project was created as a result of the interest of four parties:
1. Clinicians and nurses wanted to computerize medical records to improve care and facilitate patient data analysis.
2. The Lisbon Regional Health Administration wanted to identify provider performance profiles to bring health care costs under control.
3. The computer industry was trying to create a new market by marketing a turnkey system that satisfied the administrative needs of most health centers, but lacked application to directly support clinicians and public health teams.
4. The Ministry of Industry wanted to give Portuguese industry an opportunity in an emerging market.

A contract was established between the Lisbon Regional Health Administration, a department of the Ministry of Industry, and a private firm, Empresa de Investigaçao a Desenvolvimento de Electronica, to develop a series of five prototypes of varying degrees of complexity and size to define the specifications necessary to automate health centers. The School of Public Health, the Health Information Service, and the Directorate of PHC served as consultants to ensure the validity of the project.

SIGUS OUTPUTS

The development of SIGUS was based on two assumptions. First, it should be flexible enough to serve the needs of health centers of varied sizes and complexity. Second, any version of it should serve the needs of all four types of decision-makers at a health center: clinicians, public health teams, administrators, and the public.

The report shown in Figure 1 is meant to support the clinical decisions of physicians and nurses. It is a summarized medical record of all patients scheduled for one practitioner in one morning session. It is produced by the clinician himself and includes family and client identification, a flag warning about a preventive measure that the client has missed (e.g., a flu vaccination), the type of visit, a problem list with both code and free text areas, a risk appraisal with both code and free text, and finally a list of drugs taken by the patient on a long-term basis. This sheet operates as a reminder, very much along the lines suggested for problem-oriented medical records (Zander et al., 1978). This sheet is updated during the visit and is entered into the computer by the practitioner at the end of the day.

Each practicing team can revise its client file and demand reports to describe the patient population by sex, age, address, and risk group. It can list the number and types of problems appearing in the file, and the number and types of medications used on a long-term basis. It can identify patients who belong to a certain risk group and those who have missed a needed preventive measure. All these combined can help practicing teams in their clinical work, in applied research, and in constructing a curriculum vitae.

Because Portugal has a National Health Service, health centers cover the whole population. The client-based file therefore tends to be a population-based file. Public health teams have access to this data bank and can learn about the prevalence of disease. The health teams can identify high-risk groups and people who are in need of care but have not attended the health center in a certain period of time. They can list these groups and their addresses, and organize home visits with the attending team. A list is shown in Figure 2 of enrolled clients who belong to medium- or high-risk groups and have missed an appointment in the past 30 days. Other useful reports can be produced; for example, one report lists patients with one specific diagnosis and another lists clients who have missed a vaccine.

Administrators benefit from automated transaction monitoring. For each visit to the center, a record is produced that describes every procedure performed or ordered for the visiting client, including prescriptions, tests, referrals, and leaves of absence. These allow operations to be billed, monitored, and controlled. Every month the practicing profile of each team or practitioner is produced and outliers are informed about their profiles in the hope that they will do something about it. Patient scheduling is also automated to provide better control over patient flow and waiting lists (Figure 3).

THE SIGUS CONFIGURATION

The SIGUS project includes the construction of five different prototypes of increasing complexity and sizes, from a simple microcomputer to a minicomputer that supports multiuse and multiprocessing.

The simplest prototype (C1) is based on a personal microcomputer with 512 kilobytes of random-access memory (RAM) and a 10-megabyte hard disk. It has a backup tape drive and is linked to a monochrome video display, a 132-column dot matrix printer, and a small ticket printer.

This prototype has been in operation at the Sete Rios Health Center in Lisbon and is providing the basic specifications for building the more complex configurations. It appears suitable for a relatively small health center that serves 6,000 to 10,000 people.

When patients come into the health center, they are interviewed by an administrative clerk who can open or update family and individual records, and schedule visits and procedures. Physicians or nurses enter the clinical data base by using a restricted user identification, and produce a list of all patients, problems, and medications. As patients are seen, they update the patient list and at the end of the day they update the medical records of patients who have been seen or who have missed their appointments. As the client leaves the health center, he or she sees the administrative clerk who checks the visiting record, enters its data, and stamps prescriptions, test orders, and so forth.

THE ACCEPTABILITY OF SIGUS

Administrative clerks were the first group to accept the system. They became good users of the system with minimal training.

It has become prestigious to work with the computer. The accuracy of data entered has not been a problem, but the need for performing regular backups has had to be reinforced. Backups have not always been done frequently enough or properly. In every instance, it was possible to retrieve the data with minimal losses.

Physicians were more suspicious of the system. Enthusiasts were present from the beginning, but the leadership made it clear that it would not operate with the system if access to clinical data was not restricted to the clinicians themselves. Individual user identification keys were created and access to different areas of the data base was defined and restricted to certain professional groups (Hare, 1979). Practitioners were suspicious about operations monitoring and control but, because no administrative measures were taken against outliers, it has not caused any problem in the relationship between the management and practitioners.

The public has been curious about the system, but seems to accept it without problems. When the data base started to fill up, the system became very slow and clients often had to wait more than they were used to. They complained, as did physicians and administrators. A compiled version of dBase III had to be created and the structure of the data base was revised to give priority to those paths that were used most frequently.

Nurses have so far kept a distance from the system. They have not seen any direct benefit of the system to their everyday work. An application is currently being developed to monitor and control the vaccination program, which is a responsibility of nurses. Their support is expected as they see their workload relieved of much-hated paperwork.

THE FRAMEWORK FOR THE POST-SIGUS PROJECT

Experience gained with SIGUS has indicated areas that need more work; these areas will be dealt with in a post-SIGUS project. More has to be done to help nurses. They are a scarce resource in primary health care and so far have limited autonomy. Computer-assisted decision-making could enlarge and enrich the nursing function. One application being developed to control the National Vaccination Program is a type of clinical algorithm that guides nurses unambiguously through the decision process that leads to the scheduling and administration of vaccines to children and adolescents. A health risk appraisal algorithm is being considered that will enable nurses to identify high-risk client groups and provide public health teams with specific target groups for which special care programs can be tailored. Computer-assisted patient interviewing is next on the list of interests because it can increase the accuracy and comprehensiveness of data collection and, more importantly, it can focus the caring team in specific areas (e.g., alcohol abuse and smoking). Computer-assisted clinical decision-making and diagnosis have been shown to improve the care delivered by physicians' assistants (Sox et al., 1973) and are now compatible with microcomputer technology.

Clients must be given a more direct advantage to use the system. A portable medical record on a "smart card" would give them a clear advantage. Each citizen would become the owner of his or her health information, which would avoid those frequent and embarrassing instances when one wants to seek a second opinion, but has difficulty obtaining past medical information from the physician. Administrative work and time spent with clerks could be shortened. If a patient gets sick when traveling or on a holiday, it would be easy to learn about the patient's past history. In the case of an accident or unconsciousness, easy access to past history will also improve the quality of care that can be provided.

The development of microcomputer-based portable medical work stations would make home care more practicable. It would satisfy patients, physicians, and administrators. Patients complain about physicians who refuse to practice at the patient's home, whereas practitioners say that modern medicine cannot be practiced in the patient's home. A portable terminal could give the practioner access to data and even to knowledge stored elsewhere (e.g., an expert system). Simple electronic devices could guide patients in self-care and, for example, could assist the support self-treatment of diabetes mellitus.

Finally, communciation is still a problem within a health center, between different stations of a health center, and between different health care providers, like hospitals and laboratories. Communicating data in a network of thousands of health centers and stations is expensive.

Much clinical information is stored in pictures that consume a lot of electronic data storage and require much communications power. Clinical data is very sensitive; its communication has to be coupled with specific encoding and decoding processes.

CONCLUSION

Microcomputers have a great potential to assist decision-making at health centers. Much of the activity at a health center consists of collecting and processing data. Microcomputers are well-adapted to the needs of relatively small organizations like single practices, partnerships, or small health centers.

The SIGUS project was undertaken to make microcomputers serve the needs of primary health care administrators and, more importantly, to help direct providers like physicians and nurses. It currently provides the former with good operations monitoring and control and the latter with a population-based health information file and powerful data base management.

The project is now moving into the computer-assisted decision-making area of vaccination; its priority is to support physicians' assistants when the doctor is absent. Computer-assisted patient interviewing and health-risk appraisal are examples of microcomputer applications that could be developed with relative ease.

Medical records on "smart cards" can increase the control of patients, reduce the administrative workload, reduce waiting time, and improve communications. Finally, better and cheaper communication needs to be developed for automated primary health care information systems. Large amounts of data need to be transferred quickly and confidentially.

REFERENCES

Barnett, O.: COSTAR: Computer Stored Ambulatory Record (Washington, D.C.: DHEW Public Health Services, Health Resources Administration, NCHS 763145, 1976).

Hare, W.: Legislative Issues Surrounding the Confidentiality of Medical Records (Santa Monica, CA: Rand Paper Series, Rand Corporation, 1979)

Sox, H.C., Sox, C.H., and Tompkins, R.K.: "The Training of Physician Assistants." NEJM 288 818-824, 1973.

Zander, Beresford, and Thomas: Medical Records in General Practice, (London: RCGP Occasional Paper 5, 1978).

NAME	PACIENTS	HOURS (./PA)	APPOIN (./H?)	Est. APP (%)	Nx. APP (%)	H.CALL (./PA)	ABSENT (%)
GENERAL PRACTISE							
Dr. XXXXXXX XXXXXXX	1136	68.00 0.060	490 7.21	89 18.16	401 81.84	345 0.30	97 19.80
Dr. XXXXXX XXXX	792	0.00 0.000	0	0	0	0 0.00	0
Dr. XXXXXX XXXX XXXXX	558	0.00 0.000	136	55 40.44	81 59.56	0 0.00	0 0.00
Dr. XXXXXXXX XXXXXX	1119	0.00 0.000	16	7 43.75	9 56.25	0 0.00	0 0.00
Dr. XXXXXXXXX XXXXX	126	0.00 0.000	1	1 100.00	0 0.00	0 0.00	0 0.00
Dr. XXXXXXXXX XXXXXXXX	32	10.00 0.313	19 1.90	12 63.16	7 36.84	6 0.19	0 0.00
Dr. XXXXXX XXXXXXXX	90	0.00 0.000	4	4 100.00	0 0.00	0 0.00	0 0.00
Dr. XXXXXXX XXXXXXXX	132	0.00 0.000	3	3 100.00	0 0.00	0 0.00	0 0.00
TOTAL OF SERVICE	3965	78.00 0.020	669 8.58	171 25.56	498 74.44	351 0.09	97 14.50

APPOINTMENTS   TOTAL: 1297

CONF. APPOINT. TOTAL: 1194   PAID: 949   CASH: 28470$00

CANC. APPOINT. TOTAL: 73   PAID: 52   CASH: 1560$00

FIGURE 1 Summarized appointment record for one practitioner.

DIAGNOSIS	REGIST. PACIENTS TOTAL	M	W	ACTIV. PACIENTS	<1	1-4	5-9	10-14	15-24	25-64	65-74	75-+	FERT. AGE WOMAN
A04-ASTHENIC	1	0	1	1	0	0	0	0	0	1	0	0	1
D01-ABDOMINAL PAIN	1	0	1	1	0	1	0	0	0	0	0	0	0
D02-STOMACH PAIN	1	1	0	1	0	0	0	0	0	0	0	1	0
D03-HEARTBURN	1	0	1	1	0	0	0	1	0	0	0	0	0
D85-DUODENAL ULCER	1	1	0	1	0	0	0	0	0	1	0	0	0
D99-OTHER DIS. DIGESTIVE SYS.	2	1	1	2	0	0	0	0	0	2	0	0	1
K01-PAIN-ATTRIBUTED TO HEART	1	0	1	1	0	0	0	0	0	1	0	0	1
K76-CHR. ISCHEMIC HEART DIS.	4	2	2	4	0	0	0	0	0	2	1	1	0
K83-HEART VALVE DISEASE	1	1	0	1	0	0	0	0	0	1	0	0	0
K85-ELEVATED BLOOD-PRESSURE	1	0	1	1	0	0	0	0	0	1	0	0	1
K86-HYPERTENSION	13	5	8	13	0	0	0	0	0	10	1	2	1
K90-OTHER CERESROVASCULAR DIS	1	0	1	1	0	0	0	0	0	0	1	0	0
K95-VARICOSE VEINS OF LEG	1	0	1	1	0	0	0	0	0	1	0	0	1
L03-LOW BACK COMPLAINTS	1	0	1	1	0	0	0	0	0	1	0	0	1
L15-KNEE SYMPTOMS	1	0	1	1	0	0	0	1	0	0	0	0	0
L84-OSTEOARTHRITIS OF SPINE	8	3	5	8	0	0	0	0	0	7	0	1	0
L88-RHEUMATOID ARTHRITIS	1	0	1	1	0	0	0	0	0	0	1	0	0
L89-OSTEOARTHRITIS	4	1	3	4	0	0	0	0	0	3	0	1	0
N89-MIGRAINE	1	0	1	1	0	0	0	0	0	1	0	0	1
P72-AFFECTIVE PSYCHOSIS	1	0	1	1	0	0	0	0	0	1	0	0	1
P75-HYSTERICAL DISORDERS	1	0	1	1	0	0	0	0	0	1	0	0	0
P76-DEPRESSIVE DISORDERS	1	0	1	1	0	0	0	0	0	1	0	0	0
R02-SHORTNESS OF BREATH	1	0	1	1	0	0	0	0	0	1	0	0	0
R91-CHR. BRONCHITIS	2	2	0	2	0	0	0	0	0	1	1	0	0
R96-ASTHMA	1	0	1	1	0	0	0	0	0	1	0	0	0
S77-MALIGN. NEOPLASM OF SKIN	1	0	1	1	0	0	0	0	0	1	0	0	0
S86-SEBORRH. DERMATITIS	1	1	0	1	0	0	0	0	0	1	0	0	0
S99-OTHER SKIN DISEASES	1	1	0	1	0	0	0	0	0	0	0	1	0
T03-LOSS OF APPETITE	1	0	1	1	0	0	0	0	1	0	0	0	1
T08-WEIGHT LOSS	1	0	1	1	0	0	0	0	1	0	0	0	1
T90-DIABETES MELLITUS	4	1	3	4	0	0	0	0	0	2	1	1	0
T93-LIPID METABOLISM DIS.	3	2	1	3	0	0	0	0	0	2	1	0	0
U06-BLOOD IN URINE	1	1	0	1	0	0	0	0	0	1	0	0	0
U71-CYSTITIS	1	0	1	1	0	0	0	0	0	1	0	0	0
U95-URINARY CALCULUS	1	1	0	1	0	0	0	0	0	1	0	0	0
X11-OTHER VAGINAL DISCHARGE	1	0	1	1	0	0	0	0	0	1	0	0	1
X78-FIBROID/MYOMAS	1	0	1	1	0	0	0	0	0	0	1	0	0
Y29-OTHER MALE REP SYST SYMPT	1	1	0	1	0	0	0	0	0	1	0	0	0

FIGURE 2 Summarized diagnosis information for current patients.

PACIENT	NAME	AGE	MOT	DIAGNOSIS	RISK	THERAPEUTICS
4551/ 1	XXXXXXXXXXX XXXX	36	—	K86.1-HYPERTENSION R78.2-BRONCHITIS L88.1-RHEUMAT. ARTHRITIS K91.3-ATHEROSCLEROSIS T09.4-WEIGHT PROBLEM	B-	10/04/86 X -MODURETIC 10/04/86 1X4 -BRITACIL 10/04/86 13 -CLOROCIL
136/ 3	XXXAX XXXXXXXXXXXXXX	20	—	R79.1-BRONCHITIS T09.2-WEIGHT PROBLEM	B-	03/04/86 X -BRITACIL
5722/ 1!	XXX XXXXXXXX	72	—	K91.3-ATHEROSCLEROSIS L88.1-RHEUMAT. ARTHRITIS	B-	
5722/ 2!	XXXXXXXXX XXXXXXXX	71	—		B-	
2238/ 1!	XXXXXXXXXXX XXXX	57	—		B-	
5297/ 2!	XXXXXXX XXX	50	—		B-	
1983/ 1!	XXXXXXXXX XXXXXXX	49	—		B-	
1426/ 1!	XXXXXXXXX XXXXXXXXXXXX	60	—		B-	
136/ 1!	XXXXX XXXXXXX	60	—		B-	

ACKNOWLEDGEMENTS
================

GENERAL PRACTITIONER   _____

DATA INTRODUCTION ON SIGUS ___/___/___   _____

FIGURE 3 Analysis of appointment scheduling.

15

Computer Technology and Biomedical Instrumentation

MURRAY EDEN

This discussion of biomedical and other potential uses of microprocessor development focuses on trends in the electronic technology rather than on applications in medical technology per se. The influence of the electronic advances on the progress of biomedical instrumentation is not purely economic. It is true that less costly electronics may lead to lowering the cost of the devices that use them, but more importantly, the progress in microcircuits technology can be expected to modify the design of medical devices in fundamental ways. Furthermore, progress is expanding the scope of the devices utility within the framework of diagnosis and from diagnosis to the control of therapy.

In the United States, and probably in West European countries, when the role of the computer in the health care system is discussed, the image that comes to mind is a kind of information bank for health care institutions. This information bank takes care of all kinds of general accounts and records, scheduling, statistical analysis, billing, inventory control, and the like, and also of some medical functions in diagnostic and therapeutic decision-making. Michael Anbar discussed this latter topic in a recent issue of the *International Journal of Technology Assessment in Health Care* (Anbar, 1986).

It is also well known that computers are an indispensable

component in the modern high-technology devices of biological research and medical practice, especially in the realm of imaging devices. Indeed, computerized tomography (CT), positron emission tomography (PET), and nuclear magnetic resonance imaging (MRI) could not possibly have been realized as devices if numerical computations had to be done by hand. All medical imaging technologies developed since CT have crucially depended on numerical computation. This is as true of ultrasound scanning as it is of PET scanning, although the computer in an ultrasound imager is by no means as obvious, and as expensive, as the one in the PET scanner. It is not commonly appreciated that there is a computer in virtually every modern product of medical instrument technology.

It is in this context that the problems facing designers, manufacturers, and users of biomedical devices are addressed. The place of microelectronics in such devices is unquestionable. Nevertheless, the way in which this technology can be used needs to be understood if developments are to be cost-effective.

THE PLACE OF INSTRUMENTATION IN BIOMEDICINE

Doctors first began measuring temperature by means of the thermometer, exploring internal anatomy with the x-ray machine in the nineteenth century, and learning about the patient's physiology with the blood pressure cuff and electrocardiograph early in the twentieth century. Until 40 years ago, however, devices that measured or controlled an electrical signal were cumbersome and required close attention. The field of electronics at that time was still acquiring a strong scientific basis; the industry was then involved in manufacturing consumer products like radios and phonographs.

At the end of World War II, engineers, experimental physicists, and mathematicians began to investigate health-related sciences as fields in which to practice their skills. Advanced technology based on physical and electronic theory was first introduced into the biomedical environment by way of the research laboratory. The life science researcher, rather than the physician, first recognized that the new instrumentation could help to solve biological problems. Even so, complex and expensive devices, such as the mass spectrometer, spectrophotometer, ultracentrifuge, and the electron microscope, were still in their infancy and appeared to be useful only in basic biochemical and biophysical research and seemed to have little or no application to patient management.

Electronics made an entry into medicine perhaps because engineers and manufacturers could easily see how electronics could, in principle, improve the measurement of temperature, heart sounds, and blood pressure. These measurements were then and are still the three standard features of a physical examination. Electrocardiographic and x-ray devices had already made use of electronics.

Instruments as Sensors

Beginning with the stethoscope, virtually each instrument conceived by biomedical scientists was intended to enhance the user's perceptions by providing the eyes and ears with signals that could not be acquired directly. According to the current terminology of instrumentation science, these devices are known as sensors. Just as a tympanic, flexible-tube stethoscope senses the largely low-frequency sounds and transmits them to the physician's ears, the MRI apparatus senses proton concentrations in the body and shows them to the radiologist in a picture that bears a strong resemblance to an anatomical slice through the patient.

Instruments as Quantifiers

Merely enhancing the senses, however, is insufficient. Biomedical researchers anxious to make their field of work more scientific were also looking for objective measurements and facts that were unbiased by personal feeling or interpretation. Out of this impulse developed the need for display and the associated requirements of standardization and calibration.

Medicine continues to need tools that perform sensory extension or enhancement and tools that make numerical measurements. But scientific biomedicine requires more than objective observation.

Instruments as Logic Machines

Karl Pearson, the philosopher and mathematical statistician, urged anyone who wished to be a scientist, "above all things to strive at self-elimination in his judgements, to provide an argument which is as true for each individual mind as for his own" (Reiser and Anbar, 1984). In other words, to the extent possible, the data handling and the logical relations among data streams should also be dealt with objectively. These are processes for which the digital computer was originally conceived. It is therefore in the biomedical sciences and in the general health care system that the potential of the computer was quickly recognized and applications were developed rapidly.

Two instruments mentioned earlier illustrate aspects of the computer's significance. The production of a CT or MRI image is an exercise in sophisticated computation, but radiologists rarely use the numerical data available in the image. In daily practice they make their judgments subjectively. The computer is not essential to the stethoscope. It is, however, possible to "computerize" the stethoscope. The heart sounds could be stored for reappraisal, beats could be correlated, spectra could be made, and unusual patterns could be recognized. The data acquired by the stethoscope can now be displayed in new ways that might elicit different perceptions and stimulate novel insights.

COMPUTER TECHNOLOGY AND BIOMEDICINE

Data-Handling Requirements

Insofar as data handling is concerned, the needs in the health care sector are manifold but not particularly unusual. The instruments used in basic biomedical research are not very different from those used by research chemists or applied physicists. In fact, except for some devices of purely biological relevance—for example, the chemical machines that sequentially identify the nucleotides in a DNA strand—scientists in the different disciplines use the same machines. They measure masses of molecules (mass spectrometry), surface properties (electron microscopy), energy spectra of electromagnetic radiation from x-rays to infrared, and so forth. Clinics, hospitals, and larger health care systems have data handling needs that differ little from those of any reasonably complex industrial or commercial venture. They may well require networking capabilities, but these would not likely be as complex or have the response time specifications of an airline reservation network.

In terms of medical applications, there may be differences in the packaging of a device, but not in its data-handling specifications. Other than managing devices, most measurements are relatively slow; a 10-kilohertz sampling rate is fast enough for virtually every physiological process. The requirement for precision of measurement is not very great.

Special Sensors for Biomedicine

The instrumental needs of biomedical research and practice differ in two ways from those of other application areas: the place where the observation is made and the kind of measurement to be made. There is a continuing need for sensors to measure ions, gasses, small organic molecules, and enzyme activities in vivo. Noninvasive sensors would be much preferred, but only a very few of the variables are candidates for noninvasive measurement. Therefore, the requirement is for very small sensors that can be introduced into the body by needle or catheter without causing much trauma.

The interaction of sensor and computer technology represents an instructive example of how different technologies can influence and drive one another. As computer components have become less expensive (modern central processing unit (CPU) chips cost less than $5), it has become possible to put a great deal of computational power even into inexpensive devices without changing their cost much. Computers have also become much smaller. The chip itself can be smaller and much thinner than a small coin and can be put into places hitherto unimaginable.

The development of tiny microprocessors was driven to a large extent by the needs of military planners and space programs because computer power was needed in small spaces. However, this need was not only for very small computers to process information and control some functions, but also to reduce the size of the sensors to measure variables of interest. No special development has been required for biomedical applications as far as the hardware of the microprocessors is concerned. The availability of small and inexpensive microelectronics has instead encouraged the development of sensors to measure variables of significance to diagnosis or the control of therapy. The result has been a positive reinforcement of the development goals of small size, low cost, and high reliability.

Technology in Medicine

In a recent book that dealt with strategies for using technology in patient care, the biophysicist Michael Anbar represented the connections between science, technology, and medical practice in the diagram reproduced here (Anbar, 1984). He states:

> Health care depends more and more on technology to meet its large variety of needs. It uses technology to gather information and present it in comprehensible forms; to treat disorders effectively when diagnosed; to monitor treatment and evaluate its efficacy; and, last but not least, to prevent disease. There is practically no step in the sequence of medical actions that is not dependent on technology (Figure 1). Projections into the future predict an even greater role for technology in medical practice, especially in the applications of computers. Pattern recognition of complex physical phenomena, as provided by the electrocardiogram (ECG) or electroencephalogram (EEG), is today almost within the state of the art, and computerized recognition of two-dimensional or three-dimensional images will probably be achieved before the end of this century. Computerized diagnosis and decision analysis are not science fiction, nor are computerized monitoring of patients and automated treatment systems.

It should be noted that the diagram includes both diagnostic and therapeutic aspects. Most instrumentation was historically developed for diagnosis; microprocessor technology is used most in that area. Therapeutic devices by their very nature involve the control of a variable and the direct or indirect sensing of the variable. Microelectronic circuitry has also taken over many of the control functions in this area.

For example, Keithley produces an automatic x-ray exposure control that uses a PROM to store such calibration parameters as filtration, hVp waveform, and film-screen type. Bear Medical advertises an infant ventilator with "alert and alarm functions as well as on-line data such as actual inspiratory time, exhalation time, ventilator rate, I:E ratio on a breath-to-breath basis and mean airway pressure." Valleylab sells a microprocessor-based electrosurgical generator. The Sigma 6000 is a microprocessor-controlled, volumetric, peristaltic-infusion pump.

A particularly important example is the multiprogrammable pacemaker, a therapeutic device that is worn by literally millions of people whose hearts cannot maintain normal rhythm without electrical stimulation. As far as its microelectronics is concerned, the pacemaker differs from the great majority of medical devices in that it uses application-specific integrated circuits instead of standard chips. This application has highly specialized, biologically dictated constraints that limit the options available to the electronics designer.

Moreover, in this application and at the current state-of-the-art, telemetry is required between the in-dwelling pacemaker and the external computer-transporter. Custom-designed integrated circuitry is consequently dictated by application constraints and is economically justified by reason of the large potential market.

Among the common functions assessed in modern telemetering pacemakers are program content, model-identification battery status, and R-wave interval or actual pacing rate. Medtronic Inc., one of the leaders in the industry, has recently introduced what it claims to be "the most significant advance in pacing since the lithium battery." Its advertisement in *Medical Electronic & Equipment News* (MEEN) states that "Activitrax is the first single chamber rate responsive pacemaker that can detect the patient's activity and respond with an appropriate heart rate." (MEEN, 1986a).

It should be noted that the examples of controllers cited earlier are all "open loop" systems. Strictly speaking, this is also true of the new pacemakers, but medical technology is expected to introduce feedback controllers. The lag in development is not the fault of microelectronic technology. A sensor problem exists to some extent in how to measure cardiac output unobtrusively. Perhaps more important is the fact that little knowledge exists of the ways by which physiological functions are regulated in either normal or pathological organisms. Among other things, regulatory mechanisms can model in a highly nonlinear fashion, and there is no real agreement on that optimal "set-point," or that physiological variables should be maintained constant.

In the last decade, several research groups in the United States, notably the group in the Johns Hopkins Applied Physics Laboratory, have been developing a microprocessor-controlled, in-dwelling insulin dispenser for diabetics. The control regime can be modified by the user depending on such variables as size of meal or expected level of activity. There is reason to be optimistic about the development of an in-dwelling glucose sensor based on fiber-optic technology. However, clinical scientists are currently disagreeing about the need to maintain glucose in the bloodstream at a constant level. A consensus must first exist about the biological variable that needs to be controlled before the feedback device is worth designing.

The role of imaging systems in medicine has already been alluded to. The number of different imaging systems continues to grow. Magnetic resonance imaging and positron emission tomography have been developed and commercialized in the last 10 years. In particular, MRI is expected to have a revolutionary effect on diagnostic imaging. Both MRI and PET require substantial computer power. The commercial units are sold with a dedicated minicomputer and all the appropriate imaging software. Older imaging techniques are also being computerized. Many of the diagnostic ultrasound scanners use microcircuitry to display or enhance images.

The oldest of the imaging systems, radiology, has been turned into the basis of the technique of digital radiography. Once an image has been converted to a matrix of numbers, the picture can be transformed numerically. One radiograph can therefore be subtracted from another; the different picture reveals features of the anatomy that have changed over a period of time. Radiologists and their engineer collaborators have discovered a number of numerical operations—more complex than subtraction—that reveal new data in the x-rays. Commercially available systems currently exist for performing digital radiography.

The same imaging techniques that provided physicians with static anatomical information also provided dynamic information on physiological changes, because the physical response times of the analog detection systems are short when compared with the response time of physiological systems. This is true of fluoroscopy, x-ray cinematography, real-time ultrasonic B-scanning, and thermography. Technological developments in computational hardware have now made it possible to perform the same sorts of dynamic measurements digitally, not only with the analog devices mentioned earlier, but also with CT, MRI, and PET. For example, a specially built CT scanner at the Mayo Clinic can take adequate time-resolved slices of a beating heart.

Computation for Pattern Recognition and Statistical Correlation

Any one of the many different diagnostic tools provides the clinician with a certain set of features or values. It is then up to the clinician to determine the value of the information as it relates to the patient he is examining—in terms of whether or not it indicates disease.

There is an increasing tendency to look for correlations between abnormal values of several clinical tests and a certain disease; in other words, to look for a pattern or profile associated with a specific disorder. Such a pattern can be evaluated better with the aid of a computer that analyzes all the clinical information, identifies the independent variables, and recognizes a characteristic pattern that corresponds to a pathological state.

Studies of automated pattern recognition have been going on for about 30 years; the basic work in statistical associations was begun more than 100 years ago. As with the technology of imaging, pattern recognition remained largely an academic interest until the growth in the power, speed, and ease of use of computers made complex manipulations practical. A few real-time data-handling systems currently use pattern recognition. Flow-cell sorting instruments use microcomputers to identify clusters of normal and pathological cells in two-dimensional displays. Although they are still largely used as research tools, their use is likely to spread to general clinical practice.

Considerable interest exists in the development of interactive diagnostic systems. Once all the varieties of data have been collected, how can a clinician use these data to improve or supplement his diagnostic skills? Expert systems are not addressed here except to point out that the automation of the logic of medical diagnosis has been one of the first areas of application and continues to be an area of active development (Li and Fu, 1980).

Technical Options for the Design of Biomedical Instrumentation

The health care professional or the engineer engaged to develop tools for the health care system currently has several technological options to choose from. Before considering the options, it is worth reviewing the structure of a generalized biomedical instrument.

The block diagram shown in Figure 2 depicts the components of the system. It is taken from "Design of Microcomputer-Based Medical Instrumentation" by the biomedical instrumentation specialists, Willis J. Tompkins and John G. Webster (Tompkins and

Webster, 1981). The authors offer the following description of their block diagram.

> The stimulator block contains a stimulus source. If the instrument is going to examine a particular response, then repeated stimuli can initiate responses so that they can be studied. The next block contains the sensors. Here specialized transducers convert the various signals (of chemical, physical or physiological variables) into electrical signals. These signals travel to the processor block, where operations such as amplification, filtering, interference rejection, and computer analysis are carried out. Information then flows to the display, recorder, and distribution blocks, where the information is displayed to others in the immediate vicinity of the device, recorded on paper or other media for permanent storage, and distributed to other more distant areas. Finally, the processed data flows to a controller block to control patient treatment or patient stimulus.

It should be noted that the inputs to or outputs from the patient are analog signals. The signals to the sensors are physical quantities such as temperature, pressure, volume, and flow velocity, and bioelectrical capabilities, such as electrocardiograms, electroencephalograms, electromyograms, and electrochemicals— (pH, pO_2, and pCO_2). Much the same can be said for the stimuli and for the treatments when they begin to be delivered on the basis of feedback control. Medical instruments therefore require analog signal conditioning devices such as amplifiers and filters; beyond these points, all other functions in the diagram can be executed digitally. The A-D and D-A converters are microelectronic devices that are available as standard commercial chips. In other words, it is only at the interfaces between the patient and the instrument that there is any need to consider special electronic design.

Given the current stage of electronic technology, no biomedical instrument is likely to be designed from scratch by using resistors, capacitors, diodes, or transistors and other basic building blocks of electronic circuitry. Aside from the previously cited design needs at the analog end, a designer is likely to use one or a combination of three possible design modalities: microprocessors and standard microelectronic chips, specially fabricated integrated circuits, or personal computers with appropriate interfaces.

The terms microprocessor and microcomputer are used interchangeably in much of the technical literature, but a microprocessor is usually described as a chip that performs all the essential functions of the central processing unit (CPU) of a traditional computer, whereas a microcomputer is a device that includes a CPU chip and a variety of other chips, almost always including a clock, read-only memory (ROM), random-access memory (RAM), and input/output (I/O) ports.

The microcomputer is currently the dominant technology. An informal survey was made of recent issues of *Medical Electronics and Equipment News*, a journal that carries the slogan "Where the Medical Profession Consults Technology," to verify this impression (MEEN 1986a&b). First, all scalar measurements are displayed digitally and are therefore likely to use some sort of microprocessor. The only exceptions found were a blood pressure gauge, a radiation survey meter, and a ventilator. In any case, even if the display is analog, the special circuitry of the ventilator is microprocessor-based; the radiation meter circuitry is probably specially made for that purpose and may be an application-specific integrated circuit (ASIC).

Guided by the advertisement alone, one cannot state with certainty that the measurement and display electronics of a particular device are embodied in special circuitry or controlled by a microprocessor, but the economics of electronic design and fabrication costs strongly favor the use of microprocessor-based instrumentation. A relatively simple medical device, such as a digital electronic plethysmograph, can be designed with about a dozen chips, including an A-D converter, a CPU chip, a small RAM, ROM, I/O port, clock, data bus interface, and so forth, each of which is composed of thousands of basic electronic elements, both active transistors and passive resistors. Few chips cost more than $20, even when bought in small lots. Indeed, the cost of packaging a commercial medical electronic device is likely to be more than the cost of its components.

Microprocessor-based instrumentation has several advantages over devices made exclusively of discrete components, aside from the advantage of cost. Systems assembled from integrated circuit packages generally need fewer parts. Fewer interconnections are made by hand and prone to failure. Their small size allows them to be readily incorporated into all sorts of portable instruments or to be inserted into organisms, like pacemakers. Because microprocessors consume little power, small batteries that are able to provide energy for extended periods of time serve as power sources. All design considerations aside, the crucial advantage of a microcomputer-based circuit is that its operation can be changed by software and its function can be altered with no rewiring or component changes.

This software capability has radically altered the strategy of design engineers. This is apparent in the first sentence of the medical instrumentation textbook cited earlier: "This book will help you design medical instruments using computers." It should be noted that this sentence has two different interpretations. Either the book will show you how to design medical instruments that contain computers or the book will teach you how to use computers to design medical instruments. Both interpretations are correct.

A variety of tools for instrument development have become available over the last decade that have facilitated the writing, testing, and debugging of microprocessor programs. Three of the most common modalities are described in the following sections.

Assemblers

Assemblers permit the designer to write a program in assembly language. The assembler may be able to run on the same microprocessor for which the software is being written, in which case it is called a resident assembler. If it runs on another (usually larger and faster) computer, it is called a cross-assembler.

Development Boards

Development boards are built around a microprocessor identical to the one for the intended application and come complete with ROM and RAM. They also contain components that facilitate software and hardware development, such as keyboards, displays, and areas on the board in which extra circuitry can be connected (breadboarding). The board's supervisory software (in ROM) may also permit the user to step line-by-line through a program or to insert break points that will automatically halt the program at designated steps.

Development Systems

Development systems allow the user to use high-level languages while developing software for the microprocessor. Such languages are more like English and are a respite from the one-for-one representation of the machine codes that are characteristic of assembly languages. An emulator is a development system that maintains the same timing relationships of the microprocessor; it replaces the microprocessor in the test circuit by connecting to the circuit with a plug. The purpose of the in-circuit emulation is to mimic the functions of the microprocessor while monitoring it with surrounding circuitry that need not be included in the end product. When testing is complete, some development systems can burn the finished program into ROM.

The book by Tompkins and Webster referred to earlier is explicit about the assistance the authors intend to provide to their readers (Tompkins and Webster, 1981).

> [This book] helps you assess each medical instrument and decide whether or not it is a likely candidate for a microcomputer. It helps you select the proper microcomputer for the job and the necessary size of memory and peripherals. It explains the costs and time required to implement both hardware and software. It points out both the costs and advantages of using various software development packages. Finally, it guides you step by step through the detailed design of a complex medical instrument involving analog circuits and microcomputer hardware and software.
>
> This book is primarily intended for the biomedical or clinical engineer and will be of little value to a health practitioner who does not have some knowledge of electrical engineering. Once the scope of the microcomputer's applicability is appreciated by a health practitioner, engineers can be found with the requisite technical skill to address a novel instrumental application. The essential idea is a simple one: if it is known how to measure the relevant variables (sensors) and how to achieve a particular answer from a synthesis (usually mathematical) of these variables, then a microprocessor-based instrument can be built to produce and display the answer automatically and regularly.

The technological trends discussed earlier should have certain beneficial effects on medical technology. Consider the job of instrument repair and maintenance, a mundane and unglamorous but essential service in any health care institution. The diagnosis of instrument failures is itself capable of being automated. Cart-mounted safety test units have been developed using microprocessor technology to automatically identify the equipment under test, to test the safety parameters, and to record the test results (Wooten and Corsey, 1982).

When microprocessor-based equipment fails, it can be repaired much faster and for about the same cost as circuitry built from discrete components. The repair technician will not try to find the specific element that failed, but will simply insert a new card (an array of chips, connectors, and other electronic components mounted on a single plastic board), and might search for the defective component later. The card costs about $300, which is very high when compared with the cost of a discrete component. The hourly charge for repair personnel, however, may be as high as $100. It takes minutes to identify a card with a defective chip, but it could take hours to locate the defective chip. Furthermore, the board may have trade-in value. When labor charges justify it, the technician can search for and replace the defective component, and the board can be reused in a later repair.

Industry recognizes that repair and maintenance are important considerations. The ad for Philips Medical Systems' SDR 1550, a microcomputer-based ultrasound scanner, states that "Built-in diagnostic capability automatically verifies system functions and pinpoints problems for quick servicing" (MEEN 1986b).

Another advantage to the health practitioner is worth mentioning. The inner workings of a device are more thoroughly hidden from the practitioner. Few, if any, adjustments and controls are visible to the user. Modern microprocessor-based devices are suited to the needs of users who find the mechanical, chemical, or electronic entrails and their potential frailties to be distracting.

The construction of a device with a moderate level of complexity may sometimes justify the design and fabrication of a special chip. In commercial practice, the cost of designing and preparing to manufacture a special chip was recently about $100,000 or more. Given that most medical device markets number in the thousands instead of millions, it is rarely cost-effective to follow this course. Nevertheless, important devices are in this category. The programmable pacemaker was mentioned earlier.

Consider the different strategies of designing a special chip as opposed to using the standard chip packages and configuring them to the application. The latter strategy may be regarded as profligate in that in general only a very small portion of the potential available in standard chips will actually be required for the application at hand. The design effort, however, is much less painstaking because it is little concerned with the details of connectivity among the thousands of discrete elements hidden in the standard chip. By contrast, the specially designed chip will make much more frugal use of the semiconductor wafer upon which it is built; however, each detail and connection must be specified.

Government-Supported VLSI Circuit Design

The Division of Research Resources (DRR), of the National Institutes of Health, under its Biomedical Research Technology Resources Program, supports facilities at the University of Washington and at Washington University in St. Louis that design very large-scale integrated (VLSI) circuits (Biomedical Research Technology Resources, 1984). The rationale for such activities is given in the DRR description of resources at the University of Washington: "The capability of microelectronic technology continues to increase at decreased cost. To maintain low per-unit costs, development costs must be spread over broad markets that are not provided by biomedical laboratory automation and laboratory applications....Because of market considerations mentioned above, biomedical applications may not receive adequate consideration from commercial concerns designing new integrated circuits" (Biomedical Research Technology Resources, 1984).

The University of Washington facility has the objective of designing special circuits for relatively simple devices. The program description cites the development of "real-time on-line electrophysiological waveform discrimination." The facility also has VLSI design capabilities for very complex instruments "to improve in a practical way the accuracy of radiation treatment planning calculation" and "improved methods for collecting and analyzing time-of-flight positron emission tomography (PET) data" (Biomedical Research Technology Resources, 1984). Commercially available devices incorporate relatively powerful minicomputers in their systems for such tasks.

Despite the high cost of developing products that use specially designed chips, both technology and market conditions point to the expansion of application-specific integrated circuits (ASICs). According to Michael Schrage, a business reporter for *The Washington Post*, "ASICs represent the fastest growing segment of the troubled semiconductor business" (Schrage, 1986). Schrage cites Andrew Prophet, a semiconductor industry analyst, as noting that "prices for gate array custom chips have dropped to 10 percent of their prices a year ago." The fall in prices has come about because the design of custom chips has itself become automated. Several companies in the marketplace provide computer-aided design work stations for ASICs. Technological forces are once again providing automated, labor-saving ways to perform a tedious task.

Personal Computers

Whether they are built of commercially available chips or ASICs, microprocessor-based, stand-alone devices are not likely to have all the flexibility that their users would like. Another modern technology, the personal computer (PC) is likely to play a crucial role, especially in institutions in which it is important to the health practitioner that instrumental function can be modified and several functions can be integrated. Simply put, a PC can do anything a microprocessor-based device can do, but a PC can also be redirected to do something else by literally touching a single key at the terminal. Following a familiar pattern in technology, instrumentation engineers led the development in applying PCs to their designs. The journal *Electronic Design* recently devoted a special edition to PC-based instruments. Contributing editor Paul C. Schreier writes:

> When personal computer-based instruments surfaced a few years back, they were regarded as curiosities whose specification catered more to hobbyists than to professional engineers. But since then a remarkable thing has happened: Manufacturers, recognizing the tremendous possibilities, have cooked up add-on boards and boxes that transform the personal computer into a virtual instrument.
>
> Fitted with one or more of these boards or boxes, the personal computer suddenly becomes a digital storage scope, a spectrum or logic analyzer, a digital multimeter, a timer-counter, a function or signal generator, or an IEEE-488 instrument controller. It can replace multiple control panels, allowing users to conduct all I/O operations through the keyboard. And in multiple-instrument set-ups, system software can transfer data from the equipment to the host, which then displays all the key parameters on the screen simultaneously (Schreier, 1986).

It should be obvious, even to those who do not understand all the terminology used in this quotation, that what is being said of electronic measuring devices can be said of virtually all medical instrumentation. Only the special sensors need be added and they can be readily accommodated by the PC.

If a physician, laboratory technician, intensive care unit nurse, or clinical engineer has a home computer or has learned to use one, the opportunity to apply the same skill in the workplace is compelling. The PC profoundly changes the relationship between the user and the instrument; the "black box" loses its opacity because it is the software, understood and modified by the user, that controls the instrument or network of instruments.

Medical device companies are aware of this possibility. The preponderance of ads in *Medical Electronics and Equipment News* stress that the advertised device is a microcomputer or is microprocessor-based. The user's control of the operation is limited to the options prescribed by the manufacturer. Some advertisements accommodate the recent trend toward the incorporation of personal computers. Hewlett-Packard's low-priced Adult Patient Monitor features "an interface to a personal computer for data management" (MEEN, 1986b). The Navigator desk top electrodiagnostic system "combines a powerful IBM-PC compatible computer with advanced hardware and software" (MEEN, 1986a). The Plurimus Cardiac Evaluation System "combines the capability for sophisticated ECGs, annotated Holter evaluation and stress testing in one instrument." The economy of a single instrument versus three is said to make it a practical in-office system with the added benefit of a fully functional PC when it is not being used for cardiac evaluation (MEEN, 1986a).

Gould, a major electronics firm, claims that "the total solution to your measurement problems is here with the Gould 2000 W Recorder...with IEEE 488 and RS232C interfaces. [It] lets you interact with any computer system" or, if you prefer, "a totally integrated data acquisition that includes the 2000 W recorder, an IBM PC with keyboard, versatile software and color graphics display" (MEEN, 1986a).

Robotics

One of the latest microprocessor and computer developments to be applied to biomedical instrumentation is robotics. Laboratory robotics was introduced by the Zymark Corporation in 1983. The "Zymate" laboratory automation system is a microprocessor-controlled device for sample preparation. Lynn E. Wolfram, supervisor of the Analytical Sciences Laboratory at the Standard Oil of Ohio's Research and Development Center has described her group's experiences in a recent article (Wolfram, 1986). The tasks a robot must perform in a chemistry laboratory are likely to be much more complex than those required of an industrial robot that performs a single sequence of steps for months at a time. What is needed is a system that is versatile enough to be readily modified for many laboratory preparations and analyses. Laboratory robots therefore must be a complete system of automated (and usually microprocessor-based) devices controlled by a central computer, the robotic arm of which is only one of many parts. Dr. Wolfram writes, "The capability to reprogram the system quickly is an invaluable asset in applications requiring large numbers of samples and tests."

It is reasonable to anticipate rapid development in laboratory robotics. The costs are high; the Zymate mentioned above has a price of about $35,000. Therefore, only large, affluent laboratories are likely to experiment with their use. The Perkin-Elmer Corporation has recently entered the market. Their advertisement provides the following description, "The MasterLab System consists of a powerful IBM PC as system controller, a highly flexible 5-axis robot, robot electronics module, and communications interface. In addition, accessory modules are available for numerous applications. Part of what makes the MasterLab system so revolutionary is its amazing ease of use. PERL (Perkin-Elmer Robot Language) software is designed specifically for the analytical chemist: All you do is tell the robot what to do. In your own words. Then store your method on floppy disks. No computer expertise required. Ever." (Perkin-Elmer, 1986). Perhaps the claims of this advertisement are exaggerated, but even if a little expertise is actually required, the tool must be attractive to the analytical laboratory worker.

CONCLUSIONS

Only a detailed analysis beyond the scope of this discussion would enable one to make plausible predictions of the effect these new technologies are likely to have on health care costs. As a general rule, each stand-alone, black-box device is likely to be less costly than a flexible system, but a set of such devices would be much more expensive than a system that is capable of being modified to perform the individual functions when needed. After all, a personal computer that is capable of accommodating the flow of real-time electrical signals generated by most biomedically relevant sensors can be readily assembled out of parts that cost the hobbyist buyer about $2,000. A single PC can take the place of about a dozen of the data handlers built into stand-alone devices.

However, a number of difficult logistic, planning, and time-sharing problems should be taken into account by any facility that wants to exploit the personal computer option.

It is difficult to predict how far personal computers and networks will take over measurement and planning processes in health care systems, but it is safe to predict a growth in the number of PC-compatible devices, a growth in software-writing firms that specialize in biomedical problems, the enhanced development of networking the largely autonomous personal computer data stations, and the need for greater computer literacy among health care personnel.

REFERENCES

Anbar, M. "Penetrating the Black Box: Physical Principles Behind Health Care Technology," in Reiser, J.J. and Anbar, M., The Machine at the Bedside. Cambridge University Press, New York, 1984, pp. 23-34.

Anbar, M. Computer Assisted Clinical Decisions: Present Scope, Limitations, and Future. International Journal of Technology Assessment in Health Care, Vol. 2, pp. 168-176, 1986.

Biomedical Research Technology Resources (BRTR): A Research Resources Directory, NIH Publication No. 85-1430, Revised December 1984.

Li, C.- C. and Fu, K.S. "Machine-Assisted Pattern Classification in Medicine and Biology," Ann. Rev. Bioeng., Vol. 9, pp. 393-436, 1980.

Medical Electronics and Equipment News (MEENa), Vol. 26, No. 3, May/June 1986a.

Medical Electronics and Equipment News (MEENb), Vol. 26, No. 2, March/April 1986.

Perkin-Elmer advertisement, "For all the tasks you said a robot should do. The MasterLab System." Research and Development, p. 50, July 1986.

Reiser, J. J. and Anbar, M. "Introduction" in Reiser, J. J. and Anbar, M., Eds., the Machine at the Bedside. Cambridge University Press, New York, 1984, p. VII.

Schrage, M. "Some Experts Doubt U.S. Can Hold Edge in Specialty Chips," The Washington Post, Section D, Business, pp. 1-2, July 22, 1986.

Schreier, P.C. "PC-based Instruments Give Stand-alone Systems a Run for the Money," Electronic Design, pp. 104-118, March 13, 1986.

Tompkins, W.J. and Webster, J.G., Eds. Design of Microcomputer-Based Medical Instrumentation, Prentice-Hall, Inc., New Jersey, 1981.

Wolfram, Lynn E. "Lab Robot Prepares Analytical Samples," Research & Development, pp. 74-77, July 1986.

Wooten, C.K. and Corsey, R. "Microprocessor-Controlled Automatic Safety Testers", Journal of Clinical Engineering, pp. 241-244, July-September 1982.

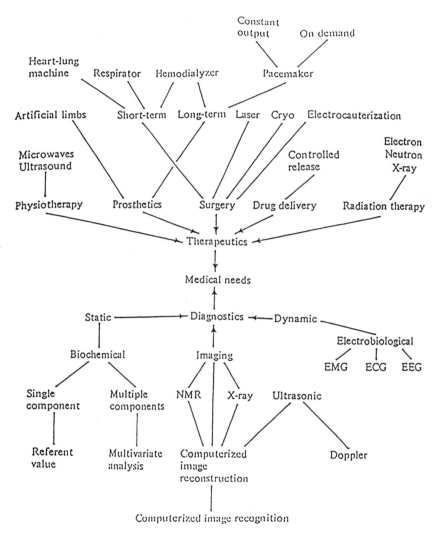

FIGURE 1 Technology networks that support diagnosis and therapy.

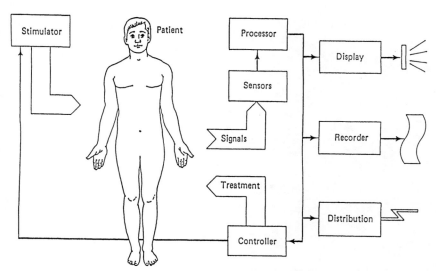

FIGURE 2 Components of a generalized medical instrument system.

16

A Distributed Processing Architecture for Real-Time Biological Data Analysis

PEDRO GUEDES DE OLIVEIRA, JOSÉ CARLOS PRÍNCIPE, and ANTÓNIO NUNES DE CRUZ

The analysis of biological signals involves the extraction of information contained in such features as waveforms and background from several channels of data. Humans perceive this information globally, but an automated system must process the same signals in a multichannel, multiobject basis and integrate the pieces in a later stage of processing.

Automated analysis is therefore oriented toward the detection and characterization of a selected catalogue of events in a single channel, such as waves or sets of waves in a signal whose peculiar shape, frequency, or amplitude may have a clinical meaning. Certain events acquire meaning only when information from several channels is confronted; several channels of data therefore must be analyzed concurrently.

This type of problem was first faced in a laboratory in which an electroencephalogram (EEG) was being studied. The signal of an EEG is intrinsically multichannelled (8 or 16 derivations should be analyzed), and it generates large amounts of data. It can be used in the study of several disorders like epilepsy and its petit mal variant or for sleep studies, all of which involve the detection of peculiar phasic events.

This framework establishes the strategy toward a two-step

procedure. A single-channel, single-object analysis called microanalysis is performed in the first step. This analysis is primarily self-contained, and it can achieve a prescreening of events to be supplied to the second step. It is in this first stage that real-time performance is most necessary.

In the second stage—the macroanalysis—interchannel relationships and the time connectivity of events are studied. This leads to the creation of new events or the rejection of events that seemed to be significant in the first step. A multiple microprocessor system called the Hierarchical Instrument for Distributed Real-Time Analysis (HIDRA) maps this strategy of analysis; it is depicted in Figure 1.

SYSTEM ARCHITECTURE

The HIDRA system is based on two buses that support a number of peripheral processors. The input bus connects a 16-channel, 12-bit analog/digital (A/D) converter to the preprocessor inputs. The 12-bit data are supplied together with a 4-bit flag for channel information and various strobe signals for different sampling rates. The common bus is the link between several preprocessors and the common memory. The common bus is a commercial standard (G64) and also supports the central unit (see Figure 2).

The peripheral units and the central unit communicate through a common mailbox memory; each preprocessor can in effect request the control of the bus and through it access the common memory for both reading and writing.

The central unit can also broadcast messages to the peripherals. An interrupt that is connected to all peripherals initiates a reading routine for a specific slot of common memory. Finally, the central unit is an 8-bit μcomputer, based on the Motorola 6809, with the usual input/output (I/O) and disk controller. The installed software ensures the macroanalysis as well as the housekeeping and user interface.

THE PREPROCESSOR

The preprocessors (Figure 3) were also built around the Motorola 6809. They are completely self-contained units with read-only and random-access memory (a total of 48 kilobytes), serial and parallel I/O ports, and two DACs that are used to supply analog versions of intermediate steps of signal analysis to the user. The preprocessors also contain the interfaces to the input and common buses; the former consists of an input latch and channel sampling rate decoder; the latter is a more complex unit. The subunit is depicted in Figure 4.

The daisy-chain arbiter is the access control to the common bus and was developed around the original proposal for G64 to which the provision of block transfer was added. Indivisible read, modify, and write operations and transfers of segments of data pertaining to the same analyzed object are enabled. A schematic drawing of the DMA controller is shown in Figure 5.

The latches allow each μcomputer performing real-time analysis to deposit the data targeted for transfer to the common memory in the local buffer without having to wait for access to the common bus. This is particularly convenient because the dominant flow of communications is from preprocessors to the central unit.

The result, however, is a more complex read operation that must be performed twice—first to put the address on the common bus and then to access the appropriate data.

CONCLUSIONS

This system has been used in the EEG analysis of sleep studies. The purpose of these studies, which are currently being performed in cooperation with clinical institutions, is to automatically assign a sleep stage to every minute of sleep according to the occurrence of certain elements (eight waveforms) in predefined derivations of the EEG. Each element of the microanalysis can be assigned to the detection and characterization of one type of event, and the macroanalysis to the global scoring.

The results thus far appear promising, but some developments are still being considered, namely at the level of the signal analysis algorithms and the global system software to provide general-purpose facilities to the user.

Finally, a dual-port memory to be used as a mailbox is being developed to provide a universal interface to other systems, such as an IBM PC. This would allow HIDRA to perform as a front-end system that feeds a general-purpose, easily available system.

REFERENCES

Binnie, C.D., Rowen, A.J., Overweg, J., Meinard, H., Wiskan, T., Kamp, A., and Lopes da Siva, F.H. "Telemetric EEG and Video Monitoring in Epilepsy." *Neurology* (Minneapolis), 1981, 31:298-303.

GESPAC - G64 and G96 Specifications Manual: Rev. 02, 1984. Guedes de Oliveira, P., Queiroc, C., and Lopes da Siva, F.H. *"Spike Detection Based on A Pattern Recognition Approach Using a Microcomputer."* Electroenceph. Clin. Neurophysiol., 1983, 97-103.

Principe, J.C. and Smith, J.R. "Automatic Recognition of Spike and Wave Bursts" in *Long Term Monitoring in Epilepsy*, ed. Gotman, Ives, and Gloor, Elsevier Science Publishers, 1985, 115-32.

Principe, J.C. and Smith, J.R. "Sleep Analyzer Microcomputer System- SAMICOS" in *Proceedings IEEE of Biomedical Engineering*, September 1986.

Smith, Jr. "Computers and Sleep Research" *Critical Reviews of Bioengineering*, CRC Press, Dec. 1978, 93-148.

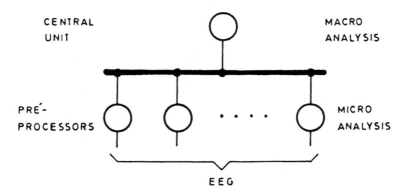

FIGURE 1   A multiple microprocessor system

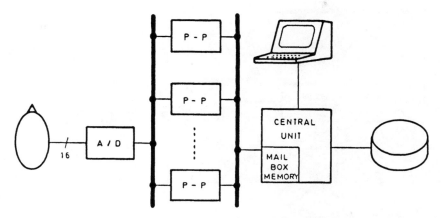

FIGURE 2 The common bus is the link between several preprocessors and the common memory.

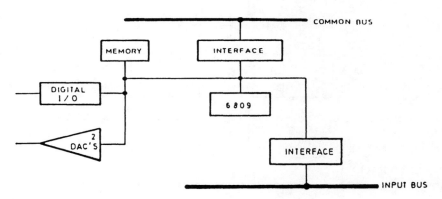

FIGURE 3 The preprocessor system.

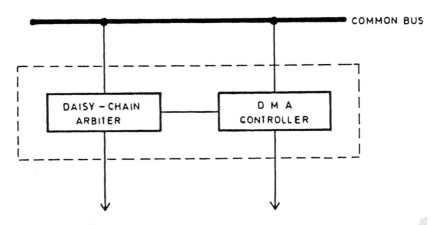

FIGURE 4 The common bus interface.

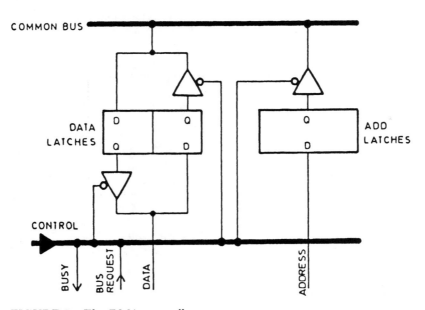

FIGURE 5 The DMA controller.

17

Natural Resource Analysis, Assessment, and Management

T. M. ALBERT

A natural resource, in a broad sense, is anything found by man in his natural environment. Resources provided by nature include rocks that contain mineral ores, energy sources, and other useful products. Also included in this category are soils, plant and animal life, elements of the landscape, surface and underground water, and the air and atmosphere. Although all elements of the natural environment can generally be regarded as natural resources, it is convenient to restrict this concept to those elements which at a given time in our stage of development have a potential use or value.

Two fundamentally different types of natural resources can be delineated: products such as minerals, oil, forests, and fish, and amenities or situations such as harbors and scenic mountains. Both types of resources are economically useful to man. Resources can be further classified as either renewable (water and forests) or nonrenewable (minerals).

The rational use of natural resources, preceded by their inventory and survey, is the basis for every country's development. The importance of natural resources in relation to development is recognized in developing countries. Together with human resources, natural resources constitute the principal economic asset of developing countries.

Countries with high standards of living usually have ample natural resources that they have put to good use. Some countries with low standards of living are held back by their lack of adequate natural resources, but low standards of living persist in many developing countries despite the existence of adequate if not abundant potentially valuable natural resources. One of the major tasks facing developing countries is to make better use of natural resources and to organize the development and productive exploitation of such resources in the interest of the entire community.

Of prime importance in developing countries is to determine which natural resources exist, evaluate them, and choose the most efficient way of using them. Furthermore, various natural resources are not independent of each other. Any changes introduced to one resource can have repercussions on another, and can affect the environment and the country's current and future economic wellbeing.

As computer technology has progressed, powerful methods have been developed to analyze various specific aspects of natural resources. Models have often involved several parameters that relate to diverse conditions. With the advent and proliferation of expert system techniques and their implementation on microcomputers, powerful and relatively inexpensive methods now exist to address even more complicated models that involve many diverse data sets and conditions. The use of these new methods must be encouraged.

ARTIFICIAL INTELLIGENCE

Artificial intelligence (AI) is the part of computer science that is concerned with the design of computer systems that exhibit characteristics associated with intelligence in human behavior, such as understanding languages, learning, reasoning, solving problems, and so forth. The term artificial intelligence originated in a 1956 conference at Dartmouth College. John McCarthy coined the term at the conference while discussing ways to simulate human intelligence and behavior through the use of computers. Early work in the field focused on the construction of general-purpose intelligent systems. A fundamental shift in direction occurred in the 1960s. Today the emphasis is on the role of specific and detailed knowledge rather than on reasoning methods. Several technologies or disciplines have become viable as a result of this emphasis and various products have reached the marketplace, including machine vision, robotics, natural language, and expert systems. Because this paper concerns natural resource assessment, only expert systems that are currently being used with some success and promise in this area will be discussed.

An expert system is a computer system that is designed to simulate the problem-solving behavior of a human who is an expert in a narrow domain. Dr. Adrian Walker of IBM's Research Division recently summarized (Walker, 1986) what an expert system should do:

- Solve an important problem that would otherwise have to be solved by a human expert;
- Be flexible in integrating new knowledge incrementally into its existing store of knowledge;
- Be able to demonstrate its knowledge in a form that is easy to read;
- Provide explanations of its advice;
- Be able to reason with judgmental or inexact knowledge about the nature of a task or how to perform the task efficiently; and
- Be able to deal with simple sentences in English or another natural language.

Three basic methodologies support the complex task of storing human knowledge in an expert system: frames, rules, and logic. Frames involve an object-centered view of knowledge representation whereby all knowledge is partitioned into discrete structures (frames) that have individual properties (slots). Rules involve structures to construct a knowledge base that consists of production rules that use "if" conditions and "then" conclusions and "if" conditions and "then" actions. Logic involves the use of predicate calculus; unlike traditional programming, which emphasizes "how" computations are performed, logic programming focuses on the "what" of objects and their behavior. The bulk of expert systems in use today involves the rule methodology.

In addition to facts and knowledge, a typical expert system also requires a domain expert and a knowledge engineer. However, an increasing number of products are currently available, called expert system shells, which come with empty knowledge bases. In this case, the system prompts and questions applications specialists and domain experts with little training in expert systems to program their own applications and input the necessary expertise. In the natural resource areas, a combination of existing, extensive detailed facts (possibly resulting from surveys), coupled with the expert system shell structure, makes for a productive approach.

Many software or expert system development tools are currently available for large computers. Even more expert systems and shells are being developed for personal microcomputers. These range in price from $50 to $1,500. The more expensive systems allow the use of a greater number of production rules. Table 1, from the spring 1986 issue of *IEEE Expert*, is a sample list of such tools. Increasingly better expert system tools are being built, but a word of caution must be noted regarding their limitations and reliability. They are limited by the information in their data and knowledge bases and by the nature of the process for entering the information. They cannot produce conclusions that are not already in their data base. Yet, with care and continual checking for reliability, they can be extremely useful analysis and decision-making tools.

The relatively low costs involved for the software and microcomputers, the ease of use and minimal training needed, and the ability to deal with increasingly larger and more diverse data sets make this technology valuable in the areas of resource analysis, assessment, and management in developing countries. Although they are not currently in extensive use, their obvious benefits in such areas as decision-making in resource management should accelerate their use.

MICROCOMPUTERS

Microcomputers are inexpensive, easy to use, and are becoming increasingly capable and powerful with greater data storage capacity. These factors, coupled with the power of expert systems and expert system shells, make microcomputers one of the most useful tools ever available to manage natural resources in developing countries. This is not only true at the national level, but also at the local village, association, and personal levels.

Low-cost AI or LISP computers are now being marketed. Such computers are almost in the microcomputer class and are designed to run the LISP programming language quickly and efficiently.

This is because LISP (the language of AI in the United States) is being implemented in firmware. Such machines will make expert systems and other AI applications much easier to implement and will improve the results obtained with such systems. As the number of rules and frames that researchers and application specialists use increases, the additional capability being offered by the LISP machines will be needed. A LISP chip and two graphic chips are also about to be marketed. The use of these chips in microcomputers will greatly enhance their capability and in many cases provide the power needed by many users for some time to come.

THE PROBLEMS OF NATURAL RESOURCE DATA

Natural resource data can generally be characterized as scientific, technical, and to some extent economic in nature; highly diverse in type and structure; and involving increasingly large volumes of detail. Individual scientists and technicians collect and structure data in a variety of ways, which emphasizes the problem of the lack of standards in naming, defining, and formatting. This results in incompatibility between data sets and difficulty in the transfer and exchange of data. The incompatibility also increases the difficulties and costs of utilizing diverse data sets together in a single model or in multidisciplinary analysis. Because the use of expert systems also requires the use of carefully digitized and reasonably reliable data, the collection, storage, dissemination, and management of natural resource data becomes a real problem. These seemingly mundane problems are often ignored in favor of the excitement and glamour of new computer hardware and software.

In the developed countries where much data has already been collected, the problem of how to deal with the data sets is receiving greater attention. Efforts to develop data standards are on the rise at the federal level, in the private sector, and in professional organizations. Other efforts concern improved data base management systems, computer operating systems that can interface with each other, common communication protocols, and common application systems that can call and handle diverse data.

In developing countries where the amount of collected data may not be as large, near-term opportunities may exist in natural resource data management, which will make the tasks of computer analysis, assessment, and management much easier, less expensive, and more comprehensive.

In regard to data sources, on-site information is collected from various surveys; satellite imagery, remote-sensed data, and maps are also major sources of data. A careful, continuing program of data digitization is necessary, as is the maintenance of a properly indexed catalog or inventory of data.

The storage and dissemination of data, particularly digitized data, becomes a problem. Communication systems may not be the best, so data sets should be carefully packed to support computer analysis on microcomputers. Magnetic storage was formerly used in support of computers, but laser optical disk storage now promises to become an important and useful tool.

Of particular interest in natural resource data sets is the use of compact disks with read-only memory (CD-ROM). The disks range from 3 1/2 in. to 5 1/4 in. in diameter and can currently contain up to 500 million bytes of storage. The disks are mastered once (for $2,000 to $5,000, but the cost is decreasing), but copies can be pressed and sold for as little as $10. The data and the disks are essentially permanent. The disks require no environmental controls and can be easily handled and sent through the mail. Reader interfaces for microcomputers are dropping in price and now cost about $200. The technology is new, but it is rapidly growing. The data from the CD-ROM would provide historical detail and can be utilized together with magnetic data input. This is only one way in which data handling can be improved.

Another important concern is the need to disseminate pertinent natural resource data and results to the scientists, technicians, and managers who will be using it. The more data available, the better the analysis; the more data available to more users, the better its reliability can be checked; and the more data available for resource assessment and analysis, the easier it is to establish an integrated country-wide plan to improve the development and use of natural resources.

The following is a sample list of the types of data found to be useful in resource analysis in the United States:

Aerial Photography	Aftershock Studies
Margin Coring Projects	Biological Analysis of
Borehole Data	Water Samples
Geophysics and Geochemistry	Carbon Content Analyses

Rangeland Classification	Geothermal Resources
Crop Analyses	Soil Analyses
Hydrogeology	Landsat Images
Water Quality	Land Use/Land Cover Data
Coal and Oil Resource Data	Maine Seismology
Earthquake Information	Digital Cartography
Paleomagnetic Data	Oil Spill Analysis
Well History	Mine Production Detail
Reservoir Files	Radiometric Age Data
Aquifer Detail	Stratigraphic Data
Irrigation and Water Use Data	Ground Water and Surface Water Resources

EXPERT SYSTEM APPLICATIONS

Natural resource management, analysis, and assessment appear to be areas in which expert systems can be used advantageously. Applications are increasing both in technical analysis and in financial and production areas.

The PROSPECTOR System

PROSPECTOR is a computer-based expert consultant system for mineral exploration and resource favorability assessment. It is intended to support geologists in evaluating the mineral potential of an exploration site or region. It was developed in the late 1970s at SRI International in Menlo Park, California, in conjunction with staff members of the U.S. Geological Survey and private consultants.

The basic idea behind PROSPECTOR is to encode ore deposit models developed by expert economic geologists in a form that allows the models to be systematically interpreted by a computer program for various purposes. Rule-based techniques were used to encode experts' knowledge of the associations between field-observable evidence and relevant hypotheses. The associations form inference networks that describe the judgmental reasoning process used by the expert to solve problems related to mineral exploration. In the early 1980s, SRI made changes and enhancements to the system. Menu choices have been added that include multiple-choice questions (see Table 2). A new format for specifying variable strength rules and the use of certainty measures to express rule strength has also been added.

The system is designed to conduct a dialogue with a geologist who has information about the general geologic setting of an area or a particular site. In a typical session, the geologist begins by entering information on existing rock types and minerals. The program matches the information against its models, requests additional information of value for making more definite conclusions, and summarizes its findings. If requested, it can provide an explanation of its reasoning in as much detail as the user desires. The PROSPECTOR system is also capable of providing additional information on the purpose of any question it poses to the user and, if further requested, the geological significance of the question.

There are currently more than 30 deposit models in PROSPECTOR with varying numbers of rules. The strategy in rule selection during the session is goal-oriented. The system reasons backward from an initial goal. A goal is achieved by applying the directly relevant rules. The need to establish the premises of those rules identifies new subgoals that are treated in the same way.

An important issue in the development of expert systems such as PROSPECTOR is to determine how expert they really are. In several different evaluations, PROSPECTOR demonstrated an ability to perform at or near the level of expert economic geologists. In one test that involved an area under exploration, the system accurately identified the location and extent of ore-grade mineralization of a previously unknown portion of a porphyry molybdenum deposit. The PROSPECTOR system requires at least a substantial minicomputer to operate. Dr. Richard McCammon of the U.S. Geological Survey is currently writing a version of PROSPECTOR to operate on a small AI or LISP computer. However, a microcomputer-based version called muPROSPECTOR was recently implemented to evaluate the mineral resources in a given geographic area. In a session with muPROSPECTOR, the geologist responds to yes/no questions. The system makes an evaluation by matching the yes/no responses with its models and summarizing its findings (see Table 3). The geologist can also add to the knowledge base. Although it lacks rule strength and other features of PROSPECTOR, muPROSPECTOR offers a low-cost entry to computer-based consultant systems. About

20 models have been developed for muPROSPECTOR (see Table 4). Although it is not microcomputer-based, an extension of PROSPECTOR has been developed by SRI International called HYDRO; it is used for problems that relate to regional water resources. Whereas PROSPECTOR is restricted to evaluating the certainty of fixed hypotheses, HYDRO encodes judgmental expertise about problems that require the computation of numeric quantities.

The muPETROL System

A prototype expert system called muPETROL has been developed to help classify and assess the petroleum resources of the world's sedimentary basins. This is the first step toward expanding muPETROL to provide an integrated expert systems approach to estimating undiscovered petroleum resources worldwide. The muPETROL system was patterned after PROSPECTOR.

Much of the early work with muPETROL has been concerned with the development of models of sedimentary basins. The system developer, Betty M. Miller of the U.S. Geological Survey, has been working with H.D. Klemme to develop the models. Klemme's world basin classification system was used. The scheme differentiates nine major basin types by their geologic frameworks and tectonic settings relative to petroleum occurrences.

The models in muPETROL are represented by inference networks that relate geologic observations. These networks are used to infer the likelihood of the occurrence of a particular basin type on the basis of the combined presence or absence of a set of geological attributes. The system is rule-based and directs a series of questions to the user that relate to the geologic base, and tectonic and depositional concepts relative to each of the basin models. Questions are answered by a "yes," "no," or "don't know." The prototype system cannot yet accept numeric answers.

The user can also request the system to print a rephrased version of the question, explain the question, access a data base to assist in answering the question, or print a summary and evaluation to that point in the analysis. The basin models are being refined to include the use of rule strengths and certainty factors that are essential when dealing with incomplete, interpretive, and uncertain data.

Experience with the prototype is encouraging and critical to the long-term objectives, which will provide for complete basin analyses to be used as inputs to a selection of petroleum resource appraisal methods for calculating the remaining undiscovered petroleum resources in a basin.

The GEOLEARN System

The GEOLEARN system developed by Meribeth Bruntz and Lynn B. Fischer of the U.S. Geological Survey is a knowledge-based system written in the LISP computer language and implemented on an IBM PC. The system uses a knowledge base that incorporates specific geologic models and a knowledge interpreter or inference engine. The knowledge base is a network representation of the domain knowledge and the knowledge interpreter is structured hierarchically. The system was developed to help a geology student learn. Although it is not strictly a sophisticated expert system, its structure and methods are similar to one. The GEOLEARN system was constructed with a knowledge of basic concepts involved in the interpretation of uranium-lead isotopic data. The system can work just as well with other knowledge bases.

The GEOLEARN system is interactive and helps a student develop interpretive skills. The major emphasis of the tutorial using CONCORDIA was to demonstrate to the student the importance of incorporating geologic constraints in the interpretation of isotope data. The system queries the student for specific information and allows for backtracking to any query in order to reevaluate it and proceed with a different mode of reasoning.

The Dipmeter Advisor System

The Dipmeter Advisor System is an expert system that was developed by Schlumberger-Doll Research and used by the parent company, Schlumberger, in a number of their Field Log Interpretation Centers. Oil well logs are made by lowering logging tools into the borehole and recording the measurements made by the tools as they are raised to the surface. Logging tools measure a number of petrophysical properties; the dipmeter tool measures the conductivity of rock in a number of directions around the borehole. Variations in conductivity can be correlated and combined with measurements of the inclination and orientation of the tool to estimate the magnitude and azimuth of the dip or tilt of various formation layers penetrated by the borehole.

The Dipmeter Advisor System attempts to emulate human expert performance in dipmeter interpretation. It utilizes dipmeter patterns together with local geological knowledge and measurements from other logs. The four central components of the system are (1) a number of production rules that are partitioned into several distinct sets according to their function; (2) an inference engine that applies rules in a forward chained manner and resolves conflicts by rule order; (3) a set of pattern detection algorithms; and (4) a menu-driven graphical user interface. Conclusions are stored as instances of 1 of 65 token types. The user can override conclusions after each subtask has been completed, and can examine, delete, or modify conclusions. The user's conclusions can be added, earlier stages of analysis can be returned to, and computations can be rerun. Much effort has been put into the provision of data displays that can be easily tailored. Before each subtask, the user is presented with a portion of the parameter knowledge base that will be used in the subtask. The user can examine current values, request descriptions of the parameters, and alter the values. The system has been used successfully and is being extended and modified as experience is gained.

Other Application Areas

Katherine Krystinik of the U.S. Geological Survey has developed a rule-based Example Expert System for Computer Interpretation of Depositional Environments. The system was constructed using the Knowledge Acquisition System (KAS) developed by SRI International. Krystinik and H. Edward Clifton have also developed an expert system for the computer interpretation of beach and near-shore facies using the same methodology.

The U.S. Geological Survey has only begun to develop and apply expert systems. The opportunities and benefits that can be expected in the natural resource areas are tremendous. Lengthy discussions have resulted in suggestions for the use of expert systems in many directions, including the following:

- Cartographic digitization;
- Interpretation of mass spectral data;
- The positioning of hydrology instrumentation;

- Ground water toxicology;
- Aquifer test interpretations;
- Log and geochemical environment analysis;
- Project management;
- Production analysis;
- Image-processing routines;
- Seismic interpretations;
- Acid rain analysis; and
- Mineral resource exploration.

GEOGRAPHIC INFORMATION SYSTEMS IN RESOURCE ASSESSMENT

In its simplest form, a geographic information system (GIS) can be viewed as a data base management system in which most of the data is spatial in nature and is spatially indexed, and upon which sets of procedures operate to structure the input and output and to answer queries about spatial entities represented in the data base. Experience suggests that the following general requirements should be satisfied in the design and implementation of most GISs:

- An ability to handle large, multilayered, and heterogeneous data bases of spatially indexed data;
- An ability to query such data bases about the existence, location, and properties of a wide range of spatial objects;
- Efficiency in handling such queries that permits the system to be interactive; and
- Flexibility in configuring the system to permit the system to be easily tailored to accommodate a variety of specific applications and users.

Effective GISs are composed of a comprehensive menu of capabilities for the entry, analysis, display, and management of geographic (spatially oriented) data. In relation to natural resource analysis and management, GISs provide an extremely powerful tool to manipulate diverse, spatially oriented data sets in combination. Multiple layers of data can be dealt with, such as surface and subsurface geology, stream flow, drainage, ground water, elevation, slope, planemetric data, and remote-sensed data. The results of queries that involve multiple data sets can be displayed graphically.

Because of the complexity of such systems, large minicomputers, at least, have been necessary to utilize them. However, with the advent of more powerful microcomputers, the GIS software is being reworked to allow its use in smaller equipment. The U.S. Geological Survey and many other organizations in the United States find such systems to be of great value.

Given the accepted value of geographic information systems, different groups have begun to involve AI techniques in the GIS's vision, pattern analysis, expert systems, and knowledge representation.

A Knowledge-based Geographic Information System

The U.S. Geological Survey has had a knowledge-based geographic information system (KBGIS) under development for more than 3 years. The research and development has been performed at the University of California, Santa Barbara. The work was begun because a very large store of earth science data of all types is constantly growing; many diverse data sets are incompatible; and more sophisticated, multidisciplinary analysis is needed. The solution to these problems involved the use of AI and GIS technology. Using the concepts of knowledge representation, a new method was developed to structure spatial data. Because it would be too expensive and time-consuming to build an in-depth expert system for each discipline, only high-level expert system rules are used. The system is designed to learn by itself by interacting with users and to retain the knowledge gained. Considering the large data sets involved, fast search methods were developed. The KBGIS architecture is shown in Figure 1.

The system has been demonstrated successfully and development and application will continue. It is now a prototype of a general-purpose intelligent data handling system that can process raster and vector data as well as remote-sensed data and other types of information. In its present form, KBGIS is a research module that needs adjustment, adaptation, and application. It also requires a super or larger minicomputer for operations; a LISP machine would be even better. However, microcomputers are becoming more powerful and LISP chips and graphics chips are being developed; as KBGIS matures, it will be adapted for powerful microcomputers.

ACCEPTANCE, UTILIZATION, AND IMPLEMENTATION OF ANALYSIS AND ASSESSMENT RESULTS

During professional meetings in the natural resources and environmental fields, a certain frustration often exists on the part of the speakers concerning the acceptance of their computer analyses and results by politicians, policy makers, and managers. Acceptance in this case means that recommended actions are implemented. This attitude may be even more pronounced in developing countries because the technologies involved are used less than in developed countries. The result is that there is less understanding of the processes involved. This is noted because the acceptance of reliable analysis and assessment is important to the further development of technology, improvement of methods, and benefits to the population. New areas of work, particularly AI in microcomputers, may be accepted even less.

It is therefore recommended that the scientist or technician bring the policy makers and managers into the system's planning process at an early stage to improve their understanding. It is also recommended that orientation talks and training programs be instituted and performed on a regular basis to appropriate audiences, including students. Cooperative projects that involve different in-country groups and groups from other countries would also be beneficial to all concerned.

For example, a village's analysis of its water supply and quality would benefit from the participation of several villages or associations in a region. The acceptance of assessments in regard to the environmental effects of new mineral recovery operations might benefit from the participation of several in-country constituencies and one or two from other countries.

SUMMARY

Three topics have been covered briefly: (1) the exploding growth and development of microcomputers; (2) the exploding growth, development, and utilization of AI methods; and (3) the combined use of these two technologies in the development and most efficient utilization of natural resources. Microcomputers are becoming more powerful with a greater capability at a relatively low cost. Artificial intelligence in the form of expert systems and expert system shells provides powerful assessment, analysis, and management tools. Expert system shells are relatively inexpensive and more and more applications are being developed.

The use and great benefit of such tools in regard to the management of natural resources is constantly being demonstrated. The problem of data collection, storage, and handling has not yet been solved. Careful approaches to the data problem are necessary because of the increasing need for multidisciplinary analysis and the transfer and exchange of data and results. Finally, the combination of AI and GIS technology has been discussed in relation to the importance of a KBGI tool in the future. With so many developments and advances currently taking place, we will all benefit by maintaining a dialogue and continuing to exchange information and ideas.

REFERENCES

Bruntz, M. and Fischer, L.B. A Knowledge-Based Design for Geologic Learning Systems, U.S. Geological Survey Open-File Report 86-290, February 1986.

Denning, P.J. Towards a Science of Expert Systems, IEEE Expert, Vol. 1, No. 2, pp. 80 - 83, Summer 1986.

Friedland, P. Introduction to Special Section on Architectures for Knowledge-Based Systems. Communications of the ACM, Vol. 28, No. 9, pp. 902 - 903, September 1985.

Gaschnig, J. Development of Uranium Exploration Models for the PROSPECTOR Consultant System, SRI Project 7856 for the U.S. Geological Survey, SRI International, March 1980.

Krystinik, K. An Example Expert System for the Interpretation of Depositional Environments, U.S. Geological Survey Open-File Report 85-30, 1985.

McCammon, R.B. Recent Developments in PROSPECTOR and Future Expert Systems in Regional Resource Evaluation, IEEE Proceedings of the 9th Pecora Symposium, Spatial Information Technologies for Remote Sensing Today and Tomorrow, Sioux Falls, South Dakota, 1984.

McCammon, R. B., Boudette, E.L., Cameron, C., Cox, L.J., and Moench, R.H. An Expert System for Mineral Resource Assessment in the Sherbrooke-Lewiston 1° × 2° Quadrangles, Maine, New Hampshire, and Vermont, U.S. Geological Survey Open-File Report 84-751, 1984.

Miller, B. M. Building an Expert System helps Classify Sedimentary Basins and Assess Petroleum Resources, Geobyte, Vol. 1, No. 2. pp. 44 - 50, 83 - 84, Spring 1986.

Montana Agricultural Experiment Station, Montana State University, National Resources Inventory Check List, Research Report 50, February 1974.

Munasinghe, M., Dow, M., and Fritz, J. Microcomputers for Development Issues and Policies, Proceedings of the First International Symposium on Microcomputer Applications in Developing Countries, June 1985.

Myers, W. Introduction to Expert Systems, IEEE Expert, Vol. 1, No. 1, pp. 100 - 109.

Reboh, R. and Reiter, J. A Knowledge-Based System for Regional Mineral Resource Assessment, SRI Project 4119 for the U.S. Geological Survey, SRI International, February 1983.

Smith, R. and Young, R.L. The Design of the Dipmeter Advisor System, Research Note Preprint, Schlumberger-Doll Research, Project SYS-009, September 1984.

Smith, R. On the Development of Commercial Expert Systems, The AI Magazine, Vol. V, No. 3, p. 61 - 73, Fall 1984.

Smith, T., Peuquet, D., Menon, S., and Agarwal, P. KBGIS-II: A Knowledge-Based Geographic Information System, University of California, Santa Barbara, Department of Computer Science, May 1986.

Suydam, W.E. AI Becomes the Soul of the New Machines, Computer Design, Vol. 25, No. 4, pp. 55 - 70, February 1986.

United Nations, Natural Resources of Developing Countries: Investigation, Development and Rational Utilization, Report of the Advisory Committee on the Application of Science and Technology to Development, 1970.

Walker, A. Knowledge Systems: Principles and Practice, IBM Journal of Research and Development, Vol. 30, No. 1, January 1986.

TABLE 1 Tools for Personal Computers

ESP Advisor from Expert Systems International, King of Prussia, Pennsylvania, runs on MS-DOS 2.0 with 256 kilobytes of memory. $895.

ExpertOPS5 was implemented by Science Applications International Corporation for ExperTelligence of Santa Barbara, California. The original OPS5 was created at Carnegie Mellon University. The current version, said by the company to be "a complete implementation," operates on a Macintosh 512 kilobytes with ExperLisp and an add-on floppy or hard-disk drive. $195.

Expert-Ease was developed by Jeffrey Perrone & Associates, Inc., San Francisco. It is written in Pascal and runs on IBM PCs and compatibles, DEC, and Victor. Perrone says that the tool enables users to produce "models" of processes that require specialized knowledge or skills. Models have been developed for property purchasing decisions, trouble-shooting, logic design analyses, preliminary diagnoses of dental pain, assistance in building code compliance, expense claims and analyses, and disciplinary action recommendations. Perrone notes that some might not consider these to be "true" expert systems. $700.

Exsys from Exsys, Inc., Albuquerque, New Mexico, accommodates up to 400 rules with 128 kilobytes of memory or 3,000 rules with 640 kilobytes. The large version runs on MS-DOS 2.0. $200.

Insight 2 is a product from Level 5 Research, Melbourne, Florida, that runs on IBM, DEC, and Victor personal computers with 192 kilobytes of memory. $495.

KDS from KDS Corporation, Wilmette, Illinois, allows for up to 16,000 rules per knowledge module. The development system requires 256 kilobytes, MS-DOS 2.0. $795.

Knowledge Workbench is based on Silog, a proprietary extension of Prolog, and comes from Silogic Inc. of Los Angeles. The system incorporates not only a knowledge-base manager and inference engine, but a natural-language interface. It is being designed to run on MC68000-based personal computers.

M.1 and M.1a are Prolog versions of Teknowledge's microcomputer tool. Both operate under MS-DOS 2.0. The M.1a version is an evaluation subset of M.1 that contains the basic features and sufficient power to develop a proof-of-concept system. M.1: $10,000; M.1a: $2,000.

Last October Teknowledge announced the conversion of M.1

to C. Rule capacity has been expanded from 200 to 1,000. Performance has improved four or five times over the original Prolog product. The Version 2 development system is priced at $5,000 and the delivery version at $500 per copy.

MicroExpert is a product of McGraw-Hill Book Co., New York. It requires 128 kilobytes and MS-DOS 2.0. $50.

Micro KES is the personal computer version of KES. It is implemented in IQLisp for the IBM PC-XT with 640 kilobytes. Software A&E says that it is functionally equivalent to KES running on a Vax, but its performance is comparable to KES on a heavily loaded Vax. Development on a personal computer is therefore difficult, but execution is believed to be adequate. $4,000.

NaturalLink Technology Package is a 1985 release from Texas Instruments for its Professional Computer. It enables a programmer to construct English sentences that the underlying application program recognizes as commands. The ultimate user constructs an input sentence not by typing, but by selecting words and phrases from lists of choices displayed in menus. $1,500.

Personal Consultant is a Texas Instruments product that runs on its Professional Computer and is compatible with PC-DOS software products. It requires at least 512 kilobytes. A user can develop an expert system of up to 400 rules using the Professional Computer. On a larger computer with a greater capacity, such as Texas Instruments' Explorer, a user can go up to more than 1,000 production rules and then run the developed system on the Professional Computer. $3,000.

RuleMaster is available from Radian Corporation, Austin, Texas. It runs under MS-DOS 3.0 on the IBM PC-XT or under Xenix on the IBM PC-AT; it requires 600 kilobytes. $5,000 to $15,000.

TIMM-PC–The Intelligent Machine Model–is supplied by General Research Corporation, McLean, Virginia. It runs on MS-DOS 2.0 with 640 kilobytes. $9,500 for the first license, less in quantity.

TABLE 2 Menu Construct

Establishing the nature of historic deposits in the region.
For which of the following do you have any information
(positive or negative):
1) fluorine
2) molybdenum
3) tungsten
4) beryllium
5) precious metals

Please type one or more of the preceding numbers
(separated by blanks): ?

[By responding with "?", the user asks for a rephrasing of the question and a list of the possible answers.]

Mines, prospects, and anomalous concentrations of valuable minerals and metals are extremely useful in judging the types of mineral deposits likely to occur within the region. To what degree do you believe that these types of deposits are present?
Legal answers are:

1. ALL [If the user has information about all choices.]
2. DISP [If the user wishes to redisplay the choices.]
3. NONE [If the user has no information about any of the choices.]
4. A list of option numbers from 1 to 5, or 0 (for NONE) [If the user wishes to provide information about a subset of the choices.]
5. A PROSPECTOR-command.

Type "?? n" for more information about Option n.
Please type one or more of the preceding numbers
(separated by blanks): *1 3 5*

14. To what degree do you believe that there are fluorine deposits in the region?-*5* [The user is sure fluorine deposits are present.]
15. To what degree do you believe that there are tungsten deposits in the region?-*4* [The user is fairly sure tungsten deposits are NOT present.]

TABLE 3

Portion of a Sample Session with muPROSPECTOR

3-ARE THE ROCKS CONSIDERED TO BE SYNOROGENIC (Y/N/?): *N*

4-ARE THE ROCKS INDICATIVE OF A RIFT ENVIRONMENT (Y/N/?): *?*

Rifts environments are indicated by tholeiitic volcanism, floor basalts, normal faulting, or 120 degree rift patterns with failed arm.

4-ARE THE ROCKS INDICATIVE OF A RIFT ENVIRONMENT (Y/N/?):*Y*

5-ARE THE ROCKS FLOWS OR SHALLOW INTRUSIVES (Y/N/?): *A*
I don't understand, please reenter.

6-IS THERE EVIDENCE EITHER OF AN EXTERNAL SULFUR SOURCE OR OF FAULTING (Y/N/?): *?*
It is necessary to establish the possibility of an external source of sulfur if the rocks are to be considered favorable.

7-IS THERE EVIDENCE EITHER OF AN EXTERNAL SULFUR SOURCE OR OF FAULTING (Y/N/?): *Y*

Based on your answers the potential for ultramafic deposits in the area is as follows:

Potential exists for deposits similar to Norilsk deposits in the USSR.

The favorable factors in order of importance are:

NO ROCKS INDICATIVE OF A STABLE PETRO-TECTONIC ENVIRONMENT

NO ROCKS CONSIDERED TO BE SYNOROGENIC

ROCKS INDICATIVE OF A RIFT ENVIRONMENT

ROCKS FLOWS OR SHALLOW INTRUSIVES

EVIDENCE EITHER OF AN EXTERNAL SULFUR SOURCE OR OF FAULTING

DO YOU WANT MORE INFORMATION (y/n/?): Y

These deposits contain Cu-Ni-PGE with byproduct Co, Au, Ag, Se, and Te.

The ores occur as high-grade lenses in the basal layer and as disseminations in the intrusives. Grades are up to 1.3 percent Ni, 2.2 percent Cu, 0.1 percent Co, and 3.8 g/t Pt.

TABLE 4 List of muPROSPECTOR Models

Model Description
1. Ni-Cr bearing laterite or placer PGE concentrate type
2. Tholeiitic Cu-Ni bearing massive sulfide type as found at Pechenga, USSR and Peura-Aho, Finland
3. Komatiitic archean greenstone Cu-Ni hearing massive sulfide type as found at Kambalda, Australia
4. Komatiitic Proterozoic Cu-Ni bearing massive sulfide type as found at Skelletea, Sweden and Thompson, Manitoba, Canada.
5. Rift-related plutonic Cu-Ni bearing sulfide type as found at Duluth, Minnesota
6. Rift-related shallow instrusive to extrusive Cu-Ni-PGE bearing sulfide type as found at Norilsk, USSR
7. Titaniferous magnetite PGE bearing sulfides of the Alaskan-zoned complex type as found at Gusevorgorsk, Urals, USSR
8. PGE bearing sulfides of the Alaskan-zoned complex type as found in the Urals, USSR.
9. Synorogenic intrusion Cu-Ni bearing sulfide type as found at Kvikne, Norway and Moxie, Maine.
10. Massive sulfide type as found in Cyprus.
11. Podiform chromite type as found in Cyprus, the Philippines, New Caledonia, and Turkey.
12. Serpentinized podiform chromite type as found in Bouazza, Morocco, Cyprus, and the Kalmiopsis area, Oregon.
13. Ophiloitic vanadiferous magnetite type.
14. Ni-Cu bearing layered intrusion of the Sudbury type.
15. Cu-Ni bearing layered intrusion of the type found in the basal zone of the Stillwater Complex.
16. Chromite-bearing layered intrusion of the type found in the lower intermediate zone in the Stillwater Complex and the Bushveld Complex.
17. PGE bearing layered intrusion of the type found in the upper intermediate zone of the Stillwater Complex and the Merensky Reef in the Bushveld complex.

18

Geographic Information Systems
VINCENT B. ROBINSON

Geographic information systems (GISs) are becoming more commonplace throughout the world. Geographic information system technology has consistently been identified as one of the significant methodologies for economic and urban development, human settlements planning (Coiner et al., 1983), rural development, resource inventory and evaluation (Schultink, 1984), and early warning and crop production forecasting (Paul et al., 1985) in the developing world. Microcomputers have also been identified as one of the leading technological innovations responsible for focusing information sciences on the problems of developing countries. A discussion is provided of the characteristics of GISs, two examples of microcomputer GISs for developing countries, and current efforts to apply expert system technology to GISs in relation to the microcomputing environment.

GEOGRAPHIC INFORMATION SYSTEMS AND DEVELOPMENT DECISION-MAKING

Geographic information systems are computer-based systems for the collection, storage, management, retrieval, analysis, and mapping of geographic data. These systems are designed to manage, integrate, analyze, and map the results of data gathered by widely disparate methods. Such integrated spatial information processing has proved to be uniquely powerful in a wide variety of applications.

Geographic information system data is typically captured from a number of differing sources with their own technological characteristics. One of the most important data sources continues to be space-borne sensors such as Landsat and AVHRR. Recent and growing interest exists in utilizing locational data provided by global positioning satellites (GPS). Aerial photographs and sheet maps continue to be two of the most common sources of data for a GIS. Regardless of the data source, a tremendous amount of data is required for an operational GIS.

Different systems use different methods to store geographic data in a variety of structures and formats. Most methods can be grouped into two categories: raster (grid cell) or vector (line or polygon). The ability of a GIS to integrate data from a satellite with data digitized from a sheet map is one of its strengths. However, this means that problems of locational registration must be solved so that all data is on a common coordinate base. Raster-to-vector and vector-to-raster conversions are also necessary for effective geographic data integration. Both of these tasks can be computationally intensive.

The ability to draw upon and integrate disparate spatial data is the single most significant characteristic of a GIS. Useful queries and analyses are based on an integrated spatial data base. One of the most common methods of exploiting the capabilities of a GIS is through a methodology generally labelled as cartographic modeling. This methodology combines query processing with the expressive power of maps.

Cartographic modeling is not the sole avenue of analysis in a GIS. Some systems incorporate sophisticated location modeling methods through the use of operations research techniques to find optimal locations for facilities on networks and develop optimal schemes to allocate the population to be served. Other systems incorporate capabilities of modeling agricultural and economic systems so that maps can be produced to show the possible outcomes of policies.

Geographic information system technology has been used to determine the location of new health facilities and services, and even new settlements (Rushton, 1984). The Comprehensive Resource Inventory and Evaluation System (CRIES) GIS (discussed later) has been used to develop agricultural potential and resource management policies (Schultink, 1986). The reliance on a number of space-borne sensors and GISs has been described by Paul (1986) as being instrumental in disaster forecasting and mitigation. Geographic information system technology is rapidly becoming an integral part of the worldwide decision-making environment in a variety of domains.

MICROCOMPUTERS AND GEOGRAPHIC INFORMATION SYSTEMS

Microcomputers have been an especially attractive GIS technology in developing countries since the late 1970s. Several interrelated reasons exist for this. It is important to realize that many local governments in developed countries find them attractive for the same reasons as developing countries.

The low cost of microcomputing hardware and software continues to be one of the primary characteristics that distinguish microcomputers from mainframes and minicomputers. Several microcomputing units can be purchased with funds that would otherwise go toward the maintenance of a mainframe environment. The presence of multiple microcomputers means that at least one backup system is available on site. Decision support information processing therefore can often continue without interruption. Software is also typically much less expensive for microcomputing systems (Coiner et al., 1983).

The reliability of microcomputing technology is a critical characteristic in many situations. These systems are able to operate under environmental conditions that would be fatal to mainframe and minicomputing systems. From the user's perspective, they are also easier to implement, expand, and use. Simplicity, interactivity, and reliability therefore contribute substantially to the cost-effectiveness and perceived responsiveness of a microcomputing GIS.

The Urban Data Management Software (UDMS) and CRIES Microcomputer Geographic Information Systems

Two systems that are widely known in the developing world are briefly reviewed to illustrate what has happened in the realm of microcomputer GIS technology. The UDMS was developed in the early days of 8080-, Z80-based microcomputers, whereas CRIES is based on today's IBM-AT. Systems that were explicitly developed as GISs (Cowen et al., 1986) have shown how AUTO-CAD, a microcomputer-based computer-assisted design (CAD) system, can be used as a GIS.

The UDMS and CRIES systems illustrate two design philosophies that are currently driving the design of future systems. The UDMS system is based on polygon/network entities and conducts locational modeling. By contrast, the CRIES-GIS system is based more on the genre of microcomputing GISs that are derived from early remote-sensing or image-processing systems. Such systems rely heavily on cartographic modeling to produce information.

The Urban Data Management Software System

The United Nations Centre for Human Settlements developed the UDMS package in 1980. It was originally developed on a Vector Graphic MZ microcomputer with 48 kilobytes of random-access memory (RAM) and two Micropolis disk drives. Based on the CBASIC language, it was used in a number of international workshops to illustrate the use of computing systems for the mapping and analysis of geographic data. Its mapping and locational modeling capabilities have since made it one of the very earliest microcomputer locational decision support systems (Densham and Rushton, 1986).

The code for UDMS has progressed from CBASIC to CB-86 so that it can be run under MS-DOS on the IBM and IBM-compatible microcomputers. However, it remains characterized by its minimum technology philosophy. The UDMS is only capable of producing line printer maps through the use of a keyboard character set. It has no special graphics drivers, but it remains one of the few packages that can both conduct location-allocation modeling on networks and present a map of the results.

The UDMS system is now distributed worldwide. It has proved to be a useful package to introduce organizations to the concept of a GIS. The strategy of using microcomputing GISs as introductory systems that lead to the establishment of larger, more capable systems has been successful for many public and commercial interests. As is noted in the following section, the limitations of microcomputing that constrained the performance of the UDMS are rapidly disappearing.

The Comprehensive Resource and Inventory Evaluation System

The CRIES project developed a GIS based on the IBM-AT (or compatible MS-DOS microcomputer) with a minimum of 256 kilobytes of RAM, an 80286 processor, and an 80287 coprocessor. Its graphics are supported with the use of the TECMAR graphics master board. The CRIES-GIS is one of the better examples of state-of-the-art operational microcomputer-based GIS technology that is being established in the developing world.

The CRIES-GIS is primarily a raster-based system that uses a kind of cartographic modeling, or grid overlay, to conduct analysis. It is therefore widely used in conjunction with data derived from space-borne sensors and aerial photographs. Unlike the UDMS, it does not provide for normative locational modeling. The system does, however, include the ability to produce three-dimensional terrain modeling.

The Food and Agriculture Organization recently supported a significant and thorough effort to evaluate the many microcomputer GISs on the market today. It concluded that CRIES-GIS was the most appropriate system for applications in the developing world. The ERDAS system was also singled out, but it was more expensive to purchase and implement.

FUTURE TECHNOLOGY FOR GEOGRAPHIC INFORMATION SYSTEMS

Current GIS technology is just beginning to exploit the larger memories, faster processors, and large-capacity disks that are becoming common in the microcomputing environment. These developments will make current systems faster and more capable of handling the real-world problems associated with large geographic data bases. However, some of the most interesting developments will come with advances in software, communications, and distributed data bases in applications that were previously thought to be beyond the capacity of microcomputing.

Automated Geographic Data Capture

One of the persistent problems of geographic information systems has been the sheer scale of the problem of geographic data capture. Specialized digitizing equipment has traditionally been considered too expensive or frivolous for purchase by developing countries. However, as more organizations begin to transform their analogy maps to digital form, automated geographic data capture will become increasingly attractive.

Microcomputing systems are increasingly being used as digitizing stations as a result of improved graphics and increased storage capacity. They are particularly well suited to this function because of their system integrity and well-developed capacity for man-machine interactions. However, automated data capture may become increasingly common with the further development of scanners and automatic line followers. Video digitization has been used for some time to instantly capture data on microcomputer image-processing systems.

The utility of these and other forms of automatic data capture will depend on the development of expert systems for GIS applications. One example is water basin delineation. Software recently has been developed to automatically delineate both streams and their basin boundaries from digital elevation files. Not only does this software automate the feature extraction process, but it does so in a manner that may lead to remarkable flexibility in dealing with multiple scales of information retrieval and analysis (Band and Robinson, 1986). Although it was originally developed in C language on a VAX 11/730 computer, this algorithm has been successfully implemented on an IBM-AT (Mark, 1986).

Location and Tracking

A system is currently being developed for automatic vehicle location and navigation that uses a 68000 microprocessor with high-resolution graphics. It is being designed for use with real-time utilization of GPS data. Utilizing a data base of digital maps, the system determines an optimal path and displays a map upon which is superimposed the location of the vehicle as it is being tracked. The dynamic map is supplemented by directions from a simple expert navigator that are currently displayed as text (Krakiwsky and Karimi, 1986). Systems such as this will certainly be using voice synthesizers to provide verbal instructions to the driver, thus reducing the need to read the screen while driving. Beyond its obvious use as a navigation aid, this system could be used to manage transport resources during natural disasters.

Expert Systems and Geographic Information Systems

Robinson et al. (1986) critically reviewed efforts to develop expert systems for GIS applications and identified significant efforts in the fields of map production, terrain and feature extraction, geographic data base management, and decision support systems.

Most of the efforts in automated map production have dealt with the name placement problem. However, little has been done that is relevant to the microcomputing environment. The programs are large and computationally intensive. Only very recently have some researchers begun to look at using artificial intelligence (AI) languages such as LISP or Prolog.

Automatic data capture technology is now being developed by various commercial concerns. Fain (1985) reported one example of the application of artificial intelligence to problems of geographic data capture from array scanning cameras. The system described by Fain not only converts raster scanning data to vector data, but it can also make decisions on how to divide the vector data into various layers. In other words, one layer of a map could include transportation routes, another layer, hydrography, and another, terrain represented as contour lines.

Terrain and feature extraction has concentrated on two major themes. One is the extraction of stream networks and basins; the other is the creation of expert land use and land cover classifiers. Although none of these efforts was reportedly done on a microcomputer, it is obvious that several could be implemented in a microcomputer environment through the use of one of the Prologs being sold. The memory requirements for a large-scale problem would call for an IBM-AT with all the memory it could hold.

Many efforts were made in the general area of geographic data base management and query processing by simply placing an intelligent query processor on a standard geographic data base. The ORBI system was a significant departure from that general trend (Pereira et al., 1982). This system provided impressive natural language query abilities for an environmental data base in Portugal. One area not yet attracting serious attention is the application of AI to distributed GIS in a microcomputer environment.

Only a few efforts have been directed at development problems in the realm of geographic decision support systems. However, activity in this area is increasing rapidly. Territorial systems planning is one area of active research and experimental application identified by Robinson et al. (1986). It is also a domain of particular relevance to development decision-makers because it deals explicitly with the interdependence of locational and spatial decisions on the form of development over a region. Work in this area will begin to produce geographic decision support systems (GDSSs) over the next decade. Many such GDSSs will be based on microcomputer workstations.

CONCLUSION

The future utilization of GIS technology in the developing world depends on the exploitation of the new tools of remote sensing, scanning, microcomputing, and artificial intelligence. Many of the previous era's expectations were not met because the tools for developing and implementing advanced GISs on small, reliable, and powerful computing systems could not be realized. As this technology matures, it will become more completely integrated into both the decision-making process and the global communications network. This maturation process will be dominated by the development of interactive intelligent systems that act as decision support workstations. These workstations will slowly become linked in a kind of globally distributed GIS.

The challenge of the distributed geographic data bases will place heavy demands on a number of areas in which little research has been done. For example, little formal work has been done on managing the geographic data interchange between different GISs. There has been talk of a "standard" or a "standard interchange" format. This is only a first step and it does not typically address issues of geographic semantic integrity and how it may vary according to application domain or country.

Nevertheless, it is becoming increasingly clear that this is to become a reality in cases in which data from a variety of sources are stored close to the source and retrieved only when needed, either from afar or simply from another microcomputer in the same building. As mass storage becomes cheaper and more reliable, such networks will become common ways to manage geographic data. Several expert systems will be needed to navigate the network, translate queries, and integrate data from a number of sensors and other sources for such a system to work. The result would be advice for a decision-maker who wants to make the most of scarce resources that are distributed over the surface of the earth.

REFERENCES

Band, L. and V. Robinson, "Automated Construction of a Hydrologic Information System from Digital Elevation Data," *Proceedings*, Workshop on GIS for Environmental Protection, US-EPA, Las Vegas, NV, 1986.

Coiner, J., I. Armillas, and V. Robinson, "Microcomputer Spatial Data Bases for Human Settlements Planning," in P.S. Glaser (ed.) *Data for Science and Technology*, North Holland: Amsterdam, pp. 198-204, 1983.

Cowen, D., M. Hodgson, L. Santure, and T. White, "Adding Topological Structure to PC-based CAD Databases," *Proceedings* 2nd International Symposium on Spatial Data Handling, pp. 132-141, 1986.

Densham, P.J. and G. Rushton, "Decision Support Systems for Locational Planning," in B. Timmermans and R. Golledge (eds.) *Behaviour Modelling Approaches in Geography and Planning*, Croom Helm, London, 1986.

Fain, M.A., "Automatic Data Capture with AI," *Computer Graphics World*, pp. 19-22, December, 1985.

Krakiwsky, E. and H. Karimi, *Automated Vehicle Location Using GPS on a Microcomputer System*, Occasional Paper, Division of Surveying Engineering, The University of Calgary, 1986.

Mark, D., Personal Communication. Department of Geography, SUNY-Buffalo, Amherst, NY, 1986.

Paul, C.K., M.L. Imhoff, D.G. Moore, and A.N. Sellman, "Remote Sensing of Environmental Change and its Link to Economic Development," Paper presented at the International Conference on Man's Role in Changing the Global Environment, Venice, Italy, October 21-26, 1985.

Paul, C.K., "Support for Geographic Information Systems in Developing Countries," in B. Optiz (ed.) *Geographic Information Systems in Government - Volume 1*, A. Deepak Publishing: Hampton, VA, pp. 7-15, 1986.

Pereira, L.M., P. Sabatier, and E. de Oliviera, *ORBI-An Expert System for Environmental Resource Evaluation Through Natural Language*, Report FCT/DI-3/82, Departmento de Informatica, Universidade Nova de Lisboa, 1982.

Robinson, V.B. and J.C. Coiner, "Characteristics and Diffusion of a Microcomputer Geoprocessing system: The Urban Data Management Software (UDMS) Package," *Computers, Environment, and Urban Systems*, 10(3/4): pp. 165-173, 1986.

Robinson, V.B., D. Thongs, A.U. Frank, and M.A. Blaze, "Expert systems and Geographic Information Systems: Critical Review and Research Needs," in B. Optiz (ed.) *Geographic Information Systems in Government - Volume 2*, A. Deepak Publishing: Hampton, VA, pp. 851-869, 1986.

Rushton, G., "Use of Location-Allocation Models for Improving Geographical Accessibility of Rural Services in Developing Countries, *International Regional Science Review*, 9(3): pp. 217-240, 1984.

Schultink, G., "Integrated Remote Sensing and Information Management Procedures for Agricultural Production Potential Assessment and Resource Policy Design in Developing Countries", *Canadian Journal of Remote Sensing*, 9(1), 1984.

Super Microcomputer Networks for a National Geographic Information System

ANTÓNIO SOUSA DA CÂMARA, ANTÓNIO DA SILVA E CASTRO, and RUI GONÇALVES HENRIQUES

Natural resources management, land use planning, and facility planning and implementation are activities that depend on the availability of an integrated set of multisectoral data related by the common reference of geographical location.

In Portugal, these thematic data and the base cartography are dispersed, stored using incompatible formats, and often outdated or nonexistent. The creation of a national geographic information system that would make geographic information accessible at central, regional, and local levels therefore has a high priority.

THE NATIONAL GEOGRAPHIC INFORMATION SYSTEM OF PORTUGAL

Objectives

The development of an integrated geographic information system that could be readily accessed by Portugal's central, regional, and local authorities is the primary goal of the Sistema Nacional de Informação Geografica (SNIG) project, which began in early 1986.

The specific objectives of the SNIG project are to digitize and continuously update Portugal's base cartography at a 1:50,000 scale (at a 1:25,000 scale in some regions); provide base thematic information at the same scale for planning tasks at the central and regional levels; provide access to base thematic information for local planning; and provide specialized information for central, regional, and local planning activities. An overall objective is to achieve these goals while minimizing cost, maximizing effectiveness, and respecting the equity among central, regional, and local users.

Philosophy

The SNIG project will attempt to accomplish these objectives in a modular and incremental fashion. The system will be predominantly decentralized despite the existence of a central coordinating unit. Flexible solutions are also being sought to accommodate rapid technological changes without significant expenditures.

Data Models

The SNIG project will store two fundamental data groups: base cartography and thematic data. Cartographic data will result from digitizing and updating military maps drawn at a scale of 1:50,000 and 1:25,000.

Thematic data are divided into the three major categories of physical, human, and biological data. These categories include several subcategories that integrate sets of variables grouped in themes (see Table 1). Each thematic variable is defined by its magnitude, relation to other variables, spatial scale and representation, temporal scale, use (central, regional, or local level; descriptive, impact analysis, or alternative evaluation type), source, producing institution, and users.

Architecture

The SNIG project will attempt to be a distributed and modular system with a network that has a centralized node and seven regional nodes in the short term. Most of the digitizing and image processing facilities will be located in the central node, and all eight nodes will have appropriate GIS hardware and software.

The SNIG users will also have access to a number of existing or developing specialized information systems that are or will be connected by way of network communications to the nodes of the network. It is hoped that this network will be increased in the middle term with local data bases to form a national information system.

TABLE 1 The Basic Structure of the SNIG Project's Thematic Data

Categories	Subcategories	Themes
Physical	Soil	Geology Geophysics Pedology
	Water	Water resources
	Air	Climate Air quality
Human	Human population	Demography Sociology
	Human activities	Economic Social Environmental Planning Political
Biological	Flora	Terrestrial Aquatic
	Fauna	Terrestrial Aquatic
	Natural areas	Natural reserves Protected Landscapes Classified objects and places

Extensions

The SNIG project will provide many research opportunities and contribute to significant advances in the state of the art of geographic information systems. One of the major extensions will be the incorporation of geographic knowledge bases that benefited from Portugal's strong artificial intelligence tradition, which has been documented by the pioneer work of Pereira et al. (1982).

Implementation Phasing

The SNIG project will begin by creating a central node and an experimental regional node. Major digitizing, image processing, and GIS facilities are planned for the central node, whereas only a GIS system will be implemented at the experimental node. These developments will be made throughout 1987. The other six regional nodes will be installed during the next 2 years.

Many implementation issues concerning hardware, software, and institutional arrangements are being studied. This discussion attempts to account for the dramatic changes taking place in the computer industry. One such change is the increasing availability of solutions for geographic information systems that involve the use of networks of super microcomputer workstations.

The Super Microcomputer Network Option

The emergence of microcomputer workstations that offer 32-bit power for central processing units, virtual memory, bit-mapped raster graphics, and the ability to communicate with other systems by way of networks is having a tremendous impact on GIS design. Leading GIS vendors are aware of these developments, and solutions are being advanced (see a review of available solutions in Waltuch, 1986).

This option is obviously of interest to the SNIG project, especially when its decentralized, distributed, and least-cost philosophy is considered. The possibility of specialized data bases existing in public agencies and municipalities through the use of microcomputer workstations is feasible because it is affordable.

The major problem with this option is that available GIS solutions are still immature. A decentralized, network-based alternative is also bound to face compatibility problems.

SUMMARY AND CONCLUSIONS

Most of the thematic data and base cartography in Portugal is dispersed, outdated, or nonexistent. The development of a national geographic information system will therefore improve the availability and accessibility of Portugal's geographic information.

The system is being planned in a modular and incremental fashion with a decentralized, distributed, and least-cost philosophy. The emergence of GIS solutions that involve the use of networks of super microcomputer workstations will contribute to achieving these goals. Much work will have to be done at the institutional level to implement such solutions in Portugal. Compatibility needs will also require the enforcement of standards for data collection and storage at central, regional, and local levels.

REFERENCES

Pereira, L.M., P. Sabatier, and E. de Oliveira, "ORBI-An Expert System for Environmental Resource Evaluation through Natural Language," Departamento de Informática, UNL, Monte de Caparica, 1982.

Waltuch, M. "Design and Implementation of a Workstation Geo-relational Information System," Master's Thesis, University of Massachusetts, Amherst, 1986.

20

Microcomputers in Agricultural Development

F.J. TILAK VIEGAS

A description is provided of the experience of the Epidemiology and Economics Research and Services Unit (UISEE) in the use of microcomputers to support a range of activities in agricultural development with emphasis on livestock production.

The UISEE was created in 1982, with a limited staff, as part of the Faculty of Veterinary Medicine of the Technical University of Lisbon. As a development-oriented unit, its objectives were markedly interdisciplinarian in character. Scientific and technical subjects were integrated that are normally treated independently, such as animal health, animal production, and agricultural economics. The creation of the UISEE resulted from the perceived need for urgent technological change in the livestock subsector at the production, service, and planning levels. Pressure to bring about these changes stemmed from the need to increase the competitiveness of Portuguese agriculture in the context of the European Economic Community (EEC). The efficiency of Portuguese agriculture had to be increased without exceeding the financial resources allocated by the EEC for agricultural development.

During the 4 years of its existence, the UISEE has operated in a multiple-objectives framework in line with its university commitments to conduct applied research, advisory, and consultancy services to the public and private sectors, and to establish a solid base for the implementation of postgraduate training programs for researchers, planners, and managers. The achievements of the UISEE, the types of problems faced both internally and with client institutions, and the prospects for the resolution of these problems are described.

LIVESTOCK DEVELOPMENT

The planning of the use of incremental resources in agriculture, like any other economic activity, requires an adequate characterization of the existing farming systems and the study of possibilities for the improvement of its land and labor productivity. These improvements should have a positive financial effect both on the farmer's budget and at the national level.

The following two aspects were emphasized in UISEE's approach to cope with the general absence of reliable and updated information on livestock production systems in Portugal:

- The development of farm management routines that are operated in direct association with farmers and farmers' organizations to allow for the collection of reliable and updated information on physical and financial parameters at the farm level; and
- The evaluation of technical assistance schemes that are operated by official and farmers' organizations.

These two sources of information were used to model livestock systems at the farm, regional, and national levels. These models are used to simulate the impact of proven technology and as an aid for decision-making through the use of a social benefit-cost analysis.

Microcomputers played a critical role in all of these activities by enabling large amounts of data to be manipulated quickly and effectively. Microcomputers also permitted the UISEE to overcome the budgetary constraints that are generally associated with university-based research and development units, particularly in the early stages of operation. The introduction of microcomputers into livestock production and management is discussed in the following section, in which organizational and training requirements as a function of local psychological and social constraints are emphasized.

MICROCOMPUTERS IN FARM MANAGEMENT

Software

The UISEE operates two farm management systems—dairy cattle and pigs—and is in the process of implementing a new system for sheep and goat production. About 40 farms are visited regularly by professional UISEE staff or associates who collect data on reproduction, production, disease patterns, feeding routines, and expenditures.

A commercial program (FARMPLAN) is used to process data for the large dairy farms; it is now being transferred to a system developed by the University of Reading (DAISY). Small-scale dairy farm data is processed through a dairy forecasting and control system developed by UISEE using Lotus 1-2-3 and a lactation curve-fitting program that was also written by UISEE in BASIC. A linear programming routine (MINRAC) and a feed budgeting program based on Lotus 1-2-3 (TURBOMARC) are used to ration feed. The impact of subclinical mastitis and brucelloses control is evaluated physically and financially using software developed by UISEE. Software developed by the University of Minnesota (PigCHAMP) is used to manage large pig farms.

The UISEE began by purchasing commercial software for its farm management operations that was later found to have the following limitations:

- The software did not adequately cover the needs of data recording for research purposes.
- There were difficulties in persuading commercial suppliers to review the programs and adjust them to the farming systems and management routines of Portugal.
- Very little software existed that was oriented toward the requirements of the smallholder farms that prevailed in a large number of countries with a developing agriculture.

These limitations led the UISEE to look for cooperative arrangements with similar units in economically developed countries as a source of software for commercial farms. At the same time, it would develop its own software for those categories of farmers who were unable to operate relatively sophisticated recording and information systems.

Information Systems

Information systems are only as good as the quality of the data recorded. The guarantee of the quality of the data must be based on the recorder's interest in accuracy. When the recorder is a commercial farmer, it is not difficult to demonstrate the negative financial consequences of having an extended calving interval or a high consumption of concentrate feed per liter of milk produced. As a result of this problem identification, the farmer will frequently tighten his management routines and cooperate more closely with the veterinarian who assists the farm regularly. This is a rewarding situation for both the farmer and the veterinarian, one that could easily be translated into financial incentives. Information systems for smallholder farmers, although not significantly different in objectives, require a consideration of the whole farming system, the limitations imposed by the scarcity of labor at peak periods, and illiteracy.

Incentives are also required to ensure the quality of data collected by government agencies and farmers' organizations. These incentives fall into the following two categories:

- *Professional satisfaction.* One of the most demoralizing factors to a technician involved in data collection is ignorance of the resulting information. Technical staff must be involved in the feedback of the information to the producer and must use this information to advise him to improve his production practices. Failure to use technical staff as a timely two-way communications channel will probably result in lack of confidence on the part of the farmer and insecurity on the side of the technician; the end result is an inaccurate data collection system.
- *Financial incentives.* The operation of information systems that result in direct financial benefits should have a built-in reward system in proportion to the volume of increments in the farm's cash flow.

Assuming that the obstacles associated with good data collection can be overcome, it is still essential to produce and use information in a timely way. The cyclic nature of the many biological activities that are essential to agriculture confers a high value on time. This means that profit functions can be calculated as a function of time lost or gained in relation to certain target values.

The information system must have a time cycle that allows the decision-maker (farmer, technical staff, etc.) to anticipate the occurrence of certain events and prepare the corresponding activity plans.

The information systems operated by the UISEE are currently office-based. The drastic reduction in the price of microcomputers and the appearance of portables and lap-tops represents a reasonable opportunity for on-farm data processing. Considerable savings can be made on the professional's time, transport costs, and the interval between data collection and the delivery of information. With a few exceptions, the UISEE is not yet considering the installation of personal computers for farmers.

MICROCOMPUTERS, PROFESSIONALS, AND INSTITUTIONS

Professionals and institutions react differently to the introduction of microcomputers and will therefore be discussed separately.

The professionals who delivered technical assistance services to farmers reacted in two different ways to the introduction of computerized information systems in farm management:

- One group regarded computerized records and aids to management as a savings of time and freedom from tedious paperwork. This group also considered the computerized outputs to be a great help in self-evaluation and in the improvement of technical skills.
- The other group felt embarrassed by poor productivity indicators and by the extra technical services required that could have been controlled by the farmer.

The latter group was clearly in need of refresher training and indicated to the UISEE the great importance of associating the introduction of microcomputers to continuing education programs. In fact, these programs are required at different levels, even for those professionals who are already performing at satisfactory levels, to allow them to keep pace with the technology. The initial steps of the introduction of microcomputers in agriculture should therefore give priority to technically oriented farmers and to technically well-equipped professionals.

Institutions also demonstrated heterogeneity in their reactions to the use of microcomputers in project management. Assuming the existence of an enlightened leadership, two situations can be identified whenever an institution requests assistance to strengthen, reorganize, or develop management routines. Either the institution already has a data processing unit (DPU) that more often than not is equipped with expensive minicomputers or mainframes, or computerized data processing has not yet been introduced to the institution.

The first situation is the most difficult to handle because national institutions are not used to contracting consulting services, and the recruitment of external expertise is often regarded as an intrusion into the DPU's territory and sphere of competence. A careful distribution of work between the DPU's staff and the external adviser is required. The programming tasks should preferably be left to the DPU, whereas the functional analysis and perhaps the program's design should be the responsibility of the adviser. It is often possible to install an independent microcomputer system and leave open the possibility of interfacing it with a larger computer in the future. Low microcomputer costs and the existence of protocols for communications between computers should have a positive effect in alleviating the often monopolistic tendencies exhibited by DPUs.

Another major advantage of microcomputers over minicomputers or mainframes in relation to institutional development is that they stimulate people to think about processing their own data and extracting relevant information without being completely dependent on the services of professional programmers. The problem of incompatibility between data bases, which is often used as an argument by the DPUs, is becoming less of an issue because it is now possible to share data files among different programs. Data processing units could also be instrumental in preventing this type of problem by supplying microcomputer users with standardized data base software.

TRAINING MICROCOMPUTER USERS

Most professionals, whether they work privately or for institutions, often have misconceptions about the usefulness of computers for their technical work. Among the most common of these misconceptions are that one needs to learn a programming language to become a microcomputer user, and that application computer programs *a priori* have almost limitless capabilities.

Both of these misconceptions can be rectified through hands-on training, particularly when trainers are able to work with user-friendly software and data with which they are technically conversant. The UISEE has successfully trained several dozen professionals in the use of farm management, data base management, and planning software in addition to the basic use of operating systems.

MICROCOMPUTERS IN AGRICULTURAL PLANNING

The planning of investment projects at the farm, regional, or national level has been one of the UISEE's primary activities, mainly through consultancies to international financing institutions. The UISEE has installed and successfully operated software for investment analysis in agriculture and in this respect collaborates closely with the World Bank/FAO Cooperative Program.

MICROCOMPUTERS AND AGRICULTURAL DEVELOPMENT: A SYNTHESIS

The UISEE is one of the pioneers in the use of microcomputers for agricultural development in Portugal. It has primarily emphasized activities in the livestock subsector, but its experience in this area could easily be transferred to other areas of agricultural production.

The range of applications introduced or developed by the UISEE covers three main areas in which microcomputers can be used in agriculture: farm management, planning agricultural development, and the monitoring and evaluation of project implementation. The feasibility of using microcomputers in each of these areas has been established, and some of the main limitations have been identified.

Substantial benefits can be realized by introducing microcomputers to the farm level if adequate precautions are taken, such as:

- The design of appropriate information systems for each type of farming system;
- The implementation of a parallel continuing education program for professionals;

- The careful selection of initial participants in the computerized farm management scheme, be they farmers or professionals; and
- The design of cost-effective information circuits.

Microcomputers are irreplaceable as tools for modeling farming systems and stimulating development scenarios. High-quality software is available to simulate productivity changes, animal disease, and other changes at the farm, regional, or national level, and to analyze their impact through social benefit-cost analyses.

A similar situation exists for the monitoring and evaluation of development projects. Whenever these activities are linked to association-building efforts, the introduction of microcomputers should be analyzed in relation to preexisting information systems.

The steadily decreasing cost of microcomputers coupled with the increase in communications capacity will more than likely serve to encourage decentralization in data processing and stimulate creativity among professionals. The widespread use of microcomputers by people who have not been previously exposed to them should be encouraged by hands-on training with user-friendly software and real-life examples drawn from the trainees' technical backgrounds.

Resource Utilization

21

Expert Systems For Design and Manufacture

DAVID C. BROWN

Artificial intelligence (AI) is the study of activities that are considered to require intelligence. It proceeds by producing theories about how humans perform these intelligent activities and then tests them using computer programs based on these theories. The resulting behavior can then be used to evaluate and modify the theory. Well-established theories and techniques are used to develop practical intelligent systems.

The idea of an expert system was based on the fact that many experts have much well-organized knowledge that they bring to bear on a problem, that they tend to do only one type of problem-solving (e.g., diagnosis), and that an AI technique (i.e., production rules) could be used to capture this activity.

An expert system, therefore, is a system that uses AI techniques to represent an expert's knowledge and problem-solving methodology. It operates in a limited domain and uses symbolic representations to explicitly capture the complexities of that domain.

Some disagreement exists about which systems are in fact "expert." For example, some lists include planning systems. Despite the fact that human problem-solving includes much planning, it is not appropriate to refer to all planning systems as expert systems. Only those planning systems that are specifically tailored to work in a particular domain and perform a task that would normally require an expert can be considered expert systems.

A REVIEW OF EXPERT SYSTEMS APPLICATIONS

Categories of Problem-Solving

Texts on expert systems (Waterman, 1985; Hayes-Roth et al., 1983) list from 6 to 10 categories of applications and often refer to them as "generic." The basic list includes monitoring, interpretation, prediction, diagnosis, design, and planning. Additional categories are control, instruction, repair, and debugging. Waterman refers to "Generic Categories of Expert System Applications," whereas Hayes-Roth refers to "Generic Tasks." The term "generic" is very misleading. It can be argued that the list of applications is not generic at all.

What can be concluded from the term "generic"? It is expected that a group of applications in a particular category should have common characteristics. It is expected that each category should be fully defined. It is also expected that once the general method of solution of a particular problem in a category is understood, then that method can be used to solve other problems in that category. It is expected that appropriate expert system techniques can be selected from a given category, and that appropriate categories can be selected for given techniques. It is expected that these categories are distinct and that every expert problem-solving task falls into one of these categories.

It appears that most, if not all, of these expectations are not the case. Common characteristics for each category would imply that all design systems, for example, should share some core set of defining characteristics. Even though the usual definition of design as "configuring objects under constraints" holds up reasonably well for conceptual design through detailed design, it is far too general to allow one to say that design problem-solving is well defined, or that that definition acts as a common characteristic. In fact, if plans are considered objects, then planning can be defined in the same way (Hayes-Roth et al., 1983). It is easy to characterize design, for example, as including both predictive and diagnostic problem-solving. It is therefore unclear that categories are distinct.

One possible solution to this confusion can be found in the work of Chandrasekaran (1986). According to his theory, "generic tasks" are the set of basic problem-solving skills that underlie an expert's problem-solving. He does not claim to have found the complete set, but a few, such as classification, state abstraction, and hypothesis matching, have been analyzed.

The point is that these generic tasks are very basic skills that can be viewed as being assembled into complex expert problem-solvers. An expert's skill can then be characterized by the main generic tasks, subordinate tasks, the structure of the relationships between tasks, and the patterns of control. For example, routine design problem-solving (Brown, 1984; Brown and Chandrasekaran, 1985) has one underlying generic task and includes two others. If it is known which techniques are suitable to implement a generic task, and a problem can be analyzed into such tasks, then the techniques that are suitable for a problem can be known.

Demonstrated Problem Types

Despite the arguments presented earlier, the rough categorization of systems into a list that includes monitoring, interpretation, diagnosis, design, and planning is a useful one for a general discussion.

The majority of working systems are diagnostic systems. This is because early funding for the investigation of expert systems came from the medical community. The MYCIN medical diagnosis system (Buchanan and Shortliffe, 1984) provided the first large and successful rule-based system. A domain-independent expert system building tool called EMYCIN (Buchanan and Shortliffe, 1984) was derived from MYCIN and is widely available in different versions on both mainframes and personal computers.

Systems have been reported in the literature from all of the previously mentioned categories. For example, because of the reported success of XCON, Digital Equipment Corporation's (DEC's) VAX computer configuration system, many researchers in industry and academia are concentrating on design-related systems.

Successful Systems

Despite the incredible increase in activity in the field of expert systems, most people estimate that no more than about 10 to

15 expert systems are currently working on a daily commercial basis with users who are not the system's developers. There are hundreds, perhaps thousands of prototype systems that have been and are being developed. Most companies are still evaluating the potential for expert systems technology.

Of about the 200 abstracted reports of expert systems presented by Waterman (1985), only about 10 are indicated as being in commercial use or very close to that state. Of these, only four are related to engineering, and only one, XCON, could be considered to be related to design or manufacturing. These figures probably represented the situation in 1984; there are probably many others now.

Some systems may be in active use but are not being publicly reported because they are used by the military or because a company believes that disclosure would jeopardize a commercial advantage. Probably the most visibly successful system is the previously mentioned XCON system (formerly called R1). Given an order from a customer, the system decides how the VAX computer should be configured. It decides and reports on the spatial layout of the components in the cabinets and will add components if necessary. It is the largest and most thoroughly tested system in existence.

The Digital Equipment Corporation has been able to save considerable amounts of money by using XCON daily since 1980 to configure all their orders for VAX computers in the United States and in Europe. It has configured more than 20,000 unique orders with about 98 percent accuracy. The XCON system ensures correctness and completeness better than human technicians, thus saving expensive time and effort that previously involved correcting mistakes or reconfiguring a system.

The development of an expert system is expensive and involves highly paid AI experts, a great amount of a valuable expert's time, unpredictable progress, extended development periods, a difficult management task, and a continuing knowledge maintenance task upon completing the system. It is not surprising that upper management is often doubtful and requires much positive evidence of the utility of expert systems before it moves out of the evaluation phase and commits resources.

When To Build an Expert System

It is appropriate to review under which circumstances an expert system should be built (Prerau, 1985). First, the system should be possible. Criteria include the existence of an expert, a well-understood task, and a task that is not too difficult. Next, one should be able to justify the system on grounds that include a high payoff for a working system, the capture of knowledge that is about to be lost, and the scarcity of experts. If it is possible and justifiable to build a system, it would be appropriate if the system requires symbol manipulation, heuristic solutions, is not too easy, is of a reasonable size, and has a practical value.

The Benefits of Building an Expert System

It should be clear that a working expert system has benefits, principally in that one now has the equivalent of another expert that does not get tired, is consistent, and will not complain about working on uninteresting problems. One also has a "clone" of the expert that can be copied and distributed to many locations. Additional benefits come in the form of side effects from the process of building the system.

The first benefit is that the expert's knowledge is captured and made explicit in order to express it for use in the system. Many people in many countries gained their initial expertise in engineering, especially manufacturing and mechanical engineering, under the pressure of wartime. They have been refining their knowledge ever since.

These experts are now retiring and taking most of their accumulated expertise with them. They are being replaced by younger, less-experienced engineers. New designers, for example, do not have the manufacturing experience that older designers had. They are consequently more inclined to design objects that are hard to manufacture.

The captured knowledge can be organized and made accessible to many other engineers. For example, handbooks can be produced of procedures to follow, heuristics to try during diagnosis, and ways to critique designs to improve manufacturability. This has the effect of increasing the capabilities of less expert workers who can absorb the expert's knowledge and approach expert status themselves if they use these handbooks long enough.

The collected knowledge can be continuously distributed if it is formed into a system for training. Students can then interact with the system. In a design situation, for example, the system can ask the student to make a design decision and then check the student's value against the decision the system made using the expert's knowledge. The student is constantly being shown the best solution and is being trained "by comparison." This interactive approach also has the advantage of showing the student the preferred ordering of subproblems within the design problem.

The expert system can be used to train by example or by discovery. In a design situation, for example, the system can be run on many different sets of design requirements and can produce results and provide examples of expert quality designs much quicker than a human expert. By repeating this in a controlled way, the student can discover how an expert would respond to variations in requirements. In addition, the expert system could be used as a standard against which to test those who claim some expertise.

Another training method, which is just starting to be used, is to have the trainees attempt to build their own expert systems. This forces them to express their knowledge explicitly and accurately so that they learn what they do and do not know. It also acts as a very rigorous and active test. It is likely that the system can solve a problem quicker than a trainee can; consequently, it is not unreasonable to consider exhaustively testing their expert system "clone" for its knowledge instead of testing them to exhaustion.

If knowledge was collected from several experts in complementary areas, a departmental or corporate record could be built of the knowledge and the types of problem-solving used, as well as a record of existing company procedures (Mittal et al., 1984).

An expert system can provide predictive power in a manufacturing situation in the form of knowledge-based simulation. It is possible to play "what if" games, try unusual cases, and even modify data or heuristics to determine the consequences. For example, one could determine the effect of a change in dimensions or a change in material on a process plan.

Another benefit from building an expert system is that the expert is relieved of the burden of having to solve simple cases. For example, it is known how to capture the mere routine cases in a system (Brown and Chandrasekaran, 1986). The expert can concentrate on cases in which actual expertise is required; and the expert's job thus becomes more challenging, stimulating, and rewarding.

SUITABILITY OF EXPERT SYSTEMS FOR DEVELOPING COUNTRIES

The amount of education people receive in a developing country is usually lower than that in a developed country, the quality of that education may be inferior, fewer experts exist, and there is less accumulated engineering experience. These are generalities and the situation varies from country to country.

The circumstances under which a system could be built were reviewed earlier. Some of these circumstances are more important than others when viewed in the context of the development of expert systems by developing countries.

It is likely that any system that has practical value will have a high payoff. The problem need not be large and complex for this to be true. Expertise is likely to be scarce, so even partially captured expertise would be beneficial. As routine cases of design and diagnosis become well understood, for example, such systems should be fairly easy to build with a high payoff. Any small expert system with reasonably expert performance would be useful. Even slightly expert systems will appear to be expert in a context in which there is less overall expertise.

The benefits of building an expert system were discussed earlier. Some of these benefits will also be more significant to developing countries. When experts are scarce, the capture of knowledge and its organization is very important. The potential for distribution and use is also very high. A good example of this can be found in China. Using imported and "home-grown" PCs, the Chinese have "implemented some one hundred medical expert systems which serve 980 million people throughout the country" (AAIR, 1986). This is a very good example of distribution of expertise.

However, this case is even more interesting because of the way such systems fit in with their culture. Experts in traditional Chinese medicine do not make their knowledge public and will not tell their patients how they reached their conclusions. Expert systems are seen as appropriate repositories for knowledge because the systems also do not reveal their methods. The Chinese greatly respect experts and tend to accept the expertise displayed by a program almost as if it were a human expert. It is unlikely that this would occur in the domains of design and manufacture. However, one should be aware of cultural influences on the acceptability and utility of expert systems.

Developing countries also have a shortage of AI specialists. This adds weight to the suggestion that they should concentrate on the development of small systems and the use of existing systems instead of developing state-of-the-art systems that require highly developed AI skills.

Experts from more highly developed countries or multinational corporations can be consulted to compensate for the scarcity of experts. Experience can be transferred between countries by way of expert systems, but the knowledge can be distributed and used within a country.

The necessity of maintaining expert systems should be noted. Products, stock, and factory organization change over time. Consequently, expert systems should not be viewed as static. People must be trained to do more than update their knowledge bases.

The increasing complexity of manufacturing and the use of new machines, processes, materials, and attributes for old processes as a result of automation (e.g., changes in tolerances and improved consistency) increase the need for expert systems and adequate maintenance.

EXPERT SYSTEMS IN ENGINEERING

Why are expert systems applicable to engineering, design, and manufacturing in particular? These domains qualify because of the existence of experts, the need for experts, and the existence of well-defined but complex subproblems.

What is the state-of-the-art? How many systems have been developed and in what areas? These questions cannot be answered in the space of this paper, but literature can be cited in which these subjects are addressed.

A Short Guide to the Literature

The journal *Computers in Mechanical Engineering* occasionally publishes articles to inform its readers of trends in engineering. A brief review of design-related systems (Dixon and Simmons, 1983) included mention of AIR-CYL (Brown and Chandrasekaran, 1983; Brown, 1984; and Brown and Chandrasekaran, 1985), their own V-belt designer (Dixon and Simmons, 1984), DEC's XCON system (McDermott, 1982), the SACON system for advice on the use of a finite element package for structural analysis (Bennett and Englemore, 1979), and the MOLGEN system for the design of experiments (Stefik, 1981).

A Bibliography of Knowledge-Based Expert Systems in Engineering (Sriram, 1984) lists about 120 references. The category architecture, civil engineering, and geology has 32 entries; chemical engineering has 42; and general design has 13. The high figure for the civil engineering category reflects the collector's affiliation, whereas the higher figure for electrical engineering reflects the great amount of attention paid to systems that assist with the very large scale integrated (VLSI) systems production.

A more recent survey of AI in engineering (Sriram and Joobbani, 1985) also divides systems into categories. It should be noted that because the abstracts were invited, current research can only be approximated roughly. The abstracts included 2 interpretation systems, 4 diagnostic systems, 1 repair and maintenance system, 3 control systems, 1 simulation system, 2 manufacturing systems, 24 design systems, and 3 data base systems. The preponderance of design systems is partly a result of the editors' research interests.

Of the systems that are not in the design category, several relate to manufacturing if VLSI manufacture is included. A system exists for diagnosis during the photolithography stage of VLSI manufacture; a computer test-engineer's assistant; a system to find the best trade-off between the price of a product, the selection of raw materials, and the life of a manufacturing machine; and a job shop scheduling system.

In the area of mechanical design, one system is concerned with air cylinder design. In the area of electrical design, there are some VLSI design systems, a circuit critic system, and a system for single-chip computer system design. In the area of civil design there are systems for kitchen layout, automatic detailing of buildings, and structural design.

The proceedings from conferences of professional societies are a rich source of information. The ASME Computers in Engineering Conference (ASME, 1986), for example, includes 20 papers on expert systems, about half of which are devoted to design. Others include interpretation of test data, material selection for injection-molded resins, manufacturability evaluation, and a simulation of an expert browsing through large manufacturing data bases.

The American Association for Artificial Intelligence had its 5th National Conference last year (AAAI, 1986), and for the first time split the sessions into science and engineering tracks. The applications section includes papers about representing the processes in semiconductor fabrication, a simulation of the glass annealing process, design for manufacturability in riveted joints, copier paper transport design, and alloy design.

Two recent books that provide reports of conferences are worthy of note. One is devoted entirely to AI in design (Gero, 1985) and includes papers on microcomputer design, structural design of high-rise buildings, architectural design, air cylinder design, and the design of process plans for rotational components. The other book (Sriram and Adey, 1986) includes drilling station design, surface treatment selection, marine system design, valve selection, and diagnosis in large industrial plants.

A Shift in Effort

The type of people who are building expert systems has changed in the last couple of years. Many more engineers are now writing systems that used to be written exclusively by computer scientists. Engineers are also starting to contribute to the AI literature. A good example of this new point of view can be found in Dixon (1986).

Several possible reasons exist for this trend. Better tools are available for almost any computer system and engineers are becoming increasingly aware that such systems have something useful to offer. However, some engineers are becoming involved because it is fashionable.

EXPERT SYSTEMS IN MECHANICAL ENGINEERING

The AIR-CYL System

Some of the author's work is appropriate to research in mechanical design. The domain of air-cylinders in particular has been used to motivate research. An initial description of a simple prototype system can be found in Brown and Chandrasekaran (1983), and a complete account of the AIR-CYL system is available in Brown (1984).

Not all design problems are routine, but a significant portion of design activity is. In routine design the designer proceeds by selecting from previously known sets of well-understood design alternatives. At each point in the design, the choices may be simple but the resulting behavior and solutions may be complex. There are simply too many possible combinations of initial requirements for a choice to be made merely by looking in a data base of designs.

The author uses the architecture of a hierarchically organized community of design agents called specialists. The problem-solving behavior that corresponds to routine design can be captured as follows. Each specialist has a repertoire of design plans to accomplish certain design tasks at its level of abstraction. It chooses from among the plans, makes some commitments, and directs specialists at lower levels of abstraction to "refine" the design. It is believed that routine design is a largely top-down activity. Failures cause different types of actions, such as choice of alternative plans, transfer of control to a parent specialist, and so forth.

The upper levels of the hierarchy are composed of specialists in the more general aspects of the component, whereas the lower levels deal with more specific subsystems or components. A hierarchy is used not because design is intrinsically hierarchical, but because people use hierarchies to manage complexity. The responsibilities and the hierarchical organization of the chosen specialists will reflect the mechanical designer's underlying conceptual structure of the problem domain.

The design activity is divided into four phases—requirements collection, rough design, design, and redesign. Requirements are obtained in the first phase and are then individually and collectively verified. Once it has been established that the requirements are acceptable, a rough design is attempted. The rough design phase is poorly understood. It has the effect of pruning the design search space because once the overall characteristics of the design are established, it reduces the number of choices of how to proceed with the rest of the design.

Once the rough design phase is completed, the design phase can proceed. Design starts with the topmost specialist and works down to the lowest levels of the hierarchy. Design plans are selected using specifications and the current state of the design. If any failures occur during the design phase, then a redesign phase is entered. If that succeeds, then the design phase can be reentered. The system attempts to handle all failures at the point of failure before it admits defeat and passes failure information up the hierarchy. This local attention to failure is an essential element of failure-handling behavior. Agents that have some control over other agents can use those agents in an attempt to correct the detected problem.

This theory of routine design has been captured in DSPL (Brown, 1985), which is a language for expressing design knowledge and building expert design systems. The acquisition of knowledge from experts and its expression in DSPL is being investigated, and it is believed that such interactions can be effectively controlled by the structure of DSPL itself. In addition, DSPL lends itself to fairly high-level, design-related explanations because each type of design knowledge in DSPL provides goals and methods and each can be expressed in different ways. This leads to a rich form of explanation.

Other Work in Expert Systems

The DOMINIC system (Howe et al., 1986) is an approach to routine design in which design is viewed as an evaluate-and-redesign cycle. It has been tested on the design of standard V-belt drive systems and extruded aluminum heat sinks. The PRIDE system (Mittal et al., 1986) is a pinch roll transport, interactive design expert. It focuses on the design of paper feeders in copiers that use pinch rolls, including the design of a smooth path for the paper, the decision on the number and location of the pinch roll stations, and the selection of material.

EXPERT SYSTEMS IN CIVIL ENGINEERING

The HI-RISE system (Maher and Fenves, 1985) performs heuristic preliminary structural design in the domain of high-rise buildings. It designs in a synthesis, analysis, and evaluation sequence. Information about designs is represented by a hierarchical description of alternatives. It produces all structurally feasible solutions with associated evaluations so that the user can determine which is best.

A more recent system is ALL-RISE (Sriram, 1986). This system is put into the framework of DESTINY, a conceptual model of an integrated structural design system. The ALL-RISE system extends HI-RISE to perform a goal-driven and constraint-based preliminary synthesis of various types of buildings.

ELECTRICAL, ELECTRONIC, AND COMPUTER ENGINEERING

Many research efforts have been undertaken in the area of electrical, electronic, and computer engineering. One active group at Rutgers has produced, among others, the REDESIGN system (Mitchell et al., 1983), which assists in the functional specification. The SADD system is used in the design of digital circuits (Grinberg, 1980). It takes the user's description of the function of a circuit and builds a model that then converts it into a plausible circuit. It tests the circuit by simulating its operation.

Computer-related systems include the XCON system, which has already been discussed, as well as TIMM/Tuner (Kornell, 1984). The TIMM/Tuner system assists with the tuning of VAX/VMS computer systems. It suggests adjustments to system parameters from the system manager's answers to its questions.

EXPERT SYSTEMS RELATED TO MANUFACTURING

The Browser System

Many processing steps are required to complete most manufactured products. Measurements are taken and tests are made during each step to keep a history of each product, ensure the quality of the product, and monitor the performance of the processing facilities. Consequently, large quantities of data can be accumulated for multiprocess products. The earliest possible detection of product or process problems is essential for the maintenance of high yield and cost-effectiveness. Sometimes the amount of data is so great that a human expert cannot effectively monitor the processing. A knowledge-based system would be useful in such situations. A theory of expert browsing in manufacturing data bases is proposed in research reported by Brown and Posco (1986). The essence of this theory is that a browsing activity consists of strategies that guide the application of diagnostic knowledge to portions of the data base. Diagnostic conclusions are collected to provide additional evidence for processing problems. Conclusions activate hypotheses about what sort of problem or problems may have caused or may be associated with the established diagnosis. These hypotheses are used by the controlling strategy to select diagnostic knowledge for further use.

The domain of application is the manufacture and test of some devices that are made by use of VLSI technology. All of the data to be used are taken from the data bases that are directly fed with information from test equipment. There are over 100 process steps and correspondingly large amounts of data to check in one application. Experts have a limited amount of time to spend on browsing and diagnosis. Even with the help of statistical analysis, a significant amount of evidence must be assembled and interpretations must be made to discover all ramifications of a discovered problem. The more subtle interactions between faults are detected by the expert's use of heuristic knowledge. Expertise derived from experience is essential to conduct fruitful investigations into the data.

The browser is organized into three main levels that are sandwiched between a user interface level and a data base interface level. The topmost level, strategy, starts the browsing by generating one or more hypotheses. The middle level, selection, controls the selection of hypotheses (i.e., those still to be investigated) and the conclusions reached. As conclusions are reached, more hypotheses are generated. The middle level is also responsible for pruning or combining hypotheses.

The lowest level, diagnosis, is responsible for trying to confirm or deny an hypothesis by using diagnostic knowledge. The diagnostic knowledge may activate other diagnoses to reach its own conclusion. The diagnosis level feeds the selection level with new conclusions and new hypotheses.

An approach to diagnosis has been adopted in which different problems are considered to be arranged in a classification hierarchy. The higher in the hierarchy, the more generic the problem. Each node in the hierarchy is responsible for acting as a specialist that determines if its problem exists. For example, one specialist may be responsible for detecting whether or not any wafer problems exist. If there are signs that problems exist, then it will ask the specialists below if they can refine the diagnosis. In this case, one specialist may say that it can diagnose a scratch, whereas another may report that it cannot find any evidence that a piece is missing from the wafer's edge.

Other Manufacturing Problems

The task of the ISIS system is to construct factory job shop schedules (Fox et al., 1983). Knowledge in the system includes due dates, costs, and the limitations of machines. The GERES system (Nielsen et al., 1986) selects plastic resins based on predesign information about required performance and cost. The program ranks the choices by cost. Process selection and planning and diagnosis machinery are other important manufacturing areas that are addressed by expert systems.

REFERENCES

AAAI, Fifth National Conference on Artificial Intelligence, aaai-86, Vol. 2 (Engineering), Morgan Kaufmann Publications, Inc., August 1986.

AAIR, Applied Artificial Intelligence Reporter, Vol.3, No.8, Intelligent Computer Systems Research Institute, University of Miami, FL, August 1986.

ASME, Proceedings of the 1986 ASME International Computers in Engineering Conference, Chicago, IL, July 1986.

J.S. Bennett & R. S. Englemore, SACON: A Knowledge-Based Consultant for Structural Analysis. In: Proceedings of the 6th International Joint Conference on Artificial Intelligence, IJCAI, Tokyo, Japan, p. 47, 1979.

D.C. Brown & B. Chandrasekaran, An Approach to Expert Systems for Mechanical Design. In: Proceedings of the Trends and Applications Conference, National Bureau of Standards, Gaithersburg, MD, May 1983.

D.C. Brown, Expert Systems for Design Problem-Solving Using Design Refinement with Plan Selection and Redesign. Ph.D. Dissertation, CIS Dept., Ohio State University, August 1984.

D.C. Brown, Capturing Mechanical Design Knowledge. In: Proceedings of the 1985 International Computers in Engineering Conference, ASME, Boston, MA, August 1985.

D.C. Brown & B. Chandrasekaran, Expert Systems for a Class of Mechanical Design Activity. In: Knowledge Engineering in Computer-Aided Design, J. S. Gero (Ed.), North Holland, pp. 259-282, 1985.

D.C. Brown & B. Chandrasekaran, Knowledge and Control for a Mechanical Design Expert System. Computer, IEEE, pp. 92-100, July 1986.

D.C. Brown & P. Posco, Expert Browsing in Manufacturing Data-bases. In: Proceedings of the 1986 International Computers in Engineering Conference, ASME, Chicago, IL, August 1986.

B. Buchanan & E.H. Shortliffe, Rule Based Expert Systems. Addison-Wesley, 1984.

B. Chandrasekaran, Generic Tasks in Knowledge-Based Reasoning: High-Level Building Blocks for Expert System Design. IEEE Expert, Vol. 1, No.3, pp. 23-30, Fall 1986.

J.R. Dixon & M.K. Simmons, Computers That Design: Expert Systems for Mechanical Engineers. Computers in Mechanical Engineering, ASME, p. 10, November 1983.

J.R. Dixon & M.K. Simmons, Expert Systems for Engineering Design: Standard V-Belt Design as an Example of the Design-Evaluate-Redesign Architecture. In: Proceedings of the 1984 ASME Computers in Engineering Conference, Las Vegas, NV, 1984.

J.R. Dixon, Artificial Intelligence and Design: A Mechanical Engineering View. In: Proceedings of the Fifth National Conference on Artificial Intelligence, aaai-86, AAAI, pp. 872-877, August 1986.

M.S. Fox, S.F. Smith, B.P. Allen, G.A. Strom and F.C. Wimberly, ISIS: A Constraint-Directed Reasoning Approach to Job Scheduling. In: Proceedings of the Trends in Applications Conference, National Bureau of Standards, Gaithersburg, MD, May 1983.

J.S. Gero (Ed.), Knowledge Engineering in Computer-Aided Design. North-Holland, 1985.

M.R. Grinberg, A Knowledge Based Design System for Digital Electronics. In: National Conference on Artificial Intelligence, aaai-80, pp. 283-285, 1980.

F. Hayes-Roth et al., Building Expert Systems. Addison-Wesley, 1983.

A. Howe, P. Cohen, J. Dixon and M. Simmons, DOMINIC: A Domain-Independent Program for Mechanical Engineering Design. In: Applications of Artificial Intelligence in Engineering Problems. D. Sriram and R. Adey (Eds.), Springer-Verlag, 1986.

J. Kornell, A VAX Tuning Expert Built Using Automated Knowledge Acquisition. In: Proceedings of the First Conference on Artificial Intelligence Applications, IEEE Computer Society, December 1984.

M.L. Maher & S. Fenves, HI-RISE: An Expert System for the Preliminary Structural Design of High-Rise Buildings. In: Knowledge Engineering in Computer-Aided Design. J. S. Gero (Ed.), North-Holland, 1985.

J. McDermott, R1: A Rule-Based Configurer of Computer Systems. Art. Intell. Jnl., North-Holland, Vol. 19, No. 1, September 1982.

T.M. Mitchell, L.I. Steinberg, S. Kedar-Cabelli, V.E. Kelly, J. Shulman, & T. Weinrich, An Intelligent Aid for Circuit Redesign. In: National Conference on Artificial Intelligence, aaai-83, pp. 274-278, 1983.

S. Mittal, D. G. Bobrow, & J. de Kleer, DARN: A Community Memory for a Diagnosis and Repair Task. Technical memo, Xerox PARC, (Palo Alto), CA, 1984.

S. Mittal, C.L. Dym, M. Morjaria, PRIDE: An Expert System for the Design of Paper Handling systems. Computer, IEEE, pp. 102-114, July 1986.

E.H. Nielsen, J.R. Dixon, & M.K. Simmons, GERES: A Knowledge Based Material Selection Program for Injection Molded Resins. In: Proceedings of the 1986 International Computers in Engineering Conference, ASME, Chicago, IL, August 1986.

D. S. Prerau, Selection of an Appropriate Domain. The AI Magazine, AAAI, Vol. VII, No. 2, Summer 1985.

D. Sriram, A Bibliography on Knowledge-Based Expert Systems in Engineering. SIGART Newsletter, ACM, No. 89, p. 32, July 1984.

D. Sriram & R. Joobbani, AI in Engineering, special issue, SIGART Newsletter, ACM, No. 92, p. 38, April 1985.

D. Sriram, Knowledge-Based Approaches for Structural Design. Ph.D. Dissertation, Department of Civil Engineering, Carnegie-Mellon University, Pittsburg, PA, 1986.

D. Sriram & R. Adey (Eds.), Applications of Artificial Intelligence in Engineering Problems. Springer-Verlag, 1986.

M. Stefik, MOLGEN. Art. Intell. Jnl., North-Holland, Vol. 16, No. 2, pp. 111-140, 1981.

G.T. Vesonder, S.J. Stolfo, J.E. Zielinski, F.D. Miller, & D.H. Copp, ACE: An Expert System for Telephone Cable Maintenance. In: Proceedings of the International Joint Conference on Artificial Intelligence, pp. 116-121, 1983.

D.A. Waterman, A Guide to Expert Systems. Addison-Wesley, 1985.

22

Microcomputers for Industrial Automation in Small- and Medium-Sized Industries in Brazil

FLAVIO GRYNSZPAN

Some aspects are discussed of the problem of using microcomputers in industrial automation in a developing country in which such issues as unemployment, level of industrial development, and scientific and technological infrastructure are also important. A description is provided of new technologies of industrial automation, the social consequences of automation, the problem of technological dependence, and three examples of automation in different industries to show the distinct characteristics of the control systems.

TECHNOLOGIES IN INDUSTRIAL AUTOMATION

The technologies used in the automation of an industrial process are presented in Table 1. They include hardware developments in field instrumentation, interfaces, peripherals, microprocessors, and automation equipment and software development in data communication, operational systems, control methodologies, system engineering, production, and project engineering. Two distinct groups are involved in process control and manufacturing automation. Process control is characterized by a continuous industrial system that processes basic materials to produce semimanufactured or intermediary products. Examples of such systems are metallurgical, steel, cement, glass, paper, chemical, and pharmaceutical industries. Manufacturing automation is characterized by a control system that is used in industries that transform intermediary products into final, discrete products. The automobile, electronic, electric, textile, footware, and mechanical industries are examples.

Electronics has always been important in the area of process control, especially at the instrumentation and analog control levels. But it was only after digital computers were introduced in automation during the 1960s that a major transformation occurred. In this first period of transformation, the industrial process was controlled by a large, central computer connected through A/D and D/A converters. Figure 1 is a simplified picture of process control, which is still important in large industrial complexes, such as steel, hydroelectric, and petrochemical industries.

The following technologies are used in process control:

- Field instrumentation, such as sensors, actuators, transducers, and regulators;
- Interfaces, such as A/D and D/A converters and input/output circuits;
- Data communication in the form of communication links, modems, communication protocols, and multiplex equipment;
- Peripherals and man-machine communication, such as printers, disk units, tape units, video terminals, plotters, and alarms;
- Architectures for real time, such as remote stations, microprocessors, computers, and local networks of distributed control;
- Software for operational systems, high-level languages, and data banks;
- Automation in the form of data acquisition, measurement, numerical control, programmed control, sequential control, supervisionary control, direct digital control, automatic test and diagnosis, automatic inspection, smart instrumentation, and robots;
- Control methodology, such as modeling, simulation, conventional control, multivariable control, adaptive control, optimum algorithms, and distributed systems algorithms;

- Systems engineering, such as modeling, optimization, estimation, prediction, simulation, and operational research; and
- Production engineering, such as production control; computer-aided design and manufacturing; technology in equipment, systems, and utilities; maintenance; quality control; and project management and control.

Microprocessors continued to increase in performance and decrease in price during the 1970s. Consequently, microprocessors were gradually introduced into control systems as part of the decision system at the local level. Microprocessors were used initially to program controllers in which they could command a few variables and communicate information to the host computer that was in charge of the global decisions of the system. This application is still made in batch or discrete processes.

Microprocessors recently have been used in distributed control, in which a great number of decisions and operations are made locally, with a corresponding decrease in the role of the "host" computer and communication channels. An example of distributed control with centralized supervision is provided in Figure 2.

The current situation suggests the following trends in the technology:

- Transmission of digital signals favors the use of distributed control.
- Central supervision is substituting for centralized control.
- The costs of distributed control are continuously decreasing.
- A specially designed and programmed chip will be used in place of the local microcomputer in distributed control.
- Intelligence will be available in all types of control equipment, especially in "intelligent instrumentation," in which some system functions such as linearization and signal processing are taken care of at the sensor level by using sensors with microprocessor power.
- New materials and methods will be available for sensors.
- New techniques of multivariable control, adaptive control, and optimum control will depend on progress in process knowledge.

- On-line process analyzers will be used as an element of control in complex systems.
- Local area networks will play a larger role in the substitution of a larger supervision computer.
- Optical data transmission with optical fibers will be used, especially in areas where safety is a priority.

The main difficulties at the current stage are related to the communication between microcomputers and the management computers of different manufacturers. Sensors and field instrumentation have also not progressed as much as the microprocessors that control them.

The goal of manufacturing automation is the efficient operation of the whole plant in the form of complete, computer-integrated manufacturing (CIM) (see Figure 3). In CIM, the control can be analyzed at three stages: preproduction, production, and manufacturing. The preproduction stage includes interfaces to computer-aided design (CAD) and computer-aided engineering (CAE) systems and off-line programming workstations. The production stage involves process and assembly systems, process and factory monitoring systems, and automation equipment, such as robots, controllers, and vision sensors. The manufacturing control includes the interfaces to the materials requirement planning (MRP) system, inventory control systems, and quality control systems in addition to the integration of the CIM.

The important element in achieving productivity improvement in manufacturing is the operational integration of machinery and process equipment in the total plan information and manufacturing systems. At the equipment level, industrial real-time control systems that use numerical control, robots, and computer-assisted operations can increase performance. At the plant manufacturing systems level, productivity is increased by such techniques as product scheduling, management information systems, materials requirement planning, and computer-aided planning.

Depending on the type of industry, a greater effort must be made at either the equipment control level or the plant control level. For example, in mechanical industries in which processes are discrete and repetitive, the effective processing time (the time the product is being machined) is only 1.5 percent of the total time, whereas the waiting time between the machines is almost 80 percent of the total time. Therefore, before any attempt is made to introduce sophisticated control of equipment in these industries, it is fundamental to optimize the times of the waiting lines and reduce the inventories. If these operations are not performed, no real gain will be made in automating the equipment.

The control of the manufacturing equipment by microcomputers gave rise to the concept of flexible systems in which the effect of the computer was to lower the costs of batch production. This results in equipment that is adapted to the operation by the computer program. It is possible to put the machines into new uses without physical adjustments simply by reprogramming the computer. This technique, which can handle short runs, is being used in computer-controlled machinery by small factories in Italy and Japan.

THE SOCIAL ASPECTS OF INDUSTRIAL AUTOMATION IN BRAZIL

Although automation is not new to the industrial sector, the introduction of microelectronics has completely affected the productive process and its social impacts. Advances in microelectronics tend toward a great miniaturization of the electronic component and a significant reduction in the costs of the processed information. Its diffusion is changing the technical base of the productive process. The automation of equipment generated the following results:

- The advent of numerically controlled machine tools resulted in a great modification of small-scale production by eliminating the need for highly qualified operators.
- Logic-programmed controllers and robots demonstrated a total physical resistance to unsafe or repetitive manual work in addition to creating more reproducible products with almost perfect quality.
- Office equipment such as computers, peripherals, and software are causing a permanent transformation in such areas as design, management, and commerce by manipulating a great amount of information, reducing routine operations, and introducing standardized information to the office.

Labor is inexpensive and employment is a permanent preoccupation in a developing country like Brazil. The introduction of automation, generally through expensive equipment, caused a great impact in the relationship between capital and labor; a reorganization of the production process is expected.

Being a capitalist economy, it is not possible for Brazil to ignore technological progress because it could cause a loss in competitiveness and, consequently, greater unemployment. Brazil must modernize at least part of its industrial production either to satisfy the internal demands of the high-income population or to maintain international competitiveness in price and quality.

One consequence of automation is not necessarily a decrease in the rate of employment because new jobs are created while others are being eliminated. The increase in productivity as a result of automation creates less need for employment for the same amount of production, which is the case in a stagnant economy. On the other hand, if the economy is expanding, an increase in productivity can cause an increase in production for the same amount of work. In this case, the remaining question is related to the correct division between capital and labor of the economic benefits of automation.

The important issues are not purely economic or technical but have social and political ramifications for all developing countries. Laws were passed in industrialized countries to protect workers against the undesirable effects of technological modernization. Labor unions in Europe have obtained shorter working hours and a greater participation in the decision-making process.

The answer to the problem of structural unemployment is reeducation. Automation creates a growing demand for new qualifications and new professional abilities. It is important that the modern industries identify the categories of workers that will be more vulnerable to automation and establish enough training facilities to recycle these workers for new jobs.

At the industrial organization level, automation causes an administrative restructuring that emphasizes planning and programming and decreases the importance of quality control and inventory. There is a relative loss of priority of production in relation to management and control. For the workers, this represents an increase in activities in the office and a decrease in the importance of the old specialists, whose knowledge was transferred to the equipment by the control system.

It is fundamental for any country, especially developing countries, that the new technologies of automation be integrated into the economy in a harmonious and socially correct form. The great challenge is to decrease the amount of unemployment by incorporating workers in more modern industries.

THE INDUSTRIAL DEVELOPMENT OF PROCESS CONTROL EQUIPMENT IN BRAZIL

The use of process control in the industrial process depends not only on the knowledge (software) of control but also on the equipment (hardware) available. Many countries use imported equipment and knowledge to satisfy the modernization needs of the user and to keep their production at an international level. This is true for countries with an export-oriented economy and a small industrial base. Brazil has decided to follow a different route.

Figure 4 depicts a general view of the relationship between the four aspects involved in industrial production: research, technological development, industrial development, and market and social demand. Developing countries are characterized by a technological dependence that tends to be maintained. No significant demand exists for national technologies from the industrial sector in developing countries. In other words, the technological demand (Route 4) is very small for the following reasons:

- It is cheaper and less risky to use technologies that have already been tested by foreign industries or multinational companies. Technology from Route 8 is preferred over technology from Route 3.
- Most companies follow a dependent industrial strategy by being a satellite or subordinate of a foreign strategy and by receiving technologies from Route 8.
- Industries that developed an initial industrial strategy especially need to make an effort in product engineering, industrial design, and some production engineering. These activities are developed in-house and do not generate an explicit demand for research and development (Route 2).
- The societies of developing countries tend to imitate developed economies by adopting their patterns of consumption and preferring the products that come from Route 9 over the national products from Route 5.
- Other economic problems of developing countries, such as external debt, tend to facilitate the international transfer

of technology, using Routes 8 and 9, through bilateral agreements, foreign investments, and supplier credits.

The supply of technology (Route 3) is inadequate for the following reasons:

- The national R&D system develops research activities that are related more to the international R&D system than to the national reality. University regulations, such as faculty promotion, peer recognition, and participation in international workshops and symposiums, are strong incentives to encourage the connection with the international R&D system (Route 7) and competition with the transfer of research results to the national productive sector (Route 1).
- When research results cause Route 1 technologies to be generated by Route 3, they generally are not stimulated by a demand for technology (Route 4). It then becomes very difficult to transfer the results to industry because either the companies are not prepared to absorb the technology or the technology does not attend to market needs.

Because of the strategic importance of computer and related sciences, which are able to produce deep social, economic, political, and cultural transformations in society, Brazil decided to establish a special policy to control imports and promote the development of its national industry to have a greater degree of economic and political independence. The policy that began as a group of resolutions from the executive is now a law that was approved by Congress at the end of 1984. According to the law, the concept of informatics involves all aspects related to the production and use of computers, including digital instrumentation and industrial automation. The Informatics Law creates a market reserve policy that protects Brazilian computer industries from import competition for a period of 8 years in sectors that have demonstrated an ability to compete with foreign products. National industries currently dominate a few sectors, such as minicomputers, microcomputers, and peripherals. In terms of market share, Brazilian industries in 1986 occupied half of the internal market (with sales around U.S. $1 billion) and multinational companies shared the other half. With a market reserve policy, there is a control of Route 8 in Figure 4 and an increase in the demand for national technology, which will probably cause a demand for internal R&D.

Because the digital equipment of process control is included in the Informatics Law, the Brazilian productive sector depends strongly on the industrial development of national equipment for process control and manufacturing automation. This industry is now growing at a rate of almost 40 percent per year and is active in many important areas, such as programming logic controllers, computer numerical command equipment (75 percent of the market), CAD/CAM robotics, and distributed digital control systems. Distributed technology is favored by the existing policy because, although microcomputers are produced locally, mainframes must be imported.

INDUSTRIAL AUTOMATION IN BRAZIL

As was shown earlier, factors other than the output of a specific process must be considered in the introduction of control systems in any industry. The control system must be understood as part of a larger organization to be effective. Its impact strongly depends on such aspects as the type, size, and management of industry; the user needs; the level of technological development; and other social and political issues.

Three cases serve as examples of this formulation; they represent real applications of industrial automation in a developing country like Brazil. The different situations of the three cases are compared by use of a general scheme, such as Figure 3. Figure 3 represents the functional organization of an industry in which the preproduction, production, and control levels are emphasized.

The first example corresponds to a typical industry of a developing country: the assembling industry. Depending on the size of the industry, little would result if some automation was introduced in the production equipment because the machine would only be used 5 percent of the total time; the rest of the time would be wasted in the waiting line. It is important to have an efficient control at the management level of this type of industry before any attempt is made to automate the equipment. The solution for a small industry that manufactured small pumps was a computer-aided production planning and control system that included materials management, demand planning, price control, production planning, facilities management, and quality control. This first stage was necessary to any consideration of future levels of automation. A Brazilian-made microcomputer was used and a computational system was developed in small, flexible modules to facilitate its absorption by industry. An important initial result was a substantial decrease in inventory.

A need sometimes exists in certain sophisticated areas, like computers, to introduce automation technologies to the preproduction level, even in small industries. For example, a CAD system could first be introduced to analyze and design printed circuits; a computer-aided manufacturing (CAM) system could later be introduced to drill the board and perform some manufacturing.

In larger assembling industries in which an effective manufacturing control system is in place (like some automobile parts industries in Brazil), automation is introduced at the production level. Logic-programmed controllers and small robots are already controlling hazardous operations like soldering and painting. Computer-controlled machine tools are being used to manufacture critical components, and quality tests commanded by microcomputers are being applied.

The second example is in the automation of a textile industry, which is another typical example of a labor-intensive industry from a developing country. Textiles are currently being exported by many developing countries and competition is growing. Automation is therefore necessary to maintain a competitive product in the foreign market. The developing countries cannot change the textile equipment to be capital-intensive, however, because they will lose the advantage of cheap labor and will also raise unemployment. The solution is to introduce a simpler level of automation by supervising the production to increase productivity.

Supervision involves the instrumentation of the manufacture, communication to a central unit, analysis of the data, and manual command (see Figure 5). The project in Brazil includes the electronic monitoring of 700 looms in which electronic sensors in each loom are connected through a network of data acquisition circuits, multiplexers, and a central microcomputer. The data are analyzed to detect in real time the reason for any machine stoppage (rupture of warp and woof or maintenance), which is also a convenient way to measure the efficiency of a machine. The system still depends on manual operation, but monitoring can substantially decrease the loss in production due to machine problems. This is an example of how productivity can be increased without creating any disruption in the labor situation. The concept of monitoring or instrumentation can serve as a first step to future process automation in many other industries.

The latter example is a more sophisticated control system that is used in a continuous process, such as the alcohol industry. In this case it is possible to have more than one level of control. For example, a central unit can supervise and control the total operation, and remote units can control the equipment and the local processes (see Figure 2), such as the grinding action, the boiler, the level of the reservoirs, the energy demand, and the distillation process. The distillation control involves four control loops that use PID conventional controllers to maintain a set point at the ideal operational condition. The boiler is controlled by regulating the level, pressure, and combustion. Each of the other controls consists of a single control loop to maintain the operation within previously defined limits.

Commercial equipment already exists for the alcohol industry, an area in which Brazilian experience is great. The architecture of each remote unit is based on microprocessors in distributed configuration, real-time data acquisition, large-scale integrated circuits, supervision functions of analog and digital inputs and outputs, and pulse counting. The central unit is composed of microprocessors that are connected in local networks and tied to the remote units through data concentrators. The central unit has an efficient man-machine interface (easy function selection, semi-graphics presentation, and report emission) and high-level programmable protocols.

These examples summarize the situation of industrial automation in Brazil, where the following important policies currently interfere with the use of control processes:

- *Industrial*: Emphasis on the internal market and industrial modernization.
- *Social*: Decrease in unemployment and better income distribution.
- *Political*: Redemocratization for the country and an increase in worker participation.
- *Technological*: Use of digital equipment from national industries.

Each country must define its priorities and choose the most convenient uses of control systems.

REFERENCES

Wadhani, R., *"Integrating Robot Power into Automated Factory Systems,"* Management Review, pp. 8-14, June 1984.

Keyes, M.A., *"Trends in Distributed Process Control,"* IANDCS - Industry and Process Control Magazine, Vol. 58 (12), pp. 23-25, November 1985.

Astrom, K. J., *"Process Control - Past, Present and Future"* - IEEE Control System Magazine, Vol. 5(3), pp. 3-10, August 1985.

Delong, L. W., *"A Structured Approach to Integrated Factory Automation"* - International Conference on Industrial Automation, Hong Kong, March 1985.

Tavile, J. R., *"Aspectos Sociais da Automação no Brasil"* - Texto para Discussão n° 84, Instituto de Economia Industrial, Universidade Federal do Rio de Janeiro, Brasil, Novembro 1985.

Jardim, E.G.M., *"Some Aspects of Modeling of Batch Production of a Grey Iron Foundry,"* Doctorate Thesis, The University of Birmingham, 1982.

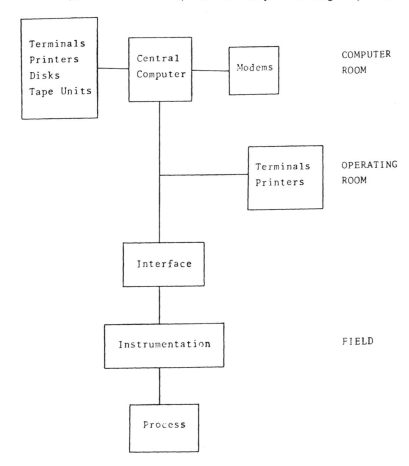

FIGURE 1 Centralized process control.

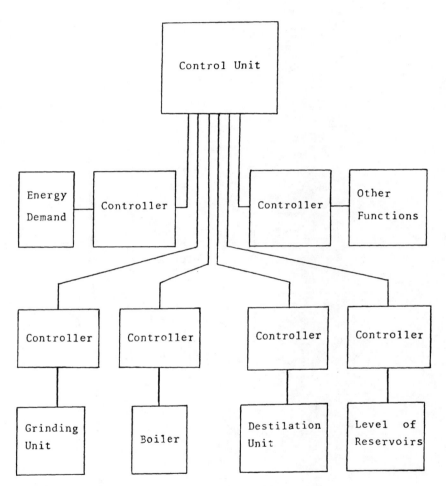

FIGURE 2 Control of an alcohol plant.

306

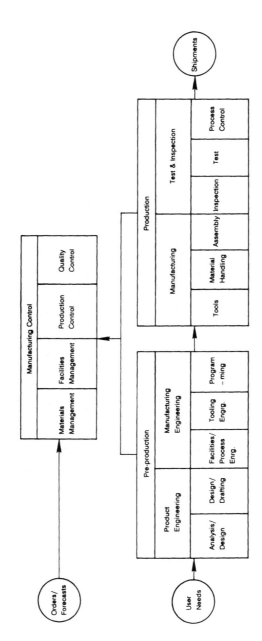

FIGURE 3 The functional organization of a factory.

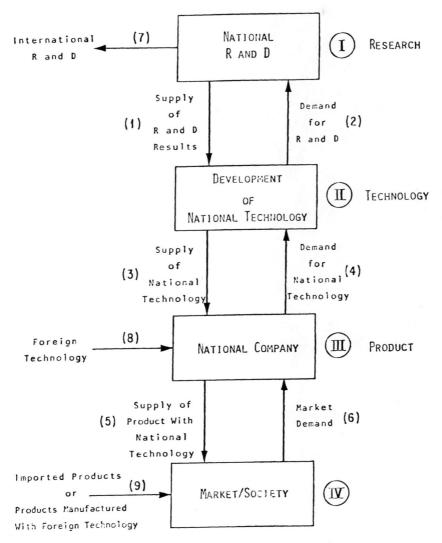

FIGURE 4 Relationships between R & D and Market/Society.

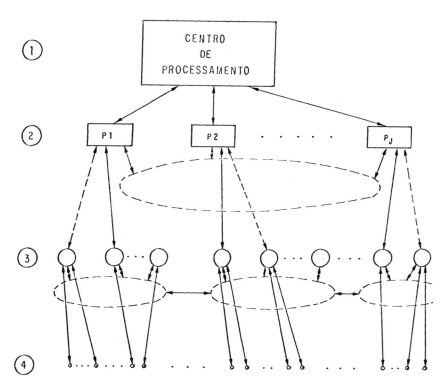

FIGURE 5 Monitoring and supervision.

23

A Microprocessor-Based Sequence Controller

ENGELBERT T. KAPUYA, R.K. APPIAH,
and S.M. KUNDISHORA

Programmable logic controllers (PLCs) are currently used to control Zimbabwean industrial processes. The devices are not only very expensive but are also difficult to modify to suit a modified process or an entirely different process. Installation, maintenance, and customization expertise is hard to find and most of it is foreign. The PLCs have to be imported, which places a heavy burden on already scarce foreign currency.

If a system could be designed that could easily be manufactured from locally available microelectronic components and materials, it would help solve the problems of local industry. One such device has been developed by the Department of Electrical Engineering at the University of Zimbabwe. The ideas presented in this paper have been applied to an actual industrial process in the Lever Brothers delinting plant in Harare. A diagram of this plant appears in Appendix A.

The basic problem in sequence control is to activate the control signals that drive a process in a controlled manner. The flow of control could depend on the feedback from the rest of the plant. Any industrial processing operation can be represented in a standard way by a state sequence diagram. The complete diagram can be considered a collection of state sequence blocks in which each state sequence block is associated with one and only one state sequence indicated by a box. One or more decision boxes may be identified in a state sequence block. Each decision box then leads to either of two state sequences: a true next state sequence and a false next state sequence. More complex state sequence diagrams can always be represented as a collection of several of these fundamental state sequence blocks. A typical state sequence block composed of one state sequence and one decision box is shown in Figure 1.

Once an industrial process has been described in this form, several microprocessor-based implementations result. One approach would be to develop a customized program to realize one particular industrial process. Although such an approach would be efficient in terms of speed and the amount of memory needed to store the program, its severe limitation is that the same hardware has to be adapted to control an entirely different process. A completely new customized program has to be developed, which requires much microprocessor programming skill and which increases the overall cost of implementation.

An alternative approach would be to program the same hardware in such a way that it is easy to transport to different industrial processes without the need for great microprocessor programming skill. The approach relies on the development of an architecture and a program that remains unchanged. The program will be driven by tables stored in read-only memory (ROM) to activate the controls necessary to drive the plant. All that needs to be done to adapt the system for different processes is to change the tables. Once the rules for compiling the tables from a standard state sequence diagram are well defined, an operator who need not know the intricate details of how a microprocessor operates can perform the adaptation. This is a very useful system attribute, considering the shortage of microelectronic skills in a developing country like Zimbabwe.

THE STATE SEQUENCE CONTROL MECHANISM

Output Control

Two main functions can be identified in state sequence control: output control and next state sequence determination.

Two tables have to be drawn up, each one dedicated to each of these main functions. The power of the arrangement can be enhanced by dedicating one read-only memory (ROM) to hold the control program and interrupt handling routines, dedicating another ROM to store the output control table, and dedicating a third ROM to storing the next state sequence table. The controller then becomes very flexible. One would replace two ROMs when one changes from one industrial process to another. Customization would then be reduced to the simple task of replacing ROMs. More drastic changes, however, may require some modification of the hardware.

Each state sequence may change the state of one or more output control signals. The change may be from a logic ZERO to a logic ONE or vice versa. A general method has to be developed to selectively change one or more control signals at any one moment. Because all control signals are formed in groups of eight to form bytes, this can be achieved by logical ANDing and ORing with predefined masks.

Consider a set of eight outputs that are concatenated to form an 8-bit byte, as shown in Figure 2. During a particular state sequence, it must be ensured that control signals OUT1 and OUT8 are in the logic ONE state and control signals OUT3 and OUT6 are in the logic ZERO state, which leaves all other control signals unchanged. This can be achieved by taking the current state of the output and ANDing it with 11011011 (DB hex) followed by ORing it with 10000001 (81 hex). These will be referred to as the AND and OR masks.

These two masks must be stored in the output table for each PIA section (peripheral data register) for each state sequence. Because eight PIA sections are in the four PIAs of the constructed hardware, 16 masks are needed for the output control table for each state sequence. It is assumed that all the peripheral lines have been configured as control outputs. The output table will contain several blocks of 16 masks for consecutive state sequences in order. To activate the control signals in a particular state sequence, the program would have to search for these masks in the output table. This task can be easily performed by pointing to the start of the output table and off-setting the state sequence code by 16 times.

The format of the output table is shown in Table 1.

Next State Sequence Determination

A similar mechanism has been employed to determine the next state sequence. Each state sequence has 18 reserved bytes. To determine the next state sequence, a condition has to be evaluated that depends on the feedback signals from the whole plant. The condition can be expressed in terms of several of these feedback inputs.

Consider eight inputs that are concatenated to form a byte read from a PIA peripheral data register, as shown in Figure 3.

The condition can be expressed as follows: IN1 and IN8 must be in the logic ONE state and IN4 and IN6 must be in the logic ZERO state for a true condition. This is the general form of the condition that has been implemented in the design of the control program because it is representative of the conditions that will be met in actual processes. It should be noted that other forms of conditions are possible. The possibility that IN1 or IN8 must be a logic ONE and IN4 or IN6 must be a logic ZERO for a true condition may generally occur; this cannot be catered to by the structure of the current program. Although it is possible to cater to all forms of conditions by a sufficiently complex program and suitable manipulation of the Boolean conditions, that approach has not been considered because of the large next state sequence tables that would result.

Returning to the condition of the example, it is apparent that the test can be performed in two steps. The first step is to complement the input byte. The next step is to OR this complement by the mask 11010111. Only if bits IN4 and IN6 are ZERO will the result be FF hex. A result other than ZERO indicates a false condition. The next step is to AND the same complement with the mask 10000001. Only if bits IN1 and IN8 are both ONE will the result be ZERO. A result other than ZERO indicates a false condition. The condition is true if both tests are passed; for example, a result of FF is followed by a ZERO result. A true condition should lead to a true next state sequence and a false condition should lead to a false next state sequence. The two next state sequence codes are stored in the last two locations of the next state table for the state sequence in question. The first 16 are dedicated to the 16 masks needed to evaluate the condition, which makes a total of 18.

The control program must locate these masks and the next

state sequence codes by pointing to the start of the next state table and off-setting by 18 times the state sequence code. The format of the next state table is shown in Table 2.

SOFTWARE

The main program has an initialization routine that is executed only once after a power-up or push-button RESET. This routine initializes the PIAs and clears a section of random-access memory (RAM) that reflects the current state of the control outputs at any one moment. It also initializes the memory location 8000 hex to FF hex, the idle state sequence code. Initialization also involves setting the system stack pointer to point at the last RAM address location, and resetting all the condition code register bits to enable all the interrupts.

The program then falls into one main loop, the primary code of which is fetched from memory location 8000 hex, which is referred to as STATEMEMLOC. If the code is FF hex (the idle code), no action is taken and the program loops back to read the state sequence code, thus effectively idling. Because this memory location was initialized to FF hex, the program will start off idling. The only way to break this loop is to find a mechanism to change the contents of the state memory location. This can be achieved by a simple interrupt service routine that changes the state sequence code to any value other than FF hex.

During normal state sequencing, in which the current state sequence code is not equal to FF hex, the main program loop fetches the current state of the output controls for the current state sequence from the RAM area of memory and modifies them by ANDing. This is followed by ORing with suitable masks fetched from the ROM area of memory. The result is written back into the memory to reflect the latest state and is also written to the peripheral data registers to effect the output controls.

The program then goes on to the next section, the primary function of which is to determine the next state sequence. This is done by reading the peripheral registers, followed by ANDing and ORing with the relevant masks to determine the condition. A true or false next state sequence code is picked from the table, depending on the result of the test. This code is saved in the memory location 8000 hex. The program then loops back to the beginning of the main loop and repeats the process. This time it finds a different state sequence code and is thus effectively in a different state.

It has been shown that the only way to break the idle loop is to interrupt the processor. The 6809 microprocessor has three interrupts. The nonmaskable interrupt (NMI) is reserved for plant start-up. Its service routine is simple; it clears the memory location 8000 hex. The state sequence diagram for plant start-up must therefore start with a state sequence code of zero. The interrupt request (IRQ) can be reserved for plant shut-down. Its service routine simply loads 01 into the memory location 8000 hex. The sequence diagram for plant shut-down must start with a state sequence code of 01 hex. The other interrupt source (fast interrupt request) can be used to handle any machine malfunctions or other fault conditions that may be detected in the process. This interrupt originates from several sources; its service routine therefore must identify the source of the interrupt and then attempt the necessary corrective measures. The corrective action can be performed by state sequencing.

The interrupt service routine for the sources interrupt will generally be complex and could be very long. A complete ROM has therefore been reserved to hold its interrupt service routine. It must be emphasized that for each process, a process engineer has to study the system and work out a schedule to correct each of the possible malfunctions and then code them as state sequence diagrams. The service routine will isolate the fault and point to the appropriate state sequence diagram.

HARDWARE

The controller is built around the 6809 microprocessor. Four PIAs are provided to cater to a maximum total of 64 inputs and outputs. The printed circuit board (PCB) layout has been structured so that each peripheral line can be independently configured as an input or output. The board is currently built so that all port As are configured as inputs and all port Bs are configured as outputs, allowing a maximum of 32 inputs and 32 outputs to be handled.

Four ROM sockets are provided to hold the TMS 2532 2-kilobyte by 8-bit ROM. These sockets are referred to as ROM1, ROM2, ROM3, and ROM4. The ROM1 socket is reserved to hold the main program and the interrupt service routines for NMI and

IRQ. It also holds the start address of the initialization program and the start addresses of the interrupt service routines. The ROM2 socket is reserved for the output table; the ROM3 socket is reserved for the next state sequence table, and the ROM4 socket is reserved for the sources service routine. Finally, a RAM socket holds the 5516 read/write memory. This socket is used as a scratch pad by the processor and as a stack and store for the current state sequence code and the current state of the PIA peripheral data registers. A memory map of the constructed hardware is shown in Figure 4.

THE DELINTING PLANT

The delinting plant at Lever Brothers in Harare is used in the production of cottonseed oil. It has a total of 58 variables that are distributed as 31 feedback inputs and 27 control outputs. A detailed description of the plant operation has been omitted. However, the complete process can be described by state sequence diagrams that enable the developed controller to be easily implemented in the process.

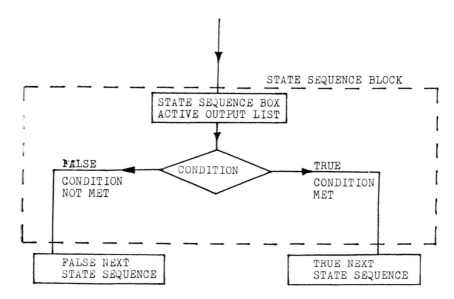

FIGURE 1 Typical state sequence block.

OUT8	OUT7	OUT6	OUT5	OUT4	OUT3	OUT2	OUT1

FIGURE 2 Output control byte.

TABLE 1 Output Table Format.

AND	MASK	PIA1A
OR	MASK	PIA1A
AND	MASK	PIA1B
OR	MASK	PIA1B
AND	MASK	PIA2A
OR	MASK	PIA2A
AND	MASK	PIA2B
OR	MASK	PIA2B
AND	MASK	PIA3A
OR	MASK	PIA3A
AND	MASK	PIA3B
OR	MASK	PIA3B
AND	MASK	PIA4A
OR	MASK	PIA4A
AND	MASK	PIA4B
OR	MASK	PIA4B

STATE SEQUENCE ZERO

AND	MASK	PIA1A
OR	MASK	PIA1A
AND	MASK	PIA1B
OR	MASK	PIA1B

STATE SEQUENCE ONE

etc.

IN8	IN7	IN6	IN5	IN4	IN3	IN2	IN1

FIGURE 3 Feedback input byte.

TABLE 2 Next State Table Format.

AND	MASK	PIA1A	
OR	MASK	PIA1A	
AND	MASK	PIA1B	
OR	MASK	PIA1B	
AND	MASK	PIA2A	
OR	MASK	PIA2A	
AND	MASK	PIA2B	STATE SEQUENCE
OR	MASK	PIA2B	ZERO
AND	MASK	PIA3A	
OR	MASK	PIA3A	
AND	MASK	PIA3B	
OR	MASK	PIA3B	
AND	MASK	PIA4A	
OR	MASK	PIA4A	
AND	MASK	PIA4B	
OR	MASK	PIA4B	
TRUE	NEXT	STATE SEQUENCE CODE	
FALSE	NEXT	STATE SEQUENCE CODE	
AND	MASK	PIA1A	
OR	MASK	PIA1A	STATE SEQUENCE
AND	MASK	PIA1B	ONE
OR	MASK	PIA1B	
		etc.	

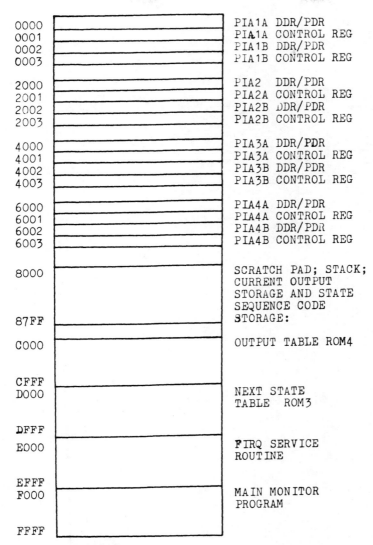

FIGURE 4 Memory map of the 6809 microprocessor controller.

PIA1 PORTA INPUTS	OE2	OC7	ORS2	OC4	OF7	OC5	ORS1	OF1F2
PIA2 PORTA INPUTS	ORF3	OC13	OF5	OC3	OC3	OS1S2	OC6	OC8
PIA3 PORTA INPUTS	ORF1	OC9	OC10	OF3	ORF2	OC11	OC12	OF4
PIA4 PORTA INPUTS	-	D3	D2	D1	S	OC1	OE1	OC2
PIA1 PORTB OUTPUTS	E2	C7	RS2	C4	F7	C5	RS1	F1F2
PIA2 PORTB OUTPUTS	RF3	C13	C14	F5	C3	S1S2	C6	C8
PIA3 PORTB OUTPUTS	RF1	C9	C10	F3	RF2	C11	C12	F4
PIA4 PORTB OUTPUTS	-	-	-	-	-	C1	E1	C2

FIGURE 5 Allocation of control signals.

320

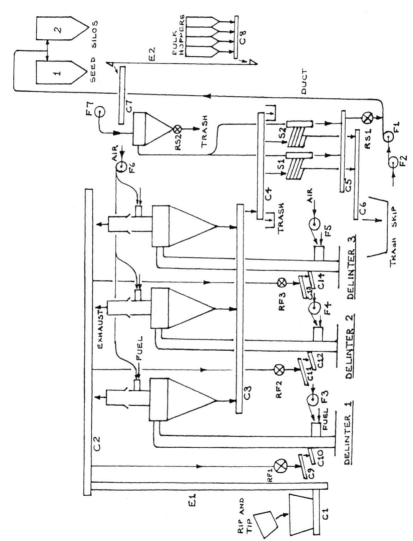

APPENDIX A Delinting plant in diagrammatic form.

24

The Field Limitations of Diagnostics in Processor-Controlled Industrial Systems

A.D.V. NIHAL KULARATNE

Current industrial systems have improved designs to avoid maintenance difficulties. Autodiagnostic software and fault-tolerant computer systems are part of the latest systems; however, rare but complicated maintenance problems still arise in these systems and pose a great challenge to field engineers. Such situations can become more complicated when there are time limits on the restoration of service. For example, a failure of a large telephone exchange because of a rare technical problem may create panic in a region of a city and service must be restored in the least possible time.

Current generations of industrial systems, such as process control systems, telephone exchanges and message switching centers, have complicated, lengthy software and miniaturized hardware that may be difficult for field maintenance groups to understand.

Several hierarchical processing levels exist in most of these systems, and all levels have large program blocks and data files. Because the hardware of the complete system is controlled by specialized lengthy and detailed software, system design details are masked from field service personnel. These systems are also by nature quite different from past generations in which individual details of the system hardware were visible.

By contrast, most current systems are well equipped with

complicated software and hardware to detect common faults and supervise overall operations, even to the extent of keeping records of the vital performance statistics of the system. Because these useful facilities are built into the system, field service personnel could become accustomed to performing only mechanical troubleshooting without concentrating on system design concepts and details. When uncommon and unusual faults occur in these machines, the repair may call for more knowledge than most field personnel possess.

Unlike such consumer products as personal computers, home entertainment systems, and watches and calculators whose chips can be easily replaced at service centers, most industrial users (such as telephone companies or other large industrial organizations) need systems with proven families of components. Because of the demand from industrial users, the manufacturers of large real-time systems use hardware and software that could be slightly behind the state of the art. Systems designed with these kinds of reliability demands can still allow a scientific approach to deep diagnostics in the field. However, a deep diagnostic approach to a problem may be limited in certain situations by trivial bottlenecks instead of the complicated nature of the system's design.

HOW TO HANDLE RARE PROBLEMS

A maintenance group's knowledge of rare faults can be useful in handling deep diagnostics in a stored program-controlled (SPC) system. Such knowledge is not gained overnight or through training programs but grows with experience on the system itself.

Rare problems on a SPC system could be the result of software errors, intermittent hardware faults, or even human operational errors. For example, when data transfer occurs between a peripheral unit and the main processor, an error may cause an abnormality, despite the use of error detection and correction algorithms built into the system. After initial data are loaded into an SPC system with cartridge tapes, floppy disks, or similar devices, an unusual system reaction may occur subsequent to a system software reload if the operator enters a wrong or outdated standby tape. In some rare situations, duplicated processing chains are working in a synchronous mode and both processing sides acquire wrong data. This could lead to a complete failure. These kinds of tricky situations are possible when large volumes of software govern the system's behavior. This is one of the reasons manufacturers should maintain detailed data on field failures. If these data are available to the field maintenance teams, they could be prepared for rare problems.

Sometimes the system may not give accurate alarm indications or maintenance messages to the operator interfaces, which may lead the maintenance teams to determine that no fault was found. In cases in which the trouble indication repeats, it could be more useful to investigate the problem in a detailed scientific manner than to follow the usual maintenance flowcharts. A reverse engineering approach to the problem may indicate that some hidden details are behind the trouble.

For example, in an on-line system that deals with a high level of analog hardware (such as process controllers, junctors, or data circuits), the original cause for an alarm may be due to a fault on the analog hardware that generates an interrupt word or a status word. The software may be just interpreting the individual bits to generate the error message or the alarm. The original interrupt word may have had several error bits at the same time (due to a possible single power failure in a multiple power supply) for which the software does not generate the correct alarm message. If the maintenance team is not properly probing the situation with in-depth analysis, it could end up making misleading corrective actions, such as changing the hardware units instead of repairing the faulty power supply.

Varied interfacing situations could exist in large communications networks in which different types of equipment are used at nodal points of the network (such as different types of exchanges in a large telephone network). Although all the central systems are working according to standard procedures and signaling formats, the processing algorithms in the central processors may respond in different ways to the faults in the links between the nodes. This kind of situation may be quite common after the initial commissioning period.

FAULTS CAUSED BY EXTERNAL FACTORS

Some rare environmental situations can create unusual faults and breakdown situations. One example is severe lightning in the vicinity of a communication system with a complex external network. In other cases, the poor condition of the available commercial power may create similar problems. In other cases, as in countries where the reliability and quality of the commercial power supply is poor, costly uninterruptible power systems (UPS) and power conditioning equipment may be called for. External conditions and their impact on new systems may not be clearly foreseen before the initial commission period. It may be very difficult to detect and correct faults using available maintenance procedures if the fault is caused by external factors.

Sometimes the repair activity may demand that the maintenance team attend to auxiliary equipment (such as the UPS) before attending to the system itself. In some cases, it may be difficult to deal with the system failures because of a main CPU failure that restricts the execution of a test program by the system. If the failure is caused by several simultaneous faults in the CPU or a similar unit that affects the execution of test programs, even swapping suspicious modules one at a time may not give quick results. Restoration times may be unusually high in such situations. Before an attempt is made to locate the fault immediately (using a trial-and-error approach), an in-depth, step-by-step scientific approach that uses available details about the nature of the fault may produce better results. This kind of approach may give clues to possible multiple faults.

For example, if the maintenance engineer analyzed and modified the test programs to determine why the expected results were not obtained, the individual faults in a situation with multiple hardware faults may be identified.

OBSTACLES TO A DEEP DIAGNOSTIC APPROACH

Inadequate Documentation

In certain large processor-controlled systems, either the buyers do not request complete systems data and a technical description of the system or the supplier does not make it an integrated part of the system. Especially in the transition period from a non-SPC system to an SPC system, the customer may not be specific about systems documents and may not request complete program listings, system flowcharts, microprogram sequences, and system timing diagrams that are irrelevant to a non-SPC system. In such situations, service personnel may detect such shortages only when a very specific need arises and time will be consumed obtaining necessary documents from a distant supplier.

Problems With Available Documentation

An attempt to tackle a difficult fault in a SPC system may depend as much on the skills of the maintenance team as on the accuracy and presentation of the documentation. Sometimes the available documentation may not provide the necessary details to approach a problem methodically. For example, in a complete stoppage situation in which data are inadequate to assess the system fault, the documentation should provide very explicit details to solve the problem. In a difficult situation such as this, it should not take unnecessary time to understand the document. The system designers (especially in certain European countries) sometimes produce original system descriptions in a language the user cannot understand. For example, French system documents may be translated into English for a particular customer. However, clarity or detail may be lost in translation. When field engineers use these documents in diagnostic procedures, they may not have all the necessary data. This kind of situation generally consumes time unnecessarily, especially when the system software or microprogram sequences are followed in a step-by-step manner to correct a tricky fault. If one is critically following a sequence of a machine code, the exact meaning of a single bit in a data word may sometimes be crucial in the selection of the next sequence in the machine code.

Trade Secrets

Highly competitive manufacturers have trade secrets or proprietary software that critically affect the performance and price margin of their systems. Some original equipment manufacturers (OEMs) are compelled to provide system details such as maintenance software to user organizations that could allow competitors to obtain sensitive information about the system. This is especially true in the case of software documentation. On the other hand, if such details are not available to the maintenance groups, they may run into difficult bottlenecks in the diagnostics.

Continuing Product Revisions

When the system manufacturers adopt changes to improve a system's performance, both the hardware and software of the system may be revised. Unlike hardware, software modifications can affect the internal behavior of a system to a large extent. In some cases, although minimal modifications may be made to hardware, the software may be completely modified. If such revisions are incorporated into existing systems, maintenance personnel may find that they impede the diagnostic process. In addition, if several systems are maintained by a single team and if different systems incorporate several revisions, the team needs to know what specific differences exist in the behavior of systems after revisions were made to hardware and software. User organizations should also be cautious to update their libraries with the revisions. Since system revisions are unavoidable, long-term maintenance problems can be avoided if customer libraries are updated accordingly. Handshake agreements with suppliers to regularly check the accuracy of available system documents would also help to avoid unnecessary bottlenecks in deep diagnostic procedures.

The Impact of New Components

Because state-of-the-art devices are often added to new systems to improve system performance and reduce its size, it becomes difficult to locate faults at the chip level. More and more component manufacturers supply customized and semicustomized multifunctional devices for industrial systems. However, when system faults are caused by failures of very large-scale integrated (VLSI) devices, it may be difficult to isolate the faulty chips on the modules in the field. In such situations, users may not have access to the expensive and complicated test gear used by manufacturers. Spares of the complex VLSI devices may also be costly. Sometimes maintenance teams may be forced to use trial-and-error procedures to detect faulty components because they lack sophisticated test gear.

Manufacturers could assist customers by providing basic details of any special devices on hardware modules. Basic functional organizations within the chips, pin assignments, and some test wave forms could be useful in such cases. They would be particularly useful for special customized and semicustomized devices in contrast to standard component families, where data could be obtained from standard data books.

Time Limits on Diagnostic Procedures

In large SPC systems that provide critical public services directly (such as telephone exchanges) or indirectly (such as railway signaling systems), there are strong pressures for restoration of service when faults occur. Such time constraints create extra burdens for maintenance teams. Extremely severe time limits may be enforced when a complete service failure has occurred.

In such disastrous situations, even the most capable maintenance experts may be nervous and unable to tackle the fault scientifically. Situations may deteriorate when higher management or those affected by the situation raise questions. Depending on the nature of the trouble (especially when it is rare), the maintenance team may need to refer to or collect a great deal of detailed information. For example, if the problem is a software fault, engineers may be forced to refer to lengthy software volumes, which could create an even greater delay. In situations in which time is critical, higher management may be forced to call for expert assistance from the supplier. This could be expensive, especially if the initial guarantee has expired.

Manpower Problems

The creation of a good maintenance team in a large SPC plant may be a challenge, especially when management policy on maintenance is not to seek the manufacturer's assistance frequently. Such situations call for the maintenance team to use deep diagnostic procedures in which in-depth details of the system must be known. Almost all SPC plants contain many more technical details than non-SPC plants. For example, when a new SPC system replaces an old non-SPC system, the maintenance team may have to understand many more software than hardware details. However, to understand an SPC system, it is extremely important to know the hardware first and then learn what the software is doing to control the hardware. This is a good learning approach for field engineers. Unlike OEM designers, who can work on hardware or software separately, field engineers always need to know both to understand the system. Field maintenance groups can, however, use their software knowledge to follow a particular sequence of events in the system. Their knowledge of computer science, software fundamentals, and programming can help them create powerful diagnostic routines by using manufacturers' system details.

Several criteria can be used to create a proper maintenance team for an SPC system:

- Properly qualified personnel;
- Initial refresher training adapted to SPC surroundings;
- Proper systems training on hardware and software;
- On-the-job training during installation and commissioning periods;
- Use of time gaps (if any) between installation and commissioning periods of a system (without live traffic) to simulate faults and make diagnostic trials; and
- Proper training on standard procedures applicable to the system.

The selection of properly qualified personnel could be the most important factor in the establishment of a proper maintenance team. For example, an engineer or technician selected for an SPC plant should have a good background in computer science and related subjects in addition to basic electronics knowledge.

Engineers should also be prepared to learn the system concepts and details by reading documentation instead of merely grasping it on the job from time to time. This is very important because documents are much more detailed in an SPC system than in a non-SPC system. Maintenance personnel also should have the courage to continue learning when they encounter details that sound new and difficult to understand.

Initial refresher training on basic subjects like digital techniques, computer architecture, and microprocessor techniques could be useful in learning about a large system. If organizations that handle these large systems have their own training centers, practically oriented refresher courses could be planned on these related subjects. The maintenance team would be better prepared for detailed systems training programs after short preliminary courses. They would also be able to follow the system's concepts more readily.

Because systems training is usually offered by manufacturers, systems engineers can learn maintenance details through them. Organizations purchasing new systems should review the manufacturer's training programs, because that is the time to request from the manufacturer exactly what they need for their field maintenance team.

On-the-job training during the installation period also plays an important role. This allows the new maintenance team to work with the expert engineers who install and commission the project to gather practical insights that could be valuable in long-term maintenance work. The testing and commissioning period in particular involves a host of acceptance tests on the system and could be an opportunity for the maintenance group to apply the theoretical knowledge they gained during systems training.

In large SPC systems, a time gap between installation and commissioning could be used by the maintenance teams (guided and supervised by the installation group) to simulate faults and test the system without live traffic.

Good training given before the new system is commissioned on applicable standard procedures (such as CITT signaling procedures in telephony) would also be useful in later diagnostic procedures. If time permits, the maintenance teams could study the system's internal software reactions to different kinds of sign calling procedures, for example, with the assistance of the installation group.

From a management point of view, it is important to ensure that maintenance teams continue to learn the system so that they will not forget useful system details during later diagnostics. It is also important to ensure that experts in the maintenance team guide others who are less experienced.

When organizations go through transition periods in which old systems are updated with new processor-controlled systems, it is not possible to drop the less qualified, but more experienced (on non-SPC machines) senior maintenance staff. But senior staff may find it difficult to adjust to new SPC surroundings and philosophies. They may also find that newcomers have a better basic knowledge of SPC fundamentals. For such senior staff, initial refresher-type training would provide an entirely new learning experience about digital systems.

THE EFFECT OF CENTRALIZED MAINTENANCE

Maintenance practices also may become quite different in situations in which a great number of communication systems, such as public telephone exchanges, are linked with a central computer for maintenance and monitoring purposes. With the advent of

SPC machines, centralized maintenance becomes easier and more cost-effective.

It is common for large organizations, such as public telephone companies, that adopt centralized maintenance practices to operate centralized technical assistance centers. When such centralized maintenance centers are prepared to analyze difficult problems at individual sites, the challenge to the on-site maintenance teams is reduced. Centralized technical assistance centers can afford to employ expert staff so that coordinated team work on difficult problems is practical. In such cases, individual maintenance centers can employ less qualified staff for day-to-day maintenance, which does not generally require expert knowledge of the systems. The technical assistance centers can also afford to maintain data banks on fault histories as well as detailed system documentation at a lower overall cost. Because these technical assistance teams have the opportunity to observe faults at different sites and can anticipate possible faults at other sites with similar hardware and software, the overall maintenance of the complete network can be more effective.

However, because centralized maintenance demands less expertise from the maintenance teams on site, they may perform maintenance work without thought to system concepts and details. When difficult problems demand quick solutions, the field staff may not be able to tackle the situation without assistance from experts at technical assistance centers. At the same time, depending on communication between the technical assistance centers and the individual sites, the response may be slow. This kind of delay may not be tolerable in the case of system stoppage or if service provided by the systems has severely deteriorated. One possible precaution to avoid such problems is to provide periodic on-the-job training for site maintenance groups at technical assistance centers.

Organizations that can afford to run centralized maintenance operations with technical assistance centers can also afford to cut the training costs, because expert training on the systems could be given to fewer system engineers, who would in turn be able to assist all sites.

25
Computer-Aided Power System Design
SRIDHAR MITTA

The development of energy sources is the key to industrial progress in developing countries. Energy development is essential to the continued improvement in the standard of living. The electrical power system is one of the tools needed to convert energy from one form to another in a convenient transportation medium. It consists of three principal subsystems: generating stations, transmission lines, and distribution systems. The transmission lines are the connecting links between the generating stations and the distribution systems. They also lead to other power systems through interconnections. The distribution systems connect all individual loads to the transmission lines at substations that perform voltage transformation and switching functions.

Most of the electrical power in developing countries is generated in steam-turbine plants. Coal is the most widely used fuel in the steam plants. Nuclear power plants are becoming operational, but their construction is slow and uncertain because of high capital costs and constantly increasing safety requirements. The voltage of large generators is usually in the range of 18 to 24 kilovolts (kv).

The generator voltage is stepped up to transmission levels in the range of 440 to 115 kv. The first step-down in voltage from transmission levels is at the bulk-power substations. The next step-down in voltage is at distribution substations that constitute the primary distribution system. Most industrial loads are fed from the primary system. The substations also supply distribution transformers that provide secondary voltages for residential use over three-phase, four-wire circuits. The voltage is either 240v or 120v, depending on the country.

Load studies are conducted to determine the voltage, current, power, and reactive power at various points in an electrical network under existing or contemplated conditions of normal operation. These load studies are essential in planning the future development of the power system. System planners also study the problems associated with the location of plants and transmission systems.

POWER DISTRIBUTION LOSSES

In most developing countries, a substantial gap exists between the supply and demand of electric power as the result of accelerated industrial growth. The power industry is also vested with the responsibility of rural electrification in line with the social and economic policies of the government. The growth in demand from existing users and the addition of new distribution networks calls for heavy adjustments and rearrangements of the distribution system.

Although the government makes additional investments to create new generation facilities, very little attention is paid to the efficient operation of generating stations and distribution systems. Consider the situation in India. Total power generation has increased from 2,300 megawatts (mw) to 36,000 mw during the last 30 years. The per capita consumption, however, is around 160 kilowatt hours (kwh), which is very low when compared to industrialized countries. Various studies have revealed that transmission and distribution losses are at a very high level of 22 percent. The prevention of power transmission and distribution losses would amount to a greater generating capacity.

Substations in rural areas are located in block headquarters. As and when a village becomes a candidate for electrification, it is connected to the nearest point of the existing network, taking into consideration geographical constraints. The incremental extension of the distribution system has resulted in feeders that run long distances in a zig-zag fashion and cause large losses of power and poor terminal voltages. The poor terminal voltages in turn affect electrical equipment, especially induction motors that are used for agricultural purposes.

Power system engineers are required to perform detailed exercises to optimize the distribution system for minimum losses during every expansion. They also conduct a continuous exercise to rationalize power distribution systems in line with ever-increasing loads. These two exercises are also coupled with a minimal capital investment.

Power system engineers in developing countries perform these exercises using conventional long-hand techniques that are tedious, inaccurate, less than optimal, and time-consuming. The use of computational techniques is limited because well-supported minicomputers are either unavailable or cost too much. However, the situation is changing fast as a result of the local availability of inexpensive, standard personal computers with graphic facilities. An opportunity therefore exists to use computer-aided power system design.

THE COMPUTER-AIDED POWER SYSTEMS IMPROVEMENT PACKAGE

The Computer-Aided Power Systems Improvement (CAPSI) package is being developed by a leading Indian computer manufacturer in association with the Indian Institute of Science, a premier research institution. The rich experience of practicing engineers is built into the system with a judicious combination of accurate mathematical models. The CAPSI package is capable of performing accurate circuit analyses of primary and secondary distribution networks. It computes voltages at every node, real and reactive power, losses at every section, and the total loss. It also provides a cost analysis of any changes that may be required to improve the system. The practical element of this package is that it offers an opportunity to use the intelligence and intuition of experienced engineers without enforcing a hypothetically optimal solution.

The CAPSI package is interactive and user-friendly; no prior knowledge of computers is required to use it. It runs on a standard personal computer with such graphic devices as a color graphic monitor, a plotter, and a digitizer. The package helps an engineer create alternate schemes of distribution networks and responds with the technical and financial consequences of such schemes. It assists in comparing alternatives to arrive at a near-optimal technological and economical solution. It can handle a network composed of 10 feeders, each feeder of which has 100 nodes. The package can be used for subtransmission and high- and low-tension distribution networks. The CAPSI package is composed of the following six modules:

- A cost file maintenance module;
- A network input module;
- A system improvement module;
- A network plotting module;
- An executive summary output module; and
- A detailed report printing module.

The cost file maintenance module is used to enter or update construction cost parameters, such as cost per kilometer, to determine the costs of new versus salvage materials and conductors, which links and conductors can be deleted, the cost of a new substation, the cost of laying a new feeder, and the cost of a capacitor per kilovolt ampere reactive (kvar). Before CAPSI is used, these cost details must be at current values.

The network input module is used to input network information. The engineer uses a scaled map of the network in which all nodes are properly numbered. The coordinates of the nodes can be entered on a keyboard or through a digitizer. The following information must be entered:

- Network identification details;
- The feeder number;
- The node number;
- The X-Y coordinates of nodes;
- Connection details;
- The power load at the nodes; and
- The conductor type.

Once these details are entered, CAPSI is ready to analyze the distribution network.

The engineer uses the systems improvement module to analyze and calculate the effects of various alternative schemes. This module can be used for a radial network or a general mesh network. The existing network, which was constructed using input data, is displayed on a graphic monitor. The engineer starts the interactive session to create a modified network aided by a number of commands that help the engineer perform the following:

- Display the whole network or a magnified part of it;
- Change the electrical parameters;
- Change the geometry;
- Compute the performance;
- Compute the cost of modifications;
- Analyze the profitability of modifications; and
- Obtain a detailed report and executive summary.

The list of commands is given in Appendix I. The engineer uses commands to try to "straighten out" the distribution lines by adding or deleting links, splitting the network, and redistributing the load, all of which depend on the condition of the terrain. For every change, CAPSI responds by giving the cost of incorporation, savings in energy, and improvement in voltage profile. The color monitor displays the existing network and the modifications under consideration in different colors. The engineer can decide to retain or discard a modification depending on its cost-effectiveness. If the voltage profile does not improve as desired, conductors may have to be changed. Network details can be stored on diskettes for future analysis and modification. The network plotting module takes the details of the existing network and the modified network and converts them to a form suitable for output onto an X-Y plotter.

The executive summary output module creates an executive summary based on the details of the existing network and the final modified network. The summary includes the following details:

- Energy savings in kwh;
- Peak demand savings in kw;
- An investment profile; and
- A cost-benefit analysis.

The detailed report printing module prints a detailed report on system improvements to the following components:

- Feeders and nodes;
- Complex voltage and RMS voltage;
- Complex current and RMS current;
- Transformer core and copper losses; and
- Network energy savings.

The CAPSI package is also being enhanced to cater to short-circuit analysis and fault detection; transmission line losses, taking corona losses into consideration; and a secondary distribution network.

CONCLUSION

In most developing countries, a gap exists between the supply and demand of electrical power as a result of industrial growth and rural electrification. Transmission losses account for about 20 percent of the power generated. Power system engineers still use manual methods to rationalize existing power systems and add new substations.

This paper describes a Computer-Aided Power System Improvement package that runs on an inexpensive personal computer. The rich experience of practicing engineers and accurate mathematical models are built into the package. The practical element of the package is that it offers an opportunity to use the knowledge of an experienced engineer without enforcing a hypothetically optimal solution. The package is interactive and does not demand computer knowledge. It allows an engineer to create alternative schemes and evaluate them on a technological and economic basis. The package can handle either mesh or tree-type networks and subtransmission, high-tension, or low-tension distribution networks.

ACKNOWLEDGMENT

The author would like to acknowledge the help rendered by S. Ramachandran, D.L. Kulakarni, and S. Karthik from Energy Industry Group of Wipro Information Technology Limited, Bangalore, India.

APPENDIX I
LIST OF COMMANDS

A) **SYSTEM PARAMETERS**
   SP View and update system parameters
   LN Display load at a node

B) **COMPUTATIONAL RESULTS**
   Below X = E for Existing Network
           M for Modified Network
   NVX Node voltage
   MVX Minimum voltage
   VPX Voltage profile
   LIX Link current
   LLX Link loss
   FRX Feeder results
   NRX Network total results
   NSX Node voltage listing
   LSX Node current listing
   TLX Transformer loss
   SM Summary results
   CG Centre of gravity

C) **MODIFICATIONS**
   AL Add link
   LC Link code change
   AN Add new node
   CF Create a new feeder
   AC Add capacitance at a node
   DT Transfer tail portion of a feeder to another
   DL Delete link
   NC Change load at a node
   TP Create tapping point
   MD Computational mode change
   DC Delete capacitance at node

D) **NETWORK DISPLAY**
   Below X = E for Existing Network
           M for Modified Network
   GRX Network display
   MGX Magnify part of network
   VCX Voltage contour
   FMX Magnify a feeder

GRX Redraw network

E) GENERAL
HC Creation of report file
EX Terminate program
NF Creation of modified data file
HE Help facility
GH Graphic help
CC Change cost help
CN Change mode of display, i.e., with node number 0 or without.

26

Applications of Microcomputers in Water Resources Engineering

Don Charles Henry Senarath

Water resources engineering deals with the use of naturally occurring water for the maximum overall benefit to mankind. Many problems are associated with obtaining the proper quantity of suitable water at the desired location and at the right time without creating the possibility of any undesirable effects in the present or future. Water resources engineering includes data collection, data analysis, design, construction, operation, and management. Each of these phases consists of many steps that are involved with the handling of large volumes of data. Unlike many other branches of engineering, the primary commodity—water—is derived from the global hydrological cycle, which is controlled by a great number of apparently independent parameters.

Until less than three decades ago, the techniques that were commonly used were geared toward simple computational tools such as slide rules or mathematical tables. The scope of handling data through the use of these methods was limited in both accuracy and speed. In some cases, specific analyses were obtained through the use of physical models or analog techniques. Although such methods were and still are used in specific cases, they are restricted by a lack of versatility, speed, and precision.

Digital computers became available in developed countries in the late 1950s and early 1960s. Data computation and handling techniques were correspondingly changed to take advantage of the new developments. However, the benefits of these computers were not generally available to developing countries because of their enormous cost. Only a few persons from developing countries who were fortunate enough to study in developed countries or enlist in special training programs had the opportunity to use these computers.

The situation remained basically unchanged until the 1970s, when mini- and microcomputers became widely available. Microcomputers with a sufficient storage capacity and speed of operation for most purposes have come within the reach of interested users. In fact, many users now own personal microcomputers. Being one of the few commodities that tend to decrease in price regardless of inflation, it is appropriate that developing countries keep abreast of the applications of microcomputers in various fields.

A few selected examples of the applications of microcomputers in water resources engineering are described. The examples selected for this paper were restricted to cases in which the underlying theoretical concepts were simple enough to be presented to an audience of diverse backgrounds.

THE USE OF THE WATER BALANCE OF A CATCHMENT AREA TO ESTIMATE GROUNDWATER RECHARGE

Groundwater recharge is the quantity of precipitation that reaches the groundwater table as a result of percolation through the layers that underlie a catchment area. Because the quantity of water that can be abstracted from the ground depends primarily on the groundwater recharge, the latter is an important parameter in evaluating the resources of an aquifer. It is also an important parameter in modeling the flow of groundwater.

A simplified scheme of the relevant processes that take place in a catchment area is shown in Figure 1. The mechanics of water balance within the soil's moisture zone are complicated by the uncertain role played by the plant roots in evapotranspiration. Several simplified models have been devised to represent the water balance in this zone. Rushton and Ward (1979) formulated a model that has produced reasonable results in many applications (Senarath and Rushton, 1984). The model is based on the following assumptions:

- The soil is considered to be at field capacity when it holds the maximum moisture content after the moisture is allowed to drain freely under gravity. The soil is considered to have a soil moisture deficit when it holds less moisture than at field capacity. The soil moisture deficit (SMD) is measured by the volume of water per unit area (usually measured in millimeters of water) that is required to bring the soil up to field capacity.
- The potential evaporation (PE) at a given location is determined by such atmospheric parameters as humidity, temperature, and wind velocity, and can be determined either from equations such as Penman's equation (Penman, 1949) or from pan evaporation data.
- When sufficient water from precipitation is available, evaporation would take place at a potential rate. When the water available from precipitation is insufficient to meet the potential evaporation, water for evaporation will be taken up from the soil through the plant roots. However, if the soil moisture deficit is above a certain value known as root constant (C), the soil will supply only a fraction (about one-tenth) of the water required for evaporation at the potential rate. When the soil moisture deficit exceeds a value known as maximum soil moisture deficit (D), no more water is extracted from the soil for evapotranspiration. Both C and D depend on the type of vegetation and are related to the root characteristics of the particular vegetation.
- When the soil reaches field capacity, any excess water that reaches the soil moisture zone results in deep percolation and a part of this component eventually becomes groundwater recharge.

A computer model suitable for microcomputers can be developed from this simplified conceptual outline of processes that occur in a catchment system. The inputs for the model are precipitation (P) and potential evaporation (PE). The outputs are stream run-off (SR), actual evaporation (AE), soil moisture deficit (SMD), and groundwater recharge (R).

The following parameters for the soil moisture zone are required:

- The fraction of the quantity of water that follows the path of surface run-off after precipitation;

- The threshold value of precipitation above which surface run-off will take place;
- The fraction of the quantity of percolating water that follows the path of interflow;
- The root constant (C); and
- The maximum soil moisture deficit (D).

The model can be calibrated in regard to these parameters by comparing the output stream run-off (SR) with the gauged stream run-off. The initial soil moisture deficit must be known. A convenient method of supplying the initial soil moisture deficit is to start the computations after a period of heavy precipitation (toward the end of winter or monsoon seasons) when the soil moisture deficit would be zero. The values of root constant and maximum soil moisture deficit have been established on an empirical basis for different types of vegetation in different climatic areas (Grindley, 1969). A flowchart for this model is shown in Figure 2.

The program was used to study the water balance of two catchment areas in different parts of the world: the area overlying the chalk aquifer in southeast England around Essex and the area covering the sand aquifer of the island of Mannar in northwest Sri Lanka.

In the catchment area in England, it was found that out of a total annual mean precipitation of around 600 millimeters, about 75 percent was lost in evaporation, and about 2.5 percent reached the chalk aquifer as recharge.

It was also revealed that when aquifer heads were high, a significant fraction of the potential recharge did not get into the aquifer, but found its way into the streams. However, when the aquifer heads were reduced as a result of abstraction from wells, increasing quantities of the potential recharge reached the aquifer.

In the catchment area in Sri Lanka, it was found that out of an annual mean precipitation of 975 millimeters, the quantity that reached the groundwater table amounted to about 12 percent. Of this quantity, almost half escaped across the perimeter into the sea.

AN ADVANCED WATER BALANCE SYSTEM

Based on the general principles outlined in the previous section, a more detailed representation (suitable for handling with a micrometer) can be formulated to incorporate a larger land area that consists of units with widely varying properties and a larger number of parameters.

The main parameters of practical interest in such a system would be those related to irrigation water requirements. In many developing countries, irrigation water is a precious commodity that is obtained with enormous capital costs. A pressing need therefore exists for its optimum use. In countries such as Sri Lanka, in which large amounts of money have been invested to establish irrigation systems, a properly monitored management scheme is needed to supply the correct quantity of water at different stages of crop growth.

A microcomputer system of moderate cost is a valuable tool that could greatly benefit the process of managing irrigation schemes. The ability to store and process large volumes of data is the essential computer requirement, not the speed of computation. A microcomputer can fulfill this requirement completely.

Such a system can also be linked to a data collection system or a data bank from which information could be transmitted through a suitable communication network. The following field data become relevant in such a system:

- Precipitation and its variation in space and time over the area considered;
- Meteorological information, such as wind velocity, humidity, solar radiation, atmospheric pressure, and temperature;
- Information related to streams, such as discharge and stage (elevation) at a number of carefully selected gauging stations within and outside the area under consideration;
- Information related to the different soil horizons, such as depth, permeability, and storage properties;
- Information related to vegetation, such as the type of crop, water requirements, and stages of growth;
- Information related to reservoirs and groundwater systems that lie in the area; and
- Information related to indigenous habits and cultural practices of the populations in different areas.

The system should also have sufficient "intelligence" to make use of past experience in making decisions for the future. Because the arithmetical operations involved in such a system are of a simple nature, the speed of computation need not be a very significant criterion. As long as the computer can store and handle a large volume of data at a moderate speed, the intended purpose would be fulfilled.

GROUNDWATER FLOW MODELS

Another application of microcomputers is to represent groundwater flow. The objective of such a representation is to assess the implications of alternative possibilities in the use of an aquifer, particularly in regard to the location of abstraction wells and the rates of abstraction. A system that represents the flow of groundwater is called a groundwater model (ASCE, 1972). In general, a groundwater model can either represent the regional flow in an aquifer within specified boundaries or the flow toward a single well from the surrounding area. The former is called a regional flow model and the latter a radial flow model (Rushton and Redshaw, 1979).

Groundwater models are generally formulated on the basis of discrete steps in space and time. The computations involve large storage requirements and considerable computer time. However, it is possible to select appropriate techniques to suit the facilities available. For example, the use of the Gaussian elimination technique to solve simultaneous equations involves a large memory requirement but comparatively little computer time. By contrast, the use of an iterative technique such as the successive over-relaxation method (Rushton, 1974) involves less memory but more computer time. The former method would be more appropriate if a microcomputer with a large memory is to be used, even if the speed of computation is not high.

Another important application of microcomputers is in the conjunctive use of groundwater with surface water. A groundwater model can be linked to a surface catchment model and used to study management options to obtain the optimum advantages of the combined system. Such a system could also be linked to a data bank or a data collection network like the one mentioned in the case of the surface water balance system.

CONCLUSION

Microcomputers play a very useful role in the management of water resource systems. Because of their low cost, microcomputers have now come within the reach of developing countries. Microcomputers can play a very significant role in the development of water resources, which is crucial to the economic development of many developing countries.

The reluctance to use new technologies and the overenthusiasm to embrace a new technology without properly examining its real usefulness in a given situation can both be harmful. However, if the need for and capabilities of available machines are properly evaluated, the use of microcomputers can significantly affect the efficiency of the overall management process in many fields. A need exists in certain areas for the development of microcomputer capabilities to cater to special requirements, such as the management of water resource systems that are linked to a data base and a data collection system.

REFERENCES

ASCE. Groundwater Management, Manuals and Reports on Engineering Practice, No. 40, New York, 1972.

Grindley, J. "The calculation of actual evaporation and soil moisture deficit over specified catchment areas," Hydrological Memorandum No. 38, Met. Office, Bracknell Berks., U.K., Nov. 1969.

Penman, H.L. "The dependence of transpiration on weather and soil conditions," Journal of Soil Science, U.K., Vol. 1, 1949.

Rushton, K.R. "Aquifer analysis using backward difference methods," Journal of Hydrology, Amsterdam, Vol. 22, 1974.

Rushton, K.R., and Redshaw, S.C. Seepage and Groundwater Flow. Numerical Analysis by analog and digital methods, John Wiley and Sons, 1979.

Rushton, K.R. and Ward, C. "The estimation of groundwater recharge," Journal of Hydrology, Amsterdam, Vol. 41, 1979.

Senarath, D.C.H. and Rushton, K.R. "A routing technique for estimating ground-water recharge," GROUND WATER, U.S.A., Vol. 22, 1984.

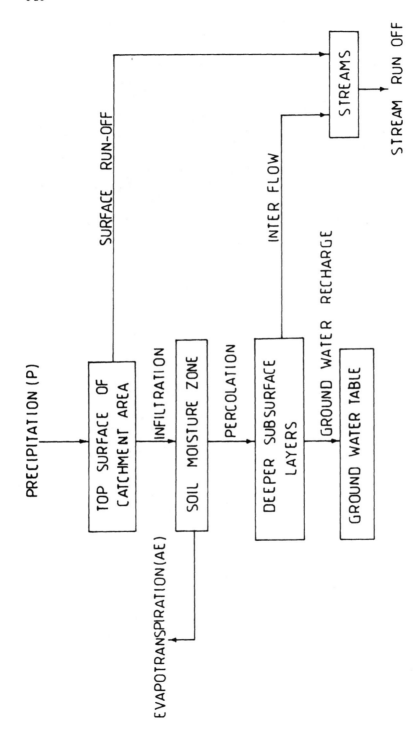

FIGURE 1 Flow distribution in subsurface layers.

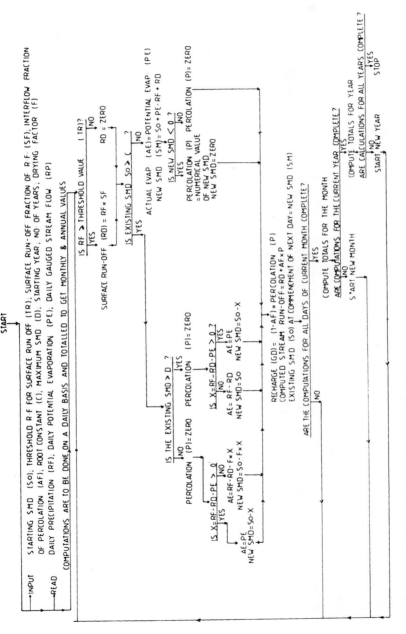

FIGURE 2 Water balance of the subsurface zones.

27

Intelligent Programs for Public Investments in Community Water Supply and Sanitation Systems

DONALD T. LAURIA

This paper is primarily concerned with public investments in community water supply and sanitation systems, but many of the concepts described also apply to other fields of investment. Water and sanitation planning in most developing countries is performed by a central agency of the national government that needs to decide when to construct and expand community systems, how large to make them, what level of service to provide, whether to make individual house connections to the water and sanitation systems or construct public taps and latrines, what the diameter of the pipe in the networks should be, whether to construct separate community systems or regional facilities, and what prices to charge the users.

The answers to these and similar questions usually depend greatly on the experience, recommendations, and standards of industrialized countries. For example, system capacity is often sufficient to meet demands for 20 or more years, as is done in the United States and Europe; house connections are preferred to public taps, as in high-income countries; the design average daily per capita flow is usually 150 liters or more; and minimum pipe sizes are seldom less than 2 inches in water networks or 6 inches in sewers.

The standards of industrialized countries are often unsuitable for developing countries because the conditions of the two are so different. In industrialized countries, labor is typically very expensive compared to capital. The social rate of discount is comparatively low, as in population growth and associated rates of demand. Industrialized countries are more concerned with expanding existing facilities than with constructing new ones. High-income countries have a greater fiscal autonomy and ability to pay, which makes them less dependent on government subsidies. Because investment is at the local instead of the national level of government, capital budgeting in industrialized countries is less restrictive.

It is widely accepted that the adoption of planning and design standards from industrialized countries by developing countries is basically unwise and can lead to serious misallocation of scarce resources. Investment decisions should instead be tailored to local economic, social, and other conditions. The most appropriate methods of obtaining appropriate solutions for a very large class of public investments are through the use of mathematical models and intelligent computer programs.

Intelligent programs are computer codes that can assist in the planning, design, and operation of systems. They assist in decision-making, which involves selecting the best course of action from a set of alternatives. The main advantage of intelligent programs is that they facilitate the rapid and efficient screening of options.

The main categories of intelligent programs of interest in this paper are optimization and simulation codes. Numerous textbooks describe the characteristics of these programs; therefore, only a few are highlighted in the following discussion.

An optimization program begins with a mathematical model in which the user identifies a set of decision variables (i.e., the things about which decisions are to be made). A mathematical objective function is then written in terms of these variables, which are to be optimized. In the field of public investment, the objective function is usually a statement of project cost, which is to be minimized. Additional mathematical statements in terms of the decision variables are written for scarce resources and other constraints of the problem, thereby completing the model, which is then read into the computer.

It is unlikely that an optimization program would ever be developed with the intention of obtaining only a single solution.

Even if the model is applied to a specific situation, the user would want to solve it several times and with different parameter values, if for no other reason than to account for uncertainty. The next phase of the optimization program therefore consists of the user reading into the computer appropriate numerical values for the parameters in the model. This is followed by the use of a mathematical optimization algorithm to solve the problem, which depends on the mathematical form of the objective function and constraints. A solution consists of obtaining optimal numerical values for the decision variables, followed by back-substitution of these values into the objective and constraints to obtain values for these functions. The search for the best solution using the algorithm is automatic; the user rarely sees the different alternatives during the screening process, only the final result.

A simple example illustrates the optimization program. Suppose the user needs to determine the optimal width x and height y that maximize the area A of a rectangle subject to the constraint that the perimeter equal P. The first step is to develop the model in parametric terms:

$$\text{Maximize } A = xy \tag{1}$$

$$\text{Subject to } 2x + 2y = P \tag{2}$$

The user then supplies numerical values for the parameters and reads them into the program. In this case $P = 100$. The computer then converts the problem into an appropriate form for optimization. Replacing P by 100 in Equation 2 and solving for x results in an expression in terms of y that can be substituted into Equation 1. The final optimization problem is:

$$\text{Maximize } 50y - y^2 \tag{3}$$

This is an unconstrained, nonlinear maximization problem for which various standard solution algorithms exist. Using one of them, the optimal value of y is found by the computer to be 25. Back-substituting into Equation 2, x is found to be 25, and from Equation 1, the calculated maximum area is 625.

A simulation program similarly starts with the identification of decision variables and mathematical statements of the objective function and constraints that constitute the model and that are read into the computer. However, instead of using an automatic optimization technique to solve the problem, the user selects trial values of the decision variables and lets the simulation program calculate the resulting values of objective function and constraints. Successive values are tried by the user until a satisfactory solution emerges that may or may not be optimal. The approach is for the user to ask "what if?" questions. Unlike optimization, the user investigates numerous alternatives in the search for the best solution. Although optimization problems can always be formulated for solutions by simulation, the reverse is not true because it is not always possible to find an automatic problem-solver for any simulation problem.

After solving the previous rectangle problem by simulation, the first task is to select values for the decision variables width and height. Assume the user selects $x = 10$ and $y = 20$. Substituting into Equation 2, P is found to be 60, and from Equation 1, $A = 200$. The user can immediately see that x and/or y need to be larger to satisfy the constraint on the perimeter. The next trial, for example, is $x = 20$ and $y = 20$ for which $P = 80$ and $A = 400$. Proceeding in this fashion with trial values of x and y, numerous solutions can be obtained, some of which may be close to the optimum, perhaps without ever finding the set values:

$$x* = 25 \text{ and } y* = 25$$

OPTIMIZATION AND SIMULATION PROGRAMS

A few different optimization and simulation programs have been written for microcomputers and are being used by water and sewer agencies in developing countries and elsewhere. Some of these programs are being distributed by the World Bank and other institutions as a service to national, regional, and local government agencies. It would be possible to describe hundreds of programs in the environmental engineering field that have been developed to assist investment planning. The following small sample is intended to provide an overview of the kinds of programs available, how they are structured, and what their capabilities are. Although these models are specific to environmental engineering investments, they are typical of a much broader class of programs and therefore illustrate a general approach to programming and problem-solving. All of the following programs have been written in BASIC or FORTRAN language for solution on the IBM PC or its compatibles.

Branched Water Networks

It is not uncommon for 60 percent or more of a community's water system costs to be tied up in the pipe network. This component is not only expensive but difficult to design. If selected pipe diameters are too large, network costs will be too high, and it will be difficult or impossible for the beneficiaries to pay and will deprive other communities of water systems because of capital budgeting constraints. If diameters are too small (which is the most common situation), it will be impossible for users to obtain target quantities of water from the network because pressures will be too low. Proper network design is therefore extremely important.[1] There are two kinds of water networks: those with and those without closed circuits. A network without closed circuits is branched; an example is shown in Figure 1. In a branched network, water from the source enters at Node 1 and is taken out at Nodes 2 and 4 to meet demands. The flow in any link of a branched network can be easily determined by inspection or simple calculation; the flow in Link 1 is Q_2+Q_4.

Water flows from points of higher pressure to points of lower pressure; the highest pressure in Figure 1 is at Node 1. Pressure is reduced as water flows along a pipe as a result of friction. If the network in Figure 2 was flat, the lowest pressures would be at Nodes 2 and 4. Well-known equations describe how the pressure in a pipe decreases as a function of the flow, pipe diameter, length, and pipe material (i.e., pipe roughness).

Once the system has been laid out, the basic problem of network design is to select the lengths and diameters of pipes in the system. A mathematical model was developed about 15 years ago to show how this could be done optimally by using linear programming (LP) (Robinson and Austin, 1976). Assume that each link in Figure 1 consists of pipes with different diameters laid

---

[1] The proper design of sewers is similarly important. They are expensive and hard to design; over- and under-design should therefore be avoided. Optimization and simulation programs for sewers (similar to those for water networks) have been developed, are in use, and are available from the World Bank.

end to end in a series; the user must select the candidate diameters for these pipes (rules of thumb are available for this). The task of design is to determine the optimal length of each different diameter pipe in each link; the lengths are the decision variables.

The objective function is an expression of total construction cost, which depends on the unknown lengths of the pipes with different diameters. The optimization problem is to find the pipe lengths that minimize cost. Two sets of constraints complete the model. The first constraint requires that the total length of all the proposed pipes in each link equal the length of the link; a separate equation is needed for each link (three in the case of Figure 1). The second set of constraints imposes hydraulic restrictions on the design. Assuming that the available pressure at source Node 1 is known, and that minimum allowable pressures have been specified for demand Nodes 2 and 4, the first hydraulic constraint requires that the pressure at Node 1 less the friction losses in Pipes 1 and 2 result in a pressure at Node 2 equal to or greater than the specified minimum. A similar constraint is written for the hydraulic pathway between Nodes 2 and 4; in other words, the pressure at Node 1 less friction losses in Pipes 1 and 3 must result in a minimum specified pressure at Node 4.

Because the network is branched and the decision variables are pipe lengths, the objective function and constraints are all linear expressions.[2] It is therefore possible to use LP as the optimization algorithm for solution. Although the previous description covers the most rudimentary considerations of network design, it is possible to expand the model to include such realistic elements as multiple sources of water supply, uneven terrain, constraints on maximum pressure (for steep elevations) and minimum pressure, and the use of parallel pipes in links to enable the networks to be expanded.

A computer program has been written for this model using the IBM PC; the program is being distributed by the World Bank (1985). The user of this program only has to specify such things as network configuration, flows at demand nodes, ground elevations at nodes, target pressures at source and demand nodes, link

---

[2] This problem could have been formulated assuming the diameter of each link for its entire length is constant. In this case, pipe diameters would be the decision variables, and solution would require nonlinear programming.

lengths, candidate diameters, and the cost per unit length for each different diameter to obtain an optimal solution (i.e., the pipe lengths that minimize cost). After reading these data into the computer, the program formulates the LP problem and then solves it using an LP algorithm. The user is informed of the final solution but does not see any of the intermediate solutions that are investigated in the search.

Looped Water Networks

Looped water networks have closed circuits; a system with a single circuit is shown in Figure 2. Input flow Q_1 is at Node 1 and demand flows are at Nodes 2, 3, and 4. Although it is clear that $Q_1 = Q_2 + Q_3 + Q_4$, it is impossible to easily determine the flows in the pipes; it certainly cannot be determined by inspection, as was possible in the case of Figure 1. This is a major difference between branched and looped networks, and it accounts for an entirely different mathematical modeling and computer programming approach to design.

Although various optimization models have been published for the design of looped networks, they are all nonlinear, which makes them difficult to solve and somewhat impractical for real-world applications, especially for large complicated networks. The preferred approach is to use computer simulation, which is briefly described in the following paragraphs.

Assume the designer knows the pressure at source Node 2 and has minimum allowable values for the other demand nodes. The supply and demand flows are known, as are pipe lengths and ground elevations. Assume further that the designer selects a trial diameter for all the pipes in the network. The computer calculates the pressures at the demand nodes using the empirical flow equations mentioned in the previous section (which are nonlinear). The pressures constitute a simulation of the system.

If the node pressures are far above the allowable minimum, the trial diameters are too large (i.e., friction losses are too small); if the pressures are too low, the trial diameters are too small. This is not uncommon. Based on judgment, the user selects a new set of pipe diameters, reduces those that seem to be too large, and enlarges those that are too small. Another submission to the computer will reveal whether or not the diameter adjustments have resulted in satisfactory pressures.

The process of selecting diameters and simulating pressures is continued until the user is satisfied. When to end the trials is a matter of judgment; a mathematically optimal solution will probably never be found, but a very good solution with minimized costs is likely. In this process of simulation, it is interesting to note that network cost is not usually considered after each trial, despite the fact that the engineering goal is to minimize cost. The supposition is that node pressures close to the minimum will result in a cost that is similarly near the minimum. Computer programs that simulate looped networks are available to national water supply agencies and others from the World Bank (1985).

Combined Optimization and Simulation

In the case of looped network design, the better the judgment of the user in selecting initial pipe diameters, the fewer the trials needed to obtain a satisfactory solution. A significant problem in developing countries, however, is that engineers frequently have little or no experience in designing networks and therefore do not have very good judgment in selecting trial diameters. This can result in the need for numerous simulations in addition to the risk that the final solution might be far from optimal.

A combination of optimization and simulation can be used to overcome this problem and obtain good network designs. The approach is to first ignore some of the links in the system to convert the looped network to one with branches. The network can be optimally designed using the LP program described earlier; little experience and judgment are needed for the primary (branched) pipes of the looped network. The next task is to select diameters for the links that close the circuits of the looped network (i.e., the ones ignored in converting the looped system to one with branches); simple rules are available to aid judgment. The looped system, with initial diameters for all pipes, can then be simulated to see if it performs satisfactorily (i.e., whether node pressures are acceptable). If the pressures are considered unsatisfactory, some diameters may have to be changed, but the number of changes to be made will usually be far fewer than if initial trial diameters were selected entirely by judgment; convergence to solution can also be very rapid.

This approach to design is illustrated by the looped network in Figure 2. It can first be seen that a branched as opposed to a looped network would be quite capable of delivering the input flow Q_1 to demand Nodes 2, 3, and 4. For example, Pipe 2 could be discarded, which would result in the branched system shown in Figure 3. The branched network shown in Figure 3 is called the primary system because the pipes in the network are the principal ones for delivering flows.

The first task is to decide which pipe to discard in forming the primary (branched) network. The general principle is to retain those pipes in the branched network that have the shortest total length needed to connect the source node (Pipe 1) with the demand nodes (Pipes 2, 3, and 4). An optimization technique called the minimum spanning tree algorithm can be used to identify this branched network. This algorithm is particularly useful for large, complicated looped systems with many circuits and is included in the package of programs distributed by the World Bank.

Once the primary branched network is identified, the optimal sizes of its pipes can be found using the LP program described earlier. The next step is to select diameter(s) for the pipe(s) omitted from the branched system. Because these pipes are mainly needed to close the circuits and not to deliver demand flows to nodes, they are called the secondary links and can often be arbitrarily selected using minimum allowable pipe diameters. The addition of these pipes to the branched network changes the network's hydraulic characteristics. It does not follow that node pressures will be satisfactory, even though the primary network has been optimally designed. For this reason, it is necessary to submit the entire looped network to the computer for simulation. Node pressures will generally be satisfactory or nearly so. If adjustments in pipe sizes are found to be needed, however, they can usually be made easily by using trial and judgment. A flowchart of the optimization and simulation process is shown in Figure 4.

RESERVOIR PROGRAMS

The first of the previous three sections described an optimization approach to design, the next described simulation, and the last described a combination of the two in which optimization is initially used to obtain an approximate solution that is then finetuned using simulation. Although the methods were described in terms of water networks, similar programs and approaches to design are used for a wide variety of public investments. Water storage reservoirs are typically very expensive to build. Their design can therefore benefit from the use of computer programs. A great deal of literature exists on optimization approaches to reservoir design.[3] A classic and powerful model was developed by Revelle et al. (1969) that uses LP for solution. The core of the model is a set of mass balance equations for the amount of water in the reservoir for each month of the planning period. Another set of equations describes the operating rule for the reservoir, which is assumed to be a linear expression. The objective is to minimize reservoir size subject to meeting demands, maintaining water volume within upper and lower bounds, and so forth. Solution is easily obtained by LP.

Just as the LP model for networks applied only to a certain class (ones without closed circuits), the LP model for reservoirs pertains only to systems in which the operating rule is linear. In cases in which a more complicated nonlinear operating rule is used, a simulation approach to reservoir design is used. As in the case of looped networks, the user must select trial values of the decision variables, which in this case are reservoir size and key parameters of the rule. The computer is then used to simulate reservoir performance, and specific attention is paid to water shortages in meeting target demands. If shortages are judged to be unsatisfactory, new trial values of size and operating parameters are chosen, and the simulation process is repeated until an acceptable solution is obtained.

In the case of looped networks, it was shown that a combination of optimization and simulation can overcome some of the problems of poor judgment in selecting initial trial values of the decision variables. A similar approach is possible with reservoirs. The LP model is used to estimate the optimal system size and operation; the result can then be fine-tuned through simulation.

PRICING PROGRAMS

Much literature exists on capital budgeting models that can assist water and other agencies to determine when and how much

---

[3]See, for example, the journal *Water Resources Research* and Loucks et al., 1981.

to borrow to implement capital improvement programs and how to change prices over time to meet target revenue requirements.[4]

Optimization models that use LP have been developed from capital budgeting. As in the case of reservoirs, the core of the model is a set of inventory equations that describes cash flow for each year of the planning period. The balance at the end of any year depends on the amount at the start in addition to income from such sources as revenues, grants, loans, and interest less expenditures for such things as construction, operation, maintenance, and debt service. Various constraints can be added to the model, such as minimum annual cash reserves and limits on fluctuations in prices. The basic set of decision variables consists of annual prices, which in the case of water is the amount charged per unit volume in each year of the planning period. Although at least a few different objectives can be formulated for the model, all include some expression of total prices or total revenue that is to be minimized.

As in the case of LP models for networks and reservoirs, optimization can be used for capital budgeting only under certain simplistic and restrictive assumptions. Networks had to be branched; reservoirs had to employ a linear operating rule; and the source of revenue for capital budgeting is from water sales, for which only a single price that remains constant in each period of the model can apply. In real situations, however, several sources of revenue usually exist, such as initial connection charges to the system, fixed monthly service fees, and monthly commodity charges that depend on sales. Furthermore, commodity charges may include increasing or declining blocks of prices instead of a single constant price, and they may be different for residential, commercial, and industrial customers as well as for places within and outside city limits.

Simulated programs are used to handle these complexities. They are extremely common in industrialized countries and almost always make use of an electronic spreadsheet. The user first selects trial fees and prices (and possibly other decision variables, such as the amounts, timing, and interest rates for loans) and then uses the program to calculate the flow of revenue shortages and surpluses. Variations of these programs are used by such international finance

---

[4] See, for example, Clark et al., 1979; and Wilkes, 1977.

institutions as the World Bank and can also calculate indicators of project viability, such as the internal rate of return.

As in the case described earlier, the combination of optimization and simulation holds the promise of identifying near-optimal solutions for complicated capital budgeting problems. An LP model can first be solved to contain an initial set of commodity prices. These can then be desegregated by judgment to account for the complexities of the real tariff structure, and a simulation can then be made to test for revenue sufficiency and other indicators of fiscal viability.

DISCUSSION

The previous descriptions of intelligent models and programs indicate that many of the ones for public investments have certain universal characteristics, despite the fact that they apply to different situations. Optimization and simulation approaches both have advantages and disadvantages.

One of the main advantages of optimization models, at least in theory, is that they can identify a globally optimal solution; that is, the unique set of decision variable values that optimize the objective function while satisfying the set of problem constraints. Simulation cannot do this; at best it can identify a near-optimal solution, assuming that the user has proposed one for investigation. The real question is how important it is to know the globally optimal solution. Although the mathematically inclined can get excited about optimization, realists might argue that with so much uncertainty in the world, deterministic problem formulation and solution are not that meaningful. Realists might be correct to believe that a mathematical optimum is a fiction. The goal should be to find one or a few very good solutions, ones that are better than solutions formulated without intelligent programs.

Optimization programs have the advantage of being easy to use. They can be treated like a black box in which the user has to do little more than read in the parameter values and get an instant solution. The user accordingly needs (or at least appears to need) little expertise or understanding of the program. Simulation programs, on the other hand, require the intelligent interaction of the user, who must scrutinize results at each step and decide which values for decision variables should be tried next.

Both of these programs have a disadvantage when placed in

the hands of uninformed users. The risk with optimization is that an inexperienced user can apply the program to situations for which it was never designed. Meaningless results can unknowingly be believed and applied with disastrous consequences. Simulation, on the other hand, forces the user to become at least somewhat knowledgeable about the problem. The risk, however, is that good solutions may be completely overlooked. If only poor alternatives are proposed, a near-optimal solution will never be found.

The time and effort required to solve a problem can be enormously different between optimization and simulation programs. The alternative problem solutions in optimization are internally generated and automatically evaluated by the computer, whereas the user must perform this function while interacting with the computer in the case of simulation. Simulation takes a long time; if the user is solely concerned with the final solution, time would appear to be spent unproductively. However, the positive aspect of simulation is that the long time needed for solution is actually devoted to educating the user. The user participates in a vicarious learning experience that in the long run improves decision-making.

A related issue in regard to solution time is the matter of sensitivity analysis. It is possible for the user to change parameter values to account for uncertainty in both optimization and simulation. However, in the case of optimization, it is generally necessary to resolve the entire problem *de novo* each time the parameters are changed, which requires the internal computerized screening of perhaps hundreds or even thousands of alternatives. In simulation, once the general region of a good solution has been found, sensitivity analysis can be rapid and straightforward.

Optimization models can be formulated for very large and complicated problems. However, the tendency is to structure them as linear problems because LP is by far the most powerful optimization technique. This in fact limits the kinds of problems that can be handled by optimization and also leads to the risk that nonlinear problems may be inappropriately modified to linear form so as to enable quick and easy solutions.

Simulation has the advantage of being nearly independent of the mathematical form of the problem, whether linear or nonlinear. For this reason, it can handle complexities that cannot be addressed by LP. As was shown in the presentation of the sample programs, simulation is often reserved for the fine-tuning of approximate LP solutions. Although they are a bit difficult to generalize, simulation programs frequently have more modest computer requirements than optimization programs, and they are not usually dependent on proprietary or sophisticated computer codes as is sometimes the case with optimization programs. However, simulation codes are generally more difficult to write than optimization codes (especially LP).

An important theoretical and often real advantage of optimization programs, especially in the case of LP, is that they supply economic information and insights into the planning problem that are simply lacking in the case of simulation. By far the most important of these insights are shadow prices that indicate the amount by which the objective function would change for marginal changes on the levels of the constraints. Indeed, shadow prices are sometimes more important for investment planning than the optimal values of the decision variables.

CONCLUSIONS

It is always difficult and dangerous to generalize. Nevertheless, when everything is considered, simulation programs for public investments in developing countries appear to hold the edge over optimization programs.

Perhaps the major advantage of simulation is that it requires users to understand their systems; this results from having to review the computer output after each iteration and make decisions for the next trial. Consequently, users quickly gain "experience," which, although vicarious, is still an excellent teacher. This can be accomplished without the agony of having to actually spend scarce resources only to learn months or years later that the project is a failure. Simulation programs can be strong aids to judgment and can make it possible to avoid absurd solutions, which is all too common in the case of optimization.

Simulation programs can handle essentially any kind of problem, linear or otherwise, constrained or not, with single or multiple objectives. They can also handle any level of detail or sophistication. This is not the case with optimization. In addition, simulation programs can often be easily changed to handle new or unusual circumstances and new planning considerations that were not foreseen at the time of program development.

Electronic spreadsheets are an important advancement in simulation modeling. They are ubiquitous and greatly facilitate program development by reducing the requirements for user expertise in programming to a minimum. Finally, simulation programs often fit more easily onto microcomputers than optimization codes and generally lend themselves to rapid sensitivity analysis, which is very important in developing countries because of the uncertainty of data.

As was indicated in this paper, optimization programs have an important role to play in developing countries and should not be ignored or discounted on the basis of the remarks in this paper. However, when model development is in doubt, simulation may be the most appropriate approach to investment planning.

REFERENCES

Clark, J. J., T. J. Hindelang, and R. E. Pritchard. Capital Budgeting: Planning and Control of Capacity Expansion, Prentice Hall, Englewood, N.J., 1979.

Loucks, D. P., J. R. Stedinger, and D. A. Haith. Water Resource Systems Planning and Analysis, Prentice Hall, Englewood, N.J., 1981.

Revelle, C., E. Joeres and W. Kirby. The Linear Decision Rule in Reservoir Management and Design, *Water Resources Research*, Vol. 5, No. 4, pp. 767-777, August, 1969.

Robinson, R. B. and T. A. Austin. Cost Optimization of Rural Water Supplies, *J. Hydraulics Div.*, ASCE, Vol. 102, No. HY8, August, 1976.

Wilkes, F.M. Capital Budgeting Techniques, John Wiley and Sons, London, 1977.

World Bank. Microcomputer Programs for Improved Planning and Design of Water Supply and Water Disposal Systems, a set of diskettes and user instructions available from the Technology Advisory Group, World Bank, Washington, D.C., 1985.

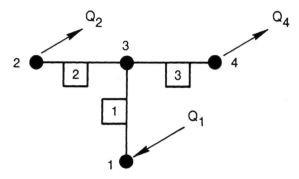

FIGURE 1 Branched network.

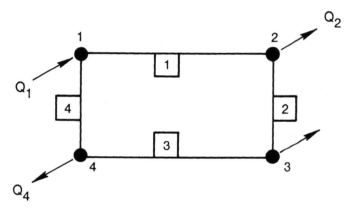

FIGURE 2 Looped network.

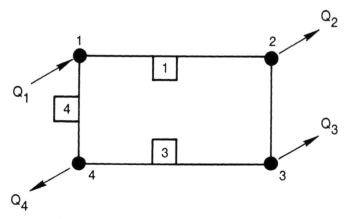

FIGURE 3 Primary (branched) network.

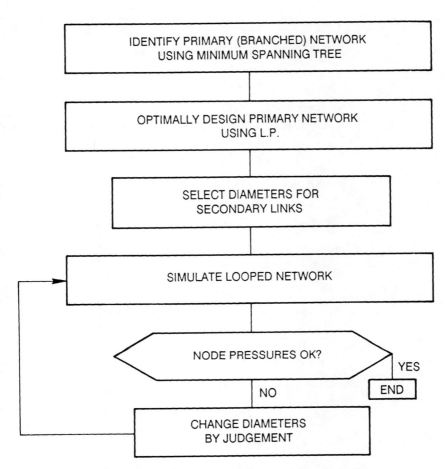

FIGURE 4 Looped network design using optimization and simulation.

28

Applications of Artificial Intelligence in Civil Engineering

BRIAN BRADEMEYER and FRED MOAVENZADEH

The traditional civil engineering process, whether planning, design, construction, operations, or maintenance, involved either an empirical/statistical or an analytical/theoretical approach to problem-solving. These approaches were limited in scope by their requisite data collection and processing burdens on the one hand, and the degree of approximation needed to obtain closed-form solutions on the other. Although computers have been used actively and effectively for several decades to remove some of these limitations, only now are they creating profound impacts on the processes and products of civil engineering.

Although the introduction of the computer greatly enhanced the power and scope of both of these problem-solving approaches, it should be recognized that, in this context, computers are only a tool to aid in civil engineering tasks. As such, their use should be justified on the basis of the benefits they provide, such as enhanced productivity, improved products, reduced resource requirements, and increased reliability. Early computer use focused largely on the design phase, in which a methodological change in analysis and component design procedures allowed reductions to be made in factors of safety. The reliability and efficiency of the designs were also improved by performing far more structural analyses with the computer than was customary with manual calculations.

However, although many of the small steps in the design process could be automated, the use of computers on these steps was often slow and disruptive of the overall design process. Improvements in productivity therefore remained elusive.

It soon became apparent that an integrative computer system approach, as opposed to raw number-crunching capability, was required. As a result, much of the early computer research performed in the Department of Civil Engineering at the Massachusetts Institute of Technology (MIT) was oriented toward improving the productivity and acceptability of computers in the design process. Systems such as COGO, STRESS, STRUDL, and PROJECT promoted a broader view of the design process. By providing a problem data base and, at least conceptually, an interactive environment, these early integrated systems allowed the engineer to create and manipulate engineering problems by applying generalized operators, such as component design and analysis functions, in an appropriate sequence. However, that work was performed when computation was expensive, interactive computer systems were not widely available, and data base management technology was in its infancy.

Recent years have seen a very dramatic set of changes that resulted from continuously improving cost-effectiveness, size reduction, and expanding capabilities in computational power that in turn resulted from microcomputers reaching a mass market position. These improvements are increasing at an accelerating pace and are creating opportunities to use computers in new and different ways. They are also increasing the general degree of computer use in civil engineering substantially. These changes in computer technology will alter the nature and structure of civil engineering organization and the processes by which facilities are planned, designed, constructed, operated, and maintained.

The cost of computational power on chips has dropped an average of 30 percent a year for the last two decades. In addition to the much greater demand for computing equipment that resulted from lower costs, cost reductions have also extended to other hardware components, such as fixed-disk systems. At the same time, a much wider variety of computer hardware is available today with drastic reductions in size. The advent of the personal computer environment has allowed software to become responsively interactive. Easy-to-use computers with inexpensive storage have finally provided the user with the computing environment that was envisioned during the development of STRUDL and other such systems.

In summary, the current computational environment is no longer constrained by hardware. The major constraints are now related to software, programming, training, and a simple awareness of what can currently be done. However, the thesis of this paper is that even greater changes will be occurring over the next 5 years, changes of a much more fundamental nature that could alter the way in which civil engineering tasks and processes are viewed.

A revolution is currently taking place in the information processing field. It involves harnessing hundreds, thousands, or even millions of microprocessors to work together on a single task. Today's fastest mainframe computing speeds may be achieved at a significantly reduced cost by utilizing many relatively inexpensive microprocessors together in a multiprocessor system. Many researchers on such new breeds of machines expect that they will enable some of computer science's most romantic and ambitious aspirations to be realized: image recognition, speech comprehension, and more intelligent behavior. The massive quantitative increase in computing power promised by the multiprocessor revolution may be a prerequisite to the much-heralded qualitative increase in the intelligence of future computers. In this environment, an engineer can ask all the "what if?" questions and the computer, using artificial intelligence techniques, can incorporate the expert reasoning processes relevant to the problem at hand.

ARTIFICIAL INTELLIGENCE, EXPERT SYSTEMS, AND MACHINE LEARNING

Artificial intelligence (AI) is the field of computer science that approaches problem-solving by replicating the manner in which people think. This approach to problem-solving is distinct from traditional algorithmic approaches, which are based on mathematical models, probability theory, optimization techniques, and the like. Artificial intelligence concepts are particularly useful in fields in which the manner in which people think is a very important part of solving a problem, in which algorithmic approaches cannot generate reasonable values for the effort, and in which these two features are combined. Elements of artificial intelligence include knowledge representation, search techniques, inference mechanisms, planning of searches, learning, and allocation of problem-solving resources.

Knowledge-based expert systems (KBES) represent the branch of AI that applies organized knowledge related to a particular area of endeavor in a skillful and cost-effective fashion. Judgment and experience often have a stronger influence than numerical calculations on the solution of civil engineering problems (e.g., the cheapest design for a factory might also be the most objectionable design to its neighbors).

Contrary to algorithmic programs, which follow a fixed sequence of steps regardless of the particular problem at hand, an expert system will attempt to solve the problem in the manner most appropriate to the current context. Such systems can simulate deductive reasoning, search through information in an intelligent way, and abandon one line of reasoning for a more promising approach. Expert systems accomplish this by exploiting a knowledge base comparable to that of human experts, including the relevant definitions, empirical observations, rules of thumb, and chain of reasoning by which experts would address a problem.

Specific features of a KBES are the domain of knowledge, the source of expertise, the manner in which knowledge is represented, the nature of the "reasoning" mechanism, the ability to reason under uncertainty, the knowledge acquisition (learning) capability, the user interface, and the explanation facility.

Machine learning includes symbolic and numeric techniques of learning from observations, explanation-based generalization, adaptive control, and qualitative reasoning. As such, it is most usefully applied in areas of science and engineering in which the understanding of the nature of knowledge is still evolving.

Learning from observations is suitable for building knowledge in evolving domains in which nature (or the system studied) supplies numerous instances of behavior that may be aligned on a success/failure criterion. The machine-learning program then tries to induce relationships that reflect the behavior under consideration, in both its positive and negative instances.

Explanation-based generalization is useful in domains in which several competing theories exist about the behavior under consideration. Such programs attempt to elaborate the details of the actual behavior using one or more of the competing theories. Coupling either or both of the previous techniques with a feedback loop of adaptive control provides a means for evaluating the induced relationships and deduced explanations.

Qualitative reasoning ensures that neither the induced relationships nor the deduced explanations are logically inconsistent with the known facts and relations in the domain with each other.

The areas of application of artificial intelligence techniques, particularly through knowledge-based expert systems, have been expanding at an accelerating pace in recent years and will undoubtedly continue to do so. Three principal reasons exist for this growing interest in knowledge-based techniques:

- The potential for enormous cost savings in computation and instrumentation;
- The continuing dramatic decline in the costs of computation in general; and
- The potential expansion and dissemination of human knowledge by making explicit the experiential and judgmental knowledge known only to the expert practitioners of a field.

Civil Engineering Applications

In solving most of the difficult and interesting problems in civil engineering, expert performance critically depends on expert knowledge as opposed to formal reasoning alone. Unfortunately, "knowledge" is a relative concept, and knowledge programming is a very complex process. Researchers are currently grappling with three interrelated issues: the representation of knowledge, which is roughly the machine equivalent of human memory; the control and use of knowledge, which corresponds to human abilities in problem-solving and planning; and the acquisition of knowledge, or learning. Although the application of expert system methodology to civil engineering problems is still in its infancy, several programs have been developed to solve various problems.

In the area of data interpretation, HYDRO was developed to help a hydrologist estimate the value of input parameters to the Hydrocomp HSPF simulation program (Gaschnig et al., 1981); SACON helps a structural analyst select appropriate modeling options in MARC, a large, general-purpose finite element program (Bennett and Engelmore, 1979). SesCon is a prototype preprocessor for the Seasam-69 structural analysis package (Fjellheim and

Syversen, 1983). In the area of problem diagnosis, SPERIL was developed at Purdue University to assess the damage to buildings after a hazardous event, such as an earthquake (Ishizuka et al., 1981).

In the area of system design, MacCallum has developed a system to design ships that uses numerical modeling at the preliminary design stage (MacCallum, 1982). Preiss describes a knowledge representation scheme for engineering design applications that uses a "frame" representation (Preiss, 1980). Nay and Logcher are devising a frame-based system to analyze construction project risks at MIT (Nay and Logcher, 1985).

Although many other civil engineering applications of AI techniques exist, this paper focuses on three applications that have enormous potential: computer-aided design, automated condition assessment, and robotics.

COMPUTER-AIDED DESIGN

One of the most promising applications of AI techniques, particularly expert systems, to civil engineering is the improvement of computer-aided design and drafting (CADD). Structural design can be broken down into three stages: the choice of a preliminary design, the analysis of the structural response to the stresses and strains of its intended environment, and the detailed design of the structure's components such that each satisfies the constraints imposed on it. Artificial intelligence techniques can assist in each stage and in integrating the results of all three stages.

It must first be recognized that the graphic representation of an object in a design often depends on the context in which it is presented. For example, a steel beam is shown very differently in the context of analysis topology, architectural layout, working drawings, or shop drawings. It is shown in some forms as a single line, whereas in others it is also shown in a width or cross-section shape. In addition, it must be realized that as the design is evolving, information about the object is increased and refined. When dealing with layout, one may not have information on size, weight, or loads on a beam, but one does have information on other geometric and design characteristics. The representation of objects in design systems must be dealt with in much more flexible ways than are possible with traditional data base management techniques.

Such representations have been one of the focal points of expert system research. For example, researchers at Carnegie-Mellon University have developed an expert system called HI-RISE to assist in the preliminary design of high-rise buildings (Fenves and Maher, 1983). The program suggests a number of possible substructures and helps the user select the configuration that will best resist gravity and lateral loads. Similar systems would be practical for the preliminary design of other structures.

Hundreds of algorithmic programs are available for the second stage of design—structural analysis. The larger programs probably have more capabilities than a single engineer could use during his or her entire career. An expert system, however, could mediate between the needs of the user and the requirements and capabilities of the program, thereby helping engineers to exploit complex algorithmic programs to the fullest.

In the third phase of design, an engineer must ensure that each component of a structure fulfills the pertinent specifications and codes, although the final choice among all acceptable components will be tempered by the resources, style, and in-house wisdom of the firm for which the engineer works. Expert systems now on the market can help designers meet universal regulations; however, few systems account for the "softer" constraints that govern design choices at a particular firm. This is one of the many areas in which expert systems for design and drafting still need improvement.

A great deal of research also is needed to integrate all three stages of design within a single system. This would require a sophisticated network of communication among architects, engineers, and contractors. It could, however, make the entire design process more efficient, and bring to workers in one discipline the expertise of workers in many related fields. An expert system proposed by researchers at Carnegie-Mellon could plan an entire chemical plant, from the choice of its location to the layouts of its pipes and the selection of its machinery. In doing so, the system would bring together the judgment and experience of engineers, designers, business administrators, and chemists.

Future CADD systems will be object-oriented in the AI sense in that they will allow procedures to be flexibly associated with CADD objects. Such procedures are now used to generate embedded objects, such as the floor framing in a building, from simple geometric data. When these systems are integrated with future expert systems techniques, the development can be foreseen of very powerful CADD systems that perform detailed design and actually assist in preliminary design. It is therefore probable that detailed design will be largely automated in the next decade.

A potential consequence of these developments is that these sophisticated programs will allow inexperienced engineers to design complex structures. This might not necessarily be undesirable, considering that expert engineers are often scarce. Because fewer experts are available to review designs that have been generated by a computer, inadequate drawings may further impede the design or construction process and cause costs and risks to increase. To prevent this, an expert system could examine a design that was produced with an algorithmic program and verify that it fulfills the standards of the best reviewers in the field.

Researchers at MIT have developed an expert system that can verify designs for reinforced concrete beams; this system could easily be expanded to verify the design of the simple girder-slab bridges that characterize most highway overpasses in the United States. The development of similar validation programs for other structural elements will probably be a growth area for future expert system applications.

AUTOMATED CONDITION ASSESSMENT

Artificial intelligence techniques will be of great service not only in designing and building new structures, but in evaluating the condition of existing structures, especially those that are buried, submerged, or hazardous. Engineers have developed many instruments for remote sensing and nondestructive testing in the past decade. Ground-penetrating radar can pinpoint a sewer line's location by reflecting a signal from a buried pipe and returning it to a receiver. In a similar way, seismic waves can determine the geophysical profile (the distribution of soil, rock, and water) of a hazardous waste site, and electromagnetic waves can show whether chemicals have spread from the waste site to a city's groundwater. If gamma rays from a nuclear emitter such as cesium are directed at pavement, the density of the pavement will reveal itself as a function of the transmitted and scattered radiation. Infrared thermography can detect the subsurface delamination of a highway. Delamination is the division of pavement into layers. Because a thin layer of asphalt absorbs less heat than a properly thick layer of pavement, the cracked pavement will reflect the sunlight's heat more readily to a heat-sensitive scanner.

The full power of such techniques has yet to be realized. First, these methods generate more data than a human operator can interpret. Most sensors currently compensate for this by simplifying their output from three dimensions to two dimensions, for instance, but at a cost of an extreme loss of detail. To be truly useful, an instrument must be able to assess miles and miles of pipelines or sewers, thousands of cubic yards of dam walls, or millions of square yards of pavements, bridge decks, or airfields and to process the data quickly and cheaply. This suggests a great need for automation.

Dr. Kenneth Maser of MIT has suggested that expert systems can be used to analyze the data from conventional processors of digital signals (Maser and Smit, 1985). One such group of instruments could detect subsurface delaminations in a bridge deck before the bridge crumbled beyond repair. A vehicle equipped with ground-penetrating radar could traverse a bridge at highway speed; the raw data could be recorded and replayed to a digital signal processor (DSP). The DSP could infer from these data the internal structure of the bridge in the form of the relations of the surface and underside of the concrete to the reinforcing bars inside. Given the DSP's "sketch" of the bridge deck, in addition to information supplied by the user about the design of the bridge and the weather, traffic, and maintenance to which it has been subjected, the expert system could gauge the deterioration of the deck. In doing so, the system would be making the sort of judgment that a dentist makes when looking at an x-ray and deciding whether the light and dark spots indicate a healthy tooth or one that needs to be filled. The analogy is not randomly drawn; expert systems were first applied in medical diagnostics.

If a sensor could measure the condition of a structure directly, if it clicked in the vicinity of subsurface corrosion the way a Geiger counter clicks in the presence of radioactivity, no expert would be needed to interpret its data. But most sensors can only measure conditions that are related to deterioration; for example, the presence of salt and water on a bridge deck makes it likely that the rebars inside have corroded. An expert is needed to infer a condition from a digital read-out; to *reliably* infer that condition demands that several experts compare their interpretations of the data.

The use of one sensor to detect a single type of flaw in a structure places a great burden on the instrument and limits its applicability. Imagine how inefficient it would be to design a program that could diagnose only one human disease; the program would have to be complex, but a doctor would need dozens of such programs to comprehensively diagnose a patient. Even so, the doctor would not be able to reach a conclusion in a reasonable time without a strong *a priori* suspicion about the patient's true ailment. To avoid this difficulty, Maser has suggested that a suite of automated sensors be integrated with an expert system to assess an entire structure. Each of the sensors in the suite would be like one of the blind men who inspected the elephant; each assessed a different aspect of part of the creature. An expert system would be needed, however, to make sense of the measurements in the form of a computer program that would know what sort of "animal" was being measured and which ailments it might be susceptible to.

A simple suite of instruments that could survey a long stretch of pavement and diagnose its condition might consist of an optical crack sensor, a transmitter and receiver of subsurface interference radar, and an acoustic profilometer, all mounted on a vehicle that is able to move at highway speeds so as not to impede traffic.

The first of these sensors would consist of two parts: a "line of sight" source positioned in such a way that a crack in the pavement would create a dark spot in the line and an array of photodiodes that could sense dark spots. The radar would reflect from interfaces at which the dielectric constant of the medium changes (e.g., the air/asphalt boundary). The time between reflections would depend in part on the depth of the interface. The analysis of a pattern of reflections might indicate a thin asphalt layer or asphalt that is riddled with voids or saturated with water.

The acoustic profilometer would use the path of an ultrasonic wave to plot a profile of the roughness and faults of the pavement surface. For a given length of highway, the sensors might show cracking and mild surface roughness, a change in thickness (or air content) of the pavement, and a subgrade anomaly. From this the expert system could deduce the presence of alligator cracking, which is a grid of intersecting cracks that resembles the scaly skin of an alligator and is related to excessive moisture in the pavement.

Sensors necessary for a more complete survey of a highway or the assessment of other structures would not be hard to develop;

many such sensors are currently available. However, the acoustic profilometer is currently the only highway-speed instrument used by maintenance crews. The demand for more sophisticated instruments has arisen only because of the recent awareness that much of the country's infrastructure is deteriorating more rapidly than it can be repaired or replaced. Even with normal maintenance schedules, most agencies are so short of trained personnel that facilities inspections are rare. In most states, even when inspectors are available, advanced equipment often is not. The inspectors therefore can do little more than look at a few miles of roads or a few bridges and guess at what lies beneath their surfaces.

Nevertheless, it is believed that surveying machines that are based on the automated analysis of multisensor data; that use programmed knowledge and judgment related to the individual sensory systems being utilized and the physical system being measured; and that operate at practical speeds have a foreseeable near-term potential. The ability of such machines to measure subsurface and surface defects at high speeds will qualitatively change the nature of the performance data available to facility managers. This in turn could revolutionize the parametric information that is most relevant to facility design and management and would make long-term performance monitoring projects based on current performance criteria unnecessary or even obsolete. The timely detection of the imminent collapse of one major structure would pay for the development costs of such machines and their support software many times over.

ROBOTICS

Automated systems have long been used to make cars, steel, and ships, but they have been applied almost exclusively to repetitive tasks in controlled environments. Conversely, most civil engineering processes are often highly responsive to local conditions, which suggests the need for flexible, responsive machinery to perform a variety of similar, but not identical tasks. Recent advances in robotics, remote control, and pattern recognition can provide the "intelligence" needed to enhance the mobility and flexibility of maintenance and rehabilitation equipment, methods, and procedures.

Such machines will be indispensable for surveying miles of highways, railways, and waterways, and for inspecting structures that are invisible or inaccessible to humans (e.g., buried pipes, off-shore platforms, submerged piers, aqueducts, and sewer lines). A system that could not only decide whether or not a repair was needed, but also perform the repair and verify that it had been done correctly would be of still greater value. Most repairs of a given type are similar to one another, but they are not identical; each must be tailored to local conditions. A machine that could perform a task repeatedly with small modifications each time would be a tremendous asset in repair work, especially on structures that are difficult for humans to reach.

Robots could also save human workers from the hazards of frigid oceans, toxic waste sites, nuclear power plants, and tunnels and blasting sites. The rate of occupational illness and injury of construction workers is higher than that of any other U.S. industry, even in most categories of mining. An extensive program of infrastructure construction or renewal would create many jobs, but such a campaign would also expose more workers to danger if robots were not used to perform the most perilous tasks.

The use of automated systems to assess and repair existing structures and to help build new structures is not far-fetched. Current technology has given us earthmovers and tunnel borers whose paths are guided by lasers, machines that line and repair water pipes *in situ*, and automated batch plants that turn out prefabricated building components. True construction robots will need vision and pattern recognition capabilities to move over large, three-dimensional, and ever-changing sites; "hands" dexterous enough to manipulate a range of construction tools; the ability to change their activities from day to day; and "expertise" that reflects the delicate judgments of skilled craftsmen and allows operations of one robot to be coordinated with another, such as a backhoe and dumptruck. However, these obstacles become much less daunting when the construction or rehabilitation site is well defined, vision is not essential, existing equipment can perform the task, and the potentials for increased productivity or decreased worker hazards are high.

One activity that fits these criteria is the inspection and repair of inaccessible structures, particularly one-dimensional systems such as pipes and sewers. Robots also might work with relative ease indoors, where conditions are less chaotic than outdoors. Some of the earliest construction robots will probably paint walls, sand floors, and lay carpet, tiles, and bricks; Japanese robots are currently being used to finish concrete and spray fireproofing onto structural steel.

Because the handling of materials makes up 80 to 90 percent of construction labor costs, robots that could move and track supplies could greatly reduce the price of many projects. Microcomputers are already being used to manipulate the loads of cranes safely and accurately. Although human operators are still necessary, cranes may one day be regarded as the ancestors of sophisticated construction robots.

A major application for more advanced robots will be in the excavation and transportation of earth. Prototypes of these robots already populate many sites in the form of commercial scrapers, the blade levels and cut depths of which are automatically monitored and controlled. Trucks that could travel a programmed circuit from an earth pile in one corner of a site to a pit in another are also foreseen. Although robot trucks would need a crude vision capability to recognize obstacles in their paths and the ability to cooperate with robot scrapers and bulldozers, their development should be within the reach of engineers who have already built the first generation of robots to repair pipes and highways. This is especially true if advances in industrial robotics and artificial intelligence continue at their current rate.

Tunneling and blasting would provide other prime opportunities for second-generation robots. Boring through soft, wet ground is dangerous because the surrounding dirt and water continually threaten to pour into the newly gouged tunnel. The raw tunnel is commonly maintained at several atmospheres of pressures to keep it from caving in, which creates a dangerous working environment that must be constantly regulated at considerable expense to the contractor. Robots could obviate the excessive risks and costs endemic to soft-ground excavation. Because boring a tunnel is a repetitive task that occurs in a one-dimensional environment in which vision is not crucial, the development of robotic tunnel-boring systems, complete with trucks to deliver the liner segments and remove the loose material, appears realistic in the medium-term future.

Blasting a tunnel through hard rock can be as dangerous and costly as tunneling through mud. A crew of robots might be able to carry out the blasting cycle more efficiently, with fewer wasted motions and idle moments, and at less risk to life than conventional blasting crews. Alternatively, cutting machines can be used to chew through the hard rock, although most cutting tools currently break down too frequently to be cost-effective. Because heating the rock makes it more pliable, robots could be used instead of human operators to reduce the heat-shielding requirements and reduce the risks to workers of shield failure.

Robots such as these are not a product of wishful thinking. When 50 technical experts from business, industry, academia, and government met recently in Washington, they concluded that automation has an "enormous" potential in construction, and that "recent developments in industrial automation have progressed to the point where it is possible to consider applications of automation technology to the more complex and unconstrained environment of the construction site." These experts predicted that within 10 years, 50 percent of new construction equipment will be controlled semiautomatically; 5 percent of digging, grading, and ditching equipment will be controlled by computer; and 5 percent of all commercial construction will use automatic systems for navigation and control.

So far, only the costs of such systems compared to their limited market has hindered their widespread adoption. But the costs of developing construction robots would be dwarfed by the tremendous gains in productivity that would be enabled in major programs of infrastructure renewal and construction of new structure and facilities. Such machines would also relieve human workers from the drudgery of monotonous tasks, the difficulties inherent in working at night or in constricted surroundings, and the dangers of hazardous environments.

THE RELEVANCE OF NEW TECHNOLOGIES TO DEVELOPING COUNTRIES

These new technologies should pose exciting potential applications for developing countries. Such countries typically lack design engineers, project managers, and maintenance and operations management personnel. In addition to this lack of expertise, historical data is often lacking, and the few skilled personnel that exist tend to be generalists rather than specialists.

In this environment, the utilization of artificial intelligence techniques, particularly expert systems, may considerably enhance the power of the limited number of skilled personnel in making the best use of available knowledge and data. However, such systems should not be used indiscriminately. In the area of computer-aided design, such systems should be used only for problems that can be satisfactorily solved by human experts at such a high level that somewhat inferior performance is still acceptable. For instance, the application of intelligent CADD systems to the design of highway overpasses and interchanges is a realistic goal, but the design of nuclear power plants is not. Nevertheless, these improved CADD systems should prove to be immensely beneficial in assisting developing countries in the design and construction of most infrastructural facilities.

In the area of automated condition assessment, certain characteristics of developing countries, aside from the overall difficulties surrounding the maintenance and rehabilitation of infrastructure networks, limit their ability to deal effectively with issues of infrastructural renewal.

First, the networks of developing countries are relatively sparse. This has several implications for maintenance management, because expansive geographical regions are under the control of relatively few skilled workers and a limited range of equipment. Because many geological, topographical, and climatic conditions may be encountered by each field engineer, the development of specialized expertise is inhibited by the large number of situations encountered. In addition, a few pieces of equipment may have to be used across these various combinations of conditions; techniques adopted from the practices of a developed country therefore might be inappropriately applied.

A second consideration is that the agencies responsible for infrastructure in developing countries are often poorly organized and motivated for maintenance and rehabilitation. Because prestige is associated more with new construction projects, the more experienced and capable personnel are drawn to those areas. Many agencies contract most or all of their maintenance work, which leaves the maintenance engineers to fill supervisory and inspection roles that do little to expand their experience and expertise.

A final consideration in the context of developing countries is the historical absence of routine and preventive maintenance on many infrastructural elements. In addition to the considerations made earlier, this results largely from the scarcity of skilled personnel in infrastructural organizations. The demands of development require that skilled resources be applied to capital investments with the result that the technical gap is widening between those responsible for designing and building a new infrastructure and those responsible for operating and maintaining it.

Tools are needed to help bridge this gap in expertise. If the considerable difficulties encountered in transferring these new computer technologies to developing countries can be overcome, the existence of intelligent tools that help central agency engineers design new infrastructural elements, supply the experience for less-experienced maintenance crews, and perform some of the more dangerous maintenance and construction tasks can be envisioned. In addition, the monitoring and assessment capabilities of the new systems should enhance the knowledge of the causes of deterioration and the effectiveness of various maintenance actions in the specific circumstances of particular countries.

REFERENCES

Bennett, J.S., and Engelmore, R.S. "SACON: A Knowledge-Based Consultant for Structural Analysis," *Proc. IJCAI-79*, pp. 47-49, 1979.

Fenves, S.J., and Maher, M.L. "HI-RISE: An Expert System for the Preliminary Structural Design of High Rise Buildings," Technical Report, Department of Civil Engineering, Carnegie-Mellon University, Pittsburgh, PA, 1983.

Fjellheim, R., and Syversen, P. "An Expert System for Seasam-69 Structural Analysis Program Selection," TR-CP-83-6010, Division for Data Technology, Computas, Norway, 1983.

Gaschnig, J., Reboh, R., and Reiter, J. "Development of a Knowledge-Based System for Water Resources Problems," TR-1619, SRI International, Menlo Park, CA, 1981.

Ishizuka, M., Fu, K.S., and Yao, J.T.P. "SPERIL-I: Computer Based Structural Damage Assessment System," TR-CE-STR-81-36, Purdue University, Lafayette, IN, 1981.

MacCallum, K.J. "Creative Ship Design by Computer," in *Computer Applications in the Automation of Shipyard Operation and Shipyard Design IV*, Rogers, Nehrling, and Kuo (Eds), North-Holland Publishing Company, Amsterdam, The Netherlands, 1982.

Maser, K., and Smit, D. "Automation of Condition and Deterioration Surveys Using Knowledge-Based Signal Processing," presented at the Second Conference on Robotics in Construction, Carnegie-Mellon University, Pittsburgh, PA, June 24-26, 1985.

Nay, L.B., and Logcher, R.D. "An Expert System Framework for Analyzing Construction Project Risks," Report CCRE 85-2, Center for Construction Research and Education, Massachusetts Institute of Technology, Cambridge, MA, 1985.

Preiss, K. "Data Frame Model for the Engineering Design Process," *Design Studies*, Vol. 1, No. 4, pp. 231-243, IPC Business Press, New York, NY, 1980.

An Expert System for Time-Series Statistical Analysis

PABLO NORIEGA B. V., CARLOS DEL CUETO M., LUIS M. RODRÍGUEZ P., and ILEANA GUTIÉRREZ R.

Various sorts of data analysis are performed in a great number of areas, such as biology, medicine, economics, finance, and quality control. However, statistical expertise is a scarce and costly resource; many of these analyses are therefore performed by users with limited statistical training. Statistical software has spurred an increase in the use of statistical tools but has done little to improve the statistical sophistication of most of its naive users. Commercially available statistical software generally offers a wide variety of methodologies. The software is powerful, flexible, and increasingly user-friendly, but it still requires that users have a good deal of knowledge and experience. The ease of use of this software sometimes causes it to be misused by improperly trained users. However, whether statisticians like it or not, statistical techniques will still be used by nonexperts. The better the tools these users have, the better they will use statistics.

This state of affairs has been acknowledged by the statistics community and alternative solutions have been proposed. A particularly attractive approach is to incorporate artificial intelligence (AI) tools into the statistical software that a nonexpert will use. As Hahn (1985) demonstrated, three levels of "intelligence" may be involved.

At the most elementary level, intelligent statistical software can provide bibliographical references to explain why a certain technique is useful, what the working assumptions are, where the algorithms needed can be found, and so forth. The unsophisticated user can then consult these references to decide whether or not a certain technique is appropriate and if the analysis is adequate.

Through the use of more intelligent software, the user can obtain specific advice on what tools to use, how good the model is, how anomalous the data are, and so forth. This kind of software behaves as a consultant that guides the user through the maze of options that a given methodology offers and helps the user judge how good the statistical analysis is.

In the third proposed level of intelligence, the software makes all the technical decisions and only requires from the user the data and a statement of the purpose of the analysis.

As Velleman and Tukey suggested in their comments to Hahn's article, and as some of the articles in Gale's book corroborated, the approach most likely to succeed is the one that corresponds to the intermediate level of intelligence. This level attempts to provide automatic consultation in narrowly defined areas of statistical expertise. In other words, the statistical software includes some functions that a human statistical expert performs when advising a nonexpert on a specific technique. In particular, an automatic consultant should at least explain statistical terminology, point out data peculiarities, determine the appropriate form of the model, recognize possible weaknesses of the analysis, and suggest an alternative or ulterior analysis.

The CEST (Consultor Estadistico en Series de Tiempo) project follows this approach. The intent is to build an expert system that will guide a nonexpert practitioner in the use of tools and techniques for the analysis of time series. Although time-series analysis is already a narrow field of expertise, the strategy has been to divide this field into even narrower modules of expertise that are associated with specific problems and techniques. Experiences with the first of such modules—the Box-Jenkins methodology for univariate time series—are described.

THE DOMAIN OF EXPERTISE

A time series is a sequence of random variables that are indexed by time. If the data in the sequence are singletons, the sequence is known as a univariate time series (as opposed to bivariate). Time series are very common. Price indexes, the flow of tourists into a country, the international price of oil, and the number of batch jobs handled in a machine are all examples of a univariate statistical time series.

A typical problem associated with time series is to find a model that describes the underlying stochastic process that generates the series. This model is then used to forecast new values of the series, detect seasonal patterns, explain apparent irregularities, and so forth.

Methodologies for time-series analysis have existed for many years. Regression analysis and Fourier filtering are two of the best-known methodologies, but the Box-Jenkins methodology has received wide attention in recent years and has proved to be extremely useful. This methodology was developed and reported by Box and Jenkins (1970) and consists of a series of steps for analyzing a given time series. These steps involve inspecting certain properties of the series, usually with the help of well-known algorithms, and taking certain actions that depend on the results of those inspections. Many commercial statistical packages, such as SPSS, S.A.S, T.S.P., and MINITAB, include the Box-Jenkins methodology as part of their tools. However, like other statistical methodologies, Box-Jenkins requires a good deal of experience and statistical sophistication. Box and Jenkins divide the process of analyzing a time series into three main stages: model selection, model estimation, and model diagnostic checking.

The issue at the model selection stage is to decide which kind of stochastic process within a specific class best represents the observations that constitute the series. Before deciding which model to choose, the series is transformed to correct the variance (make it constant), eliminate deterministic tendencies, and identify deterministic seasonalities and possible interventions. This depuration process is complex. Well-known tools produce the required transformations of the series, but judgments of how good a transformation is or how significant a certain irregularity is depend on several considerations. Subjective judgment is usually necessary for a good depuration.

After it is determined that the series is behaving properly, a model is selected. This decision is usually based on the behavior of the series, which in turn is studied through the autocorrelation and partial autocorrelation functions of the transformed series.

Criteria exist for choosing a specific model, but they are not straightforward.

Once the appropriate model is chosen, the parameters of the model are estimated through the use of well-known algorithms. One must then decide how good the estimated model is by checking for distinctive features in the statistics of the residuals. If some problems are detected, one returns to the model selection stage (with useful information). This process is repeated until one is satisfied with the selected model.

The Box-Jenkins methodology is well suited for the analysis of time series that arise in economics, manufacturing, finance, and similar areas. Important decisions are often made based on the analysis of time series, and the social and economic values of these decisions are significant. This point is discussed further elsewhere (Zellner, 1979; Guerrero, 1986).

This methodology is usually taught in universities; good textbooks have been published on it, and most of the algorithms required by it are available in commercial software. However, a user needs a good amount of practice and coaching to develop a good sense of how to apply it.

As a matter of fact, for a given series, even two experienced statisticians (applying the same methodology) may disagree on what the best model is. This disagreement may arise not only from a difference in the purpose of the analysis, (e.g., pure forecasting versus explanatory modeling), but also from the fact that many subjective decisions are made in applying the methodology. Furthermore, experienced statisticians account for what they know about the phenomenon they are modeling. For example, when modeling the price index in Mexico, a given expert may detect seasonality in the series, whereas an economically guided statistician may conclude that the seasonality is deterministic in that it is an intervention associated with the periodic rises of minimum wages. These features may seem irrelevant to a statistician who is unfamiliar with economic issues (if there is one).

Naive users may be aware of some contextually relevant features, but may be unable to assess the statistical significance of a given series or unaware of the criteria and tools needed to deal with them. Nevertheless, they may be convinced of the need to apply a time-series analysis methodology to model the problem at hand. They may then either give up modeling entirely or depend on available software and tacitly trust the quality of the results.

The foregoing discussion attempted to justify the creation of an expert system for the Box-Jenkins methodology. The following is a summary of arguments in favor of the use of expert systems:

- A well-established body of knowledge exists,
- The character of the expertise and its application is non-trivial,
- A great number of everyday situations exist in which the knowledge can be profitably applied,
- Substantial economic and social values are associated with the application of the knowledge, and
- Readily available, living experts exist.

Considerations that involved academic issues were also taken into account when the project was started.

A VIABLE SCHEME FOR A JOINT INDUSTRY-UNIVERSITY VENTURE

The IBM Corporation has recently made public its commitment to the development and use of artificial intelligence. At the time the CEST project was proposed, no project related to AI was in progress in the Scientific Center in Mexico. No one in the Center had any experience in AI, although two notable specialists, Adolfo Guzman Arenas and José Negrete, were involved with the Center at different times. The most active field of interest of the Scientific Center was theoretical and applied statistics. Among the research goals of the Center for 1986 was the start of an applied AI project.

Activity in AI research and teaching had been proceeding in Anáhuac for 3 years, but because research had been centered in the theoretical aspects of AI, a reason was needed to start an application-oriented project. Statistics, however, has been one of the main areas of specialization in the School of Actuarial Sciences.

The mutual goals and interests of the two groups resulted in the CEST project. The project was originally planned as a prototype, but extensions were contemplated at future stages. It was expected that prototyping would take the 6 months from May to November of 1986.

The IBM Corporation contributed its expertise in statistics, equipment, and funding to the project; Anáhuac contributed experience in AI and partial funding. The original group was formed by two staff members of the Scientific Center–M. Villalobos (now at Michigan State University) and Del Cueto, Professor Noriega and four students from Anahuac (Rodríguez, Gutiérrez, Carvallo, and Pacheco). Both institutions perceived the project as a starting point for a fruitful venture.

The Potential Uses of CEST

In addition to interest in its immediate applications in real-life situations, CEST is generating interest as a teaching aid. The university and IBM recognize that potential. In addition, IBM viewed CEST as a potentially useful addition to a line of products for statistical data bases that is being developed in the Scientific Center.

Research in statistics

In the process of knowledge acquisition and validation of the expert, a constant side-benefit of expert system development has been that new insights into the domain of expertise have arisen. Time-series analysis was not expected to be an exception.

A mixture of knowledge paradigms

Among the most intriguing characteristics of the domain of expertise in CEST are the various sorts of knowledge that are involved in the analysis of a time series. An expert has to deal with numeric information that comes from applying functions to data and with knowledge of a more symbolic nature, like the purpose of the analysis of the series. Furthermore, decisions depend on the graphic features of series, the interrelations of constants, and the quality of data.

It was therefore a challenge to propose an adequate knowledge representation scheme that could encompass these traits in a uniform and simple manner and that was flexible and powerful enough to code a knowledge base that could be extended to other statistical domains. The knowledge base had to interact with graphic displays of data, nontrivial mathematical computations, and users of varying degrees of statistical sophistication. The prototype was therefore viewed as an opportunity to experiment with alternative knowledge representation schemes, data models, and statistical tools in a single system architecture.

The use of a new artificial intelligence language

The interest in experimenting with a mixture of algorithmic and symbolic knowledge and new data models called for a flexible and powerful programming environment. The environment had to be one in which different data structures could be easily manipulated, complex statistical algorithms promptly coded, and alternative programming "paradigms" properly mixed. All of these features can be found in NIAL (Jenkins et al., 1986).

The similarities between NIAL and APL are apparent enough to trust the experience that both groups had in APL to be easily transferred to NIAL, thus suggesting rapid prototyping. In addition, the logic programming features recently proposed for NIAL obviated a fragment of the coding process that might otherwise have delayed its release.

Finally, NIAL appears to be an attractive alternative for other AI developments. The experience gained in this project should help decide whether or not future projects should be executed in NIAL.

THE CEST SYSTEM

The CEST system can be thought of as a collection of small expert systems. Each of these expert systems contains enough tools and knowledge to be useful in its own right, and each deals with a specific kind of expertise. It is hoped that the collection will gradually prove to be more interesting than the sum of its parts. In any case, the Box-Jenkins methodology is a good test case.

The project was defined as a prototype so that some implementation subtleties—cosmetic issues and efficiency—could be avoided but especially because the emphasis is not yet in a product, but in the experimentation that may eventually lead to a final product. The project was also defined as a module so that other developments could be added if the project was successful and, more importantly, because the addition of modules that share a critical number of common traits enables one to build other kinds of experts.

Functional Architecture

The functional features of this CEST module were divided

analogously to the three main stages of the Box-Jenkins methodology described earlier. Some of the salient points of each stage are described in the following paragraphs.

The model identification stage is the most difficult and critical stage of the Box-Jenkins methodology. Most of the algorithms in this stage are used in further stages. Practice and sensibility are essential for a "natural" identification of the model and are as important as the different statistical tests performed on the data. Simple heuristics have been coded in CEST that successfully capture some of the basic distinctions that are traditionally drawn by visual analysis and that greatly depend on the experience and sensibility of the expert.

Identification in the Box-Jenkins methodology is performed through the estimated autocorrelation and partial autocorrelation functions of the series. For these analyses to be effective, the observed behavior of the series must satisfy certain requirements, such as stability in mean and variance. If this is not the case (and in practice it often is not), certain corrections should be performed through suitable transformations.

First of all, variance instability is detected and corrected, because it may obscure the existence of a deterministic trend. At this level, the use of heuristics to select the appropiate transformations is important and depends on the intended usage of the model (forecasting, control, etc.). Bartlett's method is used because a logarithmic transformation (or common sense) is preferred when pure forecasting is not the expressed intention.

Once the variance has been stabilized, the search for a possible deterministic trend is started by using the estimated autocorrelation function and the plot of the series. If a trend exists, it is corrected by using the difference operator as many times as needed, but usually less than three times. Success has thus far been achieved in determining when to take differences by measuring the type of zero-convergence exhibited by the autocorrelation function.

After the series is suitable for a preliminary identification, it is analyzed and modeled. Well-defined patterns of behavior exist for each type of model, but they occur too frequently and are too peculiar to be kept as a static knowledge base. Expertise is a key word at this stage. New heuristics had to be developed and tested for CEST to obtain satisfactory results.

While the identification analysis is being performed, CEST

displays graphs, plots, and messages that help the user understand the analysis. To capture the type of expertise needed to identify behavioral patterns of different models in the knowledge base, the type of visual analysis that an expert performs is mimicked by generating a family of "masks" that are matched against the true autocorrelation functions. These masks are displayed and a "similarity" function is applied to each mask and the true series. Although the technical grounds for the similarity functions and the mask generation algorithms should be revised, the success rate observed thus far is surprising. This identification is not the final one. The series should be modeled and its fit checked until a satisfactory model is attained.

The model estimation stage scarcely requires any degree of expertise. This stage is mostly algorithmical and provides the system with estimates for the parameters in the selected model. The modified steepest descendent algorithm that provides maximum-likelihood estimates is used.

The model diagnostic checking stage is not that simple. No model form ever represents the absolute truth. The general philosophy in model diagnostic checking is that the model is always inadequate in one way or another. The main task in this stage is to identify what is most likely to fail so that it can be modified in the next iterative cycle. A great deal of expertise and algorithmical treatments are needed.

The residuals (observed less expected values) are obtained and their autocorrelations are calculated. A "goodness of fit" test is performed on the series of residuals to identify whether or not a structure exists that must be modeled. If one exists, the identification stage is returned to and an analysis is performed on the residuals to find an augmented model. However, the model also may be overfitted (i.e., it may involve too many parameters). The autocorrelation between each pair of parameters is calculated and if any of them are "significant" (heuristics are needed to decide this), the number of parameters involved in the model is reduced. The feasibility of each parameter is tested, and if all the tests are satisfactory, a final model is chosen.

Although it may appear to be a simple matter of testing statistical hypotheses, diagnostic checking requires a great deal of knowledge. Some would rather have an overfitted model that would best suit their needs (like forecasting) than a parsimonious one that would better explain the process associated with the data.

In addition to these features, the CEST system includes a capture module that takes care of the basic identification and incorporation of new series into the data base. Simple checks filter out series with missing values, identify periodicity and number of observations, and suggest whether or not enough data exist to perform an analysis. Forecasting with confidence intervals is also available.

Expert System Architecture

The CEST system is to be used as a consultant; in this respect, its surface architecture is expected to resemble a DSS more than a classic automatic classification expert system. The CEST system is to be built primarily as a collection of "toolboxes," the first of which is the Box-Jenkins module. Each toolbox will contain different types of tools; one type will be composed of statistical algorithms, another with knowledge. Both types of tools are closely interrelated. Rules are written in a truly "functional" first-order language in which the functional terms are evaluated with the help of the algorithmic base. The knowledge base is partitioned into fragments associated with specific tasks, and these fragments are invoked if and when the user requires advice. Finally, because the Box-Jenkins methodology is sequentially embedded in a few steps, the consultant has to keep track of pending tasks and plausible paths, but the experienced user does not have to be caught in a procedural straight-jacket.

An interesting feature of this architecture is that the degree of openness of the toolbox depends on the degree of expertise of the user. It is currently assumed that the user will be a novice and that the system will automatically perform all important tests, produce opinions on the results, and gradually build a path of analysis. In fact, some code resides in files outside the active workspace and is automatically assembled when required by the knowledge base.

The native NIAL features were used to advantage to create a statistical data base. In this release, a time series is a nested array that includes an identifier, data, statistics of the series, and other rule-relevant data, such as degrees of similarity with other models, pending analysis, and plausible alternatives. Data management operations are simple user-defined operations and transformers. Further releases should greatly improve the data model.

Rules in the knowledge base are written in Horn-clause form

but, as was stated before, functional terms are to be evaluated while the examination proceeds, either as a look-up in the series base or as a true execution of the NIAL function. It should be noted that the size of the "elementary" universe (constant terms in the language that are specific to the domain of expertise) is greatly reduced; rules therefore seldom need substitutional unification.

At this point, a decision has not been made in favor of a true many-valued logic representation. To emulate the decision process of the living experts, some ambiguity was incorporated in a few predicates (e.g., in the pattern analysis of the autocorrelation functions). Functions and comparison predicates are then used to transform the ambiguous predicates into atomic formulas of the first-order language of the knowledge base.

Some FORTRAN-coded routines that are executed by the NIAL interpreter were included in version-0 of CEST. Speed and experimentation justify their inclusion.

FUTURE DEVELOPMENTS

The most complex type of model that CEST is able to identify thus far is ARIMA (2,d,2) for any value of "d." This family of models is adequate for many series that arise in practice, although a wider family of models should be considered to develop a fully functional system.

Although the model identification heuristics developed thus far have proved to be surprisingly effective, the mask-generating processes waste information and have not been studied yet as conditional estimators. New recognition techniques with a stronger theoretical background are under study and could be a useful addition to the better kind of heuristics that have been developed so far.

At this stage of development, CEST is unable to recognize seasonal models. This type of model is often present in practice, and it is important to have the necessary tools to analyze either additive or multiplicative seasonalities.

To fully cover the Box-Jenkins methodology, transfer function modeling should be included in subsequent versions of CEST to describe the dynamic response of a process (e.g., delays).

Other Immediate Functional Extensions

An important and useful extension to the Box-Jenkins methodology is the intervention analysis proposed by Box and Tiao (1975). The CEST system is expected to perform this time-series modeling variant in its next release. The types of series that arise in economic processes are frequently subject to this kind of behavior. If CEST is expected to become a useful tool for real-life series analysis, this extension is essential.

A missing observations module is an essential feature in a time-series analysis toolbox; it is also easy to implement. Some methods require the use of complete, related series to estimate missing values of a given series, but this approach is encumbered by the need for a great amount of contextual and heuristic knowledge. Other methods (Rodríguez, 1986) have the advantage of drawing on the same techniques that already exist in CEST applied to the observed values of the incomplete series itself. Further releases of CEST can be expected to include some of the latter.

The User Interface

As was previously noted, the prototype under development was to be delivered in a short time span. To ease the development, it was decided to exclude most cosmetic aspects from the system's development. Because CEST is aimed toward use by nonexperts, it must be as user-friendly as possible. Extensive help facilities, windowing, graphics, and plot displaying are some features that will be included in further releases.

Software and Hardware Environments

The use of NIAL in an IBM/PC-XT has proved to be a remarkably interesting protoype development environment, but a rather slow one. Version 3.06 of NIAL is an interpreter with limited editing facilities and great local memory requirements. As a result of the latter, "WS FULL" messages are a constant nuisance. These factors and a limited set of available utilities have burdened the development process. The concurrence of diverse programming styles in a single environment, good host interfacing, and splendid primitive resources for nested array manipulation, however, have greatly compensated for these limitations. One of the surprising qualities of NIAL has been its readability, particularly the ease with which novice NIAL programmers can efficiently produce satisfactory code that adheres to the same shared coding conventions.

It is fair to say that the announced improvements to NIAL appear to successfully resolve most of the problems discussed earlier. The availability of NIAL for larger equipment may satisfy others. It will be interesting to experiment with a CEST version in larger workstations, like the IBM/RT, or mainframes.

REFERENCES

Box, G.E.P., and Jenkins, G. *Time Series Analysis, forecasting and control.* Holden Day, Oakland, Ca. 1970.

Box, G.E.P., and Tiao, G.C. "Intervention Analysis with Applications to Environmental and Economic Problems" *Journal of the American Statistical Association.* March 1975, No. 70, pp. 70-79.

Gale, William A. *Artificial Intelligence and Statistics.* Addison-Wesley, Reading, Mass. 1986.

Guerrero, Victor M. "Un Modelo Estadístico Util para Pronosticar y Evaluar la Inflación durante el Año de 1983." *IDEA.* Vol. 1, no. 1, Nov. 1986.

Hahn, Gerald. "More Intelligent Statistical Software and Statistical Expert Systems: Future Directions." *The American Statistician*, Feb 1985, Vol. 39, No. 1, pp. 1-16.

Jenkins, Michael A., Glasgow, Janice I., McCrosky, Carl. "Programming Styles in NIAL". *IEEE Software*, Jan 1986, pp. 46-55.

Rodríguez P., Luis Miguel. *Pronosticos Ponderados: un nuevo Método par Completar Series de Tiempo.* B.Sc. Dissertation, Universidad Anáhuac. 1986.

Zellner, Arnold. "Statistical Analysis of Econometric Models." *Journal of the American Statistical Association*, September, 1979, Vol. 74, No. 367, pp. 628-651.

Communication

30

Intelligent Interface
Andrew C. Kapusto

The purpose of this article is to intuitively discuss the problems of man-machine interface in computerized information exchange systems that are designed to be used by the general population. Some solutions that can be adopted in currently practical implementations are suggested.

THE WEAKEST LINK

Although progress is continually being made to achieve efficient communication within computer systems, the development of the user interface is proceeding much more slowly. There are many means and ways to communicate with a computer, but they are not standardized and are usually too difficult for the untrained user. As a result, the benefits of computer services are still limited to those who can afford the equipment and who possess the programming skills or application software knowledge.

Distribution of Computing

The proliferation of personal computers in recent years appeared to advance less rapidly. Few noncommercial applications exist that would justify the repetition of the learning effort required of the casual or occasional user. Unfortunately, the skills needed to efficiently operate many applications are unique to the systems in use.

Typically, user-interface-related development efforts were dedicated to the fuller utilization of the newest hardware capabilities rather than toward better compatibility with human thinking processes. Recently, available software environments are more user-oriented but still require a definite understanding of the operation principles and underlying concepts of data processing. The windows and icon-based systems are frequently graphically intensive, symbolic presentations of the same cryptic concept preferred by the programmers.

Because general concepts are best communicated with the help of a dialogue conducted in the user's own language, it is the language interface that ultimately provides not only "friendly," but "useful" results for the first-time user. Because neither acoustical nor textual implementation of such an interface would greatly benefit from graphic presentations, recent improvements in computer capabilities have little improved the user interface.

Information Networks

One of the most important potentials of personal computers—communication terminal application—has not been fully realized. Because of the relatively small number of initial (noncommercial) users of communication networks, practical implementations of general-purpose, natural-language interfaces to the existing information services were delayed. As a result, the effectiveness of accessing the data still depends on the user's knowledge of the representations and structures used by the given system. Protocol compatibility problems further limit available information systems.

An Integrated Solution

Significant progress has been made, however, in researching and developing connections between computerized information management systems and existing telephone systems. The means for natural language communications must be provided to fully exploit the tremendous synergy of the combined networks. With most of the ingredients already in place, rapid progress from concentrated research efforts can be expected. Potential markets include the entire population of telephone users.

A NATURAL LANGUAGE INTERFACE

Information management systems can rapidly organize, reference, research, and retrieve enormous quantities of data. They also fall far short of understanding natural language expressions and therefore cannot be used by nonspecialists. It should be recognized that, even with accelerated progress in artificial intelligence (AI) research, a limit will always exist in understanding the user's input. This should not, however, prevent attempts to design practical and effective language interfaces. An interface concept that is based on the language model and application domain expert system is described in the following section.

Interface Heuristics

The level of intelligence sensed by the interface user depends on the system's ability to predictably react to intuitive input responses or selections and on the ability to remember and learn from the total history of the dialogue. It is important that the system can gather additional information about erroneous inputs or at least present its interpretations to the user.

The information-seeking interface may never quite understand the relationship between what users say or type and what they want, because natural language communications are idiosyncratic. However, communication of the error feedback may indicate the source of confusion and educate the user as to the limitations of the language model or inadequate inputs. Some of the most difficult but largely psychological problems—the avoidance of word-sense ambiguities by the user—could be helped in this way. The linguistic competence of the user could be better utilized with an interface that provides information about its current state of understanding of the objective of the dialogue. The nonfunctional structure of the interface under discussion is shown in Figure 1.

Language and Dialogue Models

The input recognition module converts original user input to a thesaurus reference. The probabilistic model of the language used is based on the lexical domain required by the application. The context-interpreting module parses and processes the syntax of the input. It determines the semantic state in the dialogue domain. The probabilistic model of the dialogue determines the extent of the linguistic capabilities of the system.

It is reasonable to assume that the input recognition system will be subjected to a wide variety of forms and meanings, not only in the natural language but also in a lexically and syntactically restricted mode of communication. Because humans are imprecise in naming objects and providing instructions, these tasks will be handled by a probabilistic model that represents statistical knowledge of the likelihood of intended objects and the likely referents of the words used. One could say that, for a given linguistic domain, the problems of synonymy and polysemy could be alleviated by combining the words' prior probabilities with conditional input-output mapping probabilities.

An Application Domain Model

The output from the context interpreter is used by the goal monitoring module, which is the central decision-making element of the interface. The model of application domain is being constructed in the process of parameterizing and categorizing the linguistic context of the speech application. Rules that involve different categories are then defined. The knowledge base is represented by the set of these rules and the uncertainty factors are represented by prior probabilities or rules that were assigned priorities.

Status Feedback

As opposed to relatively constant language and application factors, knowledge base operating data are highly modifiable. Inference processing of the rules can create or eliminate rules as a result of successful hypotheses or evidence matches in forward, backward, or mixed chaining.

The operation of the interface is initiated at the beginning of the conversation to reflect the default assumption about the goal or the next communication exchange objective. If the information provided by the user is successfully recognized and interpreted, the goal change reflects only the current stage of the scenario of the dialogue. The current goal is available at any time to the user in the form of the status. Otherwise, the hypotheses are generated by the probability models and tested against the knowledge base and dialogue history. The goal is modified for error recovery needs and a new status report is provided to the user, or the best matching input is given for verification by the user. The rule base or models can eventually be processed to reflect the successful transition path.

A VOICE INTERFACE APPLICATION

The natural language interface described earlier applies to both text- and speech-based applications. A telephone interface application would require both voice recognition and voice response units when fully implemented.

Voice Recognition

The most technologically challenging, speaker-independent speech recognition can be accomplished over the telephone network. Current state-of-the-art systems are capable of recognizing numbers and a small set of control words with a high degree of accuracy. Much larger vocabularies are expected in the future. It is unlikely, however, that other than major languages will soon be fully supported. This seems to be of lesser importance now, when more and more telephone networks are capable of MF signaling. More practical natural language interfaces that operate in a user text-input mode instead of a voice-input mode are currently being implemented successfully (see Figure 2).

Voice Response

Two technologies are available for voice output functions: digitized voice response and voice synthesis. Digitized voice response is most effective for applications that require natural, human-sounding speech. Because of the rapid increase in speech storage capacities, the vocabularies of digitized voice systems are no longer limited. The latest text-to-speech algorithms greatly improve the quality of voice synthesis systems. They are similar to speech recognition systems but, unlike digitized speech-based systems, they are currently limited to a single natural language.

Application Considerations

Telephone interface implementation must account for the fact that, unlike a two-dimensional display with memory, voice output is only a one-dimensional time production, and the memory is that of the user. Short and logical menu selections and powerful repeat and help functions are always required. Prompting on both command and data levels and adaptive time-out mechanisms is also necessary.

Practical Aspects

Display terminal analogy is useful in the concept of a virtual voice terminal. Different methods are possible to provide equivalent voice cursor control, voice memory/pages, voice scroll/stop, and voice attribute control. Voice attribute control makes it possible to assign such attributes as volume, speed or pitch, and male or female to such different message categories as system output, prompt, goal report, and status report.

Input Functions

Data and commands can both be entered in the text mode using the phone keypad and several letter-to-number assignment methods. The direct numeral avoiding is the simplest one. Because natural language words are notationally redundant, they can be entered the same way as numerical data using the standard number-to-letter pattern and text/numbers switch command. For example, to enter COGNITRONICS, press 264648766427 followed by the # key. Certain collisions are possible and should be handled at the dialogue level. It was estimated that only about 10 percent nonunique encodings occur for the directories of 100,000 mostly English names.

Dialogue Design

When several users were asked to suggest a (monologue) voice response message to "best" inform on the same and objectively defined facts and situations, they would select from the wide variety of names and phrases. Although only a few of the choices offered would be commonly acceptable, the designers were very confident that their spontaneously created versions were optimal.

Because human semantic references are created by poorly understood psychological processes, it is difficult to objectively judge their informational adequacy or stylistic fitness. From this point of view, it seems that a probabilistic language model could be used again, this time to select the "most likely" and the most widely acceptable sentences or phrases automatically. It is generally not easy to build a language data base large enough to produce some statistically relevant choices.

SUMMARY AND CONCLUSION

A discussion was provided of the practical aspects of the man-machine interface in computerized information exchange systems. It was suggested that an interface based on the probabilistic model of the natural language used in the dialogue be implemented. The effectiveness of the information exchange process can be further assured by the mechanisms that continuously seek the dialogue goal and present the user with its current status in an attempt to resolve input imperfections. Details were presented of the applications of the voice communication with a computer that uses the most broadly available terminal: the telephone.

Because a limit always exists to the affordable accuracy of any model, it is important that this fact is both recognized and planned for in the process of designing natural language communication. The intelligent interface could largely eliminate the operational deficiencies of existing information systems in handling input ambiguities and could teach users about its inner workings and shorten user training.

REFERENCES

Furnas, G.W., Landauer, T.K., Gomez, L.M., Dumais, S.T., *Statistical Semantics: Analysis of the Potential Performance of Key-Word Information Systems*, The Bell System Technical Journal, Vol. 62, No. 6, July-August 1933.

Jelinek, F., *Self-Organized Language Modeling for Speech Recognition*, Continuous Speech Recognition Group, IBM T.J. Watson Research Center.

Klatt, D.H., *Text to Speech: Present and Future*, Proceedings of Speech Tech '86, pp. 221-226.

Slator, B.M., Anderson, M.P., Conley, W., *Pygmalion at the Interface*, Communications of the ACM, Vol. 29, No. 7, July 1986.

Witten, I.H., *Principles of Computer Speech*, Academic Press, 1982.

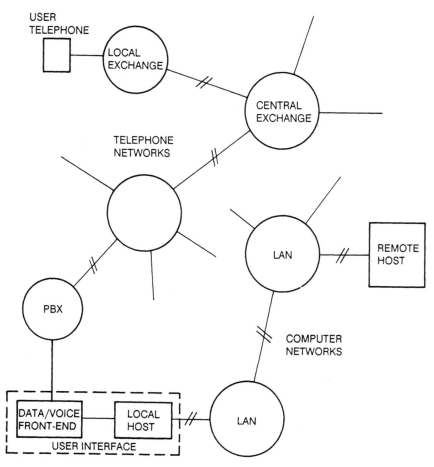

FIGURE 1 Functional diagram of an intelligent interface.

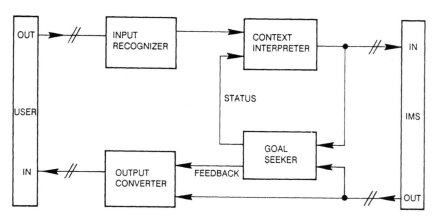

FIGURE 2 Telephone voice response interface.

31

English to Thai Machine Translation
WANCHAI RIVEPIBOON

Machine translation (MT) or computer-aided translation (CAT) research in Thailand began in 1981 when professor Bernard Vauquois, head of Group d'Études pour la Traduction Automatique (G.E.T.A.) at the Université Scientifique et Médicale de Grenoble, France, introduced the ARIANE system to researchers at the Prince of Sonkla University in Thailand.

In June of 1981, the Ministry of University Affairs in Thailand appointed a committee to undertake an English-Thai machine translation project. The committee consisted of lecturers in linguistics and computer science from almost every university in Thailand.

The aim of this project is to translate scientific and technological texts from English to Thai through the use of the ARIANE system. The results of the morphological and structural analysis of English performed by G.E.T.A. serve as the basis of the project.

THE ARIANE SYSTEM

The current version of the ARIANE system—ARIANE-78—has been in use since 1978. The algorithmic components of the system are illustrated in Figure 1.

The input text is submitted to a morphological analyzer produced by the ATEF (string-to-tree transducer) component. The results are then transformed into a multilevel intermediate structure by ROBRA. The transfer phase is divided into two steps:

- A lexical transfer by TRANSF, which is mainly a bilingual dictionary supplemented with possible solutions for lexical ambiguities, and
- A structural transfer in the form of a tree-transducing program from ROBRA.

The generation phase begins with the computation of the surface syntactic structure through the use of ROBRA, and ends with a morphological generation performed by a SYGMOR program, which is a tree-to-string transducer. Details of this system can be found in G.E.T.A (1982), Quezel-Ambrunaz (1978), Boitet et al. (1978), Quezel-Ambrunaz (1979), Quezel-Ambrunaz (1980), and Vauquois et al. (1982).

AN ENGLISH-THAI MACHINE TRANSLATION MODEL

The English-Thai MT model consists of three main phases: analysis, transfer, and generation. It has been designed to provide language independence in both the analysis and generation phases; language dependence is restricted to the transfer phase only. During the analysis phase, the characteristics of the English language are captured into logico-semantic relationships that are considered universal among languages. They will later be adapted or generated back to particular features of Thai. The transfer phase converts English lexicals to their Thai equivalents in addition to structured conversions of those lexicals peculiar to the source language for which no direct equivalent exists in the target language and for which a different structure is required. This strategy permits not only bilingual translation but multilingual translation by means of changes in the transfer phase only because the analysis and generation phases are separated from each other. Analysis and generation models therefore can be written only once for each language.

The model has adopted three levels of interpretations of a form: morphosyntactic classes, syntactic functions, and logico-semantic relations. The first level describes the properties of each terminal node of the tree structure of a sentence. Properties include terminal morphosyntactic classes (e.g., noun and verb), grammatical properties (e.g., tense and gender) derivations (e.g., verb-noun and adjective-adverb), syntactic properties (e.g., copula or modal), semantic properties (e.g., animate or instrument), and others.

The second level describes the relationship between two nodes. Information is noted on the source node of that relation. For example, the subject group is bound implicitly to the governing verb of the phrase. Examples of syntactic functions include subject, object, and governor.

The third level describes the relationship between the predicate and its arguments, between the predicate and terms that do not occupy places or arguments (e.g., circumstantials), and between terms that qualify phrases. Examples include aim, qualifier, topic, and argument places.

The third level is considered to be universal among languages. The aim of analysis is to convert a given surface structure to its deep structure or "highest structure" by means of logico-semantic relationships. Consequently, the aim of generation is to obtain a surface structure from this deep or highest structure.

An Example of Translation Results

A short sentence can serve as an example of English to Thai translation: "The reaction has an interesting application." This sentence has the following morphological analysis:

```
                    ULTXT
                   .......1
                      |
                    ULFRA
                   .......2
                      |
    _____
    |       |       |       |.      |       |
  ULOCC   ULOCC   ULOCC   ULOCC   ULOCC   ULOCC
  ....3.......5.........7........9......11....... 13


    |       |       |       |       |       |
   THIS   REACT   HAVE     A    INTEREST  APPLY
   ....4.......6.........8.......10.......12......14
                         ...2
```

English to Thai Transfer

This phase of translation depends on the two languages involved. The transfer is performed in two stages: lexical transfer and structural transfer.

Lexical Transfer The lexical transfer stage has the same function as a bilingual dictionary in which a source lexicon is converted to its target lexical item or items. The conversion can be direct, conditional, or ambiguous. The following is an example of direct conversion:

```
THIS → NII
```

In the case of conditional conversion, a source lexicon can be converted to different target equivalents, depending on certain criteria; for example:

```
If INTEREST is a noun → PRAYOOT
If INTEREST is a verb → SONCHAI
```

An ambiguous conversion means that certain source lexical items give rise to more than one target equivalent that can only be resolved at a later phase.

Structural Transfer In the structural transfer stage, all ambiguities that result from lexical transfer are resolved, and transformations are incorporated into structures for which there is no direct equivalent in the target language.

Certain morphosyntactic classes do not have direct equivalents. For example, tense is not shown in the Thai verb form. Any tense in English therefore must be mapped into only one Thai tense form, such as a neutral or infinitive form. Certain syntactic functions also have no direct equivalents. For example, postadjectives in English are transformed to relative clauses in Thai. The result of the structural analysis serves as the input for the structural transfer; the output of the transfer looks like the following:

```
            ULTXT
            ......1
               |
               |
            ULFAR
            ......2
               |
               |
            *VCL
            ......3
      _____
      |         |          |
      |         |          |
     *NP       MII        *NP
    ......4   .....7    ....8
   ____|_____          _____
   |         |          |      |          |
  NII   PATIKIRIYAA   ULO9   *AP       PRAYUK
  ......5      6       9    | 10         12
                            |
                            |
                          SONCAI
                            11
```

The output from the lexical transfer stage is not shown in this example, but it is the same as the output from the structural transfer stage. The output from the lexical transfer stage that serves as the input to the structural transfer stage is unchanged because the sentence has the same structure in both languages. It should be noted that A in English is transferred to ULO, which means there is no corresponding lexical unit in Thai.

Thai Language Generation

The Thai language generation phase of the project is still underway. Thai language generation follows a top-down design and involves two stages: multilevel generation and morphological generation.

Multilevel Generation The output from the structural transfer phase will be investigated in this example. An attempt is made to specify syntactic relations in Thai. The presence of ARG0 and ARG1 indicates that ARG0 is the subject and ARG1 is the first object. All the designations are removed to follow their governor and UL0 is eliminated. The result should look like the following:

```
                        ULTXT
                        .....1
                          |
                        ULFRA
                        .....2
                          |
                        *VCL
                        .....3
                          |
         _____|_____
         |               |               |
        *NP             MII             *NP
        .....4           7             ....8
         |                               |
    _____|_____                    _____|_____
    |         |                    |           |
PATIKIRIYAA  NII                 PRAYUK       *AP
 ..........5 ....6                .....9      ....10
                                              |
                                            SONCAI
                                            ....10
```

Morphological Generation   Although Thai is not a reflexive language, some morphological generation has to be considered, and the correct forms of Thai derivation have to be selected. For example, PRAYUK is a verb-noun derivation; a rule must therefore be set to generate the noun from:

PRAYUK → KAANPRAYUK

The same must be done for SONCAI, which is a verb-adjective derivation:

SONCAI → NAASONCAI

The final result will appear as follows:

PATIKIRIYAA NII MII KAANPRAYUK NAASONCAI

Further postediting work can proceed from this point.

CONCLUSION

The model is by no means complete. Many aspects of and types of sentences have not been covered for English and Thai. Further research is being performed to study and implement them.

REFERENCES

Boitet, C. et al. "Manipulation d'Arborescences et Parallelism: SYSTEM ROBRA."G.E.T.A., 1978.

G.E.T.A. "Le Point sur ARIANE-78 debut 1982." GETA-CAMPOLLION, 1982.

Quezel-Ambrunaz, M. "ARIANE-78." G.E.T.A., 1978.

____,"Transfer en ARIANE-78: Le Modele TRANSF."G.E.T.A., 1979.

____, "Modifications et Nouvelles Commandes sous le System ARIANE-78." G.E.T.A., 1980.

Vauquois, B. et al. "Étude de Faisabilitée d'un System de Traduction Automatisée Anglais-Français." Association Champollion, 1982.

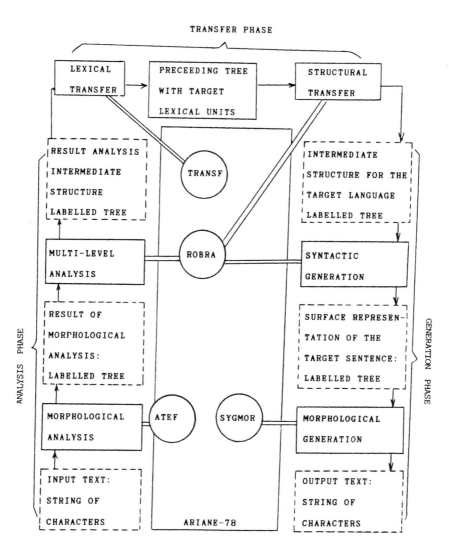

FIGURE 1 The algorithmic components of the ARIANE system.

32
The Need For Standards in Computer Graphics
JOÃO DUARTE CUNHA

The effective use of any technology depends to a large extent on the existence of national, international, or "de facto" standards.

The consequences of the lack of widely accepted standards for developing countries are examined in this paper. Computer graphics are considered in detail, and a review of recent work on graphic standards is presented.

As with many other things in this life, the importance of standards is only truly appreciated when they are lacking. The standards we have become accustomed to are taken for granted or forgotten, and we are seldom able to imagine how much work was involved in their development. However, everyday life would not be the same without the many standards that put some kind of order in our technological world.

Color television is a good example; we have not one, but at least three different standards, all of which have inherent inconveniences. Videocassette recorders (VCRs) are even more complicated when these three television standards have to be combined with different recording standards. These difficulties are well known to anyone who has tried to use VCRs where different systems prevail. One of the benefits expected from the new generation of high-resolution televisions is the creation of a single, worldwide standard.

Because developing countries have fewer resources to invest in new technologies, they are more vulnerable to the consequences of using nonstandardized technologies and are often left with useless pieces of costly equipment.

In the case of computer equipment, in which hardware and software play complementary roles, attention must be paid not only to equipment and software selection, but to the application because work developed on a computer may be used in the future.

STANDARDS IN THE COMPUTER INDUSTRY

Defining standards in fields in which continuing innovation is the rule is a difficult task; the computer industry clearly demonstrates that. One of the typical results of this situation is the so-called "de facto" standard, which originated from widely accepted products. The most recent examples are the IBM PC microcomputer and the MS-DOS operating system. The life-cycle of "de facto" standards is governed by market rules and company strategies as opposed to established bodies. These standards are therefore flexible and able to evolve with the technologies themselves. They don't, however, possess the degree of stability desirable for medium- or long-term projects.

The important contribution of the IBM PC to the microcomputer world was not in the technical innovations it created, but in the stability it provided to attract a great population of users.

What if IBM had decided to stay away from the 16-bit microcomputer business? Or, what if they had decided to use a proprietary operating system instead of one compatible with MS-DOS? Any answer to these or similar questions is purely speculative, but it may be useful to speculate on these issues to better understand the role of the few standards that already exist or are in preparation.

COBOL, FORTRAN, and BASIC account for the vast majority of all programming languages software ever written. Their strength stems not from their intrinsic quality—the weaknesses of FORTRAN have long been recognized—but from the fact that they are standardized and available almost everywhere. The real contribution of languages like Algol-60, Simula, and most of all, Pascal, was the influence they had in the development of software engineering concepts in general and new programming languages in particular.

Standards are by their very nature conservative, and revision mechanisms should remain active all the time. Nevertheless, they provide the basis for stable work and should not be replaced by whatever seems more attractive at a given moment.

Operating systems were until recently a completely nonstandardized field; each manufacturer provided its own system or systems. This fact is certainly the main reason for the dependence of users on computer manufacturers. Because the operating system helps users to interact with the computer, any change in the operating system has a great impact and therefore a very high cost. This tends to generate a very special relationship between user and manufacturer that often inhibits a critical evaluation of the relative merits of alternative solutions.

The growing interest in UNIX and the wide acceptance of CP/M and MS-DOS for microcomputers represent a significant change in this area. UNIX and MS-DOS can be considered "de facto" standards and are already having a great impact on the way people look at computers. It is impossible to speak of computer standards without mentioning the emerging network standards that are rapidly transforming the OSI model from a theoretical framework into a well-established, standardized protocol.

Developing countries are much more sensitive to the nonexistence of standards, both as users and as potential suppliers, because of the lack of resources and the distance to the large markets. Once standards are established, they can provide a medium-term basis for the development of products and therefore allow less-developed countries to work with less risk of product obsolescence.

COMPUTER GRAPHICS

The computer graphics field is nearly 25 years old; for a long time its availability was restricted because of the high cost of early equipment. The introduction of the storage tube was the first step toward popularizing this powerful technique. But it was not until large-scale integration allowed the production of low-cost, large-capacity semiconductor memories, which are an essential component of modern raster displays, that computer graphics became so popular.

Work on computer graphics standards started more than 10 years ago, but the first International Standards Organization (ISO) standard, Graphical Kernel System (GKS), was approved last year. As a result of this and other standards now under development, it should be possible to perform the following tasks:

- Write programs that generate pictures and interact graphically with the operator in a way that is independent of the hardware used;
- Store and transport graphical information between users and systems; and
- Address graphics devices in a standard way.

Graphics, perhaps more than any other computer application area, span the entire range of equipment, from the US$100 personal computer that uses a television set as a screen to the most powerful machines available (for example, those used in the movie industry).

However impressive this wide spectrum may appear, the extremes are not relevant to this discussion. Applications that can affect the high cost of sophisticated equipment usually have their own software and peripherals and will not benefit from the development of standards in the near future. Inexpensive personal computers, however, are normally used as stand-alones or are integrated into homogenous networks with compatible packages and peripherals. The need to integrate this equipment, or the work developed in them, into heterogeneous environments, whether or not they are physically connected, is uncommon. The interesting range starts with 16-bit microcomputers, includes 32-bit workstations, minicomputers, and superminicomputers, and reaches the mainframe level. This type of equipment is often used in the same institution project; the expected increase of local and wide area networks will certainly make it necessary for different computers to be able to integrate in every aspect, including graphics.

Anyone involved in this situation knows from experience that even the use of graphics packages in microcomputers (or the transport of graphic information from one system to another) is much less direct.

As emerging standards become widely used, which is expected and desired, these compatibility problems will be solved and the following will result:

- Easy transport of graphics software and computer-generated pictures between different systems;
- More effective use of graphic peripherals, some of which are still too expensive to be duplicated everywhere; and

- Less dependence on particular computer manufacturers.

A REVIEW OF RECENT WORK ON COMPUTER GRAPHICS STANDARDS

It may prove useful to briefly examine the current state of different computer graphics standards within ISO and ANSI. The information included in this section is taken from Bono (1985) and is complemented by more recent data.

The Graphical Kernel System has been an ISO and ANSI standard since 1985. It was published as IS7942 in July 1985 and approved as ANS X3.124-1985 in June 1985. The system is a procedural interface for two-dimensional graphics, including vector and raster graphics and synchronous and asynchronous input.

FORTRAN and Pascal language bindings for GKS are now in the final voting stages to become ISO standards. The Ada binding was still in the draft proposal stage within ISO. The FORTRAN binding was already approved by ANSI, and the Pascal and Ada bindings are in their final approval stages. The C language is not yet standardized, but a binding recommendation is available as an ISO technical report, and a full ANSI standard will be approved when C itself becomes an ANSI standard.

3D graphics are the object of two mutually complementary approaches—GKS-3D and the Programmer's Hierarchical Interactive Graphics System (PHIGS) (Hewitt, 1984). The first is obviously an extension of GKS to 3D, whereas PHIGS is aimed at a more sophisticated market. It uses displays that support fast image transformation capabilities and picture structures that are more complex than the one-level segment model offered by GKS.

Both are now in the draft proposal stage of ISO, but GKS-3D is slightly more advanced and should by now be entering the next stage and become a Draft International Standard (DIS). The two other standards under development are Computer Graphics Metafile (CGM) and Computer Graphics Interface (CGI).

The CGM standard will provide a mechanism for retaining and transporting graphics data and control information. It can be considered the equivalent of ASCII for graphical information, and its interest is fairly obvious (Osland and Francis, 1984). Apart from the other graphical standards, CGM bears a close relation to network standards, because networks will be used increasingly to interchange data, including graphical data. The standard includes three different methods of encoding to account for different uses: character encoding for compactness and easy transmission through networks, binary encoding for fast processing within a given computer system, and clear-text encoding for readability and transport between highly incompatible systems.

CGM is now in the DIS stage within ISO.

The Computer Graphics Interface provides a standard way of driving graphical devices, thus solving a problem that until now was only minimized by the existence of some "de facto" standards (e.g., the Tektronix 4010/4014 protocol).

CONCLUSIONS

An attempt was made to stress the importance of graphic standards in a time when 10 years of international cooperation is beginning to show its first results. The importance of these developments should not be underestimated, especially in developing countries, where investments must be protected.

Standards have a drawback in that they cannot always reflect the latest technological advances, but this should not minimize their importance.

REFERENCES

Bono, Peter R., Report of the Timberline Meeting of ISO TC97/SC21/WG2 "Computer Graphics," Computer Graphics Forum 4, 1985, pp. 383-386.

Hewitt, W. T., PHIGS - Programmer's Hierarchical Interactive Graphics System, Computer Graphics Forum 3, 1984, pp. 299-300.

Osland, C. D., and A. H. Francis, Computer Graphics Forum 3, 1984, pp. 301-303.

Network-Based Information Systems: A Role for Intelligent Workstations

JOSEPH F. P. LUHUKAY

THE DEPENDENCE ON COMPUTER TECHNOLOGY

The increasing importance of computer-based information systems in the world today has been the topic of many papers. The role of these systems in support of planning and decision-making processes has made modern executives irrevocably dependent on the computer. Computerized information systems not only help to make decision-making more effective, they have a potential to enable organizations to realize previously unattainable objectives. From a historic point of view, the potential support of computer technology to ease the labors of managers and administrators has never been this favorable. Moreover, computer technology itself—the hardware and software—is expanding and improving faster than most users can keep pace with. The fact that these developments are happening outside of most developing countries makes them all the more difficult to follow.

The Need for a Strategy

The combination of the increased dependence on information systems and the rapid advancements in computer technology has raised the need for a proper strategy. Three distinct approaches exist in the development of such a strategy in developing countries.

The first approach has to do with technology-driven developments that tend to encourage the use of a form of technology mainly because of its availability. A case in point is microcomputer technology. Application of the microcomputer frequently resulted in practical and useful systems. Initial investments brought about user satisfaction that often resulted in acceptance of subsequent expansions. Less successful examples, however, abound in many countries.

A few years ago, authorities in a developing country tried to introduce teleconferencing, a sophisticated form of telecommunications, but almost no demand has existed for this relatively expensive form of technology. Policy-driven developments, the second approach, are usually based on national priorities that also account for other economic sectors. From the macro point of view, this approach has the potential of rendering a more holistic strategy. The policy of using domestically produced and assembled microcomputers for all government-related purchases is one example of this approach. Among other things, it encourages indigenous technology development and eases after-sales support. However, a developing country can easily be trapped by the exclusive use of older computer technologies that are almost invariably lower in price/performance ratios than newer ones.

The third approach takes the form of demand-driven developments that usually result in a technology transfer process based on *vox populi*. Democratic as it may sound, this is not always feasible, especially when the predominant lack of technology awareness in developing countries is considered. However, the very rationale of the approach of basing everything on actual demands is making this approach gain popularity faster than the other two.

Experience in a number of computerization projects in a developing country indicates that the best strategy (if such a thing exists) is to use a demand-driven base, strengthened by an increase in technology awareness, and system-wide policy enforcement. This means that the users, the most important subsystem, must be equipped with the proper knowledge of alternatives to be able to rationally select the best technology to meet their demands. This process often proceeds with the support of consultants who are sometimes not properly versed in computer technology. Policies must be made with attention to detail but should be flexible enough to allow for positive competition among suppliers.

Based on user preferences and technology trends, a design

philosophy was developed to implement distributed information systems that employ computer network techniques. The strategy was based on a number of implementation cases. Subsequent test cases that involved multivendor environments further improved this strategy. The nature of information requirements in today's business environment and the division of tasks according to these specific requirements are described in this paper. Two implementation cases are briefly described. The material presented in this paper was heavily borrowed from a previous publication (Hussain and Hussain, 1981).

COMPUTERS AND INFORMATION SYSTEMS

Computers were first used in data processing about three decades ago and have since progressed beyond the stage of being regarded as mere supercalculators. Their more recent role as a management support tool is becoming increasingly pronounced. Their progress is being continually stimulated by increasingly complex human requirements and technology improvements.

A computer-based information system in an organization can be basically defined as encompassing all measurable data that pertain to the organization that can readily be recorded, stored, processed, retrieved, and communicated as required by a variety of users inside and outside the organization. Based on these data, information can be generated to support managerial and administrative tasks.

This pragmatic definition upholds unembellished data processing systems, but fails to discern requirement nuances, technology advancements, and the necessity for a global strategy. The problem with definitions is that they are invariably developed in a certain context and may therefore lack the flexibility required in the ever-changing computer field. Moreover, people trained in one school of thought may become staunch defenders of their own beliefs, which is common in any discipline. Like other branches of technology, an inclination exists among information technology practitioners to be overwhelmed by practical and proven techniques but to refrain from experimenting with fresh concepts. This attitude poses a serious problem in the computer realm mainly because of the rapidity with which new techniques develop. As computer technology continues to develop, information systems will further evolve to meet increasingly complex requirements.

COMPUTER NETWORKS

The decreasing cost of computers and the advances in data communications and computer networking technology are extending the use of this technology in many areas of business, government, and academia. Spurred on by the proliferation of microcomputers, computer networks are gaining in popularity. Both local- and wide-area networks are growing extensively in a maturing market.

The main forces that spur this increase in popularity are resource sharing and distributed processing. Although single-vendor networks were predominantly used in the past, multivendor environments will quickly prevail as the technology matures. High-speed local-area networks are enabling implementations with tighter coupling to be designed, which gives rise to sophisticated task distribution. Wide-area networks are making distances even more transparent to end-users. The continuous development of standards and the widespread adherence to them is increasing the chances of connectivity in heterogeneous environments.

The Transition to a Distributed System

During the early days of electronic data processing, data were usually accessed by means of primary keys (Martin, 1981). Because improved software are available, search keys (also called secondary keys) enable more complex searches, such as "List all second-year students whose grade-point average exceeds 3.0." The employment of high-level data base languages often increases the use of these search keys. Relational data base techniques carry this utilization method even further.

The problem with search key operations is that they frequently result in long response times. Moreover, they tend to take longer to program on larger machines in which relational data base management systems and productivity tools are still luxury items. A great number of records in the data structure may have to be searched by means of a secondary index or other mechanism. This problem exists on both mainframe and minicomputers and influences the poor overall performance in centralized environments that often results in the development of distributed systems.

At issue here is an important transition—the often traumatic change from a friendly centralized system to a multicomputer environment. With expansion comes the requirement for a wider span of control that usually results in much more complex resource and data management. Moreover, it is always preferred to maintain direct connectivity among the computers, which includes the problem of network development.

The Nature of Information Requirements

Before the implementation strategy is discussed, it is necessary to investigate the information requirement itself. There are basically two major categories of information requirements. The first category is that in which information needs are highly periodic. This kind of information tends to be well-structured in the sense that the requirements are better defined and can therefore be fulfilled with better-designed solutions. The exact nature and a good estimate of the transaction volume are known at the time when data structures are designed.

The second category involves information that is more or less nonstructured, and that is required on a much less periodic nature than the first category. The nature and frequency of queries is not known beforehand, and the data structure will have to be designed to support a variety of search procedures.

The first information category is typically used by administrators and the electronic data processing (EDP) department in production runs to generate periodic reports. The second category is used more often to aid management in decision-making and planning. Most questions that can be answered by nonstructured information are of the "what if?" type; these questions are highly unstructured and very often unpredictable.

This requirement classification is strongly supported by Martin's description of production systems and information systems. The main differences with Martin's categorization lie in the more evident distinction between user groups related to each classification, periodicity, and the structure of the requirements. Moreover, recent advancements in computer technology have made it easier to categorize the hardware and software that are needed to support the different building blocks required for network-based information systems.

Tasks Necessary to Fulfill Specific Requirements

The first information category is generally processed in batch mode, because a great amount of data is generally processed to produce this type of information. The preparation of pay slips, class rosters, and monthly balance sheets are some of the more popular examples. The data processing center is a natural choice for the batch-oriented processes that are required to produce this information. Because of the structured characteristics and periodicity of this information, EDP-center personnel will not have to make new application programs for every production run. Except for possible modifications, it is usually not necessary to redesign existing software.

The second information category, however, would be too burdensome if processed in a batch mode. Moreover, the combination of its near-unpredictability and relatively short lead times makes batch mode processing even less attractive, especially when software productivity tools are lacking. As is generally the case, the problem is further compounded by the difficulties in translating user intent into design specifications, which in turn makes lengthy output-prototyping cycles very unattractive. Another difference between the two categories is that relatively small amounts of data are usually required to generate output in the unstructured, less periodic information category. This category generally calls for an interactive processing mode with relatively short design cycles.

The following are necessary to meet the first requirement category:

- Efficiency in high-volume processing;
- Batch-work scheduling (often complex);
- On-line and data entry; and
- Support by nonrelational data base management techniques on mainframe and minicomputers.

The following are necessary to meet the second requirement category:

- Effectivity, ease of use, and direct value to end-users;
- An interactive mode with end-user language support;
- Data can often be down-loaded from a centralized file-server; and

- Use of relational data base management techniques with fourth-generation language support on microcomputers.

As is the case with distributed systems in general, data management is one of the main design issues. The extended control span of a multicomputer environment needs special attention, especially when dealing with data integrity, data down- and uploading procedures, data dictionaries, and data interchange formats.

Design Strategy

A number of issues must be addressed to augment the well-known planning steps needed to determine a corporate distributed-data strategy. This is especially true when it comes to designing and implementing this strategy into a network-based information system. A discussion of such planning steps is beyond the scope of this paper. The issues described in this paper are meant to extend the strategy planning itself; they cover various aspects that must be considered when developing network-based information systems.

The first issue concerns the design of a network architecture, which consists of defining protocols, formats, standards to which different hardware and software must conform, and network-wide security measures. This issue becomes more important when a multivendor environment is being considered. Standardization should be limited to the interface of hardware, software, and data. Man-machine interface standards must also be accounted for. The architecture should adhere to internationally accepted communication protocol standards so as to benefit from the availability of off-the-shelf equipment. Limiting the architecture of a network to conform to features and products offered by a single vendor often is the most viable alternative for rapid implementation. However, factors such as future expansion alternatives, second-sourcing, quality of vendor support, and development of in-house capabilities may be hindered in the long run. The next issue involves network task and resource distribution. Resistance to the networking concept can be expected from influential EDP centers. It is typically feared that control over information (and the organization's power play) will be lost by distributing processing tasks. Without delving further into this widely discussed problem and its implications, it is suggested that the following allocation template be used:

First Category

- File/data base, computing, and message server(s) are based on one or several mainframes or minicomputers installed at EDP center(s).
- File transfer facilities to and from second-category userstations are performed in an interactive mode (easier) or batch mode (harder).
- Production runs are mainly performed in batch mode (EDP personnel may perform development and administrative tasks in an interactive mode).
- Message-handling facilities (electronic mail and bulletinboard services) are predominantly in the interactive mode.

Second Category

- User stations are based on microcomputers (predominantly single-user units) installed at user sites.
- Corresponding file transfer facilities on these stations must support an unattended mode (preferred) and/or a real-time mode (i.e., transfers are performed while the user is logged onto the central server by way of terminal emulation).
- Processing is usually performed locally by using userfriendly microcomputer software, including relational data base techniques and related productivity tools.
- Access to message handling facilities is enabled by logging onto the appropriate server.

Results can be improved by standardizing the user stations (e.g., IBM-PC and compatibles or UNIX-based microcomputers) and software packages used on these stations. Several packages are offered on various mini-, micro-, and even mainframe computers (e.g., the ORACLE relational data base system and its productivity tools). However, the availability and affordability of these packages on microcomputers improves the likelihood of applying this approach without incurring steep initial investment costs.

The third issue addresses the problem of improving development times. From the user's perspective, it is automatically expected that the transition to a network-based system improves the design cycle. Because of the availability of productivity tools on user stations, users can be brought in early in the development process by virtue of the fast prototyping capabilities. The early involvement of management shortens the design cycle and improves computer awareness. Same-day prototyping has always been a good ice-breaker; as such, it improves the working relationship with users tremendously.

Span of control is the fourth issue encountered in developing a strategy for network-based information systems. Aside from the resource allocation template mentioned earlier, data management has a strong potential to become problematic if not handled properly. Lesser issues may also exist within specific environments. The generic rule used to solve this issue is to centralize control while distributing operations. The following principles can be applied in addition to those mentioned earlier:

- Only data on the central file/data base server(s) are valid. Other systems (including user stations) must down-load to acquire the latest valid data. Any local data updates on a user station remain invalid until properly up-loaded onto the central server.
- Data dictionaries and formats must be centrally controlled and enforced for the whole network.
- Distributed applications developments are controlled through centrally designed algorithms and formulae.

Adherence is tested through benchmarks and certification to ensure the applicability of a multivendor environment.

The fifth issue pertains to maintaining recurrent and expansion costs within reasonable limits. This may appear unrealistic, but it is usually on management's wish list. However, in addition to the rules mentioned earlier, costs can be controlled by applying the following principles:

- Improve and maintain connectivity by enhancing resource sharing. For example, peripheral sharing, which is one of the best cost and performance options to consider when expanding network services, can be realized by developing such resource servers as printer and communications servers (modems, etc.).
- Communications costs tend to dominate recurrent expenditures. The best overall cost/performance ratio can then be achieved by concentrating on telecommunications (packet-switching versus circuit-switching, international communications standards versus vendor standards, etc.).

Much has been said and written about the sixth issue—security, which is a very important subject in network-based information systems. Without lingering excessively on this popular topic, the following rules are recommended for inclusion in the strategy:

- A network-wide security arrangement should be developed as part of the network architecture. This arrangement should include resource access control, alarm generation and response management, and the application of encryption and decryption techniques.
- Extramural links (those that go into public telecommunications facilities) should always include encryption and should never be linked directly with a server whenever possible. The use of dedicated gateways that employ proper security measures to control access and encrypt and decrypt the data flow is suggested for these links.
- Intramural links, including those implemented on a local area network (LAN), should include layered access control. Sensitive data files can always be encrypted, but it may not be necessary to encrypt the data flow on the communication links.

Sample Cases

The first example of network-based information systems development involves the Central Government Agency, which is located in a 21-story office building in Jakarta's main business center. The agency uses two models of minicomputers, each with its own time-sharing terminal users, and a number of microcomputers that are scattered around the building. Applications are divided among the mini- and microcomputer systems. Management is inclined toward the development of an office automation system. Existing applications range from a personnel administration system to project monitoring, almost all of which are in the early stages of development. The systems are predominantly in the batch mode, although interactive terminal-based access is supported for a very small number of users.

A project was planned during the third quarter of 1985 to develop and implement a network-based information system. A LAN was to be installed to link various computers, and a couple of applications were to be identified and developed. It was also decided that the project team would include agency personnel who were to be trained and involved in the effort. The first stage of the project was to be completed in 7 months.

A LAN that was based on the IEEE 802.3 standard (Ethernet) was designed with communication servers that connected 24 lines based on the EIA-RS232C standard. One minicomputer was to be connected first, and the other was to be connected in the second stage of the project. On the hardware side, the interconnection problem was solved by the use of standards, as shown in Figure 1. On the software side, three different computing environments, each with its own operating and file systems, had to be made to communicate with each other. Office automation facilities included a network-wide electronic mail system, an electronic bulletin-board system, and the required file transfer facilities. Terminal emulation software was developed for each microcomputer to enable users to log onto the minicomputer, which was made to run as a first-category system. All microcomputers were placed at user sites and developed into second-category systems. File transfers were all in ASCII mode, and relational data base techniques with ample productivity tools were used on the microcomputers. Applications consisted of a personnel system that was changed from an old system into a network-based system and a monitoring system for overseas scholarship and training. The first stage, which was initially scheduled for 7 months, was completed within 4 months.

The second case involves a university with two campuses and a student body of around 15,000 that was previously served by an entirely centralized system that resided on one of the campuses. The increased affordability of microcomputers and the availability of various equipment grants gradually changed the distribution of computing facilities. The computer center, however, was overburdened by various recurrent tasks. This resulted in an inability to meet some user requirements, especially those that fell in the second category. First-category applications were extensively developed over the years, almost entirely in batch mode. The LAN of the computer center is confined to one building, but it is planned to extend it to other campus buildings.

The case in point involves one of the departments that decided to acquire its own minicomputer and a number of IBM-PC compatibles. The former was to be used for instruction and research, and the latter to support second-category requirements among the department's management. An internal project was established to design and develop these two services to complement other services currently rendered by the campus computer center. The project was started in the second quarter of 1985; its first stage was planned to take 1 year to finish. The part of the first stage in which second-category applications were developed is applicable to this discussion.

A relational data base package was acquired for the IBM-PC compatibles. One of the main criteria in the selection of the package was the availability of productivity tools and the availability of the package on other computers. This criterion was used mainly to reduce development times and improve the system's portability. Based on data that were down-loaded from the campus computer center, several second-category applications were developed, such as a student academic performance management system, an academic advisor monitoring system, and a personnel management system. These systems reside on dedicated microcomputers, all of which are equipped with a hard disk. The project's first stage was planned to run parallel to the extension of the campus network to include this particular department.

The current network encompasses one superminicomputer, two minicomputers, five supermicrocomputers, and a number of microcomputers. About nine different operating systems run on the network, all of which are capable of communicating with one another. An inter-building link was planned to connect this department to the network. However, due to unforeseen problems, the network facilities were not available at the time of this writing. In lieu of this electronic interconnection, files are transferred on diskettes. The data management schemes outlined earlier have been fully implemented to ensure overall integrity. The current and projected configuration of the system is shown in Figure 2.

Projected modifications consist of the connection of optical fibers to the campus network, the expansion of computing facilities to include a number of engineering workstations, and the improvement of second-category applications.

CONCLUSIONS

The transition from a centralized system to a distributed, network-based information system will always be difficult. The reluctance of EDP personnel to change, the increased pressure from end-users for improved services, and the availability of increasingly distributed enhanced technologies are three main problems to resolve. A strategy to develop a network-based information system must at least address the requirement for a network architecture, a proper task and reference to the source distribution scheme, an improved development cycle, a manageable span of control, the task of minimizing recurrent and expansion costs, and a sensitivity to security problems. The trend toward increasingly distributed information systems is impossible to circumvent in normal environments, and a strategy must be developed to prepare for it.

REFERENCES

Donna Hussain and K. M. Hussain, *Information Processing Systems for Management*, Richard D. Irwin, Inc., 1981.

James Martin, *Design and Strategy for Distributed Data Processing*, Prentice-Hall, 1981.

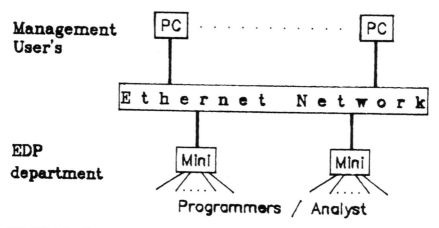

FIGURE 1 Government network-based information system.

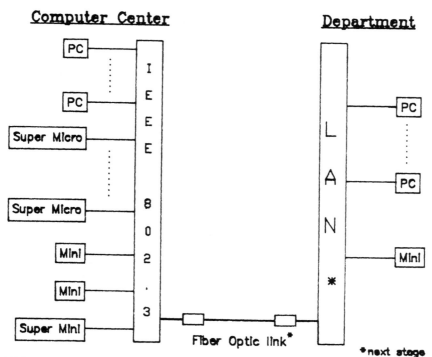

FIGURE 2 University network-based information system.

34

Application-Driven Networks

KILUBA PEMBAMOTO

A network design approach is presented that results in network solutions that are fully integrated in the associated application. Because the network design is systematically executed from the processing requirements of the application, the resulting network is efficient, easy to maintain, secure, reliable and, above all, economical.

The evolution of computers and their wide acceptance in all fields has created a *de facto* distributed processing environment. Coupled with the advances made in communication links, the distribution of processing capabilities has resulted in the transformation of every computer installation into a network system of some kind. The replacement of dumb terminals with intelligent ones, especially by microcomputers, is an example of the rapidly growing *de facto* distributed processing environment.

The advent of computer networks has not come cheaply or without compromise. As networks have become more complex and more accessible, a number of issues that once were easy to solve have now become major hurdles. For instance, computer security considerations used to be resolved simply by restricting access to the computer room; now, however, intelligent software systems must be integrated in the network to protect it against willful remote invaders. Such sophisticated software has been a major contributor to the cost of data processing; however, this has been offset somewhat by the tremendous decrease in the hardware costs of low- and medium-range computer processors and electronic equipment in general.

The future promises even more complex functional requirements on computer installations. The approach to the development and implementation of network systems is therefore becoming a major factor and a significant area of investigation. The objective is to provide networks that meet their goals economically and efficiently. This problem assumes an even stronger emphasis when viewed from a developing nation's standpoint. The stringency of the requirements and constraints, whether political, economical, or technical, in these nations does not easily lend itself to the packaged solutions that are conceived for most developed nations.

This paper will focus on this point by proposing an adaptive approach to the development of computer network systems. This approach will rely on the requirements of the applications to be supported by the network. The application-driven network (ADN) will therefore become a systematic approach for designing nonstandard networks.

NETWORK DEFINITIONS

Computer networks have generally been defined as a collection of computer systems that are interconnected by some communication facilities. The individual computing elements, also known as nodes or stations, have processing capabilities to implement a variety of functions, such as terminal concentration, routing, and support of application programs. Each such node is an addressable element of the network. The communication facilities that interconnect any two nodes are called physical links. Each physical link may be composed of a number of logical or virtual channels.

The layout of all the nodes, together with the interconnecting physical links, comprises the network's topology. Although the actual placement of nodes in the network does not affect their functionalities, the efficiency of their connectivities to other nodes may limit their performance.

Two major classes of computer networks have been defined in the literature based on the proximity concept: the local area network (LAN) and the wide area network (WAN). LANs are basically defined as networks whose nodes are physically located in a constrained area, such as a building complex, shopping center, or university campus. Because of this geographic restriction, the physical links in LANs have very high bandwidths and use new communication technologies, such as fiber optics, coaxial cables, and cable television. WANs have no such geographic limitations. The physical links between any two nodes in a WAN could span thousands of miles, thus making them dependent on existing telecommunication infrastructures, such as telephone trunks, microwave links, and satellite links. Because of the cost of high bandwidth links over such long distances, WAN physical links have mostly been restricted to low bandwidths.

Any two networks are interconnected through a common node referred to as a gateway. This node provides all the translation and conversion needed to ensure that the information content of any message is not altered as it moves from network to network, even though its data structure may have changed.

DATA COMMUNICATION TECHNOLOGIES

The transmission of information within a network is controlled through a set of transmission rules that are predefined and consistent in any two communicating nodes. The International Standards Organization (ISO) Open Systems Interconnection Standards, when fully completed, will be the most generalized and comprehensive set of rules for the seven layers of network communication. Only the first three layers are of interest in this paper; they are as follows:

Level	Layer	ISO Standard
1	Physical	X.21 (X.24, X.26, X.27)
2	Data Link	HDLC
3	Network	X.25

Communication technology has gone through a major metamorphosis with the integration of computer technology in the communication arena. This change is exemplified by such achievements as electronic switching systems, voice digitization, and packeted digital transmissions. In some quarters, a new word—compunication—has even been coined to describe the mating of computers and communications.

The packet concept has specifically given rise to a new way of utilizing shared resources in a transparent mode. Whereas the nonpacket environment requires that a point-to-point connection between the two ends be dedicated entirely to a communication session, the packet environment requires only a point-to-point dedicated connection between each end and the transport system, as illustrated in Figure 1. Many communication sessions can therefore simultaneously utilize the same hardware link. This of course requires that each message sent through the shared transport system has a destination address so that the transport system will know where to deliver it. This results in optimum utilization of transport resources.

The packet environment provides another attractive benefit in that it can hold undelivered messages until the receiving end is available. The sender and the receiver need not both be active for a session to take place. However, if the various senders that use the same transport system have a combined throughput that is higher than the bandwidth of the transport system, a backlog may appear. This is usually not acceptable for actual real-time applications such as process control or voice/image communications. The following two basic requirements must be met for a packet-based communication system to operate correctly:

- The transport system must guarantee the delivery of any and all messages to their proper destination.
- All stations must be connected to the transport system and have unique identifiers or addresses.

The packet concepts also have a few more advantages that are worth mentioning:

- A given node (station) can receive information from several sources concurrently. This is accomplished by tagging each message with an identification that is unique to the source.
- A given node can simultaneously communicate with several other nodes and can gain a broadcasting capability by using some reserved node addresses. Additional intelligence will be needed in the transport mechanism to correctly implement the broadcast function.
- Actual information format is transparent to the transport system. Various types of information can therefore share the same transport system as long as the two communicating ends are cognizant of the meanings of their messages.

DISTRIBUTED PROCESSING

The latest advances in the computer hardware industry have resulted in an unprecedented decline in the cost of small- and medium-scale computer systems. This cost reduction has been one of the major reasons that distributed processing has emerged as a viable solution. It has resulted in more processing power, redundancy through multiple units, higher availability of processing capability, and transfer of functional responsibility from the data center to the user.

In the following table a cost comparison is made of four classes of computer processors with equivalent aggregate processing power. An interconnection cost factor must be applied to make the comparison much more realistic. However, this factor was left out because cost greatly depends on the application and is quite constant over a given application.

Processor System	Unit Cost	Performance (MIPS)	Units Required (27 MIPS)	Total Cost
IBM 3090-200	4100K	27.0	1	$4,100K
VAX 8800	700K	10.0	3	2,100K
Micro VAX II	35K	.9	30	1,050K
IBM AT	4K	.3	90	360K

The cost differential in this table is better than 50 percent from one class to the next lower class. Even if an instruction set compensation factor and an interconnection cost factor were applied, the overall cost differential between any two consecutive classes will be at least 25 percent for most applications. Such savings, coupled with other advantages of distributed processing, create an enticement that is hard to overlook in appropriate situations.

The distribution of computer processing over an organization is a task that greatly depends on the application to be supported. Consider an application that requires 500 merchants, each with a single terminal so that a private inventory data base system can be updated on a mainframe. If 20 megabytes of disk storage are assumed for each merchant, 500 terminal ports, over 10 gigabytes of disc storage, tape drives, and printers are required. Given all other requirements, such a system may cost about $4,000,000 in fixed costs and $2,000,000 in recurring costs. Because no required interactions exist among the various merchants, this same application can be implemented using 500 stand-alone IBM ATs at approximately $2,000,000 in fixed costs and $500,000 in recurring costs. No interconnection equipment would be required in this case.

However, if another requirement was introduced to the application, such as printing a consolidated daily activity report, then the costs of the mainframe solution would basically remain unchanged. The microcomputer system, however, might require an additional microcomputer or minicomputer with a dial-up facility to be a data concentrator and report generator. Each of the original microcomputers would require an upgrade with dial-out capability to enable them to transfer daily reports to the data concentrator. The approximate cost for the upgrade would be around $250,000.

It can therefore be seen that the cost of distribution tends to increase with the complexity of the integration required in the application. However, the great majority of nonscientific applications are of the type in which the level of integration is directly proportionate to the organizational level at which the information is utilized. This type of integration within applications can be effectively implemented by the use of hierarchical distributed processing system structures, as shown in Figure 2. In such systems, the processing elements of the same level are all usually identical in regard to capabilities and functionalities.

The Advantages of Distributed Processing

Cost Reduction

As was shown earlier, the use of multiple but less complex computers reduces the cost of hardware equipment, system software, and application development areas. Human resources and facilities costs are other areas in which large reductions can be achieved. As in the earlier example, the mainframe solution requires a full-blown computer center with all its usual needs in addition to the space for terminals at the merchants' locations. However, the microcomputer solution does not require any more than the terminal space at merchants' sites.

Response Time

An improvement in response time is almost guaranteed because each computer is not as overloaded as the central one would be. Most less complex computers have fewer operational and processing overhead costs, which results in faster responses. Some mainframes do not have an adequate throughput capacity to efficiently serve applications that require large numbers of interactive users simultaneously. Response time can also be improved through parallel processing. Because all computers process simultaneously, some tasks will be performed faster in this environment than in the centralized one.

Backup

A backup system can be provided to any data processing complex by using the concept of n+1 modular redundancy. In the centralized case, this implies that another computer system should be acquired, thereby doubling the basic infrastructure. In a distributed processing environment, however, only a single computer system need be acquired if it is assumed that all other systems are identical. In fact, in cases in which operational tolerance exists, the latter acquisition may not even be necessary because each computer system can be backed-up by its physical or logical neighbor. Consequently, the worst-case situation requires an increase of $1/n$ in the basic infrastructure.

Resource Utilization

The distributed processing environment provides better opportunities for the efficient utilization of some data processing resources, from hardware to personnel. These resources can usually be shared among the various sites.

Processing Capacity

A distributed processing system will invariably have more actual processing power than its centralized system equivalent, mainly because of parallelism. This additional computing power can be effectively used at each local site for added functionalities or additional applications. This advantage alone is the foremost justification for using a distributed processing system. The acceptance of the need for local computing capability is also a *de facto* matter. Once the data processing needs have been established, the added local processing capacity is a bonus if the implementation is performed in a distributed mode.

It is generally agreed that distributed processing has become accepted as a default system architecture only because of the proliferation of processing units. As was mentioned earlier, the replacement of dumb terminals by intelligent ones definitely implies the delegation of some functions from the main computer center to the user's site. The current issue therefore depends more on how to configure such systems so that the resulting system's organization is adequate, efficient, and capable of supporting the application.

When distributed processing is viewed in light of the interaction between sites, then it naturally becomes a computer network. In such a system, analyses are not only required of each site's computing capacity, but of the communication bandwidth between sites, site connectivity, security considerations, and others.

APPLICATION-DRIVEN NETWORKS

Application-driven networks are a subset of special-purpose networks. As their name implies, the architectures of ADNs are tightly coupled with the application they support. Because their development is almost entirely drawn from their associated application requirements, ADNs do not possess the general functionalities that are prevalent in most networks. The attractiveness of ADNs is based on two major characteristics that are inherent in their development:

- ADNs have a minimal network overhead; they can therefore provide a better cost/performance ratio than comparable general-purpose networks.
- ADNs have minimal network general functionalities; they can therefore provide built-in, highly secure protection against unauthorized intrusions.

The Development Procedure

The design of a network is a function of identifying the hardware elements (i.e., processors and peripherals), their interconnections (i.e., communication paths and links), and the basic software that runs in the hardware elements in such a way as to produce a coherent and consistent execution of network operations. These operations may include such capabilities as information transfers between some hardware element and the remote utilization of some resources (i.e., data base, compilers, and special processors) that are available in the network. The set of executable functions in a general-purpose network is generally very large because the network provides basic functions much like an instruction set. The user or network system programmer therefore can reliably build super functions by executing basic functions in a logically devised procedure much like a program.

Application-driven networks do not provide this generality to users. The network and the application of ADNs have a one-to-one correspondence such that the only functions capable of being performed on an ADN are those that are part of the application. An ADN network can be regarded as a special-purpose installation with a well-defined application.

The ADN development procedure is based on a hierarchical approach that can be likened to structured design using a top-down methodology. The application requirements are first used to determine the basic functions and, consequently, the network's virtual topology. Some steps are then followed to transform the virtual topology into a physical one by determining which capabilities of the hardware elements are necessary to support the application. Finally, the detailed hardware and software aspects of the resulting network are determined by selecting appropriate vendors.

The systematic development procedure of ADN networks can be stated as follows:

1. Define all processing requirements in terms of virtual hardware elements. In this step, each information processor is identified as a separate block (e.g., square), and its functional requirements (or descriptions) are inscribed inside the square. Duplicate blocks are permitted at this point because they will be dealt with in the minimization procedure.

2. Identify all data flow requirements specified in the application. In this step, each data link is characterized in terms of application requirements. Factors such as data capacity, information characteristics, frequency of transmission, and any other restrictions may affect the determination of the hardware communication elements. Care must be taken to ensure that each link is individually stated.
3. Partition the processing virtual elements of each geographic requirement. This will ensure that geographically separated processing elements are not implemented in the same physical computer. The geographic separation encompasses all known requirements for physically separated, virtual processing elements.
4. For each partition of Step 3, identify all groups of virtual processing elements that can be combined into a single physical processing unit (i.e., a computer). This will identify the actual physical processing elements in each partition. The determination of whether or not any two or more virtual processing elements can be implemented in the same physical processing unit is based on the following two conditions:
    a. The physical unit must be able to support the combined requirements of the virtual elements.
    b. The physical unit must be capable of supporting all required data links. This step cannot be completed until the capabilities of the physical unit under consideration are determined. In cases in which full flexibility in the choice of physical unit exists, other factors such as cost can be used to determine the physical partitioning.
5. For each physical processing unit identified in Step 4, identify all physical communication links required to support the associated data flow links. The multiple data flows defined in Step 2 can be combined on the same physical link. Consideration should be given to the link capacity and the software link driver at both ends to avoid inconsistencies.
6. Select the appropriate product for each hardware element defined in Step 4 (processing units) and Step 5 (communication links). This selected product should at least meet the performance required by its virtual functionalities. Other factors such as cost, reliability, politics, and

economics can be considered at this point to complete the selection.
7. Identify all software needed to drive all data links and implement the applications. The identification of the software may either result in the selection of prepackaged products or in new developments that are tailored specifically to this application. The protocol and message formats will be considered at this point to ensure that the various processing elements are communicating properly.

The Advantages of Application-Driven Networks

The resulting network can be tailored for a particular application by following the previously described procedures. Application-driven networks have the following advantages:

- *High efficiency.* Efficiency is inherent in the design process through Step 5. From Step 6 on, efficiency can be easily lost if compromises are made in the selection processes of hardware and software products. This usually occurs when the market does not have products that perfectly match the requirements or appropriate products cannot be considered for other reasons. Efficiency can be maintained when a given product is specifically developed for an application, but it may not be cost-effective to do so.
- *High security.* Because the network does not allow any general-purpose functions, it is well protected from any tampering that requires functions other than those provided in the applications. Several means are available to improve the security of ADNs:
  - Security functions can be integrated into the application, which results in an inherent built-in protection against certain types of security breaches.
  - Hardware and software products and their integration can be selected in such a manner as to generate nonhomogeneous systems in which individual product shortcomings are not easily propagated throughout the network.
  - The development of in-house products to utilize nonstandard protocols, message formats, encoding schemes, and processing procedures will also provide a level of protection.

- *High reliability.* The reliability of ADNs is mostly a function of the application requirements. Any reliability functions that were integrated into the application are inherently built into the network. The reliability of a network is therefore greatly determined at the start. Even so, the various steps of the development phase provide opportunities to improve or decrease the network's reliability. The partitioning of the hardware processing elements and the selection of the physical processing and communication elements are two such steps.

The Disadvantages of Application-Driven Networks

Most of the disadvantages of ADNs result from the fact that such networks are highly specialized and application-dependent. The following are the disadvantages of application-driven networks:

- *Cost.* Cost comparisons between ADNs and standard networks cannot be easily devised. It can generally be asserted that ADNs will result in more cost-effective systems than comparable standard networks for well-defined applications. The cost-effectiveness of standard networks is lost because one generally ends up paying for more functionalities than are needed. The cost of adapting generalized functions to the application and integrating the security features usually results in even lower cost-effectiveness. The ADNs, however, provide a flexible environment in which cost and performance trade-offs can be applied in a relatively safe environment that does not directly affect the network's functionalities.
- *Adaptability.* ADN networks may not be as easy to adapt to new requirements and functions as standard networks are. The main obstacle is the one-to-one correspondence between the network and the application. If added requirements depart greatly from the original ones, it may even be cost-effective to start the development phase over again. The trade-offs between the lack of complete adaptability of ADNs and standard network generalities are a problem that can be solved only when evaluated in regard to an actual application.

The problem of adapting a given ADN to support additional applications can be viewed in the same manner as the addition of new applications in a working system. Some flexibility should be built into any developing system if the probability of expanding it later is high. However, such a system may lose some efficiency in regard to the original application.

The cost of a standard network is also dictated by economic forces. The mass production of such systems greatly contributes to the decrease in price that makes them attractive in spite of all other attributes. An ADN that utilizes off-the-shelf packages could be developed. The resulting system would not be totally application-driven, but it may be the most cost-effective solution.

CONCLUSION

Application-driven networks provide a systems solution in which the application and network support functions are fully integrated. As was discussed earlier, this integration could be operationally advantageous in appropriate applications.

The development of ADNs will continue to be spurred by two major requirements that embody cost-effectiveness:

- *Support requirements.* Because ADNs are more application-oriented, the overall support expertise of such systems can reside in the organization.
- *Security requirements.* The most secure network systems in existence are home-grown. Because these systems were not developed for general-purpose uses, they are usually ADNs of some type.

Although ADNs may not be appropriate for all organizations for a number of reasons (the most important being lack of internal technical credibility), organizations that require independence in regard to development, support, and operation in a highly secure environment cannot afford to overlook this alternative. In fact, application-driven networks may prove to be the most cost-effective solution in the long term.

REFERENCES

Black, U.D., *Data Communications Networks and Distributed Processing*, Reston Publishing Company, 1983.

Chorafas, D.N., *The Handbook of Data Communication and Computer Networks*, Petrocelli Books, Inc., 1985.

Donaldson, H., *Designing a Distributed Processing System*, John Wiley & Sons, 1979.

Goldberg, R.P., "Virtual Machine Technology: A Bridge From Large Mainframes to Networks of Small Computers", *Proceedings COMPLON*, Fall 1979, pp. 210-213.

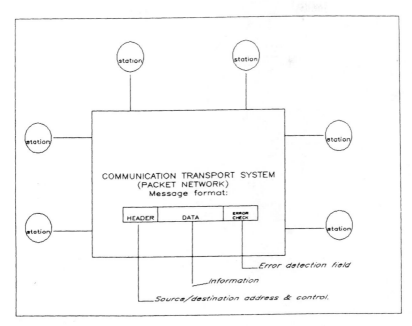

FIGURE 1 Packet communication concept.

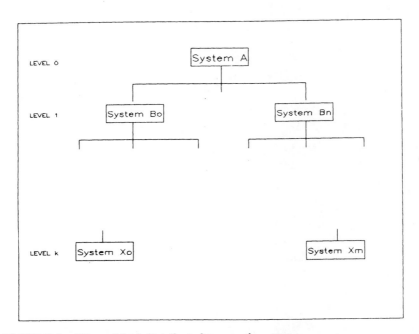

FIGURE 2 Hierarchical distributed processing system.

35

The Use of Microcomputers to Improve Telephone Service

Augusto Júlio Casaca

The complete digitalization of the telephone network at both the transmission and switching levels is an aim pursued by most telecommunication companies worldwide.

Digitalization will permit the implementation of an Integrated Services Digital Network (ISDN) that will offer a set of new services to the subscriber in a reliable and, it is hoped, inexpensive way. However, a long period of time is needed to implement a widespread ISDN, because it is necessary to substitute the analog transmission and electromechanical switching with digital transmission and digital exchanges, respectively. In the meantime, the existing equipment must continue to be used with the highest possible efficiency. This is possible by gradually introducing digital hardware in the network, especially for supervision and maintenance purposes.

Maintenance has been one of the major problems in the telephone network for a long time because it directly affects the quality of service offered to the subscriber. Maintenance aids based on microcomputers can be easily conceived and inexpensively implemented to lower maintenance costs and improve the quality of service.

Good examples of this approach are two microcomputer-based supervision and maintenance networks for crossbar exchanges and public telephone coin boxes, respectively. They are being implemented in the Lisbon area by a joint collaboration between the Telefones de Lisboa e Porto (TLP) and the Instituto de Engenharia de Sistemas e Computadores (INESC).

A MICROCOMPUTER NETWORK FOR THE SUPERVISION AND MAINTENANCE OF CROSSBAR EXCHANGES

The microcomputer network is organized in three distinct hierarchical levels. The data in the network is transmitted along leased telephone lines. As shown in Figure 1, the General Maintenance Center (GMC) is at the highest level. It is based on a minicomputer that processes the maintenance data bases and manages the lower levels of the network. At the immediate level are seven Regional Maintenance Centers (RMCs), each of which is based on a powerful microcomputer. The RMC concentrates data that originate in a group of up to 16 exchanges confined to a certain geographical area. The RMC operator chooses the exchanges under supervision by running application programs in the microcomputer.

At the lowest level—the exchange level—there is a microprocessor-based data acquisition system for local fault diagnosis and alarm indication. The system basically consists of a set of boards that contains an 8088 microprocessor, data random-access memory (RAM), program read-only memory (ROM), interface logic to acquire data from the exchange, and transmission logic to communicate with the RMC. A block diagram of the system is shown in Figure 2.

The system acquires data from the exchange whenever a fault or an alarm occurs and transmits the data to the respective RMC, where it is stored on a disk, ready to be processed by the RMC microcomputer. Data is also processed locally in the 8088 microprocessor, which allows the main characteristics of the fault to be displayed on the video screen. A message is sent to the video screen or printer to indicate which exchange organs are involved in the fault or alarm and a diagnosis of its possible origins.

The local system also accepts a set of commands that allows the local operator to perform the following functions:

- Choose the video or printer as an output peripheral;

- Hold the organs involved in the fault in their state of operation to permit a more detailed observation of the fault by maintenance personnel; and
- Obtain statistics on the number and types of faults and on the organs involved in these faults.

It is often possible to identify which organs are more likely to be faulty by studying these statistics.

The hierarchical organization of the network permits the use of maintenance personnel to be optimized. With the exception of exchanges with a large number of subscribers, the remaining exchanges are essentially supervised from the RMCs and GMC, where most maintenance teams are concentrated. A team will only have to move to an exchange to ensure local maintenance when it is judged necessary at the maintenance center.

MICROCOMPUTER-BASED CONTROL AND MAINTENANCE OF TELEPHONE COIN BOXES

A high degree of utilization, hostile environmental conditions, and vandalism can cause a low mean time between failures in many coin boxes, which affects the public image of the phone company in a negative way. An automated maintenance procedure that can give a maintenance center a real-time picture of what is happening in the coin boxes is required to deal with this situation. The maintenance system described in this paper was conceived to operate in the Lisbon area, in which about 2,000 telephone coin boxes are used. But the system is flexible enough to be easily adapted to other telephone networks.

The maintenance system consists of a set of local units (one unit per coin box) and a central unit installed in a maintenance center as shown in Figure 3. The local unit is based on a low-power, single-chip microcomputer. The unit is placed inside the coin box and has the following three functions:

- It controls the telephone calls made from the coin box, which renders the old control logic that existed in the box obsolete and achieves a higher degree of reliability.
- It automatically detects certain types of critical situations in the coin box, such as the lack of a handset, a slow dial, the rejection of too many consecutive coins, and a great number of coins in the box that need to be collected. Any

one of these occurrences is automatically transmitted as an alarm by the microcomputer to the maintenance center along the public telephone network as soon as the line is free.
- It records statistical data, such as the number of calls, the duration of the call, and the number of different types of coins, and it automatically transmits these data to the maintenance center once a day.

The central unit in the maintenance center is a standard minicomputer connected to the telephone network through a group of lines with an automatic search procedure. The main roles of the central unit are as follows:

- To collect alarms and statistical data from the local unit and broadcast these data to the maintenance personnel through a user-friendly interface; and
- To run application programs that permit the maintenance personnel to be efficiently scheduled, the collection of coins to be planned, and an overall picture of the status of the coin boxes network to be provided.

The local unit is based on an 80C31 microcomputer chip, an EPROM program, and input/output ports. It is completed with a set of two interfaces to control and acquire data in the coin box, respectively, and to transmit data along the telephone lines. Components were carefully selected to obtain a highly compact and low consumption board for the local unit, because it is mandatory in this type of application.

CONCLUSIONS

The availability of low-cost and reliable microcomputers enables the use of digital techniques to supervise the performance and aid in the maintenance of crossbar telephone exchanges and public telephone coin boxes.

The solutions adopted for the Lisbon area will improve the maintenance efficiency and the quality of telephone service and allow maintenance personnel to be better managed. These solutions are also economically advantageous to the telephone company, because the required investment is relatively low, the savings in maintenance costs is significantly high, and the public image of the company is ameliorated as a result of better service.

REFERENCES

J. Jesus, A. Casaca, J. Marques, "Microcomputer Aided Maintenance for Public Telephone Exchanges," MIMI Symposium, San Feliu de Guixols, June, 1985.

J. Jesus, "Um Sistema de Diagnóstico Automático de Avarias e Alarmes em Centrais do tipo Pentaconta 1000 A," M. Sc. Thesis, I.S.T., February 1985.

A. Casaca, N. Mamede, L. Baptista, L. Costa, "Sistema Auxiliar de Conservação para Postos Telefónicos Públicos," 2o. Workshop sobre Technologia das Comunicações, Vimeiro, October, 1985.

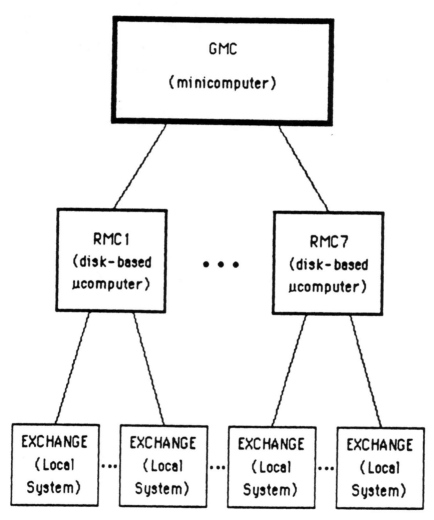

FIGURE 1 Supervision and maintenance network for crossbar exchanges.

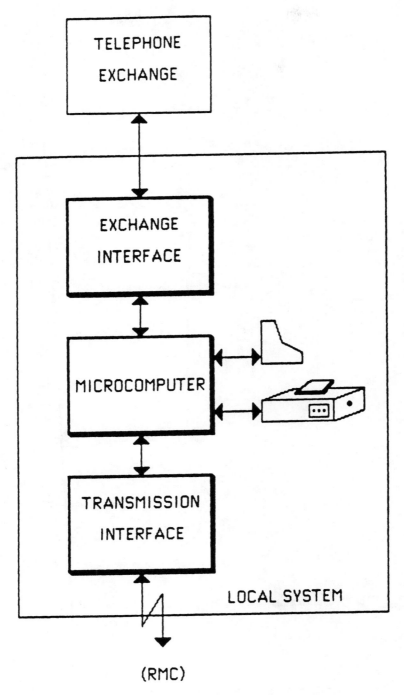

FIGURE 2 Local system block diagram.

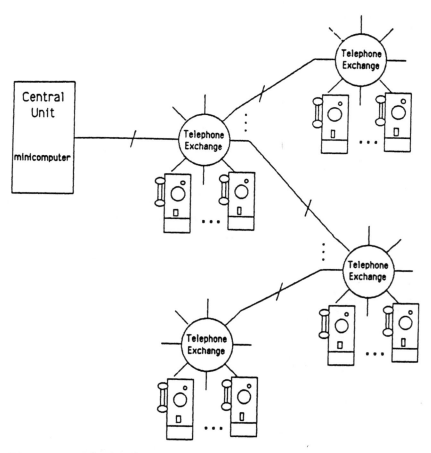

FIGURE 3 Maintenance system for public telephones.

36

Loop Signaling for PCM Equipment

VASCO LAGARTO and LUSITANA DELGADO

INTRODUCTION

Due to the use of microprocessors, the loop-signaling equipment described in this article has a set of features that allows its use not only to perform the normal functions of such equipment but also to go beyond, performing functions usually attributed to other blocks within an analog switching exchange and easily adapted to any exchange used in the Portuguese CTT network.

In the PCM structure (Rec. G732-CCITT), time slot 16 is used to convey all the signaling information of the 30 channels.

The signaling information in the Portuguese Network is usually separated from the voice information by the switching exchange, using special relay sets. Those relay sets transform the signaling information on earth potentials that are sent to the other side using only one bit. So, in those relay sets, or anywhere within the exchange, there must be the necessary "intelligence" to understand the meaning of an earth potential along the processing of a call.

Meanwhile, the PCM transmission equipment gives to any signaling channel the possibility of using 4 bits each 2 ms interval. This means that each signaling channel has an information capacity of 2 Kbits/s, a value much above the need for an analog switching exchange.

Joining the processing capability with the transmission capacity, we got a system to process and convert the signaling information from an exchange into digital information and vice-versa, substituting the functions of the traditional interfaces.

The future use of different digital switching systems in the Portuguese Network may also give rise to the need for a flexible and universal interface to easily allow the integration of the new switching exchanges into the actual network.

Connection with PCM Multiplex Equipment and the Analog Exchange

Figure 1 shows how the loop signaling equipment is connected with the analog exchange.

The communication with the PCM MUX equipment is done using a 64 Kbit contra-directional interface (Rec. G. 704-CCITT). Through this interface is given access to the time slot 16 of the PCM frame.

To the analog exchange side, an interface was designed, trying to cover all the situations existing in an outgoing to an incoming junction. This means that the same circuit is actually used to interface both types of junctions.

BLOCK DESCRIPTION

Figure 2 shows a block diagram of the equipment. This is actually done with 3 different boards (double Eurocard).

- Central office interfaces;
- Central processing; and
- Data collecting (remaining blocks).

INTERFACES

Each interface board has 6 interfaces, which can be "programmed" to be used with an incoming or an outgoing junction. All the output interface circuits are protected against short-circuits and over-voltages. In the output interfaces, optoelectronics are used.

Each interface also has the possibility to send the busy tone to the subscriber, which is important when it performs the same functions as the relay sets.

Each interface can deal with 4 wires (a and b, plus p and r wires) plus 3 more wires common to all systems.

The following functions can be performed by each interface:

- To feed the subscriber line with normal or reverse polarity;
- To detect the loop condition and the dial pulses;
- To impose a loop condition and to repeat the dial pulses;
- To send the busy tone;
- To detect a positive, negative, or an earth potential on the p or r wires; and
- To impose a positive, negative, or an earth potential on the p or r wires.

DATA COLLECTING

The data collecting board controls the 64 Kbit contradirectional interface and also the data coming from the interfaces.

In order not to overcharge the man microprocessor (8085) on the processing board, all the data coming from the interfaces or from the 64Kbit interface is analyzed in order to detect any modification from the previous sample. If there is any difference, the new value is memorized together with the information on the exact interface that changed to another state.

All this information (processed by a 8039 microprocessor) is given to the processing board to be processed one by one, as soon as the main processor is available.

It is also this card that controls the signaling frame according to the CCITT recommendations. It also generates a set of control signals needed to the other boards.

This card has 4 Kbits of ROM.

PROCESSING BOARD

The loop signaling equipment was designed to take care of all the different types of signaling on the CTT network. So it is a system that has the capability to be adapted to any specific situation.

In this board we can find a 8085-AH-2 microprocessor with 20 Kbits of ROM and 5 Kbits of RAM. It is this unit that is responsible for the performance and the different features of the equipment.

When the equipment is powered up, this unit collects the information about the type of interfaces (outgoing or incoming junctions). If the same equipment is on both sides of the connection (Figure 1), the equipment checks the configuration on both sides before service is given, giving an alarm indication if any mistake is detected.

The software is divided into very small blocks, according to the transition state diagram of the junctions.

While all the inputs are first "filtered" by the data collecting board, this unit interfaces directly with the PCM link and the exchange interfaces to send all the outcome signals from the processing.

CONCLUSION

The loop signaling equipment, due to the use of microprocessors, can be a great help in the improvement of the actual network and also to ease the transition for the digital network.

Due to its "intelligence," information such as relation between dummy traffic and real traffic, traffic by direction, and traffic carried by each junction can be obtained using this equipment, besides some maintenance facilities.

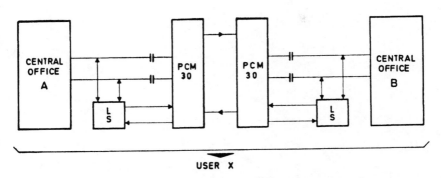

FIGURE 1 Loop signaling (LS) equipment connection with the analog exchange.

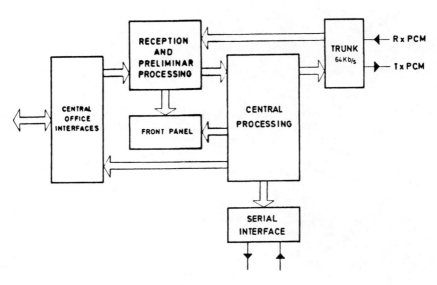

FIGURE 2 General hardware diagram.

37
Design and Manufacture of Modern Telecommunication Equipment in Portugal

CANDIDO M. LOPES MANSO

ABSTRACT

Countries with no tradition of electronic industry or telecommunications equipment design and manufacture must take a big step not to sink in the new emerging era of ISDN communications.

Although university laboratories can play a big role in this task, it is the national industry that must lead the effort; otherwise, the targeted goals shall never be fully accomplished.

Trying to illustrate Portuguese activities in this matter, we shall present some accomplished R&D projects developed at our company (Empresa de Investigação e Desenvolvimento de Electrónica, SARL), concerning digital switching equipment for the private telephonic market.

INTRODUCTION

In Portugal, the public telephone network service is currently supported with traditional electromechanical switching equipment. The same situation is true for private telephone networks (PABXs). Until the end of the seventies, the market was mostly supplied by the two national telecommunication manufacturers. However, the private switching market is very dynamic and market pressures are much more powerful; thus the national industry had to start offering modern equipment, otherwise they would gradually lose the market to trade companies selling imported products. At that time, two possible strategies for overcoming this situation were identified:

- To manufacture under license third party products; and
- To begin an R&D effort to create and develop know-how and subsequently design our own products.

The prime advantage of the first solution is the possible short time lag between the decision and the results; based on this assumption (later verified as not so exact), our company decided to initiate a licensing operation in order to be able to comply with market needs in the short term. However, at the same time we decided to initiate in parallel a broader operation of R&D, aiming for the medium term to achieve an internal know-how and technological capabilities that would result in a real capacity for producing competitive full proprietary equipment.

Although the success of the first operation—licensing/transfer of "know-how"—can give adequate results in certain situations, we can point out some major drawbacks it presents, based on our own experience:

- It is not as straightforward as it seems; if the licensed equipment involves an upgrading of manufacturing methods, it takes longer than planned.
- If the receiving team is not already familiar with the technology, the know-how it can absorb is limited compared with goals.
- In a field moving as rapidly as telecommunications is today, the licensed product, even being competitive in the beginning of the contract, can rapidly become obsolete; the absorbed know-how may not be enough to start with and maintain its technological competitiveness.
- Licensing contracts very often include market restriction clauses, which can sometimes interfere in the desirable evolution of the license company.

The second strategy, in-house expertise acquisition and development, although in my opinion is the right decision, as I will try to illustrate later by the accomplished results, presents also some difficulties that cannot be hidden:

- *Staff*: Local availability of enough technicians with adequate background education for these developments, namely in software engineering areas.
- *Information*: Difficult access to information sources, namely those related to high technology owned by private commercial companies; sometimes the same applies to brand-new electronic components.
- *Tools*: Efficient project support tools, not commercially available; this sometimes implies additional effort to develop (or miss) them.
- *Technologies*: Small countries with small markets do not justify competitive design options (e.g., custom VLSI).
- *Manufacturing*: Besides project and prototype developments, the team must also introduce new methodologies for manufacturing, tests, and quality assurance, compatible with a generation of products not traditional in the factory shop.
- *Financing*: High financing costs due to the medium term nature of this operation, involving not only high cost manpower, but also expensive project support equipment.
- *Others*: Last, we will not omit a final barrier of a cultural nature existing among consumers of many countries; they tend to underestimate home made products when faced with "international" (or multinational) ones, with traditional reputation.

Even when faced with all of those difficulties, this approach is the only solution to reach a true embedded technological capability, allowing multiplying effects; to encourage these kinds of initiatives, a global effort (or attitude) has to be developed. Public and governmental institutions, universities, and the national industry, all have a large role to play. From the outset, we claim encouragement and care for the products developed under these premises, universities, and similar institutions, can help to overcome many of the above mentioned difficulties. However, we must stress that the full goals will never be reached when universities undertake projects without a real involvement of related industry; many technological development problems arise from manufacturing difficulties, as already pointed out.

Experience shows many interesting and successful university

projects that never reached an industrial stage due to those "small" details.

RESULTS

This R&D policy undertaken in my company in the telecommunications field has already started to show some successful results. Only as a matter of illustration of preceding statements, we shall now give a brief description of the more relevant products or projects issued from these developments.

Central Exchange 12 (CX 12)

- Electronic PABX with a 12-port capacity;
- Stored program controlled;
- Analog switching solid state matrix; and
- Fully equipped with usual commercial features.

This product has been the first experiment in this area; the project was concluded by the end of 1983; production started during 1984, and it has revealed a very competitive price performance. One thousand units have already been shipped, mostly sold in the internal market with good export prospects underway.

Upgraded versions of this product have since then been developed; a sister product—Central Key System 12 (CK 12)—using more sophisticated feature phones is now starting field trials.

Residential Telephone System (RTS)

RTS is a small electronic analog PABX, with the same technology as the preceding but featured to reach the needs of domestic users. Its capacity is 5+1 or 5+2. The project was slated to end in 1986. A project has been committed to our company by a well known multinational telephone supplier, to be manufactured later in their own factory plants. We are presenting this development here because it represents, in my point of view, a milestone in this effort of know-how development.

Digital PABX's TAGID Family

The preceding projects have been presented mainly for historical reasons; they have represented a successful "soft-start" with a well known technology, mainly to test and demonstrate the feasibility of the idea. The project that involved a real step forward, due to involved technology and project size, has been the TAGID project. The goals of this project are to develop and manufacture a coherent range of digital PABXs from 50 to 1,500 ports, with all the features of third generation switching systems, including data switching. It will also be prepared to accept ISDN interfaces and services as soon as they become stable and widespread.

Although the project period is not yet concluded, we are already executing laboratory experiments with the medium model of the range (100 to 400 ports); field trials begin the first quarter of 1987, and the first shipments are planned for the last quarter of 1987.

One year later, we plan to begin the manufacture of the other two models: CX-1,500 with a capacity of up to 1,500 ports and the CX-80 aiming at a capacity of between 50 and 100 ports. The architectural modularity has been a main concern in the design phase, so that the three models share the same hardware boards and mechanical components, and the software can be reused in any of the models with only minor editing changes.

Another design concern has been architecture flexibility, under the hardware and software point of view; the objective is to allow an open path to grow towards new interfaces and services that can be envisaged in the near future to be committed to the communications node (PABX). A second phase of this project will then introduce in all of the models of this family all the features and services associated with emerging ISDN networks.

In this project, a team of about 50 people is involved, mostly university level engineers, during a period of four years, beginning at the end of 1983. Considering the investment of around 5 million US dollars necessary to finance this medium-term project, a significant push to the decision of starting it has been the support received from the NATO "Science for Stability" program, in the form of a grant important enough to allow the acquisition of project development tools mandatory to support a project of such a dimension.

Also due to the size and importance of this action, a fruitful cooperation agreement has been established under the leadership of Centrel (of which EID is a subsidiary company) with three other Portuguese institutions: Instituto de Engenharia de Sistemas e Computadores (INESC), Laboratório Nacional de Engenharia e Tecnologica Industrial (LNETI), and Correios e Telecommunicações de Portugal (CTT).

We think successful cooperation between industrial R&D departments and university or state-owned laboratories has been one of the important achievements to register. The other will be the creation in our country of a nucleus of expertise in several areas that up until now were nonexistent:

- Large project management and control;
- Telecommunications software engineering;
- Software quality assurance;
- Digital switching electronics technology; and
- Complex electronics manufacturing and testing.

This know-how, if no other exogenous factors will affect it, and the R&D policy remains coherent, will allow in the near future to create a true, well-supported telecommunications industry in Portugal.

38
The Use of Expert Systems in Educational Software
ERNESTO COSTA

Computers are an active medium for establishing communication with students. When used correctly, computers can greatly improve the teaching process. One problem that delayed the introduction of computers in schools was their price. Fortunately, the cost of a microcomputer has been continuously decreasing in recent years, and its capabilities (central memory, speed, graphics, and sound effects) have been steadily increasing. The general and widespread use of computers in education is therefore economically feasible.

Unfortunately, the educational software developed thus far is generally poor in quality (Self, 1986). The programs in use lack one of the most important qualities of a human tutor: intelligence. They know nothing about the domain being taught, the students' knowledge and skills, or teaching strategies. The part of an education program that involves solving and explaining the question asked of the student can be implemented by means of an expert system.

These programs can be used mainly in a drill-and-practice way, but they can also be ameliorated to behave as an intelligent tutor. Two simple examples of programs written in Prolog and implemented in a microcomputer demonstrate how this can be achieved.

An argument will be made in this paper in support of the thesis that computers can replace teachers to some extent; artificial intelligence techniques are needed to achieve this goal; expert systems can be used to implement intelligent drill-and-practice systems; and all this can be accomplished through the use of a microcomputer.

COMPUTERS AND EDUCATION

Education can be defined as the process by which at least two agents—a teacher and a learner—communicate in the presence of a certain environment. The goal is to increase the knowledge and performance of the learner in regard to a particular aspect of the world (Figure 1).

A good teacher has the following three characteristics:

- *Knowledge about the domain being taught.* This is an obvious point. A good teacher must be an expert in the domain being taught and must be able to solve the same problems students are expected to solve. A good teacher must also be able to analyze students' answers to establish their degree of correctness.
- *Knowledge about teaching strategies.* A teacher must define the best sequence of material to introduce a method or concept. Good teachers think about the examples they are going to use and the way in which they will interact with their students.
- *Knowledge about the students' knowledge and skills.* Even the best plan must be modified according to the students' reaction. A good teacher is one who clearly understands why students miss an important point or misunderstand a concept.

In conclusion, a teacher is permanently iterating the process of creating a plan or exposing material, solving and analyzing the questions addressed to the students, and creating a model of students' knowledge to redefine the plan, if necessary (see Figure 2).

Computers have been involved in education for a long time (O'Shea and Self, 1983). Given the previously mentioned characteristics that define a good teacher, can computers replace them? If the majority of current educational software is considered, the answer is definitely not. In fact, the educational software produced thus far has no knowledge about the domain being taught. To overcome this drawback, these programs generally adopt a principle of prestoring pairs of question and answers. But what happens if a student gives a correct answer in a different way? The programs are also unable to identify the causes of students' errors, which is a crucial point. Some programs have some planning capabilities in that they are sensitive to students' answers. But even this capability is limited; the system knows some typical wrong answers and reacts according to the one given by the student. It is clearly impossible to anticipate all students' wrong answers. This method is therefore not very effective. The remedial material produced by the system makes interpretations about the reasons that cause an answer to be given. It is known, however, that different students may have different reasons for giving the same answer. This is a point that a good human teacher is able to detect.

These programs lack the intelligence that makes human tutors so effective. The goal of artificial intelligence (AI) is to build programs that perform tasks that require intelligence. The feasibility of this project relies on the assumption that computers are symbol processors as opposed to number crunchers. It is therefore possible to represent symbolic knowledge about some aspect of the real world, because intelligence itself is the result of knowledge (representation) manipulation. Artificial intelligence techniques must be used to produce educational software. Some work has been done in this direction in recent years (Barr and Feigenbaum, 1982), (O'Shea and Self, 1983), (Sleeman and Brown, 1982). At an abstract level, they all refer to the same architecture, as shown in Figure 3 (Costa, 1986). Each of the three modules in Figure 3 is responsible for one of the three teachers' capabilities mentioned earlier.

EXPERT SYSTEMS AND EDUCATION

An expert system (ES) is a system designed to perform specific tasks that were formerly performed by a small number of human experts. It is important to stress that this expertise is acquired through experience, not by teaching. This explains why there are so few experts. Expert systems have some attractive characteristics:

- Expert systems can compete with or even surpass human experts;
- The knowledge about the domain is clearly separated from the way the system builds its inferences;
- Knowledge is represented by means of production rules that make an ES easy to modify;
- Expert systems can reason through the use of plausibility measures that allow them to be used in other than well-defined domains; and
- Expert systems currently have some form of introspection capability because they are able to explain their results.

Given these characteristics, how can an expert system be used in education? The first application could be as an active knowledge reservoir (Ennals, 1985) that can be consulted by students.

Another application involves the use of an ES as the core of an intelligent tutoring system (ITS) (Clancey, 1982). The idea behind this approach is that an ES can be used to derive an "expert solution" that can be compared to a students' solution. Another application could use the ability of the ES to evaluate and reason about partial solutions. Nevertheless, as Self (1985) pointed out, the use of an ES as the kernel of an ITS leads to emphasis being placed on conducting the learner to the level of expertise of the system, which is an impossible task. Furthermore, this is not the ultimate goal of teaching. Good teaching involves understanding the concepts a student knows, the strategies a student uses, and the misconceptions a student has, and adapting to the students' capabilities. The ES module in Figure 3 corresponds to the one responsible for solving and generating examples. It is used to support two other modules, particularly the one responsible for creating a model of the students' current state of knowledge.

Building an ITS is therefore more complicated than simply using an ES. Nevertheless, an ES can still be used to solve and explain problems posed by the student and generate problems to be solved by students. The ES can follow students' solutions in a simple way; for example, when a student fails, it can indicate which rule should have been used.

Microcomputer implementations are possible in applications of the intelligent drill-and-practice type. Two examples clarify the two applications mentioned earlier. They were both written in Prolog (Kowalsky, 1979; Bratko, 1986). Prolog was chosen because

Example One: Teaching Derivatives

The first program is a simple one that involves teaching derivatives by example. The system poses a problem for the student to solve. If necessary, the system shows the ordered sequence of rules it has applied together with the effect produced by each rule over the expression. Rules for derivation can be easily programmed, as shown.

```
d(X,X,1) :-ridentidade(X),!.
d(C,X,0) :-atomic(C),rconstante(C).
d(U+V,X,S) :-rsoma (U+V), d(U,X,A),d(V,X,B),simp(A + B,S).
d(U-V,X,S):-rdiferenca(U-V),d(U,X,A),d(V,X,B),simp(A-B, S).
d(C*U,X,S):-number(C),rprodconst(C*U),d(U,X,A),simp(C*A,S),!.
d(U*V,X,S);-rproduto(U*V),d(U,X,A),d(V,X,B),simp(B*U+A*V,S).
d(U^C,X,S) :-number(C),rexp(U^ C), Y is C - 1,
    d(U,X,W),simp(C * W * (U^Y),S).
```

A possible work session is shown next:

expression to derivate: 5 * x + 3 * x ^ 4.
in order to: x.

1) I apply the rule

   D(U + V) = D(U) + D(V) to
   D(5 * x + 3 * x ^ 4) = *D(5 * x) + D(3 * x ^ 4)

giving the partial result

der(5 * x) + der(3 * x ^ 4)

2) I apply the rule:

   D(c * U) = c * D(U) to
   D(5 * x) = 5 * D(x)

giving the partial result

5* der(x) + der(3 * x ^ 4)

3) I apply the rule:

   D(X) = 1 to

D(x) = 1

giving the partial result

5 * 1 + der(3 * x ^ 4)

or, after simplification

5 + der(3 * x ^ 4)

4)   I apply the rule:

D(c * U) = c * D(U) to
D(3 * x ^ 4) = 3 * D(x ^ 4)

giving the partial result

5 + 3 * der(x ^ 4)

This program is currently under development to build a more user-friendly interface, produce meta-level explanations in addition to explanations at a rule level, and enable the student to solve the problem and the system to analyze the answer.

Example Two: Proofs in Propositional Logic

In this example, the system can generate problems with different levels of difficulty and can give some hints to help students to solve these problems (Ferreira, 1986). The following is a possible system work session:

GIVEN

((E and G) imp (H or I))
((C or D) imp (E and G))
((A and B) imp (C or D))
(A and B)

PROVE (H or I)

1 ((E and G) imp (H or I))
2 ((C or D) imp (E and G))
3 ((A and B) imp (C or D))
4 (A and B)
5 (C or D)
6 HELP

TO CONTINUE, YOU MUST EITHER USE MODUS PONENS OR SOME TAUTOLOGY

THAT YOU CAN USE TO GENERATE NEW STEPS BY USING AGAIN MODUS PONENS.
YOU CAN ONLY USE MODUS PONENS IF YOU HAVE ALREADY PROVED
    X AND
    X imp Y, FROM WHICH YOU CAN PROVE Y
X AND Y CAN BE ANY FORMULA. CONTINUE.
1   ((E and G) imp (H or I))
2   ((C or D) imp (E and G))
3   ((A and B) imp (C or D))
4   (A and B)
5   (C or D)
6   (E and G)
7   (H or I)

DO YOU WISH ANOTHER PROBLEM? (YES/NO)
YES
WAIT A MOMENT. I AM GENERATING ANOTHER PROBLEM.
GIVEN

((N or O) imp (P and Q))
((L or M) imp (N or O))
((J and K) imp (L or M))
(J and K)

PROVE (P and Q)

1 ((N or O) imp (P and Q))
2 ((L or M) imp (N or O))
3 ((J and K) imp (L or M))
4 (J and K)
5 (L or M)
6 (N or O)
7 HELP

TRY TO USE MODUS PONENS WITH STEPS 6 AND 1
7   HELP
IF YOU USE MODUS PONENS WITH STEPS 6 AND 1
YOU'LL OBTAIN (P and Q). YOU CAN THEN CONTINUE.
8   HELP
YOU HAVE TO STUDY MORE, BECAUSE YOU FAILED A LOT.
PAY ATTENTION TO THE RIGHT PROOF AND TRY TO LEARN WITH IT.

1   ((N or O) imp (P and Q))
2   ((L or M) imp (N or O))

3   ((J and K) imp (L or M))
4   (J and K)
5   (L or M)
6   (N or O)
7   (P and Q)

DO YOU WISH ANOTHER PROBLEM? (YES/NO)
NO

The problem of determining the level of difficulty of a problem as a function of students' previous answers is being studied.

CONCLUSIONS

It has been shown that it is possible to use AI tools, particularly expert systems, to develop microcomputers that use educational software. It has been argued that an expert system alone cannot be the kernel of an intelligent tutoring system, because expert systems work precisely at an expert level. Their explanations therefore are not always understandable by a majority of students. This problem can be partly attenuated if the expert system interacts with students not at a rule level, but at a more abstract meta-level. Nevertheless, expert systems can still be useful in an intelligent drill-and-practice manner.

ACKNOWLEDGMENTS

The programs described in this paper are part of an exploratory study that involves artificial intelligence and education. The study was integrated in the national program MINERVA, and developed at the Departamento de Engenharia Electrotécnica da Universidade de Coimbra. Thanks are due to all people who are working in the group, particularly C. Bento, J. Ferreira, T. Mendes, and A. Mendes.

This research was partially financed by the European Community through COST-13 funds to the Machine Learning and Knowledge Acquisition project.

REFERENCES

A. Barr and E. Feigenbaum. 1982. *The Handbook of AI*, Vol. 2, Pittman, pp. 221-294.

I. Bratko. 1986. *Prolog Programming for Artificial Intelligence*, Addison-Wesley.

W. Clancey. 1982. Tutoring rules for building a case method dialogue, in *Intelligent Tutoring Systems*, D. Sleeman and J. S. Brown (Eds.), Academic Press.

E. Costa. 1986. AI and education: the role of knowledge in teaching, *Proceedings of the First European Session on Learning*, EWSL-86, Orsay, France.

R. Ennals. 1985. *Artificial Intelligence: Applications to Logical Reasoning and Historical Research*, Ellis Horwood Limited.

J. L. Ferreira. 1986. An examples generator in propositional logic: applications to Computer-Aided Instruction (in Portuguese), *Proceedings of the Second Portuguese Meeting on AI*, pp. 271-281, Lisboa.

R. Kowalsky. 1979. *Logic for Problem Solving*, North-Holland Publishing Co.

T. O'Shea and J. Self. 1983. *Learning and Teaching with Computers: AI in Education*, Harvester Press.

J. Self. 1985. A perspective on intelligent computer-assisted learning, *Journal of Computer Assisted Learning*, 1, pp. 159-166.

J. Self. 1986. *Microcomputers in Education: a Critical Appraisal of Educational Software*, Harvester Press.

J. Self (Ed.). *Intelligent Computer-Assisted Instruction*, Chapman and Hall, to appear in 1987.

D. Sleeman and J. S. Brown (Eds.). 1982. *Intelligent Tutoring Systems*, Academic Press.

L. Sterling and E. Shapiro. 1986. *The Art of Prolog*, MIT Press.

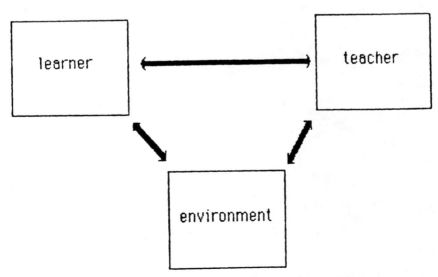

FIGURE 1 Education is the process by which a teacher and learner communicate in the presence of a certain environment.

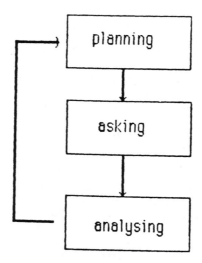

FIGURE 2 Teaching strategy requires constant revision, based on results.

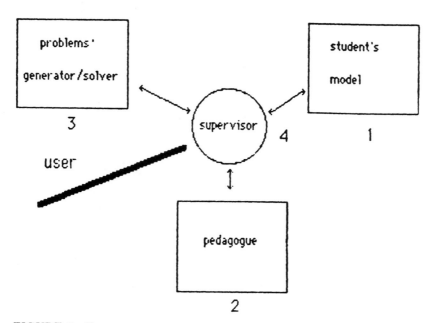

FIGURE 3 Expert systems must simulate an expert teacher to be effective in education.

CONTRIBUTORS

Alexandre Vieira Abrantes
Escola Nacional de Saude Publica
Av. Padre Cruz
1699 Lisboa Codex, Portugal

Ted M. Albert
Data Administrator
U.S. Geological Survey
801 National Center
12201 Sunrise Valley Drive
Reston, Virginia 22092, U.S.A.

Alberto Joaquim Milheiro Barbosa
EFACEC
Apartado 31
4470 Maia, Portugal

Jose Alberto Barbosa
EFACEC
Apartado 31
4470 Maia, Portugal

Eduardo Beira
IBEROMOLDES
Rua 10 de Junho, 61 - Picassinos
2430 Marinha Grande, Portugal

Brian Brademeyer
Civil Engineering Department
Room 1-230
Massachusetts Institute of Technology
77 Massachusetts Avenue
Cambridge, Massachusetts 02139, U.S.A.

Teodoro Briz
Escola Nacional de Saude Publica
Av. Padre Cruz
1699 Lisboa Codex, Portugal

David C. Brown
Artificial Intelligence Research Group
Worcester Polytechnic
Worcester, Massachusetts 01609, U.S.A.

António Sousa da Câmara
FCT - New University of Lisbon
Quinta do Torre
2825 Monte do Caparica, Portugal

Amilcar Cardoso
Departamento de Engenharia Electrotecnica
Faculdade de Ciencias e Tecnologia da
Universidade de Coimbra
3000 Coimbra, Portugal

Augusto Júlio Casaca
Instituto Nacional de Engenharia de Sistemas e Computadores
Rua Alves Redol, 9-3o
1000 Lisboa, Portugal

Ernesto Costa
Departamento de Engenharia Electrotecnica
Faculdade de Ciencias e Tecnologia da
Universidade de Coimbra
3000 Coimbra, Portugal

João Cravinho
Coordinator Innovation Programs
Junta Nacional de Investigacao Cientifica e Tecnologia
Rua da Pracas, 13-B, R/C - 1o.
1200 Lisboa, Portugal

João Duarte Cunha
Laboratorio Nacional de Engenharia Civil (LNEC)
Av. do Brasil, 101
1700 Lisboa, Portugal

John Daly
Office of the Science Advisor
Agency for International Development
Washington, D.C. 20523, U.S.A.

Luís Damas
Centro de Informatica da
Universidade do Porto
Rua das Taipas, 135
4000 Porto, Portugal

Barbara N. Diskin
International Statistical Program Center
Bureau of the Census
U.S. Department of Commerce
Scuderi Bldg., Room 602
Washington, D.C. 20233, U.S.A.

Murray Eden
Chief, Biomedical Engineering and Instrumentation Branch
Division of Research Services
Bldg. 13, Room 3W13
National Institutes of Health
Bethesda, Maryland 20892, U.S.A.

João Lourenco Fernandes
Instituto Nacional de Engenharia e Sistemas de Computadores
(INESC)
Rua Alves Redol, 9-1o.
1000 Lisboa, Portugal

A. Dias de Figueiredo
Faculdade de Ciencias e Tecnologia da
Universidade de Coimbra
Largo Marques de Pombal
3000 Coimbra, Portugal

Miguel Filgueiras
Centro de Informatica da
Universidade do Porto
Rua das Taipas, 135
4000 Porto, Portugal

Adolfo Steiger Garcao
Faculdade de Ciencias e Tecnologia da
Universidade Nova de Lisboa
Departamento de Informatica
Quinta da Torre
2825 Monte da Caparica, Portugal

Mario Rui Gomes
Instituto Nacional de Engenharia e Sistemas de Computadores
(INESC)
Rua Alves Redol, 9-1o
1000 Lisboa, Portugal

Flavio Grynszpan
President
Riotec, S.A.
Estrada RJ - 089 (via 9), 6555
Jacarepagua
Rio de Janeiro, Brazil

Glenn A. Hart
Glenn A. Hart Associates
51 Church Street
Monsey, New York 10952, U.S.A.

Harry D. Huskey
Board of Studies in Computer and Information Sciences
University of California - Santa Cruz
Santa Cruz, California 95064, U.S.A.

Anil K. Jain
Computer Science Department
A-726 Wells Hall
Michigan State University
East Lansing, Michigan 48824, U.S.A.

Andrew C. Kapusto
Cognitronics, Inc.
25 Crescent Street
Stamford, Connecticut 06906, U.S.A.

E.T. Kapuya
Department of Electrical Engineering
University of Zimbabwe
P.O. Box MP 167
Mount Pleasant
Harare, Zimbabwe

A.D.V.N. Kularatne
Research and Development Engineer
Arthur C. Clarke Center for Modern Technologies
Katubedda
Moratuwa, Sri Lanka

Vasco Lagarto
Centro de Estudos de Telecomunicacoes dos CTT
Sitio das Palhas
3800 Aveiro, Portugal

Donald T. Lauria
Department of Environmental Sciences and Engineering
School of Public Health
University of North Carolina
Chapel Hill, North Carolina 27514, U.S.A.

William J. Lawless, Jr.
Chairman
Cognitronics, Inc.
25 Crescent Street
Stamford, Connecticut 06906, U.S.A.

Joseph F. P. Luhukay
Computer Science Center
University of Indonesia
Jl. Salemba 4
P.O. Box 3442
Jakarta, Indonesia

Candido M. Lopes Manso
Empresa de Investigacao e Desenvolvimento de Electronica, S.A.
Caixa Postal 9
2825 Monte da Caparica, Portugal

Sridhar Mitta
WIPRO
Information Technology Limited
88 Mahatma Gandhi Road
Bangalore 560 001, India

Marcio H. Montagna Cammarota
Nucleo de Informatica
Secretaria Geral
Esplanada dos Ministerios - Bloco 6
70.058 Brasilia D.F., Brazil

José M. Negrete
Inteligencia Artificial en Medicina
Instituto de Investigaciones Biomedicas - UNAM
Ciudad Universitaria
04510 Mexico D.F., Mexico

Pablo Noriega B. V.
Centro de Investigacion
Escuela de Informatica y Actuaria
Universidad Anahuac
Lomas Anahuac
Mexico D.F. 11000, Mexico

Eugenio Oliveira
Faculdade de Engenharia da
Universidade do Porto
Rua dos Bragas
4099 Porto Codex, Portugal

Pedro Guedes de Oliveira
Universidade de Aveiro
3800 Aveiro, Portugal

Kiluba Pembamoto
McDonnell Douglas
Payment Systems Company
6935 Wisconsin Avenue, Suite 600
Chevy Chase, Maryland 20815, U.S.A.

Durkee Richards
3M/3M Center
Bldg. 236, ID-18
St. Paul, Minnesota 55144, U.S.A.

Wanchai Rivepiboon
Faculty of Engineering
Department of Computer Engineering
Chulalongkorn University
Bangkok 10500, Thailand

Vincent B. Robinson
Department of Surveying Engineering
University of Calgary
2500 University Drive NW
Calgary, Alberta T2N 1N4
Canada

J. C. D. Marques dos Santos
Faculdade de Engenharia da
Universidade do Porto
Rua dos Bragas
4099 Porto Codex, Portugal

D.C.H. Senarath
Department of Civil Engineering
University of Moratuwa
Moratuwa, Sri Lanka

Guilherme Silva
Faculdade de Ciencias e Tecnologia da
Universidade de Coimbra
3000 Coimbra, Portugal

Raoul N. Smith
College of Computer Science
Northeastern University
360 Huntington Avenue
Boston, Massachusetts 02115, U.S.A.

F. J. Tilak Viegas
Escola Superior de Medicina Veterinaria
Rua Gomes Freire
1199 Lisboa Codex, Portugal

OBSERVERS

Antonio Correia de Campos
Fundacao Luso-Americana para o Desenvolvimento
Rua Rodrigo da Fonseca, 178 - 5o Esq.
1200 Lisboa, Portugal

Raul Pereira da Costa
Associacao Portuguesa de Informatica (AIP)
Av. Almirante Reis, 127 - 1o. Esq.
1100 Lisboa, Portugal

Konrad Fialkowski
Chief Advanced Technologies Unit
UNIDO
Vienna International Centre
P.O. Box 400
Vienna 1400, Austria

Joseph Gueron
Information Resources Management
Agency for International Development
Washington, D.C. 20523, U.S.A.

Holger Hansen
Community Medicine
University of Connecticut Health Center
Farmington, Connecticut 06032, U.S.A.

Jose Carlos de Jesus
Instituto Nacional de Engenharia de Sistemas e Computadores
Rua Alves Redol, 9 - 1o.
1000 Lisboa, Portugal

Armando Louza
Departamento Tecnologia e Sanidos Animal
Escola Superior de Medicina Veterinaria
Rua Gomes Freire
1100 Lisboa, Portugal

Jacinto de Magalhaes
Director-Geral dos Hospitais
Ministerio da Saude
Av. da Republica, 34 - 3o. / 9o.
1000 Lisboa, Portugal

Luis Magao
Director do D.E.P.S.
Ministerio da Saude
Av. Alvares Cabral, 25 - 1o. / 2o.
1200 Lisboa, Portugal

Nuno Joao Mamede
Instituto Nacional de Engenharia de Sistemas e Computadores
Rua Alves Redol, 9 - 1o.
1000 Lisboa, Portugal

Hipolito Monteiro
Servicos Geologicos de Portugal
Rua da Academia das Ciencias
1294 Lisboa Codex, Portugal

Trygve Myhre
Operation Research Group
Oak Ridge National Laboratory
Oak Ridge, Tennessee 37831, U.S.A.

Felix Ribeiro
Grupo de Estudos Basicos de Economia Industrial (GEBEI)
Rua das Pracas, 13-B,R/C -1o.
1200 Lisboa, Portugal

Jose Pinto dos Santos
Laboratorio Nacional de Engenharia e Tecnologia Industrial
Azinhaga dos Lameiros
Estrada Praca do Lumiar, 22
1699 Lisboa Codex, Portugal

Eduardo Sousa
Instituto Superior Tecnico (IST)
Departamento de Hidraulica
Av. Rovisco Pais
1096 Lisboa Codex, Portugal

Jose Manuel Vera
Instituto Superior Tecnico (IST)
Av. Mouzinho de Albuquerque, 32 - 5o. Dto.
1100 Lisboa, Portugal

Ronald Wilson
Director, Health Programs
Aga Khan Foundation
P.O. Box 435
1211 Geneva 6, Switzerland